Building Power, Safety, and Trust in Virtual Communities

Dina Darwish
Ahram Canadian University, Egypt

IGI Global
Publishing Tomorrow's Research Today

Published in the United States of America by
IGI Global
701 E. Chocolate Avenue
Hershey PA, USA 17033
Tel: 717-533-8845
Fax: 717-533-8661
E-mail: cust@igi-global.com
Web site: https://www.igi-global.com

Library of Congress Cataloging-in-Publication Data

CIP PENDING

ISBN13: 9798369338681
EISBN13: 9798369338698

Vice President of Editorial: Melissa Wagner
Managing Editor of Acquisitions: Mikaela Felty
Managing Editor of Book Development: Jocelynn Hessler
Production Manager: Mike Brehm
Cover Design: Phillip Shickler

British Cataloguing in Publication Data
A Cataloguing in Publication record for this book is available from the British Library.

All work contributed to this book is new, previously-unpublished material.
The views expressed in this book are those of the authors, but not necessarily of the publisher.

Editorial Advisory Board

Table of Contents

Detailed Table of Contents

A Virtual Community is a network that operates inside a social network of individuals through any specific media, without any limitations based on geographical location or political restrictions. The primary objective of a virtual community is to facilitate socialization, allowing individuals to freely express their emotions, perspectives, and expertise without any limitations. Virtual communities, comprised of diverse online communities, are widely recognized as the most popular platforms for exchanging views, ideas, and fostering socialization. These types of communities are utilized for a diverse range of social and professional groups. This chapter discusses basic concepts related to virtual communities, as well as other related topics.

Enrapture, an innovative immersive tech development company based in Belgium, is one of the first businesses with a "virtual-world native" team that originally convened in Second Life a decade ago. Today, its strategic focus on user-generated content within virtual communities remains integral to its business strategy. Drawing from its extensive experience establishing leading ventures within Second Life, Enrapture facilitates seamless collaboration among virtual team members and expert partners across various time zones, aligning with the gig economy trend. This is characterized by flexible, contract-based work that challenges traditional employment paradigms. (Roy & Shrivastava, 2020). Central to the discourse on virtual immersion is the concept of the Metaverse—a sprawling landscape where virtual experiences converge with all social interactions and the commercial activities of a "creator economy" in a future version of the internet, the 3D internet.

Using Scopus as the main database, this chapter provides a thorough bibliometric study of research articles on "Exploring Social Network Sites" from 2007 to 2024. We use sophisticated analysis tools like VoSviewer, R Studio, and Biblioshiny to look at author contributions, source impacts, co-occurrences of keywords, and citation patterns. Our results demonstrate a noteworthy rise in research output over time, indicating an increase in scholarly interest. The analysis provides strategic insights for future research by highlighting prominent gaps in the subject, important contributors, and recurrent themes. This work contributes to a better understanding of the field and encourages more scholarly investigation by offering a unique mapping of the trajectory of SNS research.The findings highlight the value of ongoing investigation in SNS studies, with the goal of directing future paths and advancing the advancement of knowledge in this dynamic and ever-evolving field.

Brands need to be where their consumers are. Social networks, by providing the possibility of interaction in real time, have become excellent communication and relationship tools between organizations and their stakeholders. Football clubs, highly complex sports and social organizations cannot stay out of this new reality. This chapter aims to understand the impact that the relationship quality and the communication and engagement on Instagram have on the consumption behaviors of supporters of the football club Sport Lisboa e Benfica (SLB). To this end, a mixed data collection method was applied, with exploratory interviews to some directors of the club, analysis of the club's Instagram publications, and a questionnaire survey to supporters (n= 361). The results confirm that there is a significant relationship quality between the supporters and the club, and that the communication and engagement on Instagram stimulates the consumption of the club's products and services, which generates significant financial returns.

This chapter explores the topic of virtual community discovery in social networks. It starts with defining virtual communities. After that, the chapter goes over several network modelling strategies and community identification techniques. The significance of standardised datasets in evaluating algorithm performance is shown by a thorough analysis of benchmark networks used to test community detection techniques. The accuracy indices for assessing virtual community identification algorithms are also covered. The chapter offers common datasets needed to evaluate virtual community discovery techniques. Next, it explores community discovery using the Girvan-Newman and Louvain algorithms, two well-known techniques, to demonstrate practical applications. These illustrations explain how theoretical ideas can be applied in practical settings. Finally, this chapter provides a thorough overview of the concepts and assessment criteria for virtual community discovery in social networks, providing insightful information for both scholars and industry professionals.

This chapter explored how OpenStreetMap (OSM) enhances social inclusion and community participation in mapping. By enabling anyone to contribute, OSM leverages local knowledge for more accurate and detailed maps, addressing the limitations of traditional mapping. Community involvement is fostered through mapping parties, micro-tasking initiatives, and social media integration, promoting ownership and engagement. OSM empowers marginalized groups by documenting their communities, countering misrepresentation, and bridging the digital divide with training and resources. Despite challenges like digital literacy and data quality, solutions such as multilingual resources, robust validation, and offline tools enhance inclusivity. Ultimately, OSM supports sustainable development, disaster preparedness, and equitable resource allocation by integrating diverse perspectives and fostering community-driven mapping efforts.

This chapter explores the integration of social media platforms in e-learning environments, focusing on their roles in fostering engagement, promoting collaboration, and building trust within virtual educational communities. It analyzes how social media enhances learner interaction, discussing best practices for using platform features to encourage active participation and facilitate collaborative learning experiences. Strategies for fostering trust and community through transparent communication and inclusive practices are also examined. Drawing on theoretical frameworks of social presence and community of inquiry, this study highlights the potential of social media to create dynamic and interactive learning environments. By addressing privacy concerns and ethical considerations, the chapter offers insights into leveraging social media effectively to enhance engagement and learning outcomes in online education.

With the popularity of social media, YouTube Vlogs are playing a crucial role for travelers' hotel booking. YouTube Vloggers create videos of their travelling experiences and upload which help the novice travelers to make an informed choice about their decision on hotel booking. The current study examines what determines travelers to adopt information from YouTube Vlogs for online hotel bookings and how it influences their intentions. A research model was prepared and further, analyzed by sampling 256 Indian travelers who used YouTube Vlogs prior to their hotel booking. The hypotheses of this paper were analyzed by applying structural equation modeling (SEM) using partial least squares (PLS). The findings of this study identified that information quality, source credibility, and trust emerged as crucial factors influencing the adoption of YouTube Vlogs for hotel booking among travelers. This study expanded the information adoption model by introducing a new element, specifically the inclusion of the construct of trust.

Virtual communities have transformed the landscape of social interaction, creating dynamic and multifaceted spaces for individuals to connect, share, and collaborate across geographical boundaries. This chapter delves into the current status of virtual communities, examining their evolution from early internet forums to sophisticated social networks and online platforms. We will explore the diverse forms these communities take, including interest-based groups, professional networks, and support communities, highlighting their role in fostering social capital and collective intelligence.

Preface

The term "community" refers to a group including individuals who share particular emotions and thoughts and who join together to discuss their experiences. According to definitions, the members of this group come together with a common denominator and exhibit a comprehensive solidarity in a region that appears to have unclear limits. The concept of community, which plays a significant role in our day-to-day lives, is moving from places that are physically present to surroundings that are virtual (online) as a result of the development of technology.

It is in the literature that the idea of community is brought into contact with a created set of interpersonal connections that are founded on the shared interests of the members of the community more specifically, a shared sense of belonging to the group.

In today's world, the internet, which has emerged as a new social arena as a result of the rapid development of technology and communication technologies, is demonstrating its effect in every facet of people's lives, including the formation of relationships and the communication of ideas. Individuals' propensity to use the digital world for communication has also increased as a result of the proliferation of the internet. Time and space have been seen differently as a result of these new communication technologies, which have also resulted in the creation of a new communication environment. Reports indicate that individuals have begun to congregate in digital networks for the purpose of providing support, organization, or communication in order to safeguard and preserve their mutual interests. The enormous communities that were first formed by individuals joining together to strengthen their communication have, over the course of time, drawn the interest of businesses, which has caused many of these groups to become virtual communities. According to the contemporary conception of marketing, companies should place their clients at the forefront of their operations while making plans. When it comes to the planning of businesses, it is essential to first develop a relationship with clients and offer them with satisfaction. After that, it is crucial to generate customer loyalty by utilizing this satisfaction. Due to the fact that consumers are beginning to use the internet and, consequently, digital settings, there is a fantastic opportunity for businesses to communicate with their customers in digital environments, also known as virtual environments.

There are several computer networks located all over the world that are connected to one another through the internet, which is a substantial computer network. Through the use of the TCP/IP protocol, it connects a large number of computer systems, making it widespread and continuously expanding. Accessing and sharing information in a method that is simple, inexpensive, speedy, and safe is currently best accomplished through the use of the internet. The internet is a key component in the concept of virtual communities. This is due to the fact that virtual communities congregate in a portion of the internet that has been constructed (this portion is currently referred to as the "metaverse") rather than in physical associations. The internet is very important in today's world since it is a tool that can be used to obtain information, make communication easier, provide entertainment, and simplify business transactions. Technology was not able to provide access to information in a short amount of time prior to the advent of the internet. "Under one roof" is the term that describes the collection of all information resources, including written, audio, and video content, thanks to the internet. Since the internet was made available to the general public, it has made it possible to communicate in a variety of different ways. Internet users from all over the world, of varying ages, genders, and educational levels, have been given the option to participate in a wide range of games, which include everything from brain puzzles to gambling. Trade is the most crucial aspect of the internet, second only to the use of the internet for military purposes. The advent of the internet has made it possible for businesses operating in a wide variety of industries to conduct business on a global scale.

During the early phases of the creation of the internet, money from the federal government in the United States of America for research and development (R&D) related to defense played a significant role in the establishment of an infrastructure consisting of appropriately skilled researchers and related institutions, such as universities. In spite of the fact that researchers and engineers from a variety of countries have made significant contributions to essential research efforts that enable critical communications technologies, the scale of publicly funded research and development programs in the United States, as well as the data networks that these programs use, has exceeded the efforts that are being made simultaneously in the United Kingdom and France. In addition, the development of the internet was aided by the tight relationships that existed between people working in academics, defense, and industry.

According to Mowery and Rosenberg in 1998 and Nelson and Wright in 1990, the proliferation of the internet, which contains significant monolingual components and provides the domestic market in the United States with rapid industrial growth, as well as key features of history since 1940, brings to mind the primary themes that have appeared in the development of technology in the United States. The elimination of trade barriers, as well as the resurgence of international commerce and capital flows, led to a loss in the economic significance of this huge domestic market after 1945, according to the arguments of a few academics. Particularly noteworthy are the Hypertext Markup Language (HTML) and the Hypertext Transfer Protocol (HTTP), both of which were developed in the United States. The evolution of the internet contains a number of examples of inventions from other countries.

Today, communities have evolved into the fundamental elements that serve as the foundation for social thought. There is a reasonably deep intellectual history that occurred during the 18th and 19th centuries, and that demonstrated that they were among the most significant research subjects of the people who were influential in the fields of social theory, science, and philosophy at the beginning of the 20th century. In light of these findings, it can be concluded that virtual communities were with a growing interest on the part of customers, particularly towards the beginning of the following century.

In the field of social sciences, the community places a strong emphasis on the concept of pertaining to the existence of affiliations, conventions, and traditions, as well as the function of frameworks etc. By virtue of its inherent cohesion, the community is a group in which the elements that bring people together and foster a sense of community are substantial. It has been explained by McMillan and Chavis in 1986 that there are four fundamental components in outlining the meaning of the term "community". The components in question are as follows:

Membership is the most important factor that determines whether or not a person is a member. As to whether or not individuals are members of the community. Residents of the community view those who recognize themselves as members of the community and with whom they identify. As a result of this, individuals have a sense of emotional security and begin creating within the community. In a sense, this might be interpreted as a personal investment on your part. The term "effect" refers to the fact that individuals have an impact and contribute to the overall community. The community in which members are located can be influenced by them.

The people of the surrounding community needs can be satisfied by other members of the group. A crucial component in this context is development of a common resource by the members of the group. The values that are shared by the Community is demonstrated via thc sharing of rcsourccs and thc fulfilment of needs (whether monetary or spiritual). It is a commitment and a belief that the Standard Emotional Connection must be maintained.

Members have a similar history, a common space, and will continue to share these things. Spending time together and having experiences that are comparable. Feelings from the same connections can ensure that members have positive interaction with one another and opportunities exist. So that they can discuss their experiences, different ways of recognizing members, and participation of individuals in the community is encouraged.

The communities, in addition to the fundamental components that were mentioned earlier, in order to guarantee that some of the participants' essential requirements are met. Below is a list of these requirements:

Providing Access to Resources: Communities are associations that are located in and around Individuals that may be interested in a variety of topics, experiences, and challenges.

The exchange of information takes place concurrently with the social interaction of individuals. It is for this reason that the participants share resources in order to satisfy each other's requirements.

Strengthening Relationships: Members of the Community who are Facing Similar Challenges or experiences might become familiar to one another. Through communities, individuals are able to discuss things with other people. There is a desire among individuals to preserve their connections. When put another way, people are more likely to develop social skills because of the groups they are a part of.

Living Dreams: Communities give their members the opportunity to talk about their aspirations. In the community, members frequently have the ability to assume the role of a fictional character. In addition, members of the community can use participants communicate with one another by sharing their dreams with other members.

Commerce: Members of the community engage in the act of buying and selling goods.

The fact that these interactions are considered to be the most significant aspect of the confidence that individuals have in one another enables trade to take place more swiftly between community members. The feeling of dependence that develops among members of the group guarantees that the trading procedures are carried out in a more healthy manner.

Furthermore, the technological advancement of the internet in the direction of a participatory approach, which is referred to as Web 2.0, brought about a significant shift in the manner in which users employed the internet. This progression is characterized as being user-centered and places an emphasis on interactive forums that encourage user behaviors such as working together to create something and communicating with one another. As a result of these developments, online communities have come into existence, and people from all over the world have been allowed to freely express their opinions on topics that are of mutual interest and that are aimed at achieving the same aims by utilizing an internet platform. Furthermore, internet communities have the necessary expertise for foresight, and they could be of assistance by contributing to a more thorough grasp of the future. The fact that they possess such knowledge makes them particularly relevant for the processes of foresight; hence, the systematic integration of online communities may help lessen the amount of ambiguity regarding future developments.

On the other hand, it is not possible to assert that the great quantitative growth of the online community has coincided with the qualitative development of the knowledge that is included within it. Because of this, it is essential to take into consideration the inherent quality level of the information that is produced by the actual online community. On the other hand, the majority of research that used the data from online communities as a source of technology foresight concentrated solely on the exterior aspects of the online communities. In order to conduct public opinion mining that is reliable, it is necessary to classify online communities according to the actual intrinsic content, activities, and features of online communities. Furthermore, in order to conduct a public-based foresight process, it is currently necessary to have a framework that is both quantitative and methodical for evaluating and classifying the online community. In light of this, the research presented here suggests a new framework for evaluating the online community in terms of technology foresight. To be more specific, the purpose of this study is to conduct a quantitative analysis of the components that constitute the online communities in which debates with regard to technology take place. Additionally, in order to choose postings from a wide range of users that are relevant to technology, the selection process is based on two criteria: knowledge and diversity.

On the other hand, it is not possible to assert that the great quantitative growth of the online community has coincided with the qualitative development of the knowledge that is included within it. Because of this, it is essential to take into consideration the inherent quality level of the information that is produced by the actual online community. On the other hand, the majority of research that used the data from online communities as a source of technology foresight concentrated solely on the exterior aspects of the online communities. In order to conduct public opinion mining that is reliable, it is necessary to classify online communities according to the actual intrinsic content, activities, and features of online communities. Furthermore, in order to conduct a public-based foresight process, it is currently necessary to have a framework that is both quantitative and methodical for evaluating and classifying the online community.

The situation in cyberspace is still one in which it is quite challenging to determine what is truly taking place. When it comes to the fundamental technological structure and functionality of cyberspace, we can observe conflicting forces competing with one another. Moreover, we can observe forces that are engaged in a struggle over societal rules and institutions that are defining the framework in which the technology is used. Economic interests, such as those of large software and telecommunications corporations, as well as those of governmental and international organizations, as well as the individual user, are included in these factors.

Additionally, in the midst of this, we can find all of the Virtual Communities that are currently in existence and are grappling with a particular issue concerning the utilization and development of cyberspace. There are a variety of concerns that are at the center of these conflicts, including ownership, copyright, and the debate between open systems and standards. But this is just a small sample. Over the course of the coming years, it is likely that the ongoing investigation and production of cyberspace will give rise to an increasing number of issues that constitute concerns. For the time being, we are only getting started.

Over the course of its existence, virtual reality (VR) technology has made significant advancements. Over the course of the last two decades, we have witnessed an astonishing expansion in the capabilities and applications of virtual reality (VR).

Earlier virtual reality (VR) systems were designed primarily for use in research and military applications since they were expensive and offered a restricted range of capabilities. As a result of the introduction of consumer-oriented virtual reality (VR) devices such as the Oculus Rift and the HTC Vive, virtual reality (VR) now provides a more immersive and approachable experience for the conventional user.

Virtual reality (VR) technology is currently being utilized in a variety of professions, including gaming, education, healthcare, and even social contact. As the technology continues to advance, it is becoming increasingly clear that it has the ability to completely transform the ways in which we engage with one another and communicate. The development of virtual communities, which are digital spaces in which people may interact with one another, collaborate, and socialize, is one of the most important applications of virtual reality (VR).

In the context of online communities, the function of social interaction is important. Users interact with one another in social virtual reality (SVR) by use of avatars, which are digital representations of themselves that are placed within an immersive three-dimensional world. When compared to more conventional methods of online communication, such as text, audio, and video, service-oriented virtual reality (SVR) offers a platform for engagement that is more natural and intuitive.

The following are some of the most important features of social engagement in online communities:

Group Activities Virtual reality (VR) has the potential to host a broad variety of virtual venues, including art galleries, escape rooms, and game arenas, all of which are designed to facilitate group activities and cooperation. These settings encourage participation and facilitate the development of stronger social bonds.

When people are in the same physical place, they are able to engage with one another in a shared virtual environment. This type of interaction is known as co-located interaction. Users are able to not only connect with friends who are located in other locations, but also make memories that will last a lifetime through the experiences that they have in common.

In contrast to text-based communication, virtual reality (VR) enables users to more accurately communicate their feelings through their avatars, which is referred to as emotional presence. It is possible to transmit the user's emotional state through gestures, facial expressions, and body language, which all work together to make the experience more enjoyable overall.

As a result of the enormous development that has taken place in virtual reality over the course of the years, virtual communities have been able to come into existence.

Users are provided with improved communication capabilities and a sense of belonging through the usage of social interaction, which plays a critical part in the cultivation of meaningful connections within these communities.

In the process of developing virtual worlds for social interactions, it is of the utmost importance to build surroundings that are immersive and effectively engage users.

This can be accomplished in a number of ways, one of which is by drawing inspiration from real-world settings. This can assist users in feeling more at ease and familiar with the virtual environment. In addition, improving the sensation of immersion can be accomplished by the utilization of realistic lighting, textures, and noises.

Virtual worlds, on the other hand, make it possible to incorporate features that are one-of-a-kind and imaginative that are not present in the real world. A designer is able to construct surroundings that fascinate and inspire users because they have the flexibility to express their creativity. A sense of awe and wonder can be added to the virtual environment by the addition of features such as gravity-defying structures, floating islands, and other exotic constructions.

One further essential component of building immersive environments is making certain that the user interface is easy to understand and welcoming to anyone who uses it. Because of this, users will have an easier time navigating the virtual world and interacting with other people.

A significant number of workers, whether they are employed by software firms, research centers, universities, or as individuals, are developing software that is continually adding new capabilities and features to the realm of cyberspace. Their work serves a variety of purposes; some of them are researchers who write about their work in academic works, but the majority of them are “true” designers whose sole objective is to design and construct, either for financial gain or for personal enjoyment. This is a very significant group that is frequently overlooked in the conversations that take place regarding the research on virtual communities. It is a group that does not consider themselves to be conducting research and hence does not even contribute to the expansion of information regarding cyberspace; rather, they perceive themselves as creators of a new universe. Their fundamental viewpoint is that cyberspace is something that should be constructed by anyone who is interested in participating in that endeavor. All individuals who are “using” or living in cyberspace and in virtual communities are considered to be customers of the results that this group has produced. The findings make it possible to make use of the technology, and they are possibly the most crucial factor in determining the future possibilities for our civilization to make use of the new technology.

Numerous traditional studies on virtual communities have been conducted by academics from the social sciences, primarily sociology, psychology, anthropology, and communication studies. These studies have been compiled into a body of work that is available to the public. There is also the possibility of discovering research from the fields of computer science and information systems. The objective of these studies is to discover and/or develop knowledge on a particular facet of reality, which is the conventional purpose of academic studies. Studies that try to explain and critically assess the development of society are distinct from those that want to gain information that may be used in the future design of cyberspace and virtual communities. The most evident distinction between the two types of studies is that the former seeks to gain knowledge that could be used in the design of cyberspace and virtual communities.

People are increasingly engaging in online interactions, debating and sharing experiences, and sometimes even sharing very personal information. This trend is largely attributable to the expansion of the Internet, and in particular to the spike in the use of social networking sites. Because of this, a new sort of research has become possible, one in which data can be gathered online from a huge number of people, eliminating the limitations that are associated with conducting research in a laboratory setting. A variety of questions concerning technique and the ethical concerns that are related with it have also been brought up as a result of this. The primary problems that are typically brought up revolve on the concepts of privacy and confidentiality, informed consent, and narrative appropriation, as stated by Brownlow and O'Dell in 2002. Should the information that is generated online and provided by a number of different authors be regarded as private or should it be deemed to be on the public domain? In the event that this kind of data is going to be gathered and evaluated for the purposes of study, what are the responsibilities and obligations of the researcher? These difficulties have been examined by a number of scholars, either in a more general or in the context of their own previous work.

Studies investigating how and whether online businesses can improve their profitability through the use of online communities could be conducted using case studies. Such studies could lead to an understanding of the factors that contribute to the success or failure of virtual community institutionalization. Future research on institutionalization could develop ways to integrate the virtual community with other applications that generate profits, such as electronic commerce and customer relationship management.

This book includes several topics related to Virtual communities and how it is used to help people communicate, and to be connected. Also, this book is targeting industry experts, researchers, students, practitioners and higher education institutions interested in Virtual Communities and its influence on Society.

Book Editor,

Dina Darwish

Chapter 1
Introduction to Virtual Communities

Dina Darwish
Ahram Canadian University, Egypt

ABSTRACT

A Virtual Community is a network that operates inside a social network of individuals through any specific media, without any limitations based on geographical location or political restrictions. The primary objective of a virtual community is to facilitate socialization, allowing individuals to freely express their emotions, perspectives, and expertise without any limitations. Virtual communities, comprised of diverse online communities, are widely recognized as the most popular platforms for exchanging views, ideas, and fostering socialization. These types of communities are utilized for a diverse range of social and professional groups. This chapter discusses basic concepts related to virtual communities, as well as other related topics.

INTRODUCTION

The notion of community has undergone constant redefinition and remains remarkably elusive. After many years from Park's definition (Park, 1936), Hillery discovered a total of 94 distinct definitions of community. These definitions varied, encompassing concepts such as a group, a process, a social system, a geographic location, an attitude, a shared lifestyle, and local self-sufficiency. Hillery also noted that there is no unanimous consensus regarding the true essence of community. Hillery (Hillery, 1995) determined that the majority of definitions include three fundamental elements: (1) a distinct location, which is particularly important when studying cyberspace, (2) shared connections, which is often the least examined element, and (3) social interaction, which is the essential requirement for a com-

DOI: 10.4018/979-8-3693-3868-1.ch001

munity. While the term "community" lacks a precise definition, most sociologists agree on a traditional definition that includes three key elements. These elements, identified by Park and later confirmed by Hillery, are: a sense of belonging to a specific geographic area, shared connections among residents, and meaningful social interaction among residents. The initial component holds particular significance for virtual communities. While the notion of a community being "rooted in the soil" may appear old-fashioned in today's society, the conventional belief that a community is connected to a certain location or area remains. The concept of a virtual community appears to be excluded by the aspect of identification with location, as per its definition. The latter refers to individuals who establish communities by utilizing computer-supported social networks within the virtual realm, after engaging in extensive talks. The virtual community lacks a sense of place-based identification, but it necessitates shared connections and social engagement. Therefore, we may now reformulate our first inquiry with greater accuracy. Can the virtual community offer common bonds and social contact without a sense of belonging to a specific location? To answer this question, it is necessary to provide a thorough specification for each of these three fundamental components. The number of individuals within a community is often regarded as one of the most crucial and extensively examined aspects. and the characteristics of social relationships. The sensation of intimacy, mutual affirmation of existence, and strong bonds between us. There is a connection between us, where we have knowledge of each other and to some degree, we understand and relate to one another.

They approach one another with mutual trust and genuine goodwill. A clear and consistent reciprocal action must consistently occur. The latest expansion of the notion that community can exist independently of physical location is the concept of a virtual community thriving in cyberspace. Now, the argument is extended: not only is a local place not essential, but neither is a shared area. Consequently, physical presence is not a prerequisite for the communal bonds and social engagement typically linked to a community. Barry Wellman has consistently maintained that communities can break free from traditional physically close, tightly-knit neighborhoods and transition into a person-to-person community that is entirely detached from local physical space or shared environment. This can be achieved through technologies like wireless cell phones, enabling individuals to interact with each other regardless of their location. According to Wellman (Wellman, 1999), community can be defined as interconnected relationships that offer social interaction, assistance, knowledge, a feeling of inclusion, and social identity. Communities, as per Wellman, operate as networks rather being confined to specific areas and villages. The networks consisting of family, neighbors, friends, and co-workers are incomplete communities that are loosely interconnected and fractured. Community networks can be present in local areas, shared physical locations, and the online realm of cyberspace. Individuals adeptly utilize Internet technology to establish and maintain virtual networks, thereby fostering significant and supportive relationships in cyberspace.

BACKGROUND

A virtual community consists of individuals who are united by a common interest or motivation. They convene on a specialized online platform, where they can establish ties with one another, draw upon each other's narratives and encounters to drive advancement, and cultivate significant connections. Typically, these communities are guided by a creator or host who establishes the purpose and methods for members to develop relationships with each other while collectively pursuing a shared area of interest. Within a virtual community, individuals derive additional benefits from the ties they establish with one another. The distinguishing factor that sets virtual communities separate from social media audiences and email newsletter subscribers is the capacity for members to cultivate relationships with one another.

To comprehend the concept of a virtual community (VC), it is important to consider both of its constituent elements: virtual and community. The virtual can be defined as an entity that exists independently of physical presence, and hence lacks spatial and temporal coordinates (Van Dijk, 1999). In this context, the term "online" might be regarded as synonymous (Matzat, 2004). Contemporary sociologists conceptualize community as a symbolic fabrication (Cohen, 1985), a pseudo-community (Beniger, 1987), or an imagined community (Anderson, 1983). Community can be perceived through various lenses, depending on the chosen perspective. When individuals engage in learning activities within a community, it can be referred to as a community of practice (CoP) (Wenger, 1999). In this context, a community of practice can be seen as a social structure that encompasses a set of skills and knowledge, forming the foundation of a social learning system (Wenger, 2000). On the other hand, when people come together with a shared objective, Rheingold's definition of a virtual community is often cited by scholars as a social gathering that forms online when a sufficient number of individuals engage in public discussions with a significant level of emotional connection (Rheingold, 1993). However, there is no agreement on a universally accepted definition (Preece & de Souza, 2004). The literature identifies five attributes of virtual communities: purpose (the specific focus of discourse), place (the extent to which interaction is mediated by technology, ranging from completely virtual to partially virtual), platform (the design of interaction, including synchronous and asynchronous communication), population (the pattern of interaction, group structure, and type of social ties).

Develop a methodology that measures the return on interaction, which specifically assesses the extent to which a community generates actual economic benefit (Porter, 2004). The chosen cases can be classified as virtual communities due to their inclusion of these five characteristics. Specifically, in terms of the attribute of place, they meet the minimum requirements for designating a cyber-place with associated group-CMC (Computer-Mediated Communication) as a virtual settlement, as outlined by Jones (Jones, 1997).

A virtual community refers to an online gathering of individuals who interact and engage with each other through digital platforms. A virtual community refers to a collective of persons who utilize certain social media platforms to establish connections, often transcending geographical and political barriers, in order to pursue shared interests or objectives. Online communities functioning under social networking platforms are among the most widespread virtual communities. Howard Rheingold (Rheingold, 1993) examined virtual communities in his 1993 book, The Virtual Community. The book explores a variety of topics including Rheingold's experiences on the WELL, computer-mediated communication, social groupings, and information science. The mentioned technologies encompass Usene8t, MUDs (Multi-User Dungeon) along with their derivatives MUSHes and MOOs, Internet Relay Chat (IRC), chat rooms, and electronic mailing lists. Rheingold highlights the potential advantages of being part of a virtual community, both for personal psychological well-being and for society as a whole. Simultaneously, it has shown that work engagement has a favorable impact on the level of involvement in virtual communities of practice.

Virtual communities foster interaction, often centered around a certain hobby or for the purpose of communication. Certain virtual communities engage in both activities simultaneously. Community members have the opportunity to engage with each other through different platforms such as message boards, chat rooms, social networking websites, or virtual worlds. It is common for members to develop a strong connection to the community, frequently logging in and out of these sites throughout the day, which can potentially lead to addiction. A community is typically defined as a geographically limited entity, such as neighborhoods or villages. Virtual communities, due to their geographical dispersion, do not meet the criteria of being communities according to the original concept. Geographically connected internet communities are referred to as community websites. Nevertheless, if one defines communities as entities that have distinct boundaries separating their members from non-members, then a virtual community can indeed be considered a community. Virtual communities share similarities with real-life communities in that they offer support, information, companionship, and acceptance among individuals who are initially strangers. Within a virtual community, users are likely to experience a sense of belonging and a shared emotional connection with other members present in the virtual space.

An essential aspect of virtual communities is the ability to engage in communication across multiple media platforms or networks. With the advent of virtual communities, traditional practices like postal services, fax machines, and even telephone conversations have been rendered obsolete. Initial investigations into the presence of media-based communities focused on the fundamental nature of reality and the possibility of communities forming through media platforms. This line of inquiry aligns virtual community research with the social sciences' understanding of ontology.

Howard Rheingold's Virtual Community can be likened to Mark Granovetter's (Granovetter, 1973) seminal "strength of weak ties" paper, which was published two decades prior in the American Journal of Sociology. Rheingold translated, implemented, and disseminated Granovetter's hypotheses regarding robust and feeble connections in the digital realm. The comment on the first page exemplifies the presence of social networks in virtual society. The author describes how his seven-year-old daughter is aware that he interacts with a group of unseen acquaintances through his computer. These invisible friends occasionally manifest themselves in person, either from nearby or from a distant location. Undoubtedly, in his updated edition of Virtual Community, Rheingold explicitly states that if he had been aware of Barry Wellman's research earlier, he would have titled his book "online social networks".

This research (González-Anta et al., 2023) indicates that effective commitment, which is a psychological state that describes the connection between members and the educational virtual community, represents a long-term focus on the relationship. It influences and controls consumer behavior, leading consumers to act in accordance with the shared interests of both parties (Zhu and Xie, 2018; Pang and Yang, 2021; Yang et al., 2021). Hence, a strong level of dedication is crucial for user engagement in an educational virtual community and can potentially act as a mediator in the connection between the sense of virtual community and user engagement. Presently, there is a limited amount of research connecting the sense of virtual community, effective commitment, and user engagement in consumer behavior studies. Specifically, there is a lack of focus on the mediating role of effective commitment. Thus, this paper suggests that the virtual community established by the educational virtual community can indirectly enhance user engagement by fostering effective commitment.

This section specifically examines Virtual Communities of Practice (VCoPs). Virtual Communities of Practice (VCoPs) are groups of professionals who convene on digital platforms to share experiences, ideas, and solutions to work-related challenges, thereby improving their skills and abilities (Martínez-López et al., 2016).

Virtual Communities of Practice (VCoPs) promote collaboration, creativity, and sharing of knowledge within organizations and between experts. These communities of practice are formed through face-to-face interactions within organizations. They serve as informal institutions for efficiently sharing information, bypassing the complications of official organizational hierarchies (Kirkman et al., 2013).

Virtual Communities of Practice (VCoPs) have emerged as a crucial instrument in organizations, experiencing a global surge in adoption. However, their effectiveness and proliferation do not necessarily align with their long-term viability, occasionally resulting in unintended negative consequences for the corporations endorsing them. Additional research is required to unravel the factors that are most effective in supporting the maintenance and growth of venture capitalists (VCs) in both organizations and for-profit firms, while also taking into account other sustainability factors. Overall, this study offers a comprehensive perspective on the primary aspects that can impact members' intention to participate, which serves as an indicator of the community's sustainability. Using the TAM theory as a basis, we examined the technological, personal, and motivational variables that have been separately examined, and we combined them into a comprehensive model driven primarily by identification, interaction, and self-efficacy.

Research on user behavior in the virtual tourist community has gained significant attention. This research (Gu, and Zhu, 2023) aims to uncover the underlying mechanism behind user value co-creation behavior in tourism virtual communities, drawing from cognitive evaluation theory and organismic integration theory. Understanding this mechanism is crucial for the effective operation and growth of the tourism industry. A total of 342 valid questionnaires were collected in the survey, and structural equation modelling was used to examine the influence path. Online reviews were discovered to possess two distinct dimensions: content and qualities. The qualities of online reviews have a favorable impact on the dimensions of social connection and information exchange in social interactions. Engaging in social interactions has a beneficial impact on the behavior of creating value together. Social contact encompasses elements that have a favorable impact on user engagement. Consequently, user engagement itself exerts a beneficial influence on recommendation behavior. In summary, the study's results can encourage users to actively engage in interaction and exchange of knowledge.

Overall, the study suggests that online reviews can have a favorable impact on individuals' inclination to engage in online activities, such as socializing and exchanging information. On the other hand, visitors who actively participate in online travel groups are more inclined to increase their future involvement. Moreover, individuals' level of involvement will have an impact on their emotional and cognitive states, which in turn affect their behavior, including making recommendations. Consequently, their worth might be collaboratively generated throughout the entire procedure.

Hosting major athletic events provides hosting nations with a variety of social, economic, and reputational advantages. These events also serve as a means to display and promote the nation's brand. Participation in social media during sporting events allows community members to collaborate, select, and share the distinctive characteristics of their nation's brand. Although there has been research on the role of place-based communities in nation branding and community participation, there is less understanding of how virtual communities contribute to the nation's brand and in what specific ways. This study (Xiufang et al., 2024) aims to fill this void by investigating the virtual brand community (VBC) that revolves around the 2022 Beijing Winter Olympics. The results indicate that the extent of contributions to VBC (Virtual Brand Community) is influenced by the composition, participation, and development of discussions centered around the personality attributes of a nation brand. This conclusion is drawn from the use of social network analysis and content analysis. The conclusions of this study theoretically enhance our understanding of how to effectively utilize the characteristics of VBCs to contribute to the creation and upkeep of a genuine national brand that values community perspectives, achieved through community participation. This study expands upon existing research on digital social-level participation in virtual environments and proposes further research on participatory ways to country branding in the field of public relations. The increasing utilization of major sporting events to achieve nation branding objectives, especially in Asia and Africa, indicates that the findings of this study have significant implications at both regional and international levels. These findings can serve as a guide for public relations managers involved in organizing major events, helping them to establish sustainable VBCs (Visitor Branding Campaigns) that result in genuine place branding outcomes.

Creating a genuine brand through community-based VBC requires participatory procedures that foster conversations leading to shared meaning, within conducive settings and situations. To effectively generate content, it is essential to have a deep grasp of the local community and the specific characteristics that contribute to its composition, conversations, and participation. Community-based VBC composition refers to the inclusion of a wide range of individuals from the community, ensuring that their membership is both genuine and representative. Composition should strive to mitigate the overrepresentation of powerful groups, which may have alternative motives such as political, contentious, or misleading goals, by integrating individuals who embody varied community-based ideals.

Key Attributes of a Virtual Community

A Branded Online Community refers to a digital platform created and managed by a company or organization to foster engagement, interaction, and collaboration among its customers, users, or members. It serves as a dedicated space where individuals can connect, share information, seek support, and participate in discussions related to the brand or its products/services. A branded online community is a network where individuals with a common affiliation or goal come together to collaborate and flourish in an expanding online environment. The community in question refers to an online platform that your organization would establish to facilitate connections among its members, including consumers, workers, partners, or any other individuals involved in the community.

Characteristics of a Virtual Community

McMillan and Chavis (McMillan and Chavis, 1986) have elucidated four fundamental components in delineating the notion of community. The following elements are:

Membership is the key determinant that differentiates whether individuals belong to the community or not. Community members perceive themselves as integral to the community and establish a sense of connection with fellow members. Consequently, individuals experience a sense of emotional security, which encourages them to engage in productive activities within society. This can be interpreted as a form of individual financial commitment, to some extent.

The concept of effect suggests that individuals have the ability to create an impact and contribute meaningfully to their community. Members have the ability to influence the community in which they are situated, and their actions can have an effect on other community members.

The needs of community members can be satisfied by other members. A crucial element in this context is the members' collaborative development of a collective asset. The community's common values are demonstrated via the act of sharing resources and fulfilling both material and spiritual needs.

Normal Emotional Connection refers to the dedication and conviction that individuals have in sharing and continuing to share a collective past, a shared environment, engaging in activities together, and having comparable life encounters.

An emotional bond that is shared among individuals can guarantee favorable interaction between members, chances to exchange their personal experiences, ways to show respect to members, and the active involvement of members in the community. Communities, in conjunction with the four fundamental aspects mentioned earlier, guarantee the fulfilment of crucial requirements of its members (individuals). The following are the needs:

1-) ***Resource Sharing:*** Communities are social groups formed around specific subjects, experiences, or problems that individuals find interesting and seek to address (Flavian et al., 2005). Individuals engage in a substantial amount of information exchange during their social interactions. Consequently, the participants fulfil each other's demands by exchanging resources.
2-) ***Establishing Connections:*** Individuals within a community who share common issues or experiences might become acquainted with one another. Communities facilitate interpersonal communication among individuals. People desire to uphold their affiliations within the community and disseminate them to fellow members. Communities facilitate the formation of social interactions among individuals.
3-) ***Living Dreams:*** Communities enable members to exchange their aspirations. Community members frequently adopt a fictional persona (Flavian et al., 2005). Furthermore, community members have the opportunity to engage in dialogue and share their aspirations with fellow members.
4-) ***Trade:*** Community members engage in autonomous transactions for buying and selling. The primary characteristic of these transactions is their expedited nature, facilitated by the trust individuals have in other members of the community. The establishment of trust within the community fosters a more robust and sound execution of trade activities.

Rickman (Rickman, 1976) presents a framework consisting of four fundamental psychological components that are necessary for establishing effective knowledge sharing within a community. The following items are necessary for individuals to engage in comfortable interaction on a website:

- Individuals require a motive to access this website.
- People want a sense of boundlessness in the input and output of their shares in the places where they are situated.
- People engage in conversation more effortlessly when they possess a greater amount of leisure time.
- People tend to communicate more rapidly when they believe that the unfamiliar individuals in their vicinity are actually their neighbors. Communities provide individuals with a sense of familiarity and camaraderie.

Individuals who are not regularly involved in the field of online community platforms and strategies may find it challenging to distinguish the phrase "online community" from the numerous buzzwords associated with social networks, platforms, and tactics. Novices in the online community software sector often struggle to discern the distinctions between prominent public social media networks, such as Facebook or LinkedIn groups, and branded online communities.

While the average user may casually use public or personal social networks, members of private online communities often have a deliberate mindset and actively invest their time. They see these communities as an opportunity to engage with a specific organization's community for personal or professional development. Although these platforms have commonalities, such as the overarching goal of facilitating online connections, there are significant disparities in their functionality and behavior when it comes to devising strategies and targeting your audience. In order to foster genuine community involvement, it is imperative that users experience a profound sense of ease regarding their privacy, ability to ask questions, and sense of belonging inside the area. Disseminating and displaying their skills frequently becomes diluted on social media platforms or open-source solutions. We suggest utilizing a proprietary community platform due to various compelling factors:

Enhanced authority: By establishing your community on a social media or open-source platform, you relinquish ownership over any modifications made by the platform without your input, thus constructing your community on leased property.

Enhanced security: Community suppliers prioritize privacy as their foremost responsibility. By utilizing Facebook or LinkedIn Group, your capacity to safeguard the privacy of your members and your own personal information is restricted.

By utilizing a social media platform, you can acquire highly useful data that pertains to your community, which you would not be able to obtain otherwise, regarding your members and clients. By establishing your own online community, you will gain access to a wealth of data, enabling you to comprehend your consumers better and craft a tailored experience for them. Additional community management tools: Utilizing a community platform such as Higher Logic's, you will have access to integrated engagement tools that are specifically crafted to assist you in creating a captivating experience.

Implementing Branded Online Communities

Upon initial login, community members gain access to a branded community, which can be conveniently reached from a website. Once inside, they have the opportunity to engage in various activities, such as:

- Inquire another member regarding the methodology they employed to accomplish a task.
- Review the most prominent conversation posts from the week
- Present a recommendation for enhancing one of your offerings
- Register to be a presenter at one of your events

However, an online community is not merely a product that an organization purchases; rather, it is a platform designed to serve as a virtual gathering place for actual individuals. Your community can function as the digital hub for your organization, offering acknowledgment, assistance, and camaraderie throughout times when your customers or members require it most.

COOPERATION BETWEEN ONLINE COMMUNITIES

The authors distinguish between communication, coordination, and cooperation as distinct but interconnected processes that rely on each other. Communication refers to the exchange of information between individuals, coordination involves agreeing on and aligning group activities, and cooperation involves the production of work in a shared space with the group. Collaboration can be conceptualized as a triangular relationship in which communication, coordination, and cooperation are interconnected (Thalheim et al., 2014). Communication is essential for coordination, and coordination is necessary for collaboration to occur, involving the alignment of individuals and resources. Naturally, in reality, these classifications of processes are not as distinctly defined: for instance, communication technologies are frequently employed for the purpose of coordinating actions or engaging in collaborative efforts towards a certain objective. The model proposed by Ellis, Gibbs & Rein in 1991 (Ellis et al., 1991) incorporates several variations in nomenclature as discussed by Fuks et al. (Fuks et al., 2008). To elaborate on collaboration, it is crucial to emphasize that it takes place when a collective of independent individuals involved in a particular issue engage in an interactive procedure (Wood & Grey, 1991). Collaboration can take place through several means such as mail, telephone communication, and face-to-face interaction (Schrage, 1990).

Murphy discussed a collaboration model for online asynchronous discussion (OAD), which consists of six stages arranged in a continuum (Murphy, 2004). Initially, participants introduce themselves to others, establishing a sense of social presence. Subsequently, individuals express their viewpoint (communicating personal perspectives) and may modify their thoughts (adapting or incorporating the perspectives and meanings). In addition, they have the ability to exchange and develop shared viewpoints and meanings, as well as establish common aims and purposes, ultimately resulting in the creation of shared artefacts. In this model, which is also influenced by Schrage (Schrage, 1995), the progression goes from interaction to collaboration (Murphy, 2004), with the lower levels serving as requirements for the higher ones. Undoubtedly, interaction does not ensure collaboration. The work of Murphy (Murphy, 2004) and Thalheim et al. (Thalheim et al., 2014) can be summarized as collaboration being a joint effort where individuals come together to create a shared understanding of a process, product, or event. This collaboration takes place in a shared space, particularly in the online environment, where individuals are aware of the goals and methods being used. Murphy's approach is founded on concepts such as meaning and purposive relationship, as proposed by Schrage (Schrage,1995). On the other hand, Thalheim et al. highlight the importance of shared space, as discussed by Schrage (Schrage, 1990).

Virtual communities possess three primary attributes:

- ***A creator:*** This individual or group is responsible for uniting the community by establishing a foundational vision, creating the online platform for the community, and initiating debates.
- ***Members:*** Individuals who come together based on a common interest or motivation. Every additional member enhances the community by contributing their unique knowledge, experience, and perspective.
- ***An online community platform:*** A digital environment where the creator and members of a virtual community collaborate to collectively acquire necessary skills or knowledge. An effective online community platform will provide you with functionalities to facilitate the organization of discussions, hosting of events, implementation of membership fees, creation of subgroups, live streaming capabilities, and even the development and sale of courses. Figure 1 shows the virtual community's three primary attributes.

Figure 1. Virtual community three primary attributes

There are four key attributes that define exceptional online communities.

1. ***Effective online communities*** are constructed to foster active participation and provide empowered communal assistance. Communities vary in appearance and atmosphere, adapting to the specific requirements of their distinct members and organization. To effectively attract a wide audience to your online platform, it is crucial to consider the collective interests of all individuals engaged. This entails contemplating the advantages people will derive from participating in the community, as well as ensuring that the space is inclusive and accommodating to all.

To provide a response, let's first clarify: What is the purpose of your online community? The response will impact your approach and plans to get significant involvement. Consider your community as a distinct entity catering to a particular demographic with a defined objective. If the community is dedicated to those who utilize a particular tool or product, its objective would be to acquire knowledge, provide education, and establish connections with like-minded others. Alternatively, if the online community you establish is intended for a local riding collective, its objective may be fostering connections, organizing biking activities, and promoting bicycle safety. Regardless of the community, it operates most effectively when interactions are effortless, safe, and instinctive.

2. ***Excellent online communities are dynamic and multifaceted.*** An exceptional community is characterized by its multifaceted nature, inclusivity, and liveliness. And it flourishes due to the individuals that are involved in it. Individuals exhibit unpredictability, creativity, and diversity, making it daunting to facilitate their gathering in a setting conducive to interaction and engagement. However, it is not necessary for it to be thus - and this assembly of distinct individuals typically promotes the progress of your organization. By dismantling the conventional unidirectional transmission of knowledge and fostering open conversation, your community will provide value that exceeds expectations. By accessing individuals' distinct viewpoints and encouraging them to contribute their skills and knowledge to others, you foster engagement and establish connections that are pertinent and significant. Ultimately, you will likely find that those who perceive themselves as integral members of the community due to their unique contributions are also the ones who exhibit the highest levels of loyalty and longevity. The process of harnessing individuality and enabling individuals to have an impact on others is just one method by which a community can improve an organization's capacity to communicate, expand, and stay pertinent.
3. ***Successful online communities*** thrive when members come together around a common objective. Upon examining these various illustrations, we may now reflect upon our initial inquiry: what are the defining characteristics that constitute a community? Shared purpose refers to the collective efforts of individuals uniting with the aim of accomplishing a specific objective or resolving a particular issue. Golf enthusiasts seek guidance on selecting the most suitable golf clubs for purchase. Sephora customers desire the most up-to-date beauty advice. Marketers seek motivation for developing novel advertising tactics. While your organization may have overarching objectives such as reducing ticket volume, improving member retention, or boosting revenue, it is crucial to consistently focus on fundamental principles. We establish communities for those seeking to connect and engage in collective learning experiences. What strategies might be employed to rediscover or establish a common objective this year?
4. ***Effective online communities are meticulously moderated.*** Ensuring the safety and enjoyment of all participants on your online platforms is crucial for the sustained well-being of your community. This is when community moderation assumes significant importance. This further underscores the significance of having specialized community management. An essential aspect of excelling as an online community moderator is the ability to effectively manage discussions by maintaining order, actively participating to keep conversations engaging, and allowing members, employees, or consumers sufficient autonomy to freely express their thoughts. You desire order and coherence, yet you also wish to avoid stifling conversations at their inception.

Members should perceive the online community as a conducive space for freely expressing their knowledge and perspectives, while adhering to norms that ensure the protection of both individuals and the community.

There are eight advantages of having branded online communities. The advantages derived from a branded community have a cascading effect, leading to enhanced happiness, increased revenue, and the expansion of entire organizations, including the fostering of consumer loyalty. By forming a community, you have the ability to:

- Establish genuine ties
- Differentiate yourself from competitors by providing an enhanced customer experience
- Produce leads and obtain new members
- Enhance the quality of your products and programs by collecting and resolving feedback.
- Reduce support expenses by utilizing crowdsourcing for support.
- Enhance revenue generation by implementing in-community advertising and other strategies.
- Enhance referrals by empowering your advocates to actively participate in the community
- Expand the size and reach of your organization

Figure 2 illustrates the four key attributes that define exceptional online communities.

Figure 2. The four key attributes that define exceptional online communities

CATEGORIES OF VIRTUAL COMMUNITIES

Below are a few (but not all) examples of online communities:

- Health & wellness: centered on topics such as proper nutrition and physical fitness
- Personal development: centered on achieving personal excellence and advancing towards one's full potential
- Hobbies: Established because to a common passion for a specific activity (e.g. knitting, quilting, photography)
- Careers or entrepreneurship: centered on achieving expertise in one's profession and entrepreneurs gaining knowledge from each other
- Skill acquisition: centered on acquiring proficiency in a new skill (e.g. marketing or coding)
- Spirituality: centered on the pursuit of spiritual development or fostering a sense of community
- Healing: Members forming connections based on common hardships or traumatic experiences, such as surviving postpartum depression.

A virtual coworking community is a group of individuals who come together to share their working time. Even among these diverse societies, there can be significant diversity. Certain communities may consist of only 10 individuals, resembling a micro-community, while others boast memberships numbering in the thousands. While several virtual communities are available at no cost, others need payment for entry. However, regardless of the arrangement, these elements frequently coincide with a subscription, an online course, a mastermind group, and many other components. Virtual communities exhibit a wide range of structures and configurations. Below are many widely recognized categories of internet communities:

Brand communities are virtual communities specifically established to provide support and promote a particular brand. The objective is to cultivate a bond between the brand and the members of the community.

Learning communities encompass a wide range of formats and encompass a multitude of subjects, ranging from furniture construction to the acquisition of foreign languages. The proliferation of online personal trainers, financial consultants, and life coaches has significantly increased in recent years.

Support communities encompass various support groups that aim to assist persons facing a wide range of obstacles, such as parenthood, chronic sickness, and disability.

Communities of action are established with the purpose of advocating for a specific cause, such as environmental conservation, animal rights, or any other relevant issue.

Fan communities: Numerous individuals exhibit fervent enthusiasm for comic books, while an equal number display an intense passion for video games, and there are also others who have an insatiable appetite for numerous TV series.

Hobby communities, such as stamp collecting, photography, bird watching, quilting, gardening, and various other interests, provide a rich environment for the formation and cultivation of communities. Figure 3 and Figure 4 illustrate examples and categories of online communities.

Figure 3. Examples of online communities

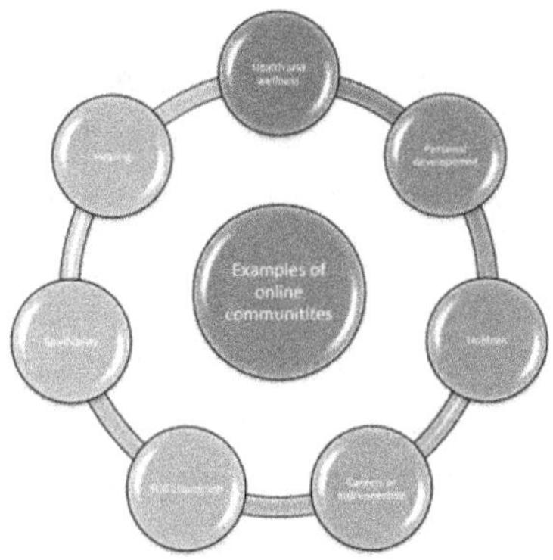

Figure 4. Categories of online communities

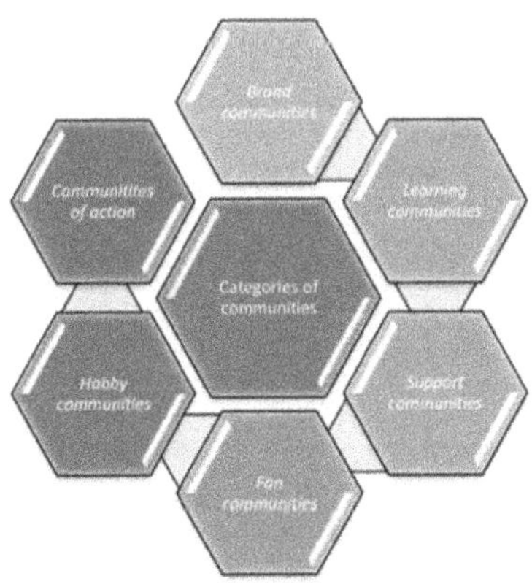

ADVANTAGES OF VIRTUAL COMMUNITIES

Below are several advantages of virtual communities, many of which are absent in traditional communities.

- ***Expand the audience:*** A virtual community has the ability to attract individuals from various locations worldwide.
- ***Diversity:*** Virtual communities have the ability to foster a wide range of individuals, experiences, and opinions due to their lack of geographical limitations.
- ***Organic member expansion:*** If you desire growth, virtual communities can automatically expand as members actively interact with each other and spread the word to their acquaintances. Virtual communities offer an excellent opportunity to establish genuine and meaningful connections with individuals from all parts of the globe, despite the misleading term "virtual."
- ***Personal development:*** In communities that prioritize learning and personal growth, undergoing transformation alongside others provides both accountability and support from others who encourage and motivate you.
- ***Portable conversations:*** Utilizing a community app such as Mighty Networks allows you to conveniently access and engage in meaningful connections wherever you go. Virtual communities that charge a membership fee generate ongoing money for their hosts.
- ***Centralized business:*** A virtual community can consolidate all aspects of an online business, including memberships, courses, and live events. Figure 5 shows advantages of online communities.

Figure 5. Advantages of online communities

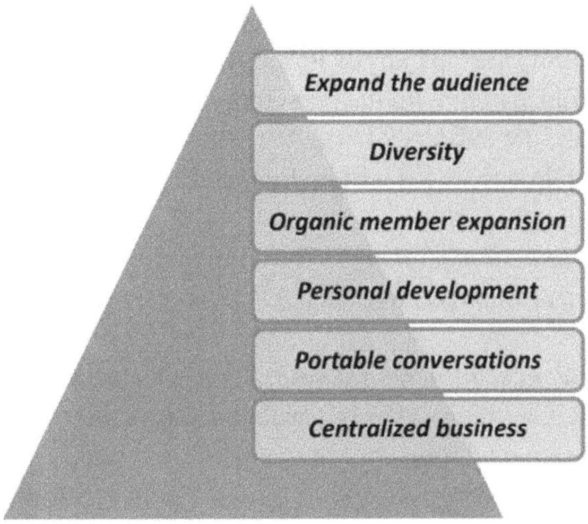

A virtual community offers a multitude of advantages for all participants, encompassing a wide array of perks.

Authentic connections: Despite the virtual nature of the platform where they are formed, the relationships established within an online community are tangible ties that frequently endure for extended periods of time.

Global reach: Membership in an online community is unrestricted by political or geographical limits. The ability to have members from any location worldwide contributes to a more vibrant and dynamic community.

Cultivating brand advocates: If you specialize in crafting custom furniture or apparel, an online network of enthusiasts and supporters has the potential to evolve into a group of influential brand advocates.

Portability: In addition to being able to attract members globally, your members have the convenience of logging in and being updated regardless of their location, be it during a lunch break, at the beach, while taking a shopping break, or even while lying in bed.

Increased revenue: The most effective community apps provide you with complete authority over the process of generating income. You have the option to provide both freemium and premium memberships, offer in-app purchases, grant access to unique content, and implement additional features.

Centralization: Depending on the nature of your business, it may be possible to consolidate all the various components, such as memberships, courses, live events, and more, into a single virtual platform.

What Are the Disadvantages or Limitations?

Virtual communities, like all things, possess drawbacks. Fortunately, the drawbacks of an online community are typically overshadowed by the advantages. Nevertheless, it is crucial to be transparent with the potential disadvantages, hence here they are:

Initial expenses: Regardless of whether your community is centered around a website or a mobile app, there will be financial obligations involved with commencing operations.

Prerequisite technical proficiency: The community host must possess a certain level of technological expertise to effectively manage, advertise, and sustain their online community.

Potential compromise of personal data: There exists a possibility that hackers may abscond with user data. This is particularly accurate if you establish your community via Facebook Groups or other costless services.

Trolls: Certain individuals engage in online forums with the sole purpose of causing distress and unhappiness to others. Having powerful content moderation technologies is necessary for this reason.

Absence of confidence: When there is a lack of visual contact between you and your staff, it can lead to a diminished sense of trust. You may feel inclined to engage in micromanagement as a means of closely monitoring the situation. Nevertheless, this might lead to a lack of engagement among employees and result in frustration for both parties involved. Therefore, it is essential to create trust right from the beginning.

Diminished team cooperation: A virtual community might be characterized by a lack of human connection, as individuals work independently and at their own convenience. Coordinating everyone's participation for a collaborative endeavor is a challenging task. Likewise, if members are situated in disparate geographical places, a time disparity may impede their advancement. Moreover, virtual communication, particularly through written messages, is prone to being misconstrued. It can result in misinterpretations that hinder the ability to effectively collaborate. There is a plethora of video conferencing software available that can be utilized to facilitate virtual team communication. To enhance the transparency of your online cooperation, you can utilize collaborative workspaces like Google Workspace tools.

Social isolation: refers to the state of being disconnected or separated from others in society. An adaptable digital setting can greatly enhance the equilibrium between work and personal life, but it can also lead to significant social isolation. Virtual workers frequently have a sense of isolation while facing a particular task and may lack knowledge on who or how to seek assistance. Team development can also be challenging, which refers to employees socializing and discussing non-work related subjects.

Concealed expenses related to technology: In order to ensure efficient management of virtual teams, it is imperative that all employees own up-to-date software, possess a comprehensive understanding of several communication channels, and have the ability to swiftly adapt to emerging technologies. Nevertheless, it is not feasible to anticipate that every current and prospective employee would have all the essential applications and resources. Therefore, it is likely that you will need to furnish them. The expenses might accumulate significantly when taking into account the various tools, applications, and integrations required by cross-functional teams, even though the cost of a single tool may appear insignificant.

Possible security vulnerabilities: The greater the accessibility of your confidential trade secrets, the higher their susceptibility. Although many firms include data protection clauses in their employee contracts, it is still possible for you to be targeted by a malware assault. Certain employees may also engage in the act of downloading company documents without implementing the required safety measures. In this scenario, if a single device belonging to a member of the virtual project team is compromised, all of your information is at risk.

Monitoring progress can be challenging: Transitioning to a virtual team may result in initial difficulties in monitoring your team's success. It is not permissible to physically approach their workstation or repeatedly request updates on a daily basis.

THE UTILIZATION OF VIRTUAL COMMUNITIES BY BUSINESSES

Although learning and support groups are widely favored for their significant impact on individuals' lives, businesses of all sizes have also recognized the advantages of cultivating a flourishing online community.

Virtual communities offer firms genuine feedback that is not available from any other source. Numerous enterprises utilize their online community as a platform for gathering feedback and opinions. They provide a unique preview of new items to community members in order to solicit their feedback, which is then used to make necessary modifications before exposing the product to the broader market. From that perspective, the online community functions as a substantial focal point for gathering feedback and insights. Businesses utilize virtual communities as a means to reduce client acquisition expenses. When community members are granted privileged access to exclusive previews and similar opportunities, they often become outspoken advocates of the brand and, whether consciously or unintentionally, promote the company to others. Such unplanned brand advocacy can significantly reduce the expense of acquiring new customers. As previously stated, an internet community possesses a worldwide reach, enabling businesses to introduce individuals from all corners of the globe to the delights of their specific offering. While customer reach was formerly confined to a city, region, or nation 50 years ago, it now has the ability to extend to individuals halfway across the globe and everyone in between.

Currently, there is a proliferation of business models being utilized within the very brief existence of E-Commerce. E-Commerce facilitates business transactions that leverage the distinct possibilities provided by the Internet and World Wide Web. These business models or companies have adopted the notion of virtual communities to expand their business, promote their products, advertise, and engage in online business worldwide. The subsequent section illustrates the correlation between E-Commerce and Community; currently, a highly essential domain in commercial enterprise for establishing an E-Commerce platform is the Virtual Community. A virtual community is a network of individuals connected through a website, which allows us to establish a connection between our business and their product or client base. If an individual develops a sense of belonging to a community, they are more inclined to adhere to the group's terms and conditions. Consequently, their purchasing behavior will be influenced.

VIRTUAL WORLDS

To obtain more extensive coverage on this subject, please refer to the article on Virtual world. A party scene from Second Life based in Hyrule. Virtual worlds are the most interactive of all sorts of virtual communities. In this particular virtual community, individuals establish connections by embodying an avatar within a computer-generated realm. Users have the ability to customize their own avatar, including selecting attire and constructing their virtual residence. They also have full control over their avatar's life and interactions with other characters in the immersive 3D virtual environment. It bears resemblance to a computer game but lacks any specific goal for the players. A virtual world provides users with the chance to construct and manage an imaginary existence within the digital domain. Characters within the virtual realm has the ability to communicate with each other and engage in interactions that closely resemble those of real-life individuals. For instance, individuals have the ability to interact and establish close connections with each other through online platforms.

This form of virtual community enables individuals to engage in real-time chats and actively interact with others. The avatars that users construct bear resemblance to human beings. Users can opt to build avatars like themselves or take on an altogether different personality than them. Character interactions involve the exchange of text-based communication and virtual experiences, such as arranging virtual dates for avatars, to foster mutual understanding. A virtual community chat room facilitates synchronous communication, enabling individuals to engage in real-time conversations with one other. Within a simulated environment, avatars have the capability to engage in shared pursuits, much to the interactions between friends in the physical world. Communities in virtual worlds closely resemble real-life communities as the characters within them coexist in the same physical space, regardless of whether the users controlling these characters are physically present or not. Second Life stands out as one of the highly favored virtual worlds on the Internet. Whyville provides a viable option for younger demographics who prioritize safety and privacy. Whyville utilizes the simulation feature of its virtual world to facilitate experimentation and acquisition of knowledge regarding diverse phenomena.

Virtual worlds have also found application in the realm of corporate communications. The utilization of virtual world technologies, including highly realistic avatars and positional sound, offers participants a more immersive experience that reduces the feeling of fatigue and enhances their sensation of presence. Enterprise controls enable the meeting host to determine the permissions of the attendees, such as who can talk or walk around, so giving the host control over the meeting environment. Zoom has shown significant growth throughout the COVID-19 outbreak and has become a widely used platform. On this platform, meeting hosts have the ability to exercise control over speaking privileges by muting or unmuting participants, as well as determining who can join the meeting. Multiple firms are developing virtual worlds for business purposes, one of which being Second Life. These business based worlds offer stronger controls and provide capabilities such as muting particular users, desktop sharing, or access lists to deliver a highly engaging and restricted virtual world to a certain organization or group. Virtual worlds designed for business purposes may offer advanced enterprise functionalities, including Single Sign-On integration with external service providers and Content Encryption.

SOCIAL NETWORK SERVICES

Social networking services are the most prominent sort of virtual community. They are a digital platform, encompassing both websites and software, dedicated to the establishment and upkeep of connections. Facebook, Twitter, and Instagram are all virtual communities. On these websites, users often create a profile or account and establish connections with others by adding friends or following them. This enables individuals to interact and seek assistance by using the social networking platform as a central meeting point. These websites frequently provide effortless monitoring of the activities of friends and acquaintances, enabling users to stay updated. Some of these platforms even offer the option of video chatting with multiple individuals simultaneously, creating a more immersive sense of togetherness. Facebook offers several features such as photo and video uploading, chatting, friend-making, reconnecting with old acquaintances, and joining groups or causes.

COMMUNITIES FOCUSED ON SPECIALIZED INFORMATION

Participatory culture significantly influences online and virtual communities. Within a participatory culture, users perceive their contributions as significant, believing that their active involvement fosters meaningful connections with fellow users. The distinctions between assuming the role of a content provider and that of a website consumer grow indistinct and intermingle. Henry Jenkins states that members of a group believe that their contributions are significant and have a certain level of social connection with each other (Jenkins et al., 2006). In order to trade and consume information effectively, individuals must possess a certain level of "digital literacy", which enables them to proficiently "archive, annotate, appropriate, transform, and recirculate media content" (Jenkins et al., 2006). Specialized information communities are platforms that bring together a distinct set of individuals that share a common interest in a certain topic. An instance of this is TasteofHome.com, the online platform associated with the publication Taste of Home, which serves as a specialized information community with a specific emphasis on baking and cooking. Users provide consumer information pertaining to their activity and engage in additional specialized groups and forums. Specialized Information Communities serve as a platform for individuals with similar interests to engage in discussions and exchange their experiences and passions.

Ethical Issues

In order to promote the utilization of the Internet and emerging online technologies, it is necessary to implement measures that enhance their safe usage and safeguard users from unwanted content. Awareness-raising initiatives should encompass various types of illicit, unsolicited, and detrimental content, such as content deemed unsuitable for minors. Additionally, these initiatives should consider relevant aspects of safeguarding consumer interests, protecting data and information, and ensuring network security against threats like viruses and unsolicited messages. These efforts must encompass content disseminated on the World Wide Web, as well as emerging forms of interactive information and communication resulting from the rapid proliferation of the Internet and mobile telephony. Internet censorship is undeniably a multifaceted problem, even if the Internet is inherently unmanageable, constantly evolving, and efforts to exert control and regulation are abundant. Attempting to limit access to the Internet is regarded as a violation of the right to freedom of expression and certainly of human rights.

Ethical principles exhibit a high degree of consistency, irrespective of the specific domain in which they are applied. Nevertheless, in every domain, particularly in the realm of information technology, novel and distinct challenges emerge, encompassing matters of secrecy and intellectual property rights. The right to privacy is being infringed upon due to the storage of personal information on networked computers, which are susceptible to unauthorized access. It is imperative for individuals to prioritize their personal security by safeguarding their accounts with passwords and potentially employing encryption software like PGP (Pretty Good Privacy). PGP is a costless encryption software that enables you to encrypt files prior to transmitting them. The recipient needs to install the PGP program as well. PGP is a software package specifically created to safeguard emails and files through the use of classical encryption and public keys. By utilizing it, one can construct safe methods of communication between individuals, without the necessity of modifying encryption keys. PGP incorporates a robust key management system, digital signature-based data authentication, and data compression.

CONCLUSION

The inherent characteristics of cyberspace imply that members of virtual communities will be freed from geographical and social limitations, form intricate social networks, become deeply engaged in shared interests, and yet maintain a psychological detachment, with only a limited responsibility towards other residents. If we define community as encompassing intimate, emotional, and comprehensive bonds, then cyberspace lacks these elements. Consequently, the cyberspace environment is less conducive to fostering genuine community compared to local and shared physical spaces. However, this does not imply that online relationships are completely opposite to real-life community relationships or that they are simply inadequate replacements for genuine community connections. The Internet should be understood as an improved method of communication, rather than a replacement for community. Its impact on community is comparable to that of the telephone. For instance, e-mail correspondence can strengthen social connections, similar to how a phone chat can, by fostering more comprehensive and intimate in-person contacts. The telephone, and now the Internet, can serve as first forms of communication in establishing stronger levels of community (e.g., when requesting a date), and they can serve as significant alternatives when in-person interactions are not feasible (e.g., when families are geographically apart). The majority of the engagement that takes place on the Internet consists of relatively limited communication focused on specific information.

While communication is an essential component of community, it is insufficient on its own to establish a sense of community. Therefore, while seeking community, the Internet can have the following effects: (1) diminish community by spending excessive time on impersonal website searches, resulting in social isolation and the absence of any form of community; (2) establish a feeble substitute for community through extensive email exchanges and chat room discussions, creating a virtual community with specialized connections and weak secondary relationships; or (3) strengthen community by facilitating initial or additional connections that lead to a community. The current ties to community are exclusively present in the digital realm, and if we consider the telephone as a suitable comparison, our increasing reliance on the Internet will continue to simultaneously diminish, substitute, and strengthen community. The pursuit of community persists in the realm of online. Nevertheless, despite several years of investigation, the notion that virtual communities devoid of physical location might supplant local communities and shared spaces as the primary source of psychological community sentiment continues to be uncertain. Currently, Internet contacts can enhance the community found in the local area and shared spaces, but they are inadequate substitutes for the type relationships found in the specific place known as The Community. Communities thrive most easily, organically, and often when individuals feel a strong connection to a certain location, such as their neighborhood, school, or business. Furthermore, direct, in-person connections remain crucial within the confines of a particular geographic region.

REFERENCES

Anderson, B. (1983). *Imagined Communities: Reflections on the Origin and Spread of Nationalism*. Verso.

Beniger, J. R. (1987). The Personalization of Mass Media and the Growth of PseudoCommunity. *Communication Research*, 14(3), 352–371. DOI: 10.1177/009365087014003005

Cohen, A. P. (1985). *The Symbolic Construction of Community*. Routledge & Kegan Paul. DOI: 10.4324/9780203323373

Ellis, C. A., Gibbs, S. J., & Rein, G. L. (1991). Groupware - Some Issues and Experiences. *Communications of the ACM*, 34(1), 38–58. DOI: 10.1145/99977.99987

Flavian, C., Guinaliu, M., & Torres, E. (2005). The Influence of Corporate Image on Customer Trust, a Comparative Analysis in Traditional versus Internet Banking. *Internet Research*, 15, 447–470. DOI: 10.1108/10662240510615191

Fuks, H., Raposo, A., Gerosa, M. A., Pimentel, M., Filippo, D., & Lucena, C. (2008). Inter- and Intra-Relationships between Communication Coordination and Cooperation in the Scope of the 3C Collaboration Model. Computer Supported Cooperative Work in Design, *12th International Conference*, 148-153.

González-Anta, B., Pérez de la Fuente, I., Zornoza, A., & Orengo, V. (2023). Building Sustainable Virtual Communities of Practice: A Study of the Antecedents of Intention to Continue Participating. *Sustainability (Basel)*, 15(21), 15657. DOI: 10.3390/su152115657

Granovetter, M. S. (1973). The strength of weak ties. *American Journal of Sociology*, 78(6), 1360–1380. DOI: 10.1086/225469

Gu, Y., & Zhu, J. (2023). The effect of online review and interaction on value co-creation in tourism virtual community. *Cogent Social Sciences*, 9(2), 2261234. DOI: 10.1080/23311886.2023.2261234

Hillery, G. A.Jr. (1955). Definitions of Community: Areas of Agreement. *Rural Sociology*, 20, 779–791.

Jenkins, H. (2006). *Confronting the challenges of participatory culture: Media education for the 21st century. An occasional paper on digital media and learning*. John D. and Catherine T. MacArthur Foundation.

Jones, Q. (1997). Virtual-Communities, Virtual Settlements & Cyber-Archaeology: A Theoretical Outline. *Journal of Computer-Mediated Communication*, 3(3), 0. DOI: 10.1111/j.1083-6101.1997.tb00075.x

Kirkman, B. L., Cordery, J. L., Mathieu, J., Rosen, B., & Kukenberger, M. (2013). Global Organizational Communities of Practice: The Effects of Nationality Diversity, Psychological Safety, and Media Richness on Community Performance. *Human Relations*, 2013(66), 333–362. DOI: 10.1177/0018726712464076

Li, X. L., Johnston, K. A., & Feng, J.Xiufang (Leah) Li. (2024). Virtual community engagement: Engaging virtual communities for nation branding through sports. *Public Relations Review*, 50(3), 102440. DOI: 10.1016/j.pubrev.2024.102440

Martínez-López, F. J., Anaya-Sánchez, R., Aguilar-Illescas, R., & Molinillo, S. (2016). Types of Virtual Communities and Virtual Brand Communities. In *Online Brand Communities: Using the Social Web for Branding and Marketing* (pp. 125–140). Springer. DOI: 10.1007/978-3-319-24826-4_8

Matzat, U. (2004). Cooperation and Community on the Internet: Past Issues and Present Perspectives for Theoretical-Empirical Internet Research. *Analyse & Kritik*, 26(1), 63–90. DOI: 10.1515/auk-2004-0104

McMillan, D. W., & Chavis, D. M. (1986). Sense of community: A definition and theory. *Journal of Community Psychology*, 14(1), 6–23. DOI: 10.1002/1520-6629(198601)14:1<6::AID-JCOP2290140103>3.0.CO;2-I

Murphy, E. (2004). Recognising and Promoting Collaboration in an Online Asynchronous Discussion. *British Journal of Educational Technology*, 35(4), 421–431. DOI: 10.1111/j.0007-1013.2004.00401.x

Pang, L. J., & Yang, Z. (2021). The Impact of Information Interaction on User Engagement Behavior in Virtual Brand Community. *Inform. Sci.*, 39, 108–115.

Park, R. (1936). Human Ecology. *American Journal of Sociology*, 17(1), 1–15. DOI: 10.1086/217327

Porter, C. E. (2004). A Typology of Virtual Communities: A Multi-Disciplinary Foundation for Future Research. *Journal of Computer-Mediated Communication*, 10(1), 00. DOI: 10.1111/j.1083-6101.2004.tb00228.x

Preece, J., & de Souza, C. S. (2004). A Framework for Analyzing and Understanding Online Communities. *Interacting with Computers*, 16(3), 579–610. DOI: 10.1016/j.intcom.2003.12.006

Rheingold, H. (1993). *The Virtual Community: Homesteading on the Electronic Frontier*. Addison-Wesley.

Rheingold, H. (1993). *The Virtual Community: Homesteading on the Electronic Frontier*. Addison-Wesley.

Rickman, H. P. (Ed.). (1976). *W. Dilthey: selected writings*. Cambridge University Press.

Schrage, M. (1990). *Shared Minds*. Random House.

Schrage, M. (1995). *No more teams: Mastering the dynamics of creative collaboration*. Currency.

Thalheim, B., Jaakkola, H., Nakanishi, T., Sasaki, S., & Schewe, K.-D. (2014). Conceptual Modelling of Collaboration for Information Systems. In Tokuda, T., Kiyoki, Y., Jaakkola, H., & Yoshida, N. (Eds.), *Information Modelling and Knowledge Bases XXV* (pp. 272–305).

Van Dijk, J. (1999). *The Network Society*. Sage.

Wellman, B. (1999). The Network Community. In Wellman, B. (Ed.), *Networks in the Global Village*. Westview Press.

Wenger, E. (1999). *Communities of Practice: Learning, Meaning, and Identity*. Cambridge University Press.

Wenger, E. (2000). Wenger (2000). Communities of Practice and Social Learning Systems. *Organization*, 7(2), 225–246. DOI: 10.1177/135050840072002

Wood, D. J., & Gray, B. (1991). Toward a Comprehensive Theory of Collaboration. *The Journal of Applied Behavioral Science*, 27(2), 139–162. DOI: 10.1177/0021886391272001

Yang, M. S., Hu, S. G., Kpandika, B. E., & Liu, L. (2021). Effects of social attachment on social media continuous usage intention: The mediating role of affective commitment. *Human Systems Management*, 40(4), 619–631. DOI: 10.3233/HSM-201057

Zhu, Y., & Xie, B. B. (2018). The relationship between the perceived climate of team Cha-xu and employee silence: Research on affective commitment and traditionality. *Acta Psychologica Sinica*, 50(5), 539–548. DOI: 10.3724/SP.J.1041.2018.00539

KEY TERMS AND DEFINITIONS

Community of Practice (CoP): Is a group of people who share a common concern, a set of problems, or an interest in a topic and who come together to fulfill both individual and group goals.

Computer-Mediated Communication (CMC): Is defined as any human communication that occurs through the use of two or more electronic devices.

Internet Relay Chat (IRC): Is a network of Internet servers that use a specific protocol through which individuals can hold real-time online conversations via PCs and other devices.

Multi-User Dungeon (MUDs): Also known as a multi-user dimension or multi-user domain, is a multiplayer real-time virtual world, usually text-based or storyboarded.

Online Asynchronous Discussion (OAD): Is considered a commonly used cooperative learning activity in distance education.

Pretty Good Privacy (PGP): Is an encryption program that provides cryptographic privacy and authentication for data communication. PGP is used for signing, encrypting, and decrypting texts, e-mails, files, directories, and whole disk partitions and to increase the security of e-mail communications.

Virtual Community (VC): Is a group of people, who may or may not meet one another face to face, who exchange words and ideas through the mediation of digital networks.

Chapter 2
Navigating the Virtual Landscape: A Beginner's Guide to Understanding Online Communities

Andi Asrifan
https://orcid.org/0000-0002-9934-6129
Universitas Negeri Makassar, Indonesia

Khaerun Nisa'a Tayibu
STKIP Andi Matappa Pangkep, Indonesia

Anita Candra Dewi
Universitas Negeri Makassar, Indonesia

Herlina Herlina
Universitas Negeri Makassar, Indonesia

Lukman Lukman
https://orcid.org/0000-0003-1679-9382
Universitas Muhammadiyah Sidenreng Rappang, Indonesia

Ira Irviana
https://orcid.org/0009-0009-2288-9086
Universitas Islam Makassar, Indonesia

ABSTRACT

This article covers online communities, their evolution, and their social impact. It explores online communities from ARPANET's late 1960s launch to the present, including wikis, MMORPGs, and virtual worlds. Virtual communities have commercial potential, but they must be built and maintained through a common identity, strong leadership, and continual participation. It also emphasizes understanding online community dynamics by examining their psychological, sociological, and ethical components. User profiles, moderation, and lurking vs. active involvement are discussed. Online communities offer informational help and social connections,

DOI: 10.4018/979-8-3693-3868-1.ch002

but they can pose privacy problems, false identities, and undesirable behavior. Case studies of successful and unsuccessful online communities offer practical advice, as do future developments like multiplayer online gaming. Understanding the complexity of online communities and their impact on the digital world begins with this article.

INTRODUCTION

There is growing evidence that people use the Internet for social and information requirements (Torous et al., 2021) (Ponnusamy et al., 2020) Simpson et al. (2021) (Yang et al., 2020). New virtual areas offer much for those who go forth. However, accessing the internet is difficult (Hoeller et al., 2024) (Nath, 2020). Some guides can help us navigate the new technology. This paper defines online community first. Next, we shall discuss online community typology. Next, we will review some of the main characteristics of online communities and then give several metaphors that represent their distinct and common traits. We will end with some tips for online community members. Online communities, each with its peculiarities, have grown rapidly and offer a unique method for people to share their opinions and communicate. As more people join online communities, it is important to understand how they affect society, relationships, and well-being (Betley et al., 2023) (Zhou et al., 2022). We will also examine the psychological components of online communities, the roles people play, and how they affect behavior and decision-making. We will also explore online community ethics, including privacy, cyberbullying, and disinformation. This will explain online communities and how they shape the digital world. In today's interconnected world, online communities shape how people communicate, share information, and develop connections. These online platforms have become a staple of social contact, allowing people from diverse backgrounds to discuss mutual interests, seek help, and have meaningful conversations. Online communities have also created new social dynamics and cultural phenomena that have changed how we view and manage the digital world (Dey et al., 2020) (Raji et al., 2024) (Mukherjee & Narang, 2023). (Dey et al., 2020) (Raji, 2024) (Mukherjee & Narang, 2023).

As we study online communities, we must understand their manifestations, from social networking sites and forums to niche interest groups and professional networks. Each manifestation contributes rules, customs, and social structures to online communities. Online community psychology illuminates the motivations, behaviors, and interactions that shape the collective experience. Understanding the psychological basis of online communities can help us understand individual roles, group dynamics, and how these interactions affect individual and collective well-being. Online communities' ethical and accountability effects on society must also be considered (Yadlin-Segal & Oppenheim, 2021). (Coghlan, 2021; Holmes, 2022). Online communities must handle ethical challenges, including digital privacy, online abuse, and spreading false or damaging information as they evolve. Critically studying online community ethics can create a more responsible and inclusive digital environment that values integrity, respect, and empathy (Herden et al., 2021).

In the end, studying online communities provides a comprehensive look at the social, psychological, and ethical factors that impact how people interact, communicate, and collaborate online. By exploring these aspects, we can better understand online communities' diversity and dynamic nature and their tremendous impact on individuals, relationships, and society. Online communities affect society, relationships, and well-being. Hence, it is important to study them as more people join. We will also examine the psychological components of online communities, the roles people play, and how they affect behavior and decision-making (Hoffner & Bond, 2022) (Das et al., 2020) (Her & Timmermans). We will also explore online community ethics, including privacy, cyberbullying, and disinformation. This will explain online communities and how they shape the digital world.

The World Wide Web, information superhighway, cyberspace, net, virtual malls, communities, or islands are common metaphors for the Internet (Maseko & Siziba, 2023) (Whyte, 2023) (Proctor, 2021). These metaphors assist in visualizing a non-physical medium and illustrate the diversity of online content and organizations. The internet's social sphere has many places where people with similar interests assemble, just like in real life. Virtual communities may have distinct rules, vocabulary, and norms of conduct than other online or real-world communities.

On the Internet, one can explore an elaborate maze of interconnected websites and digital domains, like in a buzzing city (Nikiel, 2022). Like enormous oceans, websites and online meeting places are like islands where people share ideas, communicate, and participate in various activities. Like actual cultures, these digital areas have various groups with their customs, etiquette, and engaging ways. The online world is full of virtual neighborhoods that encourage a sense of belonging and offer a rich tapestry of experiences and relationships.

1.1. Purpose and Scope of the Guide

This guide explains online communities so you can better engage. The guide focuses on bulletin boards or message boards, which are the most unmoderated online communities. Remember that online community content and rules vary depending on their purpose and members' preferences. Before publishing messages, newcomers must "lurk" (observe without engaging) to learn the community culture and decorum.

These guidelines are for all internet users—individuals, families, educators, and seniors. This tutorial is just an introduction to help you navigate the vast virtual world. Consider the Internet a big city with museums, art galleries, libraries, arcades, retail malls, and theaters. As in any city, avoid dark and unsafe spots. This guide will help you understand cyberspace, the virtual world, and online communities, including how to recognize culture and customs and keep yourself, your family, and your computer safe.

1.2. Importance of Understanding Online Communities

Whether one agrees with Howard Rheingold as the "new social frontier" or William Mitchell as an "urban metaphor" and "dubious figure of speech," people are spending more time online and engaging in various activities (Berdejo-Espinola et al., 2021; Pandya & Lodha, 2021; Langley et al., 2021). This essay quickly explores virtual communities' history and presents ideas from a social sciences perspective as a beginner's guide to online communities. It describes online community traits. Finally, it summarizes and concludes. 4.57 billion people use the internet. 59% of the world is online (Sycinska-Dziarnowska & Paradowska-Stankiewicz, 2020). This vast number of netizens requires us to move beyond cyberspace language, such as "surfing the net" and "information superhighway," to characterize online activities and connections. The virtual world has various online communities, like the actual world, with many groupings, alliances, and surroundings. Understanding online communities has various benefits (Haleem et al., 2022; Arafat, 2020). Online communities' collective expertise can help businesses create creative goods. Connecting with online groups can help politicians bridge the digital gap. Parents and educators may help kids learn by exploring internet communities.

FOUNDATIONS OF ONLINE COMMUNITIES

Virtuality is crucial to understanding online community formation and function (Asad et al., 2021) (Shao & Lee, 2020). It shows how humans develop social structures and processes to execute social functions in virtual worlds. Virtual world social groups are emerging social structures that operate as social entities and exhibit detectable social traits (Bibri et al., 2022). Dolata & Schwabe (2023)Bojic (2022). Social identity, roles, rules, and standards exist in all social groups, virtual or actual. Virtual groups' social aspects are perceived as living social structures, although they result from group interaction in a virtual environment mediated by technology.

Understanding online communities requires two fundamentals (Archambault et al., 2022). (2020, Sun et al.) (2021, Haimson et al.) First, comprehending virtuality—technology mediates human actions and changes presence, time, and place. Second, understanding the necessity to research online groups separately from face-to-face communities permits the virtual world's unique characteristics and processes to emerge. Social scientists can improve our understanding of society and benefit online community users by acknowledging that online groups are new constructs with emergent processes and unique inherent norms that allow them to function as social entities.

2.1. Definition and Characteristics

Virtual communities have internal and external worlds (Ghamrawi, 2022; Sirola et al., 2021). Users can explore and 'occupy' the inside environment like a city. Chat rooms, forums, and multi-user games create this environment. These virtual groups' physical and social underpinning is reality. Virtual community members merge despite their distance and varied communication (Morrison-Smith & Ruiz, 2020). CA: Mpofu et al. (2022) 2023. Knowing and connecting with others structures communication. Content analysis and ethnography indicate social norms in group conversations. Virtual community social identity—its history of interactions—is vital. Virtual communities offer a sense of social identity that sets them apart from online services and organizations (Kim et al., 2023) Huangfu (2022) (Ruangkanjanases, 2020). (Kim, 2023; Huangfu, 2022; Ruangkanjanases, 2020).

VR communities are common social groups (Rojas-Sánchez et al., 2023) (2022, Jovanović & Milosavljević). Internet people with similar interests work, chat, and interact online. Like other communities, virtual communities converse and share views (Jamil et al., 2022). (Liu et al., 2020). Global Internet-based virtual communities communicate. Virtual communities are remote. This attribute inspires researchers, users, and entrepreneurs to study virtual communities' social, commercial, and educational possibilities.

2.2. History and Evolution

From its inception as a small collection of computers linked to share research information, the internet has developed into a vast global electronic information highway. Today, millions of individuals use the Internet for a wide variety of purposes, such as gathering news and information, seeking employment, engaging in commercial transactions, and communicating with others via email, chat groups, and newsgroups (Li & Zheng, 2022) (Dadaczynski et al., 2021) (Zakar et al., 2021). In addition, growing numbers of individuals are participating in virtual communities that are established and maintained on the Internet. These communities, which typically focus on special interests or support groups, are forums for discussion, sharing information, and helping each other. The willingness of people to share their experiences and knowledge in free-flowing conversations within online communities has made the Internet a dynamic source of information. Many experts in the field of information and technology are studying and implementing systems for selecting, filtering, and transferring information from the Internet to outside parties.

The development of the Internet began in the late 1960s with the creation of the Advanced Research Projects Agency Network (ARPANET), which was funded by the U.S. Department of Defense (Packard, 2020) (Packard, 2023). In the 1970s and 1980s, growth in the use of the Internet was fueled mainly by academic and research institutions. The emergence of the World Wide Web in the early 1990s as a user-friendly interface for the Internet provided much easier access to the net and introduced multimedia capabilities (Taneja, 2021) (Raper, 2020) (Duka et al., 2023). Expansion of the use of the internet continues to grow at a very rapid rate.

2.3. Types of Online Communities

Wikis let users easily add, remove, and amend content. Wikipedia, the most popular free online encyclopedia, lets anybody write or edit pages (with few restrictions). There are also many smaller wikis for certain video games or TV shows (Jacobson, 2021). Wikis are considered online communities because individuals interact and communicate to build and maintain the content.

Besides social media and forums, MMORPGs, wikis, and virtual worlds are also online communities (Wang et al., 2023) (Poor, 2022). Thousands of characters interact in persistent multiplayer online role-playing games (MMORPGs). Immersion is a hallmark of MMORPGs (Kokkini et al., 2022) (Zhang, 2023). Gamers join a virtual civilization with an economy, political system, and social structure. This takes time since player characters must repeat in-game behaviors to level up. MMORPGs include World of Warcraft, EverQuest, and Final Fantasy XI.

KEY CONCEPTS AND TERMINOLOGY

The vast virtual landscape of the internet comprises many online communities (Sahu, 2022). These communities may vary from groups of individuals linked by a common interest, such as science fiction or car repair, to people brought together by cultural or national ties to those linked by electronic means within an organization.

Virtual web-like communities provide a medium where people can communicate and share information at a previously unimaginable level (Talukder, 2020) (Dowd, 2022). For a newcomer, the complexity of this virtual web can be overwhelming. This paper aims to guide a beginner and help you understand online communities' key concepts and structures (Larson & DeChurch, 2020) (Gacs et al., 2020). With this knowledge, you can better participate in online communities and support your organization's presence in the virtual world. The Internet is a global network connecting millions or even billions of computers worldwide. It operates over the standard Internet protocol suite, enabling interconnected networks to link. Various online communities have emerged, establishing connections between web users across the globe and fostering communication, information sharing, and collaboration (Jamil et al., 2022) (Akpuokwe et al., 2024). The significance and impact of online communities are undeniable, shaping how people interact and share knowledge. As the internet continues to expand and evolve, it is crucial for both individuals and organizations to understand the dynamics of virtual communal spaces and to leverage the power of these communities for personal and professional growth.

3.1. User Profiles and Avatars

Browse and communicate in online communities to see many various reputations (Brogan & Smith, 2020) (Knott et al., 2022). Some users will be helpful and knowledgeable, earning esteem. Conversely, some users cause pandemonium everywhere. Several sites display these reputation levels (Popenoe et al., 2021) (Eyal, 2021).' Every user has a community-facing name and a reputation. This enables conversation and interaction. They usually feature a link to their profile and, in forums, a list of recent remarks. Advanced user pages generally include current activity, friends, private messages, and the opportunity to invite the user into a more direct interaction (Schou et al., 2022).

Profiles collect user-specific data on various sites. The user decides how much to share, but most provide basic information to construct an online presence. Giving more often means receiving more 'benefits' from the community. Users decide if personalized help and improved user-to-user engagement are worth the privacy trade-off. In most online communities, most users have profiles (Antonelli et al., 2022). Overall, profiles let users connect to the community. Profiles also hold community members accountable. Users who distrust their identities are less likely to act out.

3.2. Moderation and Community Guidelines

If you construct your online community as part of a bigger project or on dedicated platforms, you should define community norms to mold its culture. Community guidelines should address member behavior without being too restrictive (Hoicka et al., 2021). Patel et al. (2024) (Alexander, 2020). Avoid discussing politics and religion to avoid overregulation. Highlighting experienced community members and letting them report offensive content enables peer moderation. You may want to hire moderators if you expect a lot of new users or have a huge community. To maintain trust and community success, be upfront about moderating and explain your reasons.

Members of online groups with similar interests and aspirations self-regulate (Yu et al., 2020) (Bellhäuser, 2022). Larger virtual places often have community administrators, moderators, or guidelines. Online community moderation keeps everyone secure and respectful (El et al., 2020). It prevents and resolves disagreements. Content moderation on most platforms ranges from spam filtering to discussion direction control. The site owner, members (peer moderation), or professional specialists can moderate material. Industry estimates suggest that 15-25% of social media accounts are false, designed to boost likes and promote commercial and political messaging (Al, 2022). Most sites still have online harassment and hate speech issues.

3.3. Lurking vs. Active Participation

Active online community members offer comments, ask questions, answer others' inquiries, or share information or resources. Online communities thrive on active members (Trivedi et al., 2023) (Ufholz, 2020). They foster unity among members and preserve and develop the community's knowledge. Most online communities have a small number of highly active players, a larger group that contributes occasionally, and a large population that rarely or never contributes. Most online groups have this top-heavy activity distribution.

In online communities, individuals can pick their level of engagement (Dille & Røkenes, 2021; Szymkowiak et al., 2021). Some people absorb what others say and do without contributing. This is “lurking.” According to research, most online community members start as lurkers before becoming active. Some like to listen and read without discussing. Lurkers sustain online networks through passive activity (Mousavi & Roper, 2023). Lurking lets users experience the community's culture, norms, and engagement without the risks of active participation.

BENEFITS AND CHALLENGES OF ONLINE COMMUNITIES

Online communities also have drawbacks. One issue is that you never know who you are talking to. Someone's claims to be a university professor, a 35-year-old housewife, or a 13-year-old student may not be accurate. Many people adopt "fake identities" in online forums for privacy, security, or more sinister reasons (Sands et al., 2022) (Celliers & Hattingh, 2020). This problem is serious, especially for those seeking counsel or crisis support. It is comforting to know that the person you are talking to is who they say they are, but online identity verification is challenging. While an online community may offer useful advice, getting a second opinion is always a good idea, especially if the matter is critical.

Online communities can also provide information (Chen et al., 2020; Mirzaei & Esmaeilzadeh, 2021). According to many, connecting with others who have gone through a health crisis online is more useful than any other source of assistance. Professional counsel is crucial, but only someone who has "been there" can comprehend the emotions and concerns of a health crisis. Online communities are often "self-help" groups that support members with a specific issue (Lainas, 2023) (Harkin et al., 2020). Most of these groups provide "emotional" or "peer" support. Many find that an online self-help group is more effective than a face-to-face group since the members are sympathetic and empathetic, and because the group is "virtual," there is no need to feel embarrassed or self-conscious (Duhne et al., 2022). (Sudarshan et al., 2024; Neamţu & Faludi, 2021).

Can online communities help their members, or are they just computer geek clubs? What benefits someone who spends time and energy in an online group? Anyone seeking online community involvement should ask these questions. Online communities' "virtual" character allows people worldwide to share their interests, concerns, and issues. A 24-hour computerized "drop-in center" makes participation easier (Abbas et al., 2022)." Many people like online communities because they can connect with others who share their interests or worries. This is hard to do in the "real world," especially for remote persons or those with unique interests or health issues.

4.1. Benefits for Individuals and Groups

Virtual communities revolve around shared interests rather than people. These interest-based groups might be tiny, large, or short-lived. Hobby, health, and religion are popular online interests, and over 8,000 Usenet newsgroups cover over 1,300 hobbies (Van et al.2020). These communities are popular because they allow people with similar interests to communicate regardless of geography. Many people utilize the Internet to locate others who like a rare music genre or an uncommon passion, like collecting vintage vacuum cleaners (Scherr & Wang, 2021) (Carpenter et al.,

2022) (Hjorteset & Böcker, 2020). Thus, virtual communities can expose people to more perspectives and beliefs than their real environment.

Most people can benefit from virtual communities. All demographics join online communities to exchange knowledge, support, and advice. A virtual community's feedback and diverse opinions can help people solve personal issues, receive encouragement in a safe environment, and learn new information from others in similar situations (Sundararaj & Rejeesh, 2021) (Ismagilova et al., 2021) (Aichner, 2021). New women join online parenting forums for guidance from experienced parents. Job seekers share job ads and support each other while improving resumes and interview skills.

4.2. Challenges and Risks to be Aware of

Virtual communities' anonymity can bring out the best and worst in people (Abbas et al., 2023) (Duvall, 2020). Members often create bogus identities and pretend to be others. Deception can erode confidence among members who want to help each other. Giving thousands of members a voice implies that not all contributions will be favorable. Members should expect criticism and hostility. Public relations damage from angry customers discussing products online can be difficult to control for commercial organizations (Pöyry & Laaksonen, 2022). A "mole" could infiltrate any society to steal data. Be wary of requests for personal information or links to seemingly innocent websites.

Finding a virtual group about a topic you like may be thrilling and educational. Online, things are not always good. Virtual communities have distinct challenges and threats that all members should know. Knowing what to expect will help you appreciate a community of interest and handle any emerging challenges.

There are approaches to address privacy, cyberbullying, and misinformation in online groups. Start with stringent privacy policies and data protection education to reduce privacy issues. Second, clear community norms and proactive moderation prevent cyberbullying and build respect. Advanced AI systems can notify platforms of dangerous information before it spreads. Promote digital literacy to assist people examine information and reduce misinformation. These solutions make online communities safer and more helpful, fostering meaningful relationships and enjoyable interactions.

BUILDING AND SUSTAINING ONLINE COMMUNITIES

Long-term success in an online community requires a common identity (Billiet et al., 2021). Bowe et al. (2020). Consistent site branding, rituals, inside jokes, and other community-specific characteristics can achieve this. Collaboration and group activities can also improve communal bonds (Luger et al., 2020). (Miković et al., 2020). Managing an online community requires good leadership. This may include site founders, paid staff, volunteers, or community power users. Maintaining community order requires clearly defined roles and responsibilities and leader behavior guidelines. Fair power distribution and member trust in leaders help communities survive.

Developing an online community requires more effort than just opening a website (Rizvanović et al., 2023) (Kang & Lou, 2022) (Redjeki & Affandi, 2021). Nurturing an online community helps it expand. Administrators and moderators lead debates, create new topics, and enforce rules. Promoting the site on social media and other methods can also generate community. Community development includes responding to user comments and upgrading the site's features and functionality (O'Keefe et al., 2020) (Molinillo, 2021). User engagement and community loyalty increase when they feel heard and see their suggestions implemented.

5.1. Creating a Community Mission and Values

Maintain honesty and avoid over-promising. Your goal statement should appropriately describe your community and its conversations and activities. Remember, your mission statement is your community's foundation for recruiting and retaining members.

In addition to a mission statement, you may want to create a brief elevator pitch: a concise and convincing overview of your community to attract new members. A clear, specific, and unique mission statement and value proposition are essential. A clearer community mission is more likely to recruit and keep members with similar interests (Yin & Mahrous, 2022; Gartenberg & Zenger, 2023; Kristof-Brown et al., 2023). When writing your mission statement and key principles, ask yourself: Why are you building this community? What need does it meet? What are your community's objectives? What do you want to achieve by gathering folks here? Along with a mission statement, you should create core values to govern community conduct and inform your community's rules and ethos. Before creating an online community, you should write a mission statement that explains its purpose and the goals you aim to achieve by bringing people together (Cornelissen et al., 2021). Make your mission statement count—it is the first thing community members will see.

5.2. Engagement Strategies and Activities

Online communities offer many forums for users to discuss their interests (Jamil et al., 2022). Discussions might be unstructured or planned around specific subjects. You can join online community discussions and address other members' concerns, needs, and interests to engage them. You may create a positive community culture that encourages participation by including and valuing other members' perspectives and ideas.

Effective online community engagement needs regular effort and active participation (Martin & Borup, 2022) (Mirzaei & Esmaeilzadeh, 2021). Engaged and connected members contribute and benefit from the community. Open-ended questions, personal stories, and gratitude for others' efforts can boost engagement (Roberson & Perry, 2022) (Nguyen et al., 2022) (Hemphill et al., 2020) (Chudyk, 2023). Facilitating or participating in community events, group activities, or joint projects can also strengthen relationships and foster a sense of belonging. Stay proactive and use multiple engagement tactics to keep the community supportive and active.

5.3. Tools and Platforms for Community Building

Our web experience includes online communities (Szymkowiak et al., 2021). Some societies live long after the virtual world ends. What makes an online community last? Web pioneer Howard Rheingold says, "Virtual communities employ language to create, accomplish, and collaborate. They create artifacts that reflect the group's developing culture (Mystakidis, 2022) (Ritterbusch & Teichmann, 2023). To develop a successful online community, you must first understand virtual communities and why people participate. With this information, you can surf the internet and develop online communities.

Most websites make Community creation possible (Hacker et al., 2020). Community-building is easy with email, chat rooms, and message boards. Newer tools like blogs, podcasts, and vlogs diversify communities. MySpace, Facebook, and LinkedIn offer various tools to develop and sustain online communities. Internet evolution creates new community-building tools. Understanding that community creation is not about tools (Hysa et al., 2021) is crucial. People who use tools matter. No matter the tool, online community building strives to unite people with similar interests, goals, or values.

CASE STUDIES AND EXAMPLES

Many conceptual conceptions of online "community" exist. From commercial services to bed and breakfast inns, some observers think any site with active users is a community. The word is sometimes overused, but a "virtual community" that defines certain dynamics helps generalize from one example to another. Electronic work requires high validation because the Web is full of 'fake' sites built by marketers for 'click-through' mass audiences (Kshetri et al., 2023) (Haleem, 2022).

A single community case study can reveal several aspects. However, any sociological notion must incorporate multiple social settings or communities within the same setting to be generic enough (De Haas, 2021) (Grutzpalk and Jarolimek2024). In quantitative survey data, "multiple-case" studies are difficult to collect and design, so most validation evidence comes from comparisons with other aggregations of communities or ' meta' communities, such as hobby or professional associations. Large-scale surveys will make assembling sets of true multiple case studies easier (Kasauli et al., 2021) (Marx, 2023). Until then, cautious qualitative researchers must validate concepts. Single-community research will likely disprove some of our understanding of the electronic community. Refutations imply additional variations or enhancements.

6.1. Successful Online Communities in Various Sectors

The Knot, a US-based website, offers discussion rooms for engaged couples (Basinger et al., 2023) (Castro-Cosío, 2023). Local receptions and sex are frequent subjects in the forums. Informational value is their major use. Members exchange wedding planning tips, making it easier and more fun. The Knot, a wedding services company, has created social networking around its main business. Discussion forums increase brand loyalty, and users are more inclined to buy from Knot advertisers.

The Alzheimer's Society runs a dementia caregiver forum online (Borchard et al., 2023) (Vermeer, 2020). The forum provides emotional support and knowledge. Its emotional value makes it popular. Caring for a dementia patient can be lonely and stressful. Carers can communicate with others in similar situations on the forum. Sharing emotions can be healing. The community also shares practical advice. It can inspire caring and inform about local services. The forum is a prime example of an affinity space that offers emotional support and knowledge sharing to assist individuals in overcoming challenges (Łapniewska, 2022; Na & Staudt, 2022).

For social purposes, the RSPB (Royal Society for the Protection of Birds) maintains a member-only community where people may discuss birds, animals, and the organization (Minter et al., 2024) (Turnbull et al., 2023). Introduce yourself, engage in off-topic chats, and create relationships in the community. This community succeeds because individuals love animals, and the community fosters this interest. Members renew and introduce others to the RSPB more often. The community is a cheap way for the RSPB to retain members. Social media helps RSPB members connect with the organization.

Setting up an online community might be difficult. What should you do for community success? Success means what? You must answer these questions when starting a community or taking over one. Start by learning about online communities and their success. One of the finest methods is to observe other communities in the same or different sectors. This chapter examines successful online communities in various domains.

6.2. Lessons Learned from Failed Communities

The first lesson is creating and nurturing a community. Administrators, managers, and leaders must guide members and start participation-promoting initiatives to build the community. Group members must feel ownership to share and interact. When the community disintegrates, people log off, and the group dies.

Hundreds of online groups are founded daily, with varied degrees of effectiveness (Finlay et al., 2021). Several communities will fail. Why does a community die? Put, people! Communities fail when creators do not spend enough time or money managing them, members stop participating and communicating, or the group dynamic turns negative and devolves into flame wars and personal assaults.

Throughout the history of the internet, people have created online communities to share opinions, interests, and information (Yulia, 2020) (Rogers, 2020) (Lynch et al., 2021). People have created online communities to share opinions, interests, and information since the internet's inception (Yulia, 2020) (Rogers, 2020) (Lynch et al., 2021). Virtual spaces, like real ones, have distinct cultures, rules, and systems. Community administrators and participants must understand how online communities work and how to avoid frequent mistakes and failures.

CONCLUSION

Overall, individuals are at the center of online communities, both in creating and maintaining these virtual social spaces and contributing to the shared sense of identity at the heart of every online community. Therefore, no matter how overwhelming or intimidating the virtual landscape may seem, anyone can become a more informed and empowered member of the online community space with some basic knowledge and a willingness to explore. In doing so, they can connect with others and share the purpose of bringing an online community to life.

In conclusion, online communities result from technology-mediated social interactions, and people are connected through a shared interest, idea, or purpose. As virtual spaces with complex social dynamics, rules, and structures, online communities offer a unique social environment that creates opportunities and challenges for community members. By understanding the key characteristics and elements that comprise online communities and the guiding principles that influence their functioning, individuals can more effectively and meaningfully participate in the various online communities they are a part of.

7.1. Summary of Key Takeaways

In this article, 'virtual landscape' refers to the digital or virtual environment through which online communities are connected. This landscape comprises websites, the internet, intranets, and other platforms allowing online connections and communications. Online communities travel through this virtual landscape with the help of web pages, web servers, domain names, website addresses, and other key elements. These digital tools help online communities to move from one place to another, to stay together and remain connected, and to perform specific types of tasks and activities. This chapter provides a beginner's guide to understanding how online communities make use of the virtual landscape to perform their functions and activities. To help explain these processes, concepts, and technologies are described using analogies with real-world landmarks and recognizable navigation tools.

This chapter introduces the concept of virtual environments where online communities are hosted. It examines the virtual landscape comprising websites, the internet, intranets, and other online platforms. The chapter explores the use of virtual environments by online communities through the hosting of web pages, the use of web servers, and the creation of domain names and website addresses. Key concepts and processes are explained by analogy with real-world landmarks and navigation tools that help travelers find their way around unfamiliar territories. The chapter provides a beginner's guide to understanding the technology and processes underpinning online communities' functioning in virtual environments.

REFERENCES

Abbas, N., Whitfield, J., Atwell, E., Bowman, H., Pickard, T., & Walker, A. (2022). Online chat and chatbots to enhance mature student engagement in higher education. International Journal of Lifelong Education, 41(3), 308-326. https://doi.org/tandfonline.comDOI: 10.1080/02601370.2022.2066213

Abbas, S., Alnoor, A., Yin, T. S., Sadaa, A. M., Muhsen, Y. R., Khaw, K. W., & Ganesan, Y. (2023). Antecedents of trustworthiness of social commerce platforms: A case of rural communities using multi-group SEM & MCDM methods. [HTML]. *Electronic Commerce Research and Applications*, 62, 101322. DOI: 10.1016/j.elerap.2023.101322

Aichner, T., Grünfelder, M., Maurer, O., & Jegeni, D. (2021). Twenty-five years of social media: a review of social media applications and definitions from 1994 to 2019. Cyberpsychology, behavior, and social networking, 24(4), 215-222. https://doi.org/ liebertpub.comDOI: 10.1089/cyber.2020.0134

Akpuokwe, C. U., Chikwe, C. F., & Eneh, N. E. (2024). Innovating business practices: The impact of social media on fostering gender equality and empowering women entrepreneurs. Magna Scientia Advanced Research and Reviews, 10(2), 032-043. https://doi.org/ magnascientiapub.comDOI: 10.30574/msarr.2024.10.2.0042

Al Shehab, N. A. (2022). the dark side of social media: Spreading misleading information during covid-19 crisis. Advances in Data Science and Intelligent Data Communication Technologies for COVID-19 [HTML]. *Innovative Solutions Against COVID*, 19, 277–306. DOI: 10.1007/978-3-030-77302-1_15

Alexander, R., Ravi, A., Barclay, H., Sawhney, I., Chester, V., Malcolm, V., ... & Langdon, P. E. (2020). Guidance for the treatment and management of COVID-19 among people with intellectual disabilities. Journal of Policy and Practice in Intellectual Disabilities, 17(3), 256-269. https://doi.org/ wiley.comDOI: 10.1111/jppi.12352

Antonelli, M., Penfold, R. S., Merino, J., Sudre, C. H., Molteni, E., Berry, S., ... & Steves, C. J. (2022). Risk factors and disease profile of post-vaccination SARS-CoV-2 infection in UK users of the COVID Symptom Study app: a prospective, community-based, nested, case-control study. The Lancet Infectious Diseases, 22(1), 43-55. https://doi.org/ thelancet.comDOI: 10.1016/S1473-3099(21)00460-6

Arafat, S. Y., Kar, S. K., Menon, V., Alradie-Mohamed, A., Mukherjee, S., Kaliamoorthy, C., & Kabir, R. (2020). Responsible factors of panic buying: an observation from online media reports. Frontiers in Public Health, 8, 603894. https://doi.org/frontiersin.orgDOI: 10.3389/fpubh.2020.603894

Archambault, L., Leary, H., & Rice, K. (2022). Pillars of online pedagogy: A framework for teaching in online learning environments. [HTML]. *Educational Psychologist*, 57(3), 178–191. Advance online publication. DOI: 10.1080/00461520.2022.2051513

Asad, M. M., Naz, A., Churi, P., & Tahanzadeh, M. M. (2021). Virtual reality as pedagogical tool to enhance experiential learning: a systematic literature review. Education Research International, 2021, 1-17. https://doi.org/hindawi.comDOI: 10.1155/2021/7061623

Basinger, E. D., Delaney, A. L., & Williams, C. (2023). Uncertainty management in online sexual health forums. [HTML]. *Health Communication*, 38(5), 875–884. Advance online publication. DOI: 10.1080/10410236.2021.1980253 PMID: 34605355

Bellhäuser, H., Liborius, P., & Schmitz, B. (2022). Fostering self-regulated learning in online environments: positive effects of a web-based training with peer feedback on learning behavior. Frontiers in psychology. https://doi.org/frontiersin.orgDOI: 10.3389/fpsyg.2022.813381

Berdejo-Espinola, V., Suárez-Castro, A. F., Amano, T., Fielding, K. S., Oh, R. R. Y., & Fuller, R. A. (2021). Urban green space use during a time of stress: A case study during the COVID-19 pandemic in Brisbane, Australia. People and Nature, 3(3), 597-609. https://doi.org/ wiley.comDOI: 10.1002/pan3.10218

Betley, E. C., Sigouin, A., Pascua, P. A., Cheng, S. H., MacDonald, K. I., Arengo, F., ... & Sterling, E. J. (2023). Assessing human well-being constructs with environmental and equity aspects: A review of the landscape. People and Nature, 5(6), 1756-1773. https://doi.org/wiley.comDOI: 10.1002/pan3.10293

Bibri, S. E., Allam, Z., & Krogstie, J. (2022). The Metaverse as a virtual form of data-driven smart urbanism: platformization and its underlying processes, institutional dimensions, and disruptive impacts. Computational Urban Science. https://doi.org/springer.comDOI: 10.1007/s43762-022-00051-0

Billiet, A., Dufays, F., Friedel, S., & Staessens, M. (2021). The resilience of the cooperative model: How do cooperatives deal with the COVID-19 crisis?. Strategic Change. https://doi.org/ nih.govDOI: 10.1002%2Fjsc.2393

Bojic, L. (2022). Metaverse through the prism of power and addiction: what will happen when the virtual world becomes more attractive than reality?. European Journal of Futures Research. https://doi.org/ springer.comDOI: 10.1186/s40309-022-00208-4

Bowe, M., Gray, D., Stevenson, C., McNamara, N., Wakefield, J. R., Kellezi, B., ... & Costa, S. (2020). A social cure in the community: A mixed-method exploration of the role of social identity in the experiences and well-being of community volunteers. European Journal of Social Psychology, 50(7), 1523-1539. https://doi.org/wiley.comDOI: 10.1016/j.futures.2023.103258

Brogan, C. & Smith, J. (2020). Trust agents: Using the web to build influence, improve reputation, and earn trust. amazonaws.com

Calzada, I. (2023). Disruptive technologies for e-diasporas: Blockchain, DAOs, data cooperatives, Metaverse, and ChatGPT. Futures. https://doi.org/ sciencedirect.comDOI: 10.1016/j.futures.2023.103258

Carpenter, J., Tani, T., Morrison, S., & Keane, J. (2022). Exploring the landscape of educator professional activity on Twitter: An analysis of 16 education-related Twitter hashtags. [HTML]. *Professional Development in Education*, 48(5), 784–805. DOI: 10.1080/19415257.2020.1752287

Castro-Cosío, A. (2023). 'Informal' Financial Practices in the South Bronx: Family, Compadres, and Acquaintances. [HTML]. *Journal of Family and Economic Issues*. Advance online publication. DOI: 10.1007/s10834-023-09912-0

Celliers, M., & Hattingh, M. (2020). A systematic review on fake news themes reported in literature. In Responsible Design, Implementation and Use of Information and Communication Technology: 19th IFIP WG 6.11 Conference on e-Business, e-Services, and e-Society, I3E 2020, Skukuza, South Africa, April 6–8, 2020 [Springer International Publishing. nih.gov]. *Proceedings*, 19(Part II), 223–234.

Chen, L., Baird, A., & Straub, D. (2020). A linguistic signaling model of social support exchange in online health communities. [HTML]. *Decision Support Systems*, 130, 113233. Advance online publication. DOI: 10.1016/j.dss.2019.113233

Chudyk, A. M., Stoddard, R., McCleary, N., Duhamel, T. A., Shimmin, C., Hickes, S., & Schultz, A. S. (2023). Exploring patient and caregiver perceptions of the meaning of the patient partner role: a qualitative study. Research Involvement and Engagement, 9(1), 106. https://doi.org/springer.comDOI: 10.1186/s40900-023-00511-9

Coghlan, S., Miller, T., & Paterson, J. (2021). Good proctor or "big brother"? Ethics of online exam supervision technologies. Philosophy & Technology. https://doi.org/springer.comDOI: 10.1007/s13347-021-00476-1

Cornelissen, J. P., Akemu, O., Jonkman, J. G., & Werner, M. D. (2021). Building character: The formation of a hybrid organizational identity in a social enterprise. Journal of Management Studies, 58(5), 1294-1330. https://doi.org/ wiley.comDOI: 10.1111/joms.12640

Dadaczynski, K., Okan, O., Messer, M., Leung, A. Y., Rosário, R., Darlington, E., & Rathmann, K. (2021). Digital health literacy and web-based information-seeking behaviors of university students in Germany during the COVID-19 pandemic: cross-sectional survey study. Journal of medical Internet research, 23(1), e24097. https:// doi.org/ jmir.orgDOI: 10.2196/24097

Das, K. V., Jones-Harrell, C., Fan, Y., Ramaswami, A., Orlove, B., & Botchwey, N. (2020). Understanding subjective well-being: perspectives from psychology and public health. Public Health Reviews, 41, 1-32. https://doi.org/springer.comDOI: 10.1186/s40985-020-00142-5

De Haas, H. (2021). A theory of migration: the aspirations-capabilities framework. Comparative migration studies. https://doi.org/springer.comDOI: 10.1186/s40878-020-00210-4

Dey, B. L., Yen, D., & Samuel, L. (2020). Digital consumer culture and digital acculturation. *International Journal of Information Management*, 51, 102057. brunel. ac.uk. DOI: 10.1016/j.ijinfomgt.2019.102057

Dille, K. B. & Røkenes, F. M. (2021). Teachers' professional development in formal online communities: A scoping review. Teaching and Teacher Education. https:// doi.org/ sciencedirect.comDOI: 10.1016/j.tate.2021.103431

Dolata, M. & Schwabe, G. (2023). What is the Metaverse and who seeks to define it? Mapping the site of social construction. Journal of Information Technology. https://doi.org/sagepub.comDOI: 10.1177/02683962231159927

Dowd, A. (2022). Vanishing acts: The crisis of our loss of kinship with the more-than-human world. [HTML]. *The Journal of Analytical Psychology*, 67(5), 1270–1295. Advance online publication. DOI: 10.1111/1468-5922.12863 PMID: 36440726

Duhne, P. G. S., Delgadillo, J., & Lutz, W. (2022). Predicting early dropout in online versus face-to-face guided self-help: A machine learning approach. Behaviour Research and Therapy. https://doi.org/sciencedirect.comDOI: 10.1016/j. brat.2022.104200

Duka, M., Sikora, M., & Strzelecki, A. (2023). From Web Catalogs to Google: A Retrospective Study of Web Search Engines Sustainable Development. Sustainability. https://doi.org/mdpi.comDOI: 10.3390/su15086768

Duvall, S. S. (2020). Too famous to protest: Far-right online community bonding over collective desecration of Colin Kaepernick, fame, and celebrity activism. [HTML]. *The Journal of Communication Inquiry*, 44(3), 256–278. Advance online publication. DOI: 10.1177/0196859920911650

El Morr, C., Maule, C., Ashfaq, I., Ritvo, P., & Ahmad, F. (2020). Design of a Mindfulness Virtual Community: A focus-group analysis. Health informatics journal, 26(3), 1560-1576. https://doi.org/sagepub.comDOI: 10.1177/1460458219884840

Eyal, P., David, R., Andrew, G., Zak, E., & Ekaterina, D. (2021). Data quality of platforms and panels for online behavioral research. Behavior research methods, 1-20. https://doi.org/springer.comDOI: 10.3758/s13428-021-01694-3

Finlay, J. M., Kler, J. S., O'Shea, B. Q., Eastman, M. R., Vinson, Y. R., & Kobayashi, L. C. (2021). Coping during the COVID-19 pandemic: a qualitative study of older adults across the United States. Frontiers in public health, 9, 643807. https://doi .org/ frontiersin.orgDOI: 10.3389/fpubh.2021.643807

Gacs, A., Goertler, S., & Spasova, S. (2020). Planned online language education versus crisis-prompted online language teaching: Lessons for the future. [HTML]. *Foreign Language Annals*, 53(2), 380–392. Advance online publication. DOI: 10.1111/flan.12460

Gartenberg, C. & Zenger, T. (2023). The firm as a subsociety: Purpose, justice, and the theory of the firm. Organization Science. https://doi.org/ informs.orgDOI: 10.1287/orsc.2022.1650

Ghamrawi, N. (2022). Teachers' virtual communities of practice: A strong response in times of crisis or just another Fad?. Education and information technologies. https://doi.org/ springer.comDOI: 10.1007/s10639-021-10857-w

Goh, Z., Eva, N., Kiazad, K., Jack, G. A., De Cieri, H., & Spreitzer, G. M. (2022). An integrative multilevel review of thriving at work: Assessing progress and promise. Journal of Organizational Behavior, 43(2), 197-213. https://doi.org/ umich.eduDOI: 10.1002/job.2571

Gramates, L. S., Agapite, J., Attrill, H., Calvi, B. R., Crosby, M. A., Dos Santos, G., ... & Strelets, V. B. (2022). FlyBase: a guided tour of highlighted features. Genetics, 220(4), iyac035. https://doi.org/oup.comDOI: 10.1093/genetics/iyac035

Greenhow, C., Graham, C. R., & Koehler, M. J. (2022). Foundations of online learning: Challenges and opportunities. [HTML]. *Educational Psychologist*, 57(3), 131–147. Advance online publication. DOI: 10.1080/00461520.2022.2090364

Grutzpalk, J., & Jarolimek, S. (2024). The importance of police public relations in assembly situations. In *Public Order Policing: A Professional's Guide to International Theories, Case Studies, and Best Practices* (pp. 399–411). Springer International Publishing. [HTML], DOI: 10.1007/978-3-031-43856-1_18

Hacker, J., Vom Brocke, J., Handali, J., Otto, M., & Schneider, J. (2020). Virtually in this together–how web-conferencing systems enabled a new virtual togetherness during the COVID-19 crisis. European Journal of Information Systems, 29(5), 563-584. https://doi.org/ tandfonline.comDOI: 10.1080/0960085X.2020.1814680

Haimson, O. L., Dame-Griff, A., Capello, E., & Richter, Z. (2021). Tumblr was a trans technology: the meaning, importance, history, and future of trans technologies. Feminist media studies, 21(3), 345-361. https://doi.org/ tandfonline.comDOI: 10.1080/14680777.2019.1678505

Haleem, A., Javaid, M., Qadri, M. A., Singh, R. P., & Suman, R. (2022). Artificial intelligence (AI) applications for marketing: A literature-based study. International Journal of Intelligent Networks, 3, 119-132. https://doi.org/ sciencedirect.comDOI: 10.1016/j.ijin.2022.08.005

Haleem, A., Javaid, M., Qadri, M. A., & Suman, R. (2022). Understanding the role of digital technologies in education: A review. Sustainable Operations and Computers, 3, 275-285. https://doi.org/sciencedirect.comDOI: 10.1016/j.susoc.2022.05.004

Harkin, L. J., Beaver, K., Dey, P., & Choong, K. A. (2020). Secret groups and open forums: defining online support communities from the perspective of people affected by cancer. Digital Health. http://dx.doi.org/sagepub.comDOI: 10.1177/2055207619898993

Hemphill, R., Forsythe, L. P., Heckert, A. L., Amolegbe, A., Maurer, M., Carman, K. L., ... & Esmail, L. (2020). What motivates patients and caregivers to engage in health research and how engagement affects their lives: qualitative survey findings. Health Expectations, 23(2), 328-336. https://doi.org/wiley.comDOI: 10.1080/1369118X.2020.1764606

Her, Y. C. & Timmermans, E. (). Tinder blue, mental flu? Exploring the associations between Tinder use and well-being. Information. https://doi.org/ tandfonline.comDOI: 10.1080/1369118X.2020.1764606

Herden, C. J., Alliu, E., Cakici, A., Cormier, T., Deguelle, C., Gambhir, S., . . . Edinger-Schons, L. M. (2021, March). “Corporate Digital Responsibility” New corporate responsibilities in the digital age. In Sustainability Management Foruml NachhaltigkeitsManagementForum (Vol. 29, No. 1, pp. 13-29). Berlin/Heidelberg: Springer Berlin Heidelberg. https://doi.org/ springer.comDOI: 10.1007/s00550-020-00509-x

Hjorteset, M. A., & Böcker, L. (2020). Car sharing in Norwegian urban areas: examining interest, intention and the decision to enrol. Transportation research part D: transport and environment, 84, 102322. https://doi.org/sciencedirect.comDOI: 10.1016/j.trd.2020.102322

Hoeller, D., Rudin, N., Sako, D., & Hutter, M. (2024). Anymal parkour: Learning agile navigation for quadrupedal robots. [HTML]. *Science Robotics*, 9(88), eadi7566. Advance online publication. DOI: 10.1126/scirobotics.adi7566 PMID: 38478592

Hoffner, C. A., & Bond, B. J. (2022). Parasocial relationships, social media, & well-being. [HTML]. *Current Opinion in Psychology*, 45, 101306. Advance online publication. DOI: 10.1016/j.copsyc.2022.101306 PMID: 35219157

Hoicka, C. E., Lowitzsch, J., Brisbois, M. C., Kumar, A., & Camargo, L. R. (2021). Implementing a just renewable energy transition: Policy advice for transposing the new European rules for renewable energy communities. Energy Policy, 156, 112435. https://doi.org/ sciencedirect.comDOI: 10.1016/j.enpol.2021.112435

Holmes, W., Porayska-Pomsta, K., Holstein, K., Sutherland, E., Baker, T., Shum, S. B., ... & Koedinger, K. R. (2022). Ethics of AI in education: Towards a community-wide framework. International Journal of Artificial Intelligence in Education, 1-23. https://doi.org/ springer.comDOI: 10.1007/s40593-021-00239-1

Huangfu, Z., Ruan, Y., Zhao, J., Wang, Q., & Zhou, L. (2022). Accessing the influence of community experience on brand loyalty toward virtual Brand Community: developing country perspective. Frontiers in Psychology, 13, 865646. https://doi .org/frontiersin.orgDOI: 10.3389/fpsyg.2022.865646

Hysa, B., Karasek, A., & Zdonek, I. (2021). Social media usage by different generations as a tool for sustainable tourism marketing in society 5.0 idea. Sustainability. https://doi.org/ mdpi.comDOI: 10.3390/su13031018

Ismagilova, E., Rana, N. P., Slade, E. L., & Dwivedi, Y. K. (2021). A meta-analysis of the factors affecting eWOM providing behaviour. *European Journal of Marketing*, 55(4), 1067–1102. http://dx.doi.org/https://doi.org/10.1108/EJM-07-2018-0472. DOI: 10.1108/EJM-07-2018-0472

Jacobson, J. (2021). The essential guide to the business & law of esports & professional video gaming. https://doi.org/[HTML]DOI: 10.1201/9781003143963

Jamil, K., Dunnan, L., Gul, R. F., Shehzad, M. U., Gillani, S. H. M., & Awan, F. H. (2022). Role of social media marketing activities in influencing customer intentions: a perspective of a new emerging era. Frontiers in psychology, 12, 808525. https://doi.org/frontiersin.orgDOI: 10.3389/fpsyg.2021.808525

Jovanović, A. & Milosavljević, A. (2022). VoRtex Metaverse platform for gamified collaborative learning. Electronics. https://doi.org/mdpi.comDOI: 10.3390/electronics11030317

Kang, H. & Lou, C. (2022). AI agency vs. human agency: understanding human–AI interactions on TikTok and their implications for user engagement. Journal of Computer-Mediated Communication. https://doi.org/ oup.comDOI: 10.1093/jcmc/zmac014

Kasauli, R., Knauss, E., Horkoff, J., Liebel, G., & de Oliveira Neto, F. G. (2021). Requirements engineering challenges and practices in large-scale agile system development. Journal of Systems and Software, 172, 110851. https://doi.org/sciencedirect.comDOI: 10.1016/j.jss.2020.110851

Keaton, W. & Gilbert, A. (2020). Successful online learning: What does learner interaction with peers, instructors and parents look like?. Journal of Online Learning Research. learntechlib.org

Kim, D. J., Salvacion, M., Salehan, M., & Kim, D. W. (2023). An empirical study of community cohesiveness, community attachment, and their roles in virtual community participation. [HTML]. *European Journal of Information Systems*, 32(3), 573–600. DOI: 10.1080/0960085X.2021.2018364

Knott, E., Rao, A. H., Summers, K., & Teeger, C. (2022). Interviews in the social sciences. Nature Reviews Methods Primers, 2(1), 73. https://doi.org/nature.comDOI: 10.1038/s43586-022-00150-6

Kokkini, V., Tseliou, E., Abakoumkin, G., & Bozatzis, N. (2022). "Immersed in world of warcraft": A discursive study of identity management talk about excessive online gaming. [HTML]. *Journal of Language and Social Psychology*, 41(5), 590–612. DOI: 10.1177/0261927X211067820

Kristof-Brown, A., Schneider, B., & Su, R. (2023). Person-organization fit theory and research: Conundrums, conclusions, and calls to action. Personnel psychology. https://doi.org/ wiley.comDOI: 10.1111/peps.12581

Kshetri, N., Dwivedi, Y. K., Davenport, T. H., & Panteli, N. (2023). Generative artificial intelligence in marketing: Applications, opportunities, challenges, and research agenda. [HTML]. *International Journal of Information Management*, 102716. Advance online publication. DOI: 10.1016/j.ijinfomgt.2023.102716

Lainas, S. (2023). Self-help/mutual aid groups for health and psychosocial problems: Key features and their perspectives in the 21st century. American Journal of Community Psychology. https://doi.org/ wiley.comDOI: 10.1002/ajcp.12718

Langley, D. J., van Doorn, J., Ng, I. C., Stieglitz, S., Lazovik, A., & Boonstra, A. (2021). The Internet of Everything: Smart things and their impact on business models. Journal of Business Research, 122, 853-863. https://doi.org/ sciencedirect.comDOI: 10.1016/j.jbusres.2019.12.035

Łapniewska, Z. (). Solidarity and mutual aid: Women organizing the "visible hand" urban commons. Gender. https://doi.org/ wiley.comDOI: 10.1111/gwao.12833

Larson, L. & DeChurch, L. A. (2020). Leading teams in the digital age: Four perspectives on technology and what they mean for leading teams. The leadership quarterly. sciencedirect.com

Li, J. & Zheng, H. (2022). Online information seeking and disease prevention intent during COVID-19 outbreak. Journalism & Mass Communication Quarterly. https://doi.org/ sagepub.comDOI: 10.1177/1077699020961518

Liu, S., Xiao, W., Fang, C., Zhang, X., & Lin, J. (2020). Social support, belongingness, and value co-creation behaviors in online health communities. [HTML]. *Telematics and Informatics*, 50, 101398. Advance online publication. DOI: 10.1016/j.tele.2020.101398

Luger, T. M., Hamilton, A. B., & True, G. (2020). Measuring community-engaged research contexts, processes, and outcomes: a mapping review. The Milbank Quarterly. wiley.com

Lynch, M., Sage, T., Hitchcock, L. I., & Sage, M. (2021). A heutagogical approach for the assessment of Internet Communication Technology (ICT) assignments in higher education. International Journal of Educational Technology in Higher Education, 18(1), 55. https://doi.org/ springer.comDOI: 10.1186/s41239-021-00290-x

Martin, F., & Borup, J. (2022). Online learner engagement: Conceptual definitions, research themes, and supportive practices. [HTML]. *Educational Psychologist*, 57(3), 162–177. Advance online publication. DOI: 10.1080/00461520.2022.2089147

Marx, V. (2023). Method of the year: long-read sequencing. Nature Methods. nature.com

Maseko, B. & Siziba, L. (2023). On the dialectics of policy and practice: Multilingualism and the virtual linguistic landscape of a South African university. Cogent Arts & Humanities. https://doi.org/tandfonline.comDOI: 10.1080/23311983.2023.2268395

Miković, R., Petrović, D., Mihić, M., Obradović, V., & Todorović, M. (2020). The integration of social capital and knowledge management–The key challenge for international development and cooperation projects of nonprofit organizations. [HTML]. *International Journal of Project Management*, 38(8), 515–533. DOI: 10.1016/j.ijproman.2020.07.006

Minter, M., Mason, L. R., Burgess, M. D., Peach, W. J., & Hughes, J. (2024). Understanding stakeholder perceptions on the impacts of gamebird releasing on or near UK protected sites. Journal for Nature Conservation, 126581. https://doi.org/sciencedirect.comDOI: 10.1016/j.jnc.2024.126581

Mirzaei, T., & Esmaeilzadeh, P. (2021). Engagement in online health communities: Channel expansion and social exchanges. [HTML]. *Information & Management*, 58(1), 103404. Advance online publication. DOI: 10.1016/j.im.2020.103404

Mmbaga, N. A., Mathias, B. D., Williams, D. W., & Cardon, M. S. (2020). A review of and future agenda for research on identity in entrepreneurship. [HTML]. *Journal of Business Venturing*, 35(6), 106049. DOI: 10.1016/j.jbusvent.2020.106049

Molinillo, S., Aguilar-Illescas, R., Anaya-Sánchez, R., & Liébana-Cabanillas, F. (2021). Social commerce website design, perceived value and loyalty behavior intentions: The moderating roles of gender, age and frequency of use. [HTML]. *Journal of Retailing and Consumer Services*, 63, 102404. DOI: 10.1016/j.jretconser.2020.102404

Morrison-Smith, S. & Ruiz, J. (2020). Challenges and barriers in virtual teams: a literature review. SN Applied Sciences. https://doi.org/ springer.comDOI: 10.1007/s42452-020-2801-5

Mousavi, S. & Roper, S. (2023). Enhancing relationships through online brand communities: Comparing posters and lurkers. International Journal of Electronic Commerce. https://doi.org/ tandfonline.comDOI: 10.1080/10864415.2022.2158596

Mpofu, P., Asak, M. O., & Salawu, A. (2022). Facebook groups as transnational counter public sphere for diasporic communities. Cogent arts & humanities. https://doi.org/tandfonline.comDOI: 10.1080/23311983.2022.2027598

Mukherjee, S. & Narang, D. (2023). Digital economy and work-from-home: The rise of home offices amidst the COVID-19 outbreak in India. Journal of the Knowledge Economy. https://doi.org/ springer.comDOI: 10.1007/s13132-022-00896-0

Mystakidis, S. (2022). Metaverse. Encyclopedia. https://doi.org/ mdpi.comDOI: 10.3390/encyclopedia2010031

Na, H., & Staudt Willet, K. B. (2022). Affinity and anonymity benefitting early career teachers in the r/teachers subreddit. [HTML]. *Journal of Research on Technology in Education*, 1–18. DOI: 10.1080/15391523.2022.2150727

Nath, K. (). Evolution of the internet from web 1.0 to metaverse: The good, the bad and the ugly. TechRxiv Powered by IEEE. https://dx.doi.org/ figshare.comDOI: 10.36227/techrxiv.19743676.v1

Neamţu, N. & Faludi, C. (2021). Learning Effectiveness of Social Work Methods With Groups, in Online and Face-to-Face Contexts. Frontiers in Psychology. https://doi.org/ frontiersin.orgDOI: 10.3389/fpsyg.2021.649691

Nguyen, C. Q., Kariyawasam, D., Alba-Concepcion, K., Grattan, S., Hetherington, K., Wakefield, C. E., ... & Farrar, M. A. (2022). 'Advocacy groups are the connectors': Experiences and contributions of rare disease patient organization leaders in advanced neurotherapeutics. Health expectations, 25(6), 3175-3191. https://doi.org/ wiley.comDOI: 10.1111/hex.13625

Ni, M. (2022). *Digital Participation for Inclusive Growth: A Case Study of Singapore's Collaborative Digital Governance Model.* Design for Vulnerable Communities. [HTML], DOI: 10.1007/978-3-030-96866-3_17

Nikiel, J. (2022). The Forever Now: Foretelling the Present in William Gibson's Bigend Trilogy. It Takes a Storyteller to Know a Storyteller. https://doi.org/ [HTML] DOI: 10.1163/9789004533288_004

O'Keefe, L., Rafferty, J., Gunder, A., & Vignare, K. (2020). Delivering High-Quality Instruction Online in Response to COVID-19: Faculty Playbook.. Online Learning Consortium. ed.gov

Packard, N. (2020). Three Kinds of Demand Pull for the ARPANET into the Internet. Cogent Social Sciences. https://doi.org/tandfonline.comDOI: 10.1080/23311886.2020.1720565

Packard, N. (2023). Internet prehistory: ARPANET chronology. Cogent Social Sciences. https://doi.org/ tandfonline.comDOI: 10.1080/23311886.2023.2245237

Pandya, A. & Lodha, P. (2021). Social connectedness, excessive screen time during COVID-19 and mental health: a review of current evidence. Frontiers in Human Dynamics. https://doi.org/ frontiersin.orgDOI: 10.3389/fhumd.2021.684137

Patel, P. S., Desai, N. D., Shah, S. H., & Shah, S. N. (2024). Lived experiences of bereaved family members during COVID-19 pandemic in a tertiary care hospital with special reference to imposed restrictive COVID guidelines—a qualitative study. OMEGA-Journal of Death and Dying, 89(1), 404-420. https://doi.org/ sagepub.comDOI: 10.1177/00302228221075207

Ponnusamy, S., Iranmanesh, M., Foroughi, B., & Hyun, S. S. (2020). Drivers and outcomes of Instagram Addiction: Psychological well-being as moderator. [HTML]. *Computers in Human Behavior*, 107, 106294. DOI: 10.1016/j.chb.2020.106294

Poor, N., Skoric, M., & Lampe, C. (2022). Death of a child, birth of a guild: Factors aiding the rapid formation of online support communities. [HTML]. *The Information Society*, 38(3), 188–199. Advance online publication. DOI: 10.1080/01972243.2022.2071219

Popenoe, R., Langius-Eklöf, A., Stenwall, E., & Jervaeus, A. (2021). A practical guide to data analysis in general literature reviews. Nordic journal of nursing research, 41(4), 175-186. http://dx.doi.org/sagepub.comDOI: 10.1177/2057158521991949

Pöyry, E. & Laaksonen, S. M. (2022). Opposing brand activism: triggers and strategies of consumers' antibrand actions. European Journal of Marketing. http://dx.doi .org/ emerald.comDOI: 10.1108/EJM-12-2020-0901

Proctor, D. (2021). The social production of internet space: Affordance, programming, and virtuality. [HTML]. *Communication Theory*, 31(4), 593–612. Advance online publication. DOI: 10.1093/ct/qtz036

Raji, M. A., Olodo, H. B., Oke, T. T., Addy, W. A., Ofodile, O. C., & Oyewole, A. T. (2024). Digital marketing in tourism: a review of practices in the USA and Africa. International Journal of Applied Research in Social Sciences, 6(3), 393-408. https:// doi.org/fepbl.comDOI: 10.51594/ijarss.v6i3.896

Raper, J. (2020). *Progress towards spatial multimedia*. Geographic Information Research. [HTML] DOI: 10.1201/9781003062691-41

Redjeki, F. & Affandi, A. (2021). Utilization of digital marketing for MSME players as value creation for customers during the COVID-19 pandemic. International Journal of Science and Society. https://doi.org/ researchgate.netDOI: 10.200609/ ijsoc.v3i1.264

Ritterbusch, G. D. & Teichmann, M. R. (2023). Defining the metaverse: A systematic literature review. Ieee Access. https://doi.org/ieee.orgDOI: 10.1109/ACCESS.2023.3241809

Rizvanović, B., Zutshi, A., Grilo, A., & Nodehi, T. (2023). Linking the potentials of extended digital marketing impact and start-up growth: Developing a macro-dynamic framework of start-up growth drivers supported by digital marketing. Technological Forecasting and Social Change, 186, 122128. https://doi.org/ sciencedirect.comDOI: 10.1016/j.techfore.2022.122128

Roberson, Q. & Perry, J. L. (2022). Inclusive leadership in thought and action: A thematic analysis. Group & Organization Management. https://doi.org/umich .eduDOI: 10.1177/10596011211013161

Rogers, R. (2020). Deplatforming: Following extreme Internet celebrities to Telegram and alternative social media. European Journal of Communication. http://dx .doi.org/ sagepub.comDOI: 10.1177/0267323120922066

Rojas-Sánchez, M. A., Palos-Sánchez, P. R., & Folgado-Fernández, J. A. (2023). Systematic literature review and bibliometric analysis on virtual reality and education. Education and Information Technologies, 28(1), 155-192. https://doi.org/ springer.comDOI: 10.1007/s10639-022-11167-5

Ruangkanjanases, A., Hsu, S. L., Wu, Y. J., Chen, S. C., & Chang, J. Y. (2020). What drives continuance intention towards social media? Social influence and identity perspectives. Sustainability, 12(17), 7081. http://dx.doi.org/mdpi.comDOI: 10.3390/su12177081

Sahu, A. S. (2022). Assessing internet and web services based webdom and virtual web-data-centric geographical study. GeoJournal. https://doi.org/springer.comDOI: 10.1007/s10708-021-10549-5

Sands, S., Ferraro, C., Demsar, V., & Chandler, G. (2022). False idols: Unpacking the opportunities and challenges of falsity in the context of virtual influencers. [HTML]. *Business Horizons*, 65(6), 777–788. Advance online publication. DOI: 10.1016/j.bushor.2022.08.002

Scherr, S., & Wang, K. (2021). Explaining the success of social media with gratification niches: Motivations behind daytime, nighttime, and active use of TikTok in China. [HTML]. *Computers in Human Behavior*, 124, 106893. Advance online publication. DOI: 10.1016/j.chb.2021.106893

Schou, P. K., Bucher, E., & Waldkirch, M. (2022). Entrepreneurial learning in online communities. Small Business Economics. https://doi.org/springer.comDOI: 10.1007/s11187-021-00502-8

Shao, D. & Lee, I. J. (2020). Acceptance and influencing factors of social virtual reality in the urban elderly. Sustainability. http://dx.doi.org/mdpi.comDOI: 10.3390/su12229345

Simpson, S., Richardson, L., Pietrabissa, G., Castelnuovo, G., & Reid, C. (2021). Videotherapy and therapeutic alliance in the age of COVID-19. Clinical psychology & psychotherapy, 28(2), 409-421. https://doi.org/ wiley.comDOI: 10.1002/cpp.2521

Sirola, A., Savela, N., Savolainen, I., Kaakinen, M., & Oksanen, A. (2021). The role of virtual communities in gambling and gaming behaviors: A systematic review. Journal of Gambling Studies, 37(1), 165-187. https://doi.org/springer.comDOI: 10.1007/s10899-020-09946-1

Sudarshan, S., Mehrotra, S., & Thirthalli, J. (2024). Effectiveness of Blended Internet-based Self-help and Face-to-face Intervention for Depression: A Pilot Study from India. Indian Journal of Psychological Medicine, 02537176241238289. https://doi.org/sagepub.comDOI: 10.1177/02537176241238289

Sun, B., Mao, H., & Yin, C. (2020). Male and female users' differences in online technology community based on text mining. Frontiers in Psychology. https://doi.org/ frontiersin.orgDOI: 10.3389/fpsyg.2020.00806

Sundararaj, V., & Rejeesh, M. R. (2021). A detailed behavioral analysis on consumer and customer changing behavior with respect to social networking sites. [HTML]. *Journal of Retailing and Consumer Services*, 58, 102190. Advance online publication. DOI: 10.1016/j.jretconser.2020.102190

Sycinska-Dziarnowska, M., & Paradowska-Stankiewicz, I. (2020). Dental challenges and the needs of the population during the covid-19 pandemic period. Real-time surveillance using google trends. International journal of environmental research and public health, 17(23), 8999. http://dx.doi.org/mdpi.comDOI: 10.3390/ijerph17238999

Szymkowiak, A., Melović, B., Dabić, M., Jeganathan, K., & Kundi, G. S. (2021). Information technology and Gen Z: The role of teachers, the internet, and technology in the education of young people. [HTML]. *Technology in Society*, 65, 101565. DOI: 10.1016/j.techsoc.2021.101565

Talukder, A. K. (2020). The Next Generation Web: Technologies and Services. In Big Data Analytics: 8th International Conference, BDA 2020, Sonepat, India, December 15–18, 2020, Proceedings 8 (pp. 209-229). Springer International Publishing. [HTML]DOI: 10.1007/978-3-030-66665-1_14

Taneja, B. (2021). The digital edge for M-commerce to replace E-commerce. In *Emerging challenges, solutions, and best practices for digital enterprise transformation* (pp. 299–318). IGI Global. [HTML], DOI: 10.4018/978-1-7998-8587-0.ch016

Torous, J., Bucci, S., Bell, I. H., Kessing, L. V., Faurholt-Jepsen, M., Whelan, P., ... & Firth, J. (2021). The growing field of digital psychiatry: current evidence and the future of apps, social media, chatbots, and virtual reality. World Psychiatry, 20(3), 318-335. https://doi.org/wiley.comDOI: 10.1002/wps.20883

Trivedi, M. H., Minhajuddin, A., Slater, H., Baronia, R., Blader, J. C., Blood, J., ... & Wakefield, S. M. (2023). Texas Youth Depression and Suicide Research Network (TX-YDSRN) research registry and learning healthcare network: Rationale, design, and baseline characteristics. Journal of affective disorders, 340, 88-99. https://doi.org/ sciencedirect.comDOI: 10.1016/j.jad.2023.07.035

Turnbull, J., Searle, A., & Lorimer, J. (2023). Anthropause environmentalisms: Noticing natures with the self-isolating bird club. Transactions of the Institute of British Geographers, 48(2), 232-248. https://doi.org/ wiley.comDOI: 10.1111/tran.12569

Ufholz, K. (2020). Peer support groups for weight loss. Current Cardiovascular Risk Reports. https://doi.org/springer.comDOI: 10.1007/s12170-020-00654-4

Van Engen, K. J., Dey, A., Runge, N., Spehar, B., Sommers, M. S., & Peelle, J. E. (2020). Effects of age, word frequency, and noise on the time course of spoken word recognition. Collabra: Psychology, 6(1), 17247. https://doi.org/nih.govDOI: 10.1525%2Fcollabra.17247

Wang, K., Tai, C. F., & Hu, H. (2023). Social influence processes within MMORPG guilds: A mixed-methods approach of nomological network analysis. [HTML]. *Information Technology & People*. Advance online publication. DOI: 10.1108/ITP-09-2022-0726

Whyte, C. (2023). Cyberspace is what states make of it: The social construction (and deconstruction) of strategic concepts. [HTML]. *Comparative Strategy*, 42(1), 128–151. Advance online publication. DOI: 10.1080/01495933.2022.2158031

Yadlin-Segal, A. & Oppenheim, Y. (2021). Whose dystopia is it anyway? Deepfakes and social media regulation. Convergence. https://doi.org/sagepub.comDOI: 10.1177/1354856520923963

Yang, H. L., Wu, Y. Y., Lin, X. Y., Xie, L., Zhang, S., Zhang, S. Q., ... & Zheng, X. D. (2021). Internet use, life satisfaction, and subjective well-being among the elderly: evidence from 2017 China general social survey. Frontiers in Public Health, 9, 677643. https://doi.org/ frontiersin.orgDOI: 10.3389/fpubh.2021.677643

Yin, E., & Mahrous, A. (2022). Covid-19 global pandemic, workplace spirituality and the rise of spirituality-driven organisations in the post-digital era. Journal of Humanities and Applied Social Sciences, 4(2), 79-93. http://dx.doi.org/emerald.comDOI: 10.1108/JHASS-11-2021-0177

Yu, X., Wang, C. X., & Spector, J. M. (2020). Factors that impact social networking in online self-regulated learning activities. [HTML]. *Educational Technology Research and Development*, 68(6), 3077–3095. DOI: 10.1007/s11423-020-09843-9

Yulia, H. (2020). Online learning to prevent the spread of pandemic corona virus in Indonesia. ETERNAL (English Teaching Journal). upgris.ac.id

Zakar, R., Iqbal, S., Zakar, M. Z., & Fischer, F. (2021). COVID-19 and health information seeking behavior: digital health literacy survey amongst university students in Pakistan. International Journal of Environmental Research and Public Health, 18(8), 4009. https://doi.org/ mdpi.comDOI: 10.3390/ijerph18084009

Zhang, Y. (2023). The Influence of Game-Enhanced Communication on EFL Learners' Pragmatic Competence in Compliment Responses. [HTML]. *Applied Linguistics*, amad082. Advance online publication. DOI: 10.1093/applin/amad082

Zhou, Z., Wang, R., & Zhan, G. (2022). Cultivating consumer subjective well-being through online brand communities: A multidimensional view of social capital. [HTML]. *Journal of Product and Brand Management*. Advance online publication. DOI: 10.1108/JPBM-12-2020-3267

KEY TERMS AND DEFINITIONS

Cyberbullying: It is a form of online abuse where individuals use digital platforms to harass, intimidate, or harm others. Addressing cyberbullying is a significant ethical challenge for online communities.

Lurking: A behavior where individuals observe the interactions and content within an online community without actively participating. Lurkers often start as passive members and may eventually become active contributors.

Metaphors for the Internet: Commonly used terms like "World Wide Web," "information superhighway," and "cyberspace," help visualize the Internet's vast, non-physical medium and the diversity of online content and communities.

Moderation: The process of overseeing and regulating the behavior and content within an online community to maintain order, safety, and respect among members. Moderation can be conducted by community administrators, moderators, or through peer moderation.

Online Community: A virtual space where individuals with common interests or goals interact, share information, and build relationships. Online communities can range from social networking sites to forums, professional networks, and niche interest groups.

Social Identity: Individuals' sense of self develops through interactions within a virtual community. This identity is shaped by the community's history, norms, and social structures.

Virtuality: Virtuality is the concept of human actions being mediated by technology, which changes the experience of presence, time, and place. Understanding virtuality is crucial in understanding how online communities form and function.

Chapter 3
How Virtual Communities Work

Jignesh Patil
https://orcid.org/0000-0001-5377-928X
MCT Rajiv Gandhi Institute of Technology, India

Kartik Mistry
https://orcid.org/0009-0000-8748-7779
MCT Rajiv Gandhi Institute of Technology, India

ABSTRACT

A community is a group of people working together to achieve a common goal. Social media connects people virtually through seven layers: text, networks, actions, hyperlinks, locations, search engine, and applications. A virtual community is an interconnected group of online personal relationship networks, forming communities of interest like sports, entertainment, or travel. These communities share activity-related information and can be weak or strong, with specific duties assigned to members. Each community has its own regulations, reducing communication gaps and allowing individuals to actively connect and participate in discussions worldwide..

HOW VIRTUAL COMMUNITIES WORK?

In the great expanse of the digital age, virtual communities have evolved as the busy town squares of the internet, where people from all over the world gather, connect, and form bonds that transcend physical boundaries. What were once isolated

DOI: 10.4018/979-8-3693-3868-1.ch003

pixels on a screen have grown into lively communities, with the digital landscape teeming with human connection, cooperation, and shared experiences.

As the Internet continues to develop, virtual communities are also advancing at an astronomical rate. Since the beginning, the Internet has been centered around the idea of community. Scientists have been exchanging messages, sharing data, and working together on research projects via the Internet for a long time. Essentially, researchers established engaged online communities rather than on actual campuses. Millions of computer users throughout the world have recently started experimenting with the Internet and for-profit online services like America Online and Prodigy. Many people have been involved in one or more of the communities that have emerged to meet the requirements of consumers for entertainment, information, and communication. The Well is one of the first online communities; it was started in 1985 by a group of IT enthusiasts based mostly in the San Francisco area. Thousands of computer users have interacted with one another through the Well over the last ten years, and as a result, they have grown close offline over time.

Now, let's delve into the working of virtual communities:

Virtual communities function as dynamic, interactive platforms where individuals with shared interests, goals, or experiences come together online. Here's an in-depth look at how they operate:

1. Foundation and structure:

The first and the foremost step in the working of virtual communities is the establishment of a base foundation and structure. First is the selection of a Virtual, third party, centralized and a legitimate platform. Platforms are selected in such a way that they meet the user requirements and their interests. Usually, virtual communities are hosted on various platforms such as forums, social media groups, chat applications, and dedicated community websites. Examples include Instagram, WhatsApp, Facebook groups, Discord, and specialized forums like Stack Overflow.

Second thing to build a structure is the membership. These communities can be open to anyone or restricted to a select group of individuals. Only individuals with common interest would be allowed to enter a community. Membership may require registration, invitations, or acceptance by moderators or the group admin. This is required so that no unauthorized person enters the group/community.

2. Formation and Growth:

After the foundation, the community has to be formed and for this the individuals with a common interest, goals, or identities, such as hobbies, professional fields, support groups, or fan clubs are brought together via a message or an online poster.

Also, the person who wants to be a member of a community can request the admin of the group to add him/her to the group.

As the community is formed, it should be grown and expanded so that more individuals can be a part of it. To attract individuals, some strategies need to be followed. Initial growth is often fueled by the quality and relevance of content, active participation, and effective outreach or marketing strategies. This will help individuals all over the world to connect with each other virtually.

3. Interactions and communications:

There must be a mode of interaction between the members of a virtual community. This was the main purpose of forming a community. This can be done through various communication modes such as posts, comments, direct messages, video calls, and live chats. Using these modes, communication between the members is possible without any issues.

There are two types of communication in the virtual community – Asynchronous and Synchronous. In asynchronous mode the communication can be done by posts, comments, email etc. whereas in the synchronous mode the communication is done by real-time chat, video calls, direct messages etc., (Abarca, Palos-Sanchez, & Rus-Arias, 2020).

4. Roles and Governance:

The community is formed, and communication has started. But there should be a decorum maintained in the community by the members of it. To ensure this there is an admin or a moderator present in the circle that takes care of it. Moderators and administrators oversee the community, enforce rules, manage content, and resolve conflicts. They ensure that discussions remain respectful and on-topic, (Mockaitis, Rose, & Zettinig, 2012).

For example, in WhatsApp, to form a group, there is an admin and has the authority to add or remove a person from the group and checks if everyone is following the guidelines of the group.

As said above, the members should adhere to the guidelines. Therefore, clear rules and guidelines are established to maintain order and foster a positive environment. These rules cover acceptable behavior, content standards, and conflict resolution procedures. For example, on Discord, there is a channel with multiple groups and in each group, guidelines are specified which are to be followed by all the members of the channels. This is verified by the group owner.

5. Engagement and Participation:

Members participate by sharing some relatable and valuable content pertaining to the community. Members contribute by posting articles, sharing media, asking questions, and providing answers. This content is curated by moderators using the voting system ensuring that the information is easily available.

Active participation of the members is highly appreciated in the community. It is encouraged through interactive features like upvotes, likes, shares, and comments. Engagement keeps the community vibrant and evolving. It also helps the members to understand what type of content is most preferred by the target audience.

Participation can also be achieved by conducting online events and activities. Regular events, such as webinars, Q&A sessions, competitions, and meet-ups (virtual or physical), foster deeper connections and active involvement. This leads to the buildup of trust in the community and the bond between members becomes stronger.

6. Knowledge Sharing and Collaboration:

The collective intelligence of the members in the community can help find a solution to a problem. Members pool their knowledge, skills, and experiences, creating a collective intelligence that benefits the entire community. This is particularly evident in professional and technical communities such as Stack Overflow, GitHub where one can post the query and the members provide different solutions for the query. Collaborative problem-solving is a key feature, where members seek advice, troubleshoot issues, and brainstorm solutions collectively, (Yuan, Deng, & Zhong, 2021).

7. Emotional Support and Social Bonding:

After a while the members of the community develop trust within themselves and can even share their discomforts and happenings of their respective lives. Many virtual communities provide emotional support, especially in health, wellness, and personal development spaces. Members offer empathy, advice, and solidarity. This can help a member to cope with daily struggles with some advice provided by the community members.

The connection becomes strong and social bonding occurs as members build friendships and networks, often extending beyond the virtual space into real-life interactions.

8. Feedback and Improvement:

Members' continual feedback drives community evolution. This feedback helps to enhance the platform, content quality, and community experience. Using the feedback, the community can grow and prosper successfully.

Virtual vs Physical Communities

The traits and interactions of online and real-life groups are very similar. Both types of communities are created around common interests and purposes, and they share the same social environment. However, online communities have the ability to complement or replace physical links in real communities with virtual interactions, resulting in the formation of convergent communities. These convergent communities have great emotional involvement among members but may lose some traditional community characteristics due to their virtual nature. Online communities also play an important role in knowledge sharing and issue solving, with the ability to extract and assess meaningful information from community chats. Furthermore, online networks can have a tangible offline impact and encourage joint successes. Therefore, while there are similarities between online and real-life communities, online communities have unique characteristics and dynamics that differentiate them from traditional communities.

Figure 1. Virtual vs physical communities

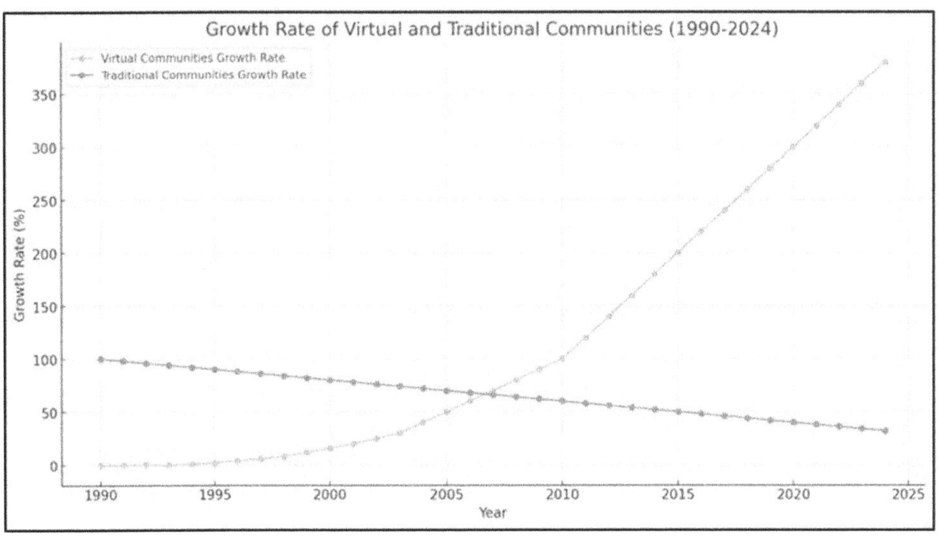

Table 1. Difference between virtual community and physical community

Parameter	Virtual Community	Physical Community
Geography	Global reach, transcends physical location.	Localized, geographically bound.
Membership	Open or closed, self-selection based on interest.	Proximity & shared experiences.
Interaction	Asynchronous & synchronous communication (text, voice, video).	Face-to-face interaction, nonverbal cues.
Social Cues	Limited by technology, relies on emoticons & text cues.	Richer communication through body language & expressions.
Persistence	Persistent content, archives conversations & history.	Ephemeral interactions, relies on memory & shared experiences.
Accessibility	Accessible from anywhere with internet.	Limited by physical location and mobility.
Diversity of Thought	Potentially wider range of viewpoints.	Primarily local perspectives.
Scalability	Can grow very large.	Limited by physical space.
Information Archiving	Discussions and resources easily searchable and stored.	Information sharing relies on individual memory or physical archives

Platform Based Virtual Communities

Virtual communities require some social media platforms as their base. Virtual communities on social media platforms such as Instagram, Facebook, and Twitter operate with unique dynamics and leverage the strengths of each platform. Let's have a discussion about these platforms in detail:

1. Instagram:

Instagram is a free photo and video sharing app available on iPhone and Android. People can upload photos or videos to our service and share them with their followers or with a select group of friends.

In Instagram, we have 3 main features that benefit the motto of virtual community – Visual Interaction, Fans and Followers and Collaborative Features.

Instagram is a platform where one can share videos, photos, and information. These are the key elements of interaction and engagement. Also, hashtags play an important role in building and expanding the community. Users can follow and use specific hashtags related to their interests and can connect with similar people.

The news of the daily events in every sector is available thereby allowing the members to share moments and ideas.

Another important feature is Fans and followers. Influencers create and lead communities around specific topics such as fashion, fitness, travel, technology, etc. Followers access influencer content and participate in conversations. Likes, comments, direct messages (DMs), and live events are the primary interaction tools that allow community members to communicate directly with content creators and each other.

Features such as co-authored posts allow multiple users to create collaborative content, fostering a sense of community and authority. Long-form videos and live events promote deep engagement and real-time interaction, strengthening social cohesion.

2. Facebook:

Facebook allows users to send messages, post status updates, share photos, share links, comment on friend's profile pages, and more. It also supports group pages, fan pages, and business pages. Facebook has 4 features that enable it to be a part of building a virtual community.

Firstly, it can create different types of groups – public groups and private groups. Facebook groups can be public, private or hidden. The program of each group is different, from community participation to specific programs. It has an add-on option of marketplace where one can buy and sell products. Pages that represent a brand, organization, or audience can provide social interaction through posts and events. Events bring together members of the immediate and physical community, (Malthouse *et al.,* 2013).

Secondly, it provides multimedia communication. Texts, photos, videos, gifs can easily be shared between individuals and in a community.

Posts create a rich environment for discussion. Comments on such posts are the main form of interaction. Even group chat and Messaging can be done via Facebook Messenger which enables group chats and promotes interactive and personal interactions.

As said earlier, there should be community management features available in a virtual community. This is a compulsory feature which is provided by Facebook. Group managers and moderators manage information, enforce rules, and maintain the health of the community using tools such as boosting posts and restricting members. Admins can create polls to collect feedback and create announcements to inform the community and act.

Another feature available in Facebook is Knowledge sharing and support. Features such as file sharing and training modules (in learning groups) promote knowledge sharing and structure. Groups focused on health, wellness, and recreation provide a platform for members to find and provide support, share experiences, and build relationships.

3. Twitter:

Twitter (presently known as X) is a free social networking site where users broadcast short posts known as tweets. These tweets can contain text, videos, photos, or links. Twitter's main purpose is to connect users and allow them to share their thoughts with their followers and others. It can be a source of news and entertainment, and can also be used as a marketing tool for businesses. Twitter encourages users to follow and interact with different individuals, brands, and media outlets, and to post updates as they happen to create a real-time stream of messages tailored to their interests.

Twitter has the following features which are necessary for a social media application to build a virtual community.

Firstly, twitter has real time interaction. Twitter works on real-time interaction using short messages (tweets) of less than 280 characters. Retweets amplify your message throughout the community. Also, one can tag a specific/trending topic. Tags organize conversations around specific topics, while trends display popular conversations, allowing you to build communities around current events.

Secondly, it provides a public and open exchange of ideas. Conversations are mostly public, with replies creating threaded discussions visible to everyone, promoting open community dialogue. Users can add their comments to retweets, fostering additional layers of discussion and engagement. This is how different people can get different points of views regarding a trending topic.

Another important feature of Twitter is the Follower Dynamics. Users follow accounts of interest and can create lists to categorize and follow specific groups of users, such as experts, friends, or organizations. This allows the user to connect with people who have similar thoughts and ideas. Also, Twitter has 'Twitter Spaces' an audio chat feature, allows for real-time, voice-based discussions, adding a new dimension to community interaction.

Instagram, Facebook, and Twitter all provide distinct environments for virtual communities, using their different strengths in visual material, various group interactions, and real- time communication. These platforms enable the creation of dynamic, engaging communities where users can interact, exchange, and collaborate based on common interests and goals.

Algorithms Used in Virtual Communities

Various algorithms are employed to construct virtual communities. One such algorithm is the Feed Ranking algorithm. Feed ranking algorithms utilize machine learning and statistical techniques to rate information depending on its likelihood of engaging a user. Using this strategy, the user can join a virtual community that matches his or her interests.

Simple Ranking Formula

$$\text{Score}=\alpha \cdot \text{ES} + \beta \cdot \text{RS} + \gamma \cdot \text{CQS}$$

- **Engagement Score(ES):** Based on the user's past interactions with similar content.
- **Recency Score**(RS): Decreases as the content gets older.
- **Content Quality Score (CQS):** Higher for original and high-quality content.
- **α, β, γ\alpha\beta\gamma:** Weights assigned to each factor, tuned based on user feedback and model performance.

Algorithm for Feed Ranking

Collect Data:

- Gather data around each post, counting the number of likes, comments, and offers it has received.
- Note the date and time each post was made.
- Determine if the post is unique substance or a reshare.
- Identify the sort of substance (e.g., video, picture, text).

Calculate Engagement Score

- For each post, calculate an engagement score based on how much individuals connected with it.
- Use a straightforward equation: Engagement Score = (Likes * 0.5) + (Comments * 1.0) + (Offers * 1.5).
- The thought is that comments and offers might be more profitable intuitive than likes.

Calculate Recency Score

- Determine how later each post is.
- Calculate how much time has passed since the post was made.
- Assign a score that diminishes as the post gets more seasoned. For illustration, a post made nowadays gets a tall score, whereas one from a month prior gets a lower score.
- Use an equation like: Recency Score = max (0, 1 - (days since post / 30)).

Calculate Substance Quality Score

- Assess the quality of the substance based on its creativity and type.
- Give a higher score to unique substance and certain sorts of substance, such as videos.
- Use a basic run the show: Unique substance gets a base score of 1.0, whereas reshared substance gets 0.5. Alter for substance sort, e.g., recordings get a multiplier of 1.5, pictures 1.2, and content 1.0.
- Example equation: Substance Quality Score = (Creativity Score) *(Substance Sort Multiplier).

Combine Scores

- For each post, combine the three scores (Engagement, Recency, Substance Quality) to get a add up to score.
- Use a weighted entirety to emphasize diverse components agreeing to their significance. For instance: Total Score = (0.4 * Engagement Score) + (0.3 * Recency Score) + (0.3 * Substance Quality Score).
- The weights (0.4, 0.3, 0.3) can be balanced based on what you think is most important.

Rank Posts

- Once all posts have an add up to score, sort them from most elevated to least score.
- The post with the most elevated score shows up at the beat of the nourish, taken after by the other most elevated, and so on, (Zhang *et al.*, 2020).

Display Positioned Feed

Show the posts to clients in the arrange of their scores, guaranteeing the most significant, locks in, and opportune substance shows up to begin with.

Facebook

Facebook's News Feed algorithm is a sophisticated system of numerous algorithms working together. These algorithms accomplish a variety of functions.

- Choosing posts to display in a user's News Feed.
- Filtering posts with disinformation or clickbait.
- Identifying a user's frequent interactions with friends and topics.
- Ranking posts based on their expected relevance to users.

Facebook has a personalized ranking algorithm that takes into account both the likelihood of a user engaging with a post and its relevance score. The relevancy score considers if the post is clickbait, leads to a low-quality page, or is misleading. Facebook also rates postings higher if they are deemed authentic and accurate. To improve your posts' performance, you can use Facebook Insights to measure their reach and impressions, and then adjust your posting strategy.

Instagram

Instagram looks at a user's previous activity, such as likes, shares, comments, and saves, as well as how they interact with the person who posted. Instagram also rewards engagement by boosting the ranking of posts that receive the most interactions. You may personalize your feed by adding accounts to your Favorites list and interacting with the information you appreciate. You can also try using different post types, such as pictures, carousels, Reels, Stories, and Lives, to reach a larger audience.

Virtual Communities Working on Social Media

The term "**virtual community**" refers to a social collective of online personal relationship networks that converse, talk, chat, converse, know each other somewhat, are highly emotional, and exchange specific expertise. Participation in sharing ideas across online communities grows within people worldwide.

A digital community is a social platform in which members with interests, targets, or behaviors communicate to share knowledge and information in social environments. The internet is a tool that instructs people, stimulates social engagement, keeps society up-to-date, offers rapid access to government information, speeds up elections, and provides an atmosphere for discussing public-interest events, (Fayez, Ismail, & Aboelnagah, n.d.) The internet led to an era of democracy that is direct, granting users more authority. Thus, instead of acquiring information from biased media groups, everyone has the chance to develop a social network and communicate what they really believe with other people.

Today, nearly all of society utilizes online platforms to share and promote brands and products across various communities, a phenomenon known as online brand communities. Since virtual communities have the widest global content reach today, they play a crucial role. Virtual communities build little ego networks with the entire network on social media platforms, focusing on relationships, interests, and similarity based on a single node (profile). For example, Roy has a school network, a college network, a company network, and a relative network on social media, thus Roy is the **ego**, and the networks to which Roy is linked rely on the connection are the **alters**. So, developing communities on virtual platforms provides virtual communication to many people in a few minutes. The **centralities** illustrate how each node is close to another node, and the nodes assess which node is the closest and longest from the center node in a network, (Óskarsdóttira *et al.,* 2020).

The steps involve building virtual communities on social media platforms are the following:

- Importance of Virtual Communities: The digital world ought to understand the functions of virtual communities and the advantages of venture capital in the modern era. Why are virtual communities necessary in the digital world? What businesses or applications can benefit from virtual communities?
- Surveys on online platforms: The virtual communities serve as a need of the age of technology, therefore making the communities online is a challenging one, because it requires the data or information referring to how significantly the local groups anticipate being part of the community after the development of the social networks.

Even yet, local groups are required to uphold community rules and regulations because they all face different challenges. As an effect, one must uphold an identical minimum program or user-based interest. When it comes to the digital age, survey data must be unambiguous and unbiased because it may be altered or handled incorrectly. Real sentiment analysis of the local groups' attitudes regarding the communities is offered through the surveys.

- Understand the structure: Structure is extremely important since it determines how survey data will be integrated into platforms. Sometimes local groups must ensure structure and comprehend how structure will interact with society. In such, community administrators must take care of local groups, and local groups must consider the degree of centrality in the groupings.

Figure 2. Basic structure for communities creation

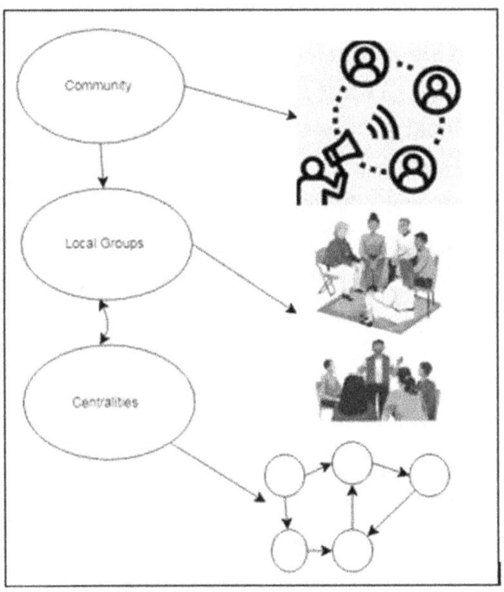

The figure above depicts how communities connect groups with identical opinions about communities, and how groups connect the centralities that have the highest **degree of centrality** with the nodes associated with the groups.

- **Create a roadmap:** Communities have to determine a goal and vision. How the world will connect with communities and how it should join with them in the projected future based on of recent updates
- **Assign Roles:** The community-building process begins with giving roles to users so that they can communicate with communities and local organizations to keep them updated. Communities' roles are to create channels to guide local groups and ensure that norms and regulations are followed. These positions are defined by the community's head or administrator, who has a broad understanding of technical vocabulary and logical reasoning for tough scenarios in the community. When local groups gather, the virtual roles provide technical assistance and timely community updates.
- **Create Communities on digital platforms:** Social topics, news, entertainment, sports, technology, and so forth can all be used to build communities. Communities are formed by experiencing and visualizing a certain location, using various location analytics tools to see where communities are developing and trailing. After assessing the location communities, the data or information is transmitted to the nodes with the highest degree of centrality using a recommendation algorithm.
- **Virtual Communities chain analysis:** Sentiment analysis of local groups and insights into local groups both before and after joining virtual communities, Chain Break (consider why local groups are not participating in and leaving the communities), Communities are being rebuilt.
- **Use of Social media analytics tools:** Patterns on the digital map will be tracked using various social media layers to gather insights about the communities.

Tool for Analyzing Communities Using Google Data Studio

Google created Google Data Studio, sometimes referred to as Data Studio, a free reporting, and data visualization application. It enables users to compile, alter, and distribute educational reports made from different data sources. Whether you work as an analyst, marketer, or business owner, Data Studio can make presenting data easier.

Figure 3. Various parameters used to determine various community social media use

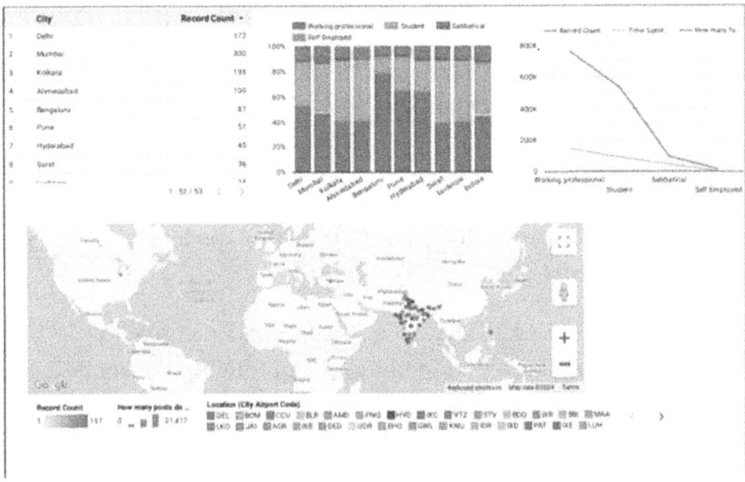

The example above illustrates the various parameters that are used to determine how various communities use social media platforms, including locations and the number of followers and posts that are active at any one time. The communities are visualized using various sets and data sets according to the target audience. Here, we can see how many working professionals, self-employed, and student communities use the social media platforms.

REFERENCES

Abarca, V. M. G., Palos-Sanchez, P. R., & Rus-Arias, E. (2020). Working in Virtual Teams: A Systematic Literature Review and a Bibliometric Analysis. *IEEE Access : Practical Innovations, Open Solutions*, 8, 168923–168940. DOI: 10.1109/ACCESS.2020.3023546

Fayez, O., Ismail, H., & Aboelnagah, H. (2023). Emerging virtual communities of practice during crises: A sustainable model validating the levels of peer motivation and support. *Sustainability*, 15(7), 5691.

Malthouse, E. C., Haenlein, M., Skiera, B., Wege, E., & Zhang, M. (2013). Managing customer relationships in the social media era: Introducing the social CRM house. *Journal of Interactive Marketing*, 27(4), 270–280.

Mockaitis, A., Rose, E., & Zettinig, P. (2012). The power of individual cultural values in global virtual teams. *International Journal of Cross Cultural Management*, 12(2), 193–210. DOI: 10.1177/1470595812439868

Óskarsdóttira, M. *, Cristián Bravob, Wouter Verbekee, Carlos Sarrautef, Bart Baesensc,d, Jan VanthienencSocial "Network Analytics for Churn Prediction in Telco: Model Building, Evaluation and Network Architecture" arXiv:2001.06701v1 [cs.SI] 18 Jan 2020

Yuan, L., Deng, X., & Zhong, W. (2021). Encouraging Passive Members of Online Brand Communities to Generate eWOM Based on TAM and Social Capital Theory. *IEEE Access : Practical Innovations, Open Solutions*, 9, 12840–12851. DOI: 10.1109/ACCESS.2021.3050162

Zhang, Y., Xia, X., Xu, X., Yu, F., Wu, H., Yu, Y., & Wei, B. (2020). Robust Hierarchical Overlapping Community Detection With Personalized PageRank. *IEEE Access : Practical Innovations, Open Solutions*, 8, 102867–102882. DOI: 10.1109/ACCESS.2020.2998860

Chapter 4
Second Life and the Immersion Into Virtual Communities

Javier Gonzalez Nuñez
https://orcid.org/0009-0000-5393-0103
Ipade Business School, Mexico

Manuel Bolognesi
Enrapture, Belgium

Jane Godbehear
Enrapture, Belgium

ABSTRACT

Enrapture, an innovative immersive tech development company based in Belgium, is one of the first businesses with a "virtual-world native" team that originally convened in Second Life a decade ago. Today, its strategic focus on user-generated content within virtual communities remains integral to its business strategy. Drawing from its extensive experience establishing leading ventures within Second Life, Enrapture facilitates seamless collaboration among virtual team members and expert partners across various time zones, aligning with the gig economy trend. This is characterized by flexible, contract-based work that challenges traditional employment paradigms. (Roy & Shrivastava, 2020). Central to the discourse on virtual immersion is the concept of the Metaverse—a sprawling landscape where virtual experiences converge with all social interactions and the commercial activities of a "creator economy" in a future version of the internet, the 3D internet.

DOI: 10.4018/979-8-3693-3868-1.ch004

INTRODUCTION

Enrapture, an innovative immersive tech development company based in Belgium, is one of the first businesses with a "virtual-world native" team that originally convened in Second Life a decade ago. Today, its strategic focus on user-generated content within virtual communities remains integral to its business strategy. Drawing from its extensive experience establishing leading ventures within Second Life, Enrapture facilitates seamless collaboration among virtual team members and expert partners across various time zones, aligning with the gig economy trend. This is characterized by flexible, contract-based work that challenges traditional employment paradigms. (Roy & Shrivastava, 2020).

Central to the discourse on virtual immersion is the concept of the Metaverse—a sprawling landscape where virtual experiences converge with all social interactions and the commercial activities of a "creator economy" in a future version of the internet, the 3D internet. Recent developments, such as Metaverse events featuring prominent artists and brands, underscore the transformative potential of immersive platforms. Through case studies and industry insights, this chapter aims to delineate the evolving contours of the Metaverse and its role as a nexus of entertainment, commerce, and cultural expression.

Enrapture's original team members chose Second Life as a platform for their virtual-world products simply because that is where they met in a fortuitous way. In effect, the "virtual-world native" term indicates how the team started with avatars meeting in virtual worlds with a shared goal to work on. That goal is to create virtual products that have a deep and cathartic impact on the real-life users behind the avatars. They understood that behind a successful Second Life product, there is a deep real-life need that can be exceptionally well solved in the virtual. Hence their motivation to power the world's most realistic maternity and parenting simulation, catering to the family-roleplay aspect of Second Life and couples who could not conceive in real life. Products like Hands On Mommy and Hands On Care Maternity, quickly became the standard in terms of realism on the platform and attracted attention from real-life maternal psychology labs and medical professionals. Partnering with real-life medical professionals across different countries to ensure their realism, the maternity and parenting simulation allowed dozens of thousands of couples to overcome challenging times of COVID-19 restrictions, brought closure to personal traumas, and even inspired some to pursue a medical career in real life. Having navigated the Second Life landscape and become proficient in all the different areas of the platform, a real-world company with goals across multiple virtual worlds was formed. Nowadays, Enrapture has over 100.000 active virtual–world clients. Here, the focus shifted from mere product creation to the establishment of a business model, developing and using remote working solutions (such as Meetwork.ai) and accommodating diverse timelines. This strategic pivot not only facilitates Enrapture's adaptation to contemporary work trends but also enables it to assist other brands in catering to virtual worlds and in engaging with new generations.

SECOND LIFE: A PREDICTION OF THE SHIFT TOWARDS A 3D INTERNET

Second Life, owned by Linden Labs, is among the earliest virtual worlds, having been established over 20 years ago. Over time, it has evolved into one of the most intricate and sophisticated virtual environments, boasting developed and complex societal dynamics that are mostly unmatched by newer platforms.

Within Second Life, a vibrant community has flourished, crafting a distinct world with its own set of norms and regulations. This community often operates under concealed real identities, utilizing alter-ego accounts and engaging in entrepreneurial endeavors shaped by unique demand patterns exclusive to the platform. These dynamics offer valuable insights into the potential trajectory of social interactions within the future 3D internet landscape.

Bardzell and Shankar (2007) argued that the emergence of multiplayer online platforms and virtual worlds such as "Second Life" has blurred the distinction between work and leisure, ushering in novel opportunities for digital immersion, interaction, and education. Nowadays, the exponential expansion of platforms like Roblox, with its staggering statistics of over 60 million daily active young users, around 40 million games, and a vibrant community of 9 million individual game developers, indicates that the pertinent inquiry is not whether this trend will persist but rather the apex it will attain (Bui, 2023).

In the early 2000s, Second Life gained popularity among both educators and non-educators. The former was drawn to Second Life for its perceived ability to manipulate space and time, bound only by imagination (Inman et al., 2010). Additionally, major corporations, including tech giants like IBM and Cisco Systems, took notice and invested substantial resources to establish a virtual environment for their employees and potential clients. While anonymity in Second Life cultivates a unique camaraderie based on personality rather than physical appearance or status, the necessity of truth and trust becomes paramount in business interactions involving significant financial stakes. This underscores a first critical issue that warrants attention in achieving successful immersion within virtual communities.

Virtual worlds like Second Life are complex, multi-layered information platforms that accommodate several media, including text, photography, videos, interactive animations, and chat. In Second Life, users may choose to design or build their own objects, environments, and characters. Rather than consuming the pre-ordained scripts of other authors, they may create their own synthetic scenarios, spaces, products, and events. This process is allowed by the creativity of users who upload and download information across powerful computer networks. Research has shown how the virtual ecology of Second Life can enable tacit knowledge creation and design collaboration, therefore contributing to improved design innovation (Rive, 2012).

Estimates suggest that only between 2004 and 2014, Second Life users have spent the equivalent of 217,266 years of time online (Hassouneh & Brengman, 2014). This book posits that time operates differently within the virtual realm. In Second Life, the passage of time appears accelerated, allowing couples to meet, marry, and start families within a span of mere weeks. Virtual pregnancies can be completed in a matter of weeks, and an avatar with just a decade of experience on the platform is already perceived as seasoned, or even old. Such observations suggest the emergence of "timeless time" and "spaceless space" within the Metaverse, where human interactions are not bound by conventional temporal or spatial constraints. It is not uncommon for Second Life "residents" to be involved in multiple roleplay families at one time, have several parents, grandparents, and several avatars to fit their daily moods.

Yet, the use of avatars can create a sense of detachment from one's own identity, blurring the lines between existence and non-existence as an individual; known as a dissociative effect of virtual immersivity (Gilbert et al., 2014). This psychological gap, coupled with the potential for anonymity in online environments and evolving social norms, may facilitate the occurrence of inappropriate behavior. While there is a certain societal pressure in virtual worlds to maintain a consistent primary identity, students appear to experience a profound sense of physical presence in educational settings that is beneficial to their learning skills (Alenezi & Shahi, 2015). This emergent utilization of Second Life in educational contexts has prompted investigations into its effectiveness (Gallego et al., 2016). . For instance, Sarac (2014) and Lin et al. (2014) scrutinized its use for language acquisition. Grenfell (2013) explored the potential of Second Life in art education. Additionally, Sutcliffe and Alrayes (2012) analyzed its role in collaborative learning, revealing its positive impact on motivation and socialization.

Second Life also serves as a potent environment for community building and collective action (Huvila et al., 2010). In an era where digital immersion blurs the boundaries between reality and virtuality, living in virtual environments has become increasingly tangible (Kim et al., 2008). Through an interdisciplinary lens, we examined the evolving nature of virtual engagement, its economic implications, and the societal dynamics shaping this transformative landscape.

Distinguishing itself from other massively multiplayer online role-playing games (MMORPGs), Second Life operates without conventional gaming elements such as point systems, winners or losers, levels, leaderboards, bosses, or strategic gameplay.

Instead, Second Life residents inhabit the virtual world as an integral part of their lives; they have the freedom to explore virtual cities and landscapes, engage socially with fellow residents, participate in various individual and group activities (like playing music), and engage in commerce by creating, buying, and selling products and services to one another.

THE COMPARISON BETWEEN SECOND LIFE AND ROBLOX

Early Success of Second Life

During the early 2000s, Second Life was a pioneering platform where brands like Adidas, Dell, AOL, Reebok, Sears, American Apparel and Wells Fargo, as well as universities created immersive virtual spaces (Callaghan, 2011; Barnes et al., 2015). These initiatives aimed to capitalize on Second Life's mostly user-generated environment, which allowed for extensive customization and interactive experiences.

The decline in brand engagement with Second Life over the years can be attributed to several factors. Despite being ahead of its time in offering immersive virtual experiences, users perceived lower practical and logical value in virtual brand interactions compared to real-life ones (Barnes et al., 2015). The platform's user base did not grow as rapidly as anticipated, limiting audience reach. Additionally, technical limitations and a steep learning curve created barriers to maintaining effective virtual brand spaces, leading brands to reconsider their investments in Second Life. Nonetheless, Second Life's efforts set the stage for future advancements in digital brand engagement and the platform still hosts a thriving virtual-world native creator economy.

Unique Ecosystems

The immersive digital landscapes of Second Life and Roblox offer unique ecosystems that cater to different demographics and serve distinct purposes. Roblox, due to its record-breaking popularity, offers creators a concrete possibility of making real-life returns from virtual-world earnings through game passes, user-generated content (UGC) collectibles, "Engagement-Based Payouts," and marketplace sales. Despite this potential, Roblox's predominantly young population may restrict this possibility. As of 2024, 42.3% of Roblox's daily active users are under the age of 13, while 56.98% are over 13 years old (Backlinko, 2024; Demand Sage, 2024). This skew towards young users necessitates stringent safety and civility measures, including AI-monitored chat censorship, privacy guidelines, and parental controls.

Like Second Life, Roblox's economic model leverages its internal currency, Robux, which can be earned, spent on the platform, and traded for real-world currency.

Safety and Moderation

Both platforms face challenges regarding safety and trust, particularly in business operations. Roblox employs AI to monitor chat for offensive content and offers extensive parental controls, automatically obscuring offensive language. However, players can still communicate using external platforms such as Discord and WhatsApp, complicating monitoring efforts.

Roblox's robust tools for user-generated content, easier development processes, and effective moderation systems make it an attractive choice for brands. This has led to successful branded experiences such as Nike's Nikeland, Walmart's Walmart Land, and Ikea's Co-worker game, which are designed to be engaging and attract modern audiences. This shift reflects a broader trend in marketing where consumer-led content and engagement through interactive experiences are prioritized over traditional advertising models.

Recent announcements from Roblox Corporation about introducing a "safe" voice chat feature indicate ongoing efforts to enhance user safety, despite concerns about censorship from its young user base. Additionally, Roblox recently introduced 17+ experiences to cater to its consistently larger number of older users. These experiences include non-sexual expressions of love and affection but still prohibit real-world romantic relationships and explicit content (Roblox 17+ Policy Standards, 2023).

Security, Trust Mechanisms & Power Dynamics

Second Life offers a vibrant and less censored environment that appeals to a more adult-oriented audience and a successful creator economy that has virtually no boundary to creativity. The open nature of Second Life enables a flourishing virtual marketplace where users can buy, sell, and trade items, services and experiences of any kind, contributing to the platform's economic success that is still ongoing in 2024.

However, Second Life is not inherently designed for team-based activities, which can create potential risks when delegating tasks. For example, allowing others to sell products or return specific items on one's land often requires granting them access to your account, posing significant security risks. These issues, though present in Roblox, are mitigated to some extent by the separate Roblox Studio software designed for collaborative work. Ethical considerations arise from the potential misuse of access by collaborators, highlighting the need for robust trust mechanisms, contractual safeguards and a focus on power dynamics.

The power dynamics within virtual worlds like Second Life and Roblox influence users' psychological experiences, including feelings of control and fears of rejection, such as being banned from a virtual land ("sim"). In these virtual lands, landlords can create their own rules, employ others, write codes of conduct, and manage object permissions, creating an illusion of control. Illusion because the ultimate power rests only with the companies that created these virtual worlds. These platforms' terms of service grant significant power to the platform owners, impacting users' autonomy and the enforcement of community standards. The psychological divide between avatars and their real-life counterparts further complicates trust and safety issues.

ENRAPTURE: THE FUTURE OF BRAND AND AUDIENCE ENGAGEMENT IN 3D

Enrapture stands as a European tech innovator company, spearheading the development of Metaverse solutions that redefine digital experiences. Specializing in a diverse array of offerings, Enrapture's portfolio encompasses branded virtual worlds, training simulations, music experiences, 3D shopping, and AI immersive workrooms that aim to captivate and engage users.

Enrapture believes that, whether through centralized or decentralized technology, the concept of ownership will be paramount in the future 3D internet to foster a robust creator economy. The essence of the Metaverse is bridging the virtual and real worlds meaningfully. In this regard, Second Life exemplifies how virtual environments can profoundly impact emotions and address psychological traumas (Gorini et al., 2008). In the Metaverse, successful products will address significant real-world issues at their core.

As outlined by Bolger (2021), the Metaverse will also be driven by Artificial Intelligence at its core. According to this vision, artificial intelligence will serve as the connecting force, integrating all aspects of the world across domains of knowledge, social interaction, and geographic dimensions. Enrapture's recent introduction of Meetwork.ai, a virtual immersive office and AI workroom solution, leverages collaborative generative AI tools and AI Non-Playable Characters to foster a contemporary office environment, aspiring to become the go-to virtual platform for professionals.

The American Academy of Pediatrics released a report in 2018. In this report, they mention: "Play is not frivolous: it enhances brain structure and function and promotes executive function" (Sahlberg & Doyle, 2019). The report goes on to recommend that doctors prescribe "play every day" to all their young patients. With this in mind, Enrapture also envisions the future of brand engagement being gamified and in 3D. As brands and entertainment increasingly find younger generations on gaming platforms like Roblox, Enrapture strives to craft immersive worlds for any brand or artist prepared for this future. A future where customers or brand enthusiasts will not merely interact with brands via smartphone screens or passive social media feeds. On the contrary, they will become integral participants in 3D dynamic virtual worlds or gaming experiences built around a brand. This paradigm shift suggests a future where brand-customer communication pivots towards a more customer-centric approach, with customers actively shaping and contributing to brands' 3D presence. Here, they can advance in ranks, forge communities around brands of interest, and even earn monetary rewards through participation in the game's creator economy and business models.

By integrating and empowering individuals within their fan communities, brands may bolster their credibility, authenticity, and trustworthiness, ultimately leading to improved sales performance.

Virtual Worlds vs. Gaming: The entrepreneurial economy of emotions

The true Metaverse will be about people. Envisioning collaboration in this future realm, humans will seamlessly inhabit it, transitioning between virtual and augmented realities, perceiving an increasingly immersive blend of the digital and physical worlds (Bolger, 2021). This immersive blend of digital and physical worlds will facilitate streamlined team performance assessments through synchronized workflow and seamless data collection (Davis et al., 2009). This is pictured as an ever-active space, ready to allow feelings of human presence, ready to promote business (through digital currencies) and play (Bolger, 2021; Ko et al., 2021).

Virtual worlds offer spaces where there is no goal, but rather a platform for socialization and virtual commerce. Philip Rosedale, Second Life's founder, was determined Second Life would not become a video game filled with quests and errands. He wanted creativity to be user-generated, not prescribed—a place, perhaps, where people might try out new identities, proclivities, and modes of escapism (Parkin, 2023).

Games limit freedom, entrepreneurship, and creation, virtual worlds encourage them. Successful virtual worlds distinguish themselves from games by nurturing emotions and creativity. They facilitate easy content creation, uphold clear property rights, encourage financial support among creators, promote live collaboration, collective ownership, enable circular trading, and prioritize free access for diversity and experimentation (Rosedale, 2022).

The cornerstone of virtual worlds' success also hinges on their provision of freedom, reduced legal obstacles, and lowered barriers to entrepreneurship. These factors empower individuals to monetize user-generated content. Virtual immersive platforms also facilitate corporate utilization by fostering engaging team interactions and collaborative virtual businesses, with avenues for monetization including v-commerce, advertising, cost-effective marketing research (33% lower than real-world equivalents), and human resources management (Kaplan and Haenlein, 2009).

Conclusion: Embracing Digital Dualities

In conclusion, this chapter delves into the dynamics of immersion within virtual communities, where individuals seamlessly navigate between the physical and digital realms, embracing opportunities for connection, creativity, modern audience engagement, and commerce. Enrapture emerges as a compelling case study, tracing its origins from the pioneering days of Second Life, where it created leading products and gathered a virtual-world native team, to its current involvement across various virtual-world platforms like Roblox and Meetwork.ai.

The comparison between Second Life and Roblox offers a nuanced understanding of the unique ecosystems these platforms support. Second Life, with its mature and intricate societal dynamics, continues to provide a rich environment for creative expression and community building. Its social maturity and uncensored communication make it an exemplary case study for understanding the future of the 3D internet from a social perspective. The platform's lack of conventional gaming elements allows users to engage in open-ended exploration, social interaction, and virtual commerce, fostering a vibrant creator economy that has remained robust for over two decades.

In contrast, Roblox represents a phenomenon of today, attracting a younger and rapidly growing demographic. Emphasizing safety, creativity, and economic opportunity through game development and user-generated content, Roblox has become particularly appealing to brands and artists. Its economic model, driven by the internal currency Robux, mirrors the financial mechanisms of Second Life while catering to a distinct user base with unique needs and expectations.

Both platforms face challenges in ensuring safety and trust, particularly in business operations and user interactions. Roblox employs advanced AI to monitor and moderate content, providing a safer environment for its predominantly young users. Meanwhile, Second Life relies more on user autonomy and self-regulation. These differing approaches underscore the broader implications of platform design and governance in shaping user experiences and community dynamics.

Ultimately, the exploration of virtual immersion extends beyond technological advancements, encompassing realms of economics, sociology, and cultural studies.

Through Enrapture's particular journey, we witness the transformative potential of virtual worlds, where innovative solutions arise from the gaps in real-life experiences, fostering unprecedented creativity and an all-hybrid type of demand. It becomes evident that in virtual environments, individuals do not merely replicate their real selves; rather, they find avenues for growth and learning, transcending physical limitations to manifest dreams and aspirations with low barriers to entry and legal limitations. The essence lies not in the avatar mimicking the real person, but rather in the real person drawing purposefulness, inspiration, knowledge, and psychological aid from the avatar's experiences. While gaming often revolves around structured narratives and gameplay mechanics, virtual worlds foster boundless freedom and agency, empowering users to shape their experiences and interactions. This refers to broader qualities within the virtual-world landscape, highlighting the intrinsic value of creative freedom, collaborative ownership, and inclusive participation.

REFERENCES

Alenezi, A. M., & Shahi, K. K. (2015). Interactive e-learning through second life with blackboard technology. *Procedia: Social and Behavioral Sciences*, 176, 891–897. https://www.sciencedirect.com/science/article/pii/S1877042815005923. DOI: 10.1016/j.sbspro.2015.01.555

Backlinko. (2024). Roblox User and Growth Stats You Need to Know in 2024. Retrieved from https://backlinko.com/roblox-users

Bardzell, S., & Shankar, K. (2007, July). Video game technologies and virtual design: a study of virtual design teams in a metaverse. *In International Conference on Virtual Reality* (pp. 607-616). Springer, Berlin, Heidelberg. Retrieved from https://link.springer.com/chapter/10.1007/978-3-540-73335-5_65

Barnes, S. J., Mattsson, J., & Hartley, N. (2015). Assessing the value of real-life brands in Virtual Worlds. *Technological Forecasting and Social Change*, 92, 12–24. https://www.sciencedirect.com/science/article/abs/pii/S0040162514003035. DOI: 10.1016/j.techfore.2014.10.017

Bolger, R. K. (2021). Finding Wholes in the Metaverse: Posthuman Mystics as Agents of Evolutionary Contextualization. *Religions*, 12(9), 768. https://www.mdpi.com/2077-1444/12/9/768. DOI: 10.3390/rel12090768

Bui, T. (2023). How Roblox can attract more adult players: a case study of a Finnish start-up.https://www.theseus.fi/handle/10024/851390

Callaghan, V. (2011). *Immersive Education: Taking K-12 Distance Learning to the Next Level*. Springer Science & Business Media. Retrieved from https://books.google.be/books?hl=en&lr=&id=Idgbf828DdsC&oi=fnd&pg=PA83&dq=Adidas+and+universities+in+Second+Life&ots=fpNsMqWcND&sig=LzSPQSHuO2B710i_cysmmECwzgg&redir_esc=y#v=onepage&q=Adidas%20and%20universities%20in%20Second%20Life&f=false

Davis, A., Murphy, J. D., Owens, D., Khazanchi, D., & Zigurs, I. (2009). Avatars, people, and virtual worlds: Foundations for research in metaverses. *Journal of the Association for Information Systems*, 10(2), 90–117. https://digitalcommons.unomaha.edu/cgi/viewcontent.cgi?referer=https://scholar.google.com.tw/scholar?hl=nl&as_sdt=0%2C5&q=study+on+working+relations+in+metaverse&oq=working+&httpsredir=1&article=1021&context=isqafacpub. DOI: 10.17705/1jais.00183

Demand Sage. (2024). Roblox Statistics For 2024. Retrieved from https://www.demandsage.com/how-many-people-play-roblox/

Gallego, M. D., Bueno, S., & Noyes, J. (2016). Second Life adoption in education: A motivational model based on Uses and Gratifications theory. *Computers & Education*, 100, 81–93. https://www.sciencedirect.com/science/article/abs/pii/S0360131516301105. DOI: 10.1016/j.compedu.2016.05.001

Gilbert, R., Thadani, V., Handy, C., Andrews, H., Sguigna, T., Sasso, A., & Payne, S. (2014). The psychological functions of avatars and alt (s): A qualitative study. *Computers in Human Behavior*, 32, 1–8. https://www.sciencedirect.com/science/article/abs/pii/S0747563213004287. DOI: 10.1016/j.chb.2013.11.007

Gorini, A., Gaggioli, A., & Riva, G. (2008). A second life for eHealth: Prospects for the use of 3-D virtual worlds in clinical psychology. *Journal of Medical Internet Research*, 10(3), e1029. https://www.jmir.org/2008/3/e21. DOI: 10.2196/jmir.1029 PMID: 18678557

Grenfell, J. (2013). Immersive interfaces for art education teaching and learning in virtual and real world learning environments. *Procedia: Social and Behavioral Sciences*, 93, 1198–1211. https://www.sciencedirect.com/science/article/pii/S1877042813034617. DOI: 10.1016/j.sbspro.2013.10.016

Hassouneh, D., & Brengman, M. (2014). A motivation-based typology of social virtual world users. *Computers in Human Behavior*, 33, 330–338. https://www.sciencedirect.com/science/article/abs/pii/S0747563213003117. DOI: 10.1016/j.chb.2013.08.012

Huvila, I., Holmberg, K., Ek, S., & Widén-Wulff, G. (2010). Social capital in second life. *Online Information Review*, 34(2), 295–316. https://www.emerald.com/insight/content/doi/10.1108/14684521011037007/full/html. DOI: 10.1108/14684521011037007

Inman, C., Wright, V. H., & Hartman, J. A. (2010). Use of Second Life in K-12 and higher education: A review of research. *Journal of Interactive Online Learning*, 9(1). https://www.ncolr.org/jiol/issues/pdf/9.1.3.pdf

Kaplan, A. M., & Haenlein, M. (2009). The fairyland of Second Life: Virtual social worlds and how to use them. *Business Horizons*, 52(6), 563–572. DOI: 10.1016/j.bushor.2009.07.002

Kim, H. M., Lyons, K., & Cunningham, M. A. (2008). Towards a theoretically-grounded framework for evaluating immersive business models and applications: Analysis of ventures in Second Life. *Journal of Virtual Worlds Research*, 1(1). Advance online publication. https://jvwr-ojs-utexas.tdl.org/jvwr/article/view/289. DOI: 10.4101/jvwr.v1i1.289

Ko, S. Y., Chung, H. K., Kim, J. I., & Shin, Y. (2021). A Study on the Typology and Advancement of Cultural Leisure-Based Metaverse. *KIPS Transactions on Software and Data Engineering*, 10(8), 331–338.

Lin, T. J., Wang, S. Y., Grant, S., Chien, C. L., & Lan, Y. J. (2014). Task-based teaching approaches of Chinese as a foreign language in Second Life through teachers' perspectives. *Procedia Technology*, 13, 16–22. https://www.sciencedirect.com/science/article/pii/S2212017314000140. DOI: 10.1016/j.protcy.2014.02.004

Parkin, S. (2023, June 10). Who needs the metaverse? Meet the people still living on Second Life. *The Guardian*.https://www.theguardian.com/technology/2023/jun/10/who-needs-the-metaverse-meet-the-people-still-living-on-second-life

Rive, P. B. (2012). *Design in a Virtual Innovation Ecology: A Cybernetic Systems Approach to Knowledge Creation and Design Collaboration in Second Life* (Doctoral dissertation, Open Access Te Herenga Waka-Victoria University of Wellington). https://openaccess.wgtn.ac.nz/articles/thesis/Design_in_a_Virtual_Innovation_Ecology_A_Cybernetic_Systems_Approach_to_Knowledge_Creation_and_Design_Collaboration_in_Second_Life/17004709

Roblox 17+ Policy Standards. (2023). Retrieved from https://en.help.roblox.com/hc/en-us/articles/15869919570708-Roblox-17-Policy-Standards

Rosedale, P. (2022, July 8). Value creation in virtual worlds. *Medium*. https://medium.com/@philiprosedale/value-creation-in-virtual-worlds-696604a694d1

Roy, G., & Shrivastava, A. K. (2020). Future of gig economy: opportunities and challenges. *Imi Konnect, 9*(1), 14-27.January-March 20.cdr (imik.edu.in)

Sahlberg, P., & Doyle, W. (2019). *Let the children play: How more play will save our schools and help children thrive*. Oxford University Press., https://books.google.be/books?hl=en&lr=&id=ny8DEAAAQBAJ&oi=fnd&pg=PP1&dq=%E2%80%9CPlay+is+not+frivolous:+it+enhances+brain+structure+and+function+and+promotes+executive+function%E2%80%9D&ots=ox84L6kTb3&sig=4igeE94L3cM04W-t-btsiB0HCgs&redir_esc=y#v=onepage&q=%E2%80%9CPlay%20is%20not%20frivolous%3A%20it%20enhances%20brain%20structure%20and%20function%20and%20promotes%20executive%20function%E2%80%9D&f=false

Sarac, H. S. (2014). Benefits and challenges of using Second Life in English teaching: Experts' opinions. *Procedia: Social and Behavioral Sciences*, 158, 326–330. https://www.sciencedirect.com/science/article/pii/S1877042814061886. DOI: 10.1016/j.sbspro.2014.12.095

Sutcliffe, A., & Alrayes, A. (2012). Investigating user experience in Second Life for collaborative learning. *International Journal of Human-Computer Studies*, 70(7), 508–525. https://www.sciencedirect.com/science/article/abs/pii/S1071581912000262. DOI: 10.1016/j.ijhcs.2012.01.005

Chapter 5
Unveiling the Web: A Comprehensive Bibliometric Exploration of Investigating Social Network Sites

Anisha Arora
https://orcid.org/0009-0004-4685-6565
Chandigarh University, India

Prashant Kumar Siddhey
https://orcid.org/0000-0002-4236-0966
Chandigarh University, India

ABSTRACT

Using Scopus as the main database, this chapter provides a thorough bibliometric study of research articles on "Exploring Social Network Sites" from 2007 to 2024. We use sophisticated analysis tools like VoSviewer, R Studio, and Biblioshiny to look at author contributions, source impacts, co-occurrences of keywords, and citation patterns. Our results demonstrate a noteworthy rise in research output over time, indicating an increase in scholarly interest. The analysis provides strategic insights for future research by highlighting prominent gaps in the subject, important contributors, and recurrent themes. This work contributes to a better understanding of the field and encourages more scholarly investigation by offering a unique mapping of the trajectory of SNS research.The findings highlight the value of ongoing investigation in SNS studies, with the goal of directing future paths and advancing the advancement of knowledge in this dynamic and ever-evolving field.

DOI: 10.4018/979-8-3693-3868-1.ch005

1. INTRODUCTION

Social networking sites (SNSs) have become essential channels for communication, engagement, and information sharing in the modern digital world. The dynamics of social interactions, community building, and even geopolitical movements have undergone a fundamental transformation thanks to these online platforms, which are typified by giants like Facebook, Twitter, and Instagram. As social media continues to pervade every aspect of daily life, academics are focusing more and more on comprehending the complex ramifications of SNSs. A thorough bibliometric examination of the body of research on social networking sites is presented in this study. We hope to identify important research, rising areas of interest, trends, and major themes in this quickly developing discipline by methodically mapping the scholarly landscape(Firdaniza et al., 2022; Hartman & Simova, 2021; Lohtia et al., 2013).

People's connections, sharing, and information consumption have changed dramatically as a result of the widespread use of SNSs. These platforms now play a crucial role in both personal and professional life, impacting everything from everyday interactions to world events. Because SNSs are widely used, a lot of data and insights have been produced, which has led researchers to investigate the social, psychological, and technological effects of these platforms. Consequently, there is an enormous amount of literature on SNSs that comes from a variety of fields, including computer science, psychology, sociology, and communication studies. The intricacy of these platforms and the requirement for a comprehensive grasp of their ramifications are highlighted by the interdisciplinary nature of SNS research(Grover et al., 2022; Studies et al., 2012).

By using a quantitative method to examine bibliographic material, bibliometric analysis provides insightful information on the development and theoretical underpinnings of many study topics. This approach identifies openings and topics for more research when it comes to social network sites (SNSs), while also highlighting important contributions and foundational initiatives. This study uses cutting-edge bibliometric tools and techniques to increase our understanding of the academic discourse surrounding SNSs. These observations help academics, professionals, and decision-makers navigate the intricate digital environment. The statistical analysis of books, papers, and other publications known as bibliometrics offers a comprehensive picture of the state of research by exposing citation networks, publishing trends, authorship patterns, and the importance of specific publications(Sağkaya Güngör & Ozansoy Çadırcı, 2022; Zarei & Jabbarzadeh, 2019).

The widespread influence of social networking sites (SNSs) on cultural norms and behaviours highlights the importance of this research. A comprehensive bibliometric investigation offers a fundamental comprehension that can guide future studies, policy creation, and the tactical advancement of digital communication platforms as these platforms progress and become more ingrained in daily life. By using this lens, we hope to shed light on the scholarly endeavour of comprehending social networking sites and provide a thorough review that adds to the larger conversation on social interaction and digital communication (Abbas et al., 2022; Javid et al., 2019).

Tracking the evolution of social network site (SNS) research throughout time is one of the main goals of this study. We can evaluate the increase and diversity of interest in this area by looking at publishing trends. Early studies on SNS mostly concentrated on how well they might link people and promote communication. The study focus has broadened to cover topics like privacy problems, the psychological effects of social media use, and the role of SNSs in political activity, though, as these platforms have developed. Finding these trends makes it easier to put recent research into perspective and point out areas that could need more research.

Additionally, the goal of this bibliometric analysis is to pinpoint the authors and publications that have had the most influence on SNS research. We can determine important research clusters and comprehend how academics from various disciplines collaborate to answer challenging SNS-related topics by mapping co-authorship networks. The regional distribution of research endeavours can also be ascertained using this data, highlighting the nations and establishments that are at the forefront of SNS research.

The study also looks for new themes and directions for SNS research in the future. We can find fresh areas of interest that are gaining popularity among scholars by conducting a keyword and topic analysis of the literature. The study of false information propagated on social media, the effect of algorithms on user behaviour, and the moral ramifications of data privacy on SNSs are a few examples of current developments. For scholars hoping to stay in the field, recognizing these rising themes is crucial.

It is critical for funding organizations seeking to promote cutting-edge research as well as for researchers trying to maintain their position at the forefront of their fields to recognize these developing themes.

This report presents a thorough bibliometric exploration that offers strategic insights for different stakeholders in addition to mapping the current state of SNS research. This technique provides researchers with a road map for navigating the large corpus of literature and finding possible partners. The findings draw attention to important issues that need regulation, such as misinformation and data privacy, for legislators. Platform developers can create features that reduce negative consequences and encourage beneficial social interactions by taking into account scholarly discourse.

Social media platforms have grown to be an essential component of contemporary communication, and it is critical for both academic and practical reasons to comprehend the wide range of effects they have. This bibliometric analysis sheds light on historical accomplishments, present trends, and future directions by offering a thorough and organized summary of the state of SNS research. By doing this, it promotes the continuous advancement of knowledge in this exciting sector and adds to the continuing conversation regarding social media's role in society.

2. LITERATURE REVIEW

Social media platforms (SMSs)

Social networking sites (SNSs) are becoming commonplace in contemporary society, offering venues for community development, information sharing, and social engagement. Social media sites like Facebook, Instagram, TikTok, and Twitter have had a significant impact on professional networking, interpersonal connections, and even political environments. SNSs have consequently grown to be an important topic of scholarly inquiry. Examining contemporary research on social networking sites (SNSs), this overview of the literature focuses on the psychological effects, social capital, privacy issues, information sharing, algorithmic influence, political involvement, economic ramifications, and upcoming trends.

Social Media's Effect on Mental Health

The focus of the current study has been on the psychological effects of social networking use. The impact of SNSs on mental health, self-esteem, and general well-being has been the subject of numerous studies. For example, Valkenburg, Beyens, Pouwels, van Driel, and Keijsers' meta-analysis from 2022 discovered that, depending on the type and context of use, SNS use is linked to both favorable and unfavourable effects on mental health. Good relationships and encouraging remarks can improve wellbeing, while bad things like social comparison and cyberbullying can make anxiety and depression worse.

Kross et al. (2022) demonstrated in a longitudinal study that compared to active use (posting and commenting), passive SNS use (scrolling and lurking) is more likely to have detrimental psychological effects. They contend that while active participation can promote social support and constructive social relationships, passive use can exacerbate feelings of loneliness and lower life satisfaction.

Social Networks and Social Capital

Social networks have played a pivotal role in moulding social capital, characterised as the assets amassed by interpersonal connections. According to Ellison, Vitak, Gray, and Lampe (2022), social networking sites (SNSs) help with social capital bridging (connecting with disparate groups) as well as bonding (strengthening ties within a group). Their research revealed that SNS use, especially among marginalized groups, improves social cohesion and access to resources and information.

Brooks and Hogan's (2021) recent study examined the function of social networking sites (SNSs) in business networking. They discovered that professional social capital is greatly enhanced by websites such as LinkedIn, which present job satisfaction and career growth chances. According to their research, LinkedIn users actively using the platform are more likely than non-users to receive job offers and career prospects.

Their results underline the importance of LinkedIn for professional development, showing that active users are more likely than non-users to obtain job offers and career possibilities.

The Spread of False Information on Social Network Sites

Social networking sites (SNSs) are essential for the spread of information and for influencing public opinion. They do, however, also make it easier for false information to proliferate quickly. Vosoughi, Roy, and Aral (2018) discovered that on Twitter, incorrect information travels more quickly and reaches a larger audience than accurate information. Politics, social stability, and public health are all significantly impacted by this.

Platforms have taken several actions in reaction to the dissemination of false information. According to Pennycook and Rand (2021), straightforward interventions can considerably slow the spread of erroneous information. One such intervention is to ask users to think about the accuracy of information before sharing it. Their research showed that encouraging self-reflection on accuracy can improve the calibre of content that is shared on social networking sites.

Data Security and Privacy Issues

Privacy concerns are still quite important when it comes to SNSs. There are moral and legal concerns about the gathering, use, and possible abuse of personal information by SNSs. The 2018 Cambridge Analytica controversy highlighted the weaknesses in data security and user privacy. It involves the unapproved collection of Facebook data for political advertising (Cadwalladr & Graham-Harrison, 2018).

Shin and Biocca (2020) looked at how users' activity on SNSs is impacted by privacy concerns. They discovered that more people utilize privacy settings and provide less information as a result of growing privacy concerns. This emphasizes how SNSs must improve user control over personal data and openness to sustain participation and confidence.

Algorithmic Impact and Reverberation Chambers

SNS content curation algorithms greatly impact what users view and interact with, resulting in highly customized feeds. Although this improves the user experience, it also helps create "filter bubbles" and echo chambers where people are only exposed to material that confirms their preexisting opinions. This deliberate exposure has the potential to polarize people by confirming their preconceptions.

In 2015, Bakshy, Messing, and Adamic conducted research on how exposure to a variety of news items was affected by Facebook's algorithm. They discovered that although algorithms do play a part in selective exposure, user action is more important in the formation of echo chambers. To counteract these impacts, Levy (2022) recommended increased algorithmic openness and the inclusion of a variety of viewpoints in content recommendations.

Engagement in Politics and Social Activism

Social networking sites (SNSs) have become effective instruments for political and social activism. They make it possible for people to rally, form groups, and promote a variety of causes. SNSs can support widespread social and political mobilization, as seen by movements like the Arab Spring, Black Lives Matter, and #MeToo (Howard & Hussain, 2011; Freelon, McIlwain, & Clark, 2018).

A meta-analysis on the connection between SNS use and political engagement was carried out by Boulianne (2020). According to the study, using social media is positively correlated with participating in politics in a variety of ways, such as voting, protesting, and having political conversations. This is especially true for young people, who are more likely to get their political information and engagement from SNSs than from any other source.

Marketing and Economic Consequences

Social networking sites have significant economic effects on business models, customer behaviour, and marketing tactics. SNSs give companies the means to connect and interact with customers using brand communities and customized advertising. Specifically, influencer marketing has emerged as a crucial tactic for companies looking to capitalize on the popularity and authority of social media influencers.

Chen, Fay, and Wang's (2021) study looked at influencer marketing's efficacy on social media networks. They discovered that consumers' intentions to make purchases are greatly influenced by influencers who have high engagement rates and genuine connections. According to the survey, trust and authenticity are essential components of influencer marketing success.

By improving customer relationship management and facilitating direct-to-consumer sales, SNSs have also revolutionized conventional company methods. The consumer path from discovery to purchase can be streamlined by firms selling products directly through social media platforms like Facebook and Instagram, which have integrated e-commerce functionalities.

New Developments and Prospects

There are still research opportunities and challenges due to the rapid advancement of SNSs. User interactions on social networking sites (SNSs) are changing as a result of emerging trends including the emergence of ephemeral material (like Instagram Stories), the incorporation of augmented reality (AR) and virtual reality (VR), and the growing significance of visual and video content.

With the advent of AR and VR technologies, SNSs are seeing an increase in user interaction and engagement with content. Virtual reality (VR) has the potential to improve social presence and engagement on social networking sites (SNSs). Van Esch and Black (2023) hypothesized that these technologies might completely transform online social interactions.

The use of machine learning and artificial intelligence (AI) to improve content moderation on social networking sites (SNSs) and improve user experiences is growing. The ethical ramifications of using AI for content curation, such as concerns about bias and transparency, were emphasized by Gillespie (2018). It is critical to address these ethical issues and make sure AI technologies are used appropriately as SNSs continue to develop

The breadth and diversity of the literature on social networking sites reflect the complexity and dynamic nature of these platforms. The psychological effects of SNS use, the function of SNSs in the development of social capital, issues with disinformation and privacy, algorithmic influence, political engagement, and economic ramifications are just a few of the major themes and findings from recent research that have been emphasized in this study.

Research must continue to fully comprehend the effects of SNSs on people and society as they develop. Subsequent research endeavours ought to tackle nascent patterns and technology, investigate the moral ramifications of social networking sites, and devise tactics to alleviate adverse consequences while augmenting affirmative input. We can better navigate the potential and difficulties posed by SNSs in the digital age by deepening our awareness of them.

3. RESEARCH METHODOLOGY

For this bibliometric investigation, a protracted procedure was followed. A focused search query was created, starting with the decision to use Scopus as the preferred database: TITLE-ABS-KEY ("Exploring" AND "Social Network Sites") AND PUBYEAR > 2006 AND PUBYEAR < 2025. The purpose of this query was to get pertinent research articles that examined different facets of social media platforms that were published between 2007 and 2024. To guarantee data accuracy and remove duplicates, extensive data cleaning was carried out after 188 relevant documents were retrieved. Then, using R Studio, a variety of analytical methods including trend analysis, descriptive statistics, and visualization revealed patterns in publishing, prolific writers, and institutional contributions.

To further enhance the investigation, VOSviewer made it easier to create bibliometric networks that exposed patterns of author collaboration, thematic clusters identified by keyword co-occurrence, and significant works identified by citation analysis. In the end, this methodological framework highlighted important themes, significant contributors, and developing avenues for further scholarly investigation, allowing for a comprehensive view of the state of research on social network sites today.

4. RESULTS AND DISCUSSION

Figure 1. Keywords occurrence 1111 keywords (Source Vos Viewer)

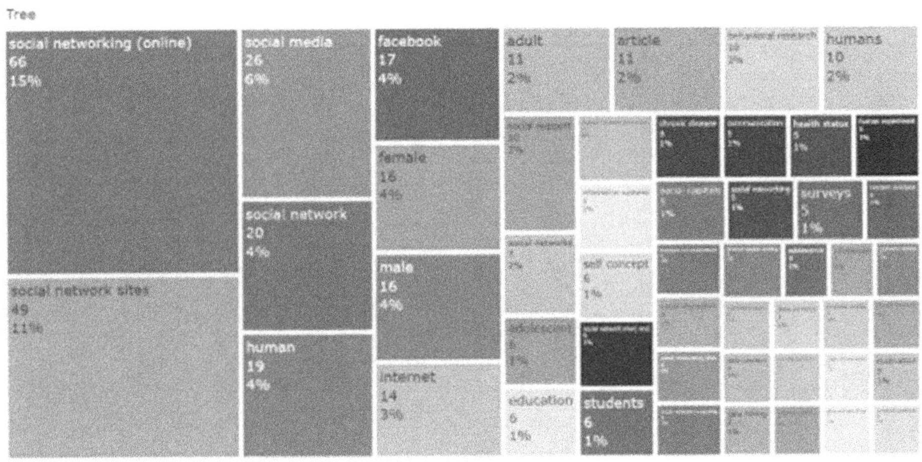

This graphic displays a network depiction of the co-occurrence of keywords from research papers about social media websites. The size of the nodes, which stand in for terms in the dataset, reveals how frequently the keywords occur. Bigger nodes like "internet," "behavioural research," "social network sites," "Facebook," and "human" imply that these are major themes in the literature. The correlations between terms' co-occurrences are shown by the edges joining the nodes. Typically, the colours of the nodes and edges in a dataset correspond to distinct groupings or themes. For instance, although one cluster would concentrate on the technological components of social networks, another might concentrate on their behavioural features. The multidisciplinary nature of research in this discipline is demonstrated by the dense clustering around key phrases, which implies a high degree of inter-related research topics.

Figure 2. Bibliographic coupling authors -168 (Vos Viewer)

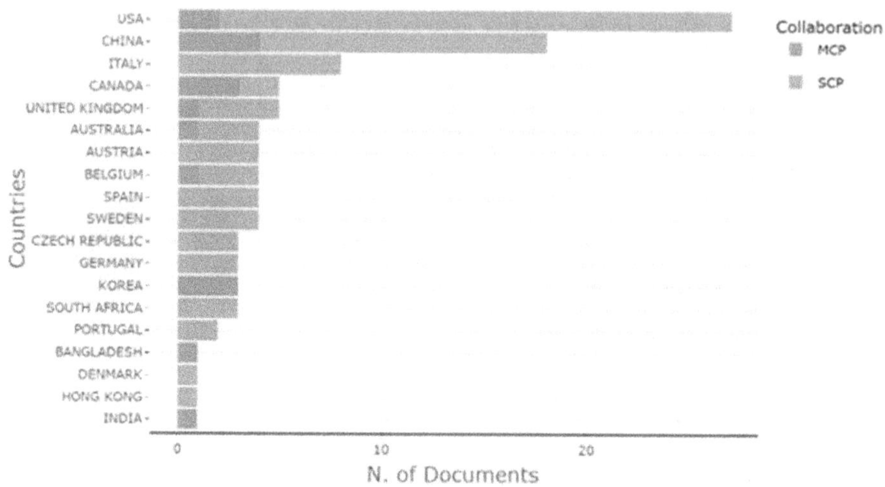

This image depicts a heatmap of author co-citations, showing the frequency with which authors are cited together. The nodes represent authors, and their size indicates the number of times they have been cited. Authors such as "Vitak J.," "Ellison N.B.," and "Nabi R.L." are prominently featured, indicating their significant contributions to the field. The heatmap colouration indicates the density of co-citation; brighter areas show higher co-citation frequencies. This visualization helps identify key influencers in the field and the relationships between various research works through their shared citations. It provides insight into the intellectual structure of the research area by highlighting prominent authors and their connections.

Figure 3. Bibliometric coupling documents 188 (Vos Viewer)

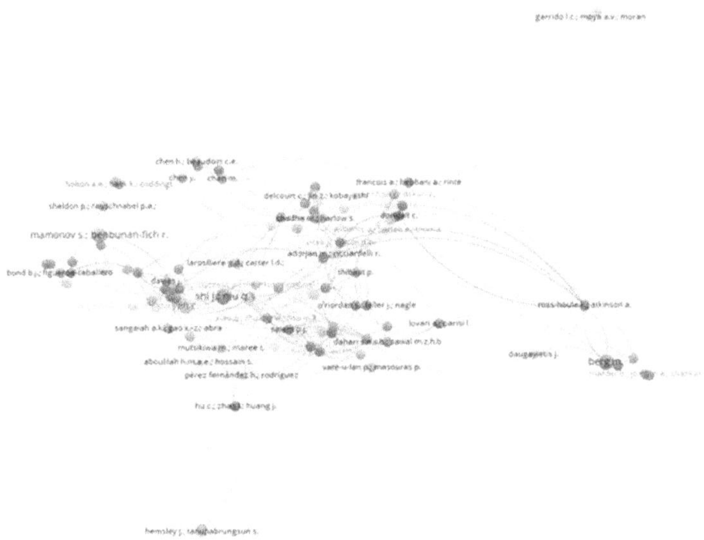

A network of bibliographic linkage between documents is seen in this figure. Individual research documents are represented as nodes, and the number of mutual references between them is shown as edges. Based on the amount of common references, the size of the nodes represents the significance or impact of the papers. Frequent coupling authors/documents: "Mamonov S.," "Benbunan-Fich R.," and "Garrido L.C." are examples of central nodes with a large number of connections. The colours indicate several groups or clusters of texts with comparable references, suggesting the same theme. This network illustrates how different studies are connected through their bibliographies and shows the relationships between research works based on their reference patterns.

Table 1. Main information

Description	**Results**
MAIN INFORMATION ABOUT DATA	
Timespan	2007:2024
Sources (Journals, Books, etc)	141
Documents	188
Annual Growth Rate %	8.5
Document Average Age	7.43

continued on following page

Table 1. Continued

Description	Results
Average citations per doc	26.05
References	8516
DOCUMENT CONTENTS	
Keywords Plus (ID)	746
Author's Keywords (DE)	531
AUTHORS	
Authors	429
Authors of single-authored docs	29
AUTHORS COLLABORATION	
Single-authored docs	31
Co-Authors per Doc	2.47
International co-authorships %	15.43
DOCUMENT TYPES	
article	111
book	1
book chapter	15
conference paper	42
conference review	13
erratum	1
note	1
review	4

(Source- R studio edited by Authors)

The collection, which includes 188 articles from 141 different publications and books, covers social network site research from 2007 until 2024. The scholarly influence of these works is demonstrated by the study field's 8.5% annual growth rate, average document age of 7.43 years, and an average of 26.05 citations per document. With 746 Keywords Plus (ID) and 531 Author's Keywords (DE), the research covers a wide range of keywords, and the dataset has a sizable number of references (8516). The authorship data indicates a collaborative research environment with 15.43% international co-authorship, with contributions from 429 people, 29 single-authored documents, and an average of 2.47 co-authors per document. There are 111 articles, 15 book chapters, 42 conference papers, 13 conference reviews, and a few more types of documents like books, errata, notes, and reviews among the many document categories.

Table 2. Most relevant sources

Sources	Articles
COMPUTERS IN HUMAN BEHAVIOR	8
18TH AMERICAS CONFERENCE ON INFORMATION SYSTEMS 2012, AMCIS 2012	6
LECTURE NOTES IN COMPUTER SCIENCE (INCLUDING SUBSERIES LECTURE NOTES IN ARTIFICIAL INTELLIGENCE AND LECTURE NOTES IN BIOINFORMATICS)	5
COMMUNICATIONS IN COMPUTER AND INFORMATION SCIENCE	4
NEW MEDIA AND SOCIETY	4
COMMUNICATION RESEARCH REPORTS	3
INTERNATIONAL JOURNAL OF INFORMATION MANAGEMENT	3
TELEMATICS AND INFORMATICS	3
ACM INTERNATIONAL CONFERENCE PROCEEDING SERIES	2
BEHAVIOUR AND INFORMATION TECHNOLOGY	2

(Source- R studio edited by Authors)

The dataset presents a wide range of papers from the most pertinent sources that have contributed to the study of social network sites. Computers in Human Behavior, which emphasizes the study of human interactions with technology, tops the list with eight articles. Six essays from the 18th Americas Conference on Information Systems (AMCIS 2012) are included, demonstrating the information systems community's major contributions. Five new articles have been added to the Lecture Notes in Computer Science series, which includes subseries on bioinformatics and artificial intelligence and reflects an interdisciplinary approach to computer science. Four articles are contributed by each of Communications in Computer and Information Science and New Media and Society, with the former concentrating on advances in computer science and the latter on the effects of new media on society. The International Journal of Information Management and Telematics and Informatics each contribute three articles emphasizing their focus on information management and communication technologies, while Communication Research Reports provides three articles outlining succinct findings in communication studies. Furthermore, two publications each from Behavior and Information Technology and the ACM International Conference Proceeding Series highlight the behavioral and technical elements of social networks.

Table 3. Most relevant authors

Authors	Articles	Articles Fractionalized
HANUSCH F	3	1.50
KLIMOVA B	3	2.00

continued on following page

Table 3. Continued

Authors	Articles	Articles Fractionalized
LEE R	3	1.17
WU Y	3	1.00
BENBUNAN-FICH R	2	1.00
BERG M	2	2.00
BRENGMAN M	2	0.67
CHEN H	2	1.00
ELLISON NB	2	0.70
GARRIDO LC	2	0.67

(Source- R studio edited by Authors)

The dataset finds the authors who have written the most articles about social network sites and have made the greatest fractional contributions. With a fractionalized contribution of 1.50 across three publications, Hanusch F. demonstrated noteworthy but collaborative authorship. In addition, Klimova B. made significant contributions to three papers, as evidenced by her higher fractionalized total of 2.00. With three articles to his credit and a fractionalized total of 1.17, Lee R. may have contributed less overall. Wu Y. received a total score of 1.00 for her three equal contributions. With equal fractionalized contributions of 1.00 for each of their two publications, Benbunan-Fich R. and Chen H. demonstrated balanced authorship. With a full fractionalized contribution of 2.00 for 2 papers, Berg M. stands out as the major or lone author. The fractionalized totals of 0.67 for Brengman M. and Garrido LC., who each contributed to two articles, indicate minimal or shared authorship. A fractionalized total of 0.70 indicates that Ellison NB. contributed to two publications as well, indicating lower individual contributions. This research focuses on the breadth of authors' contributions to the area as well as their prolific output.

Figure 4. Corresponding author's countries (R Studio)

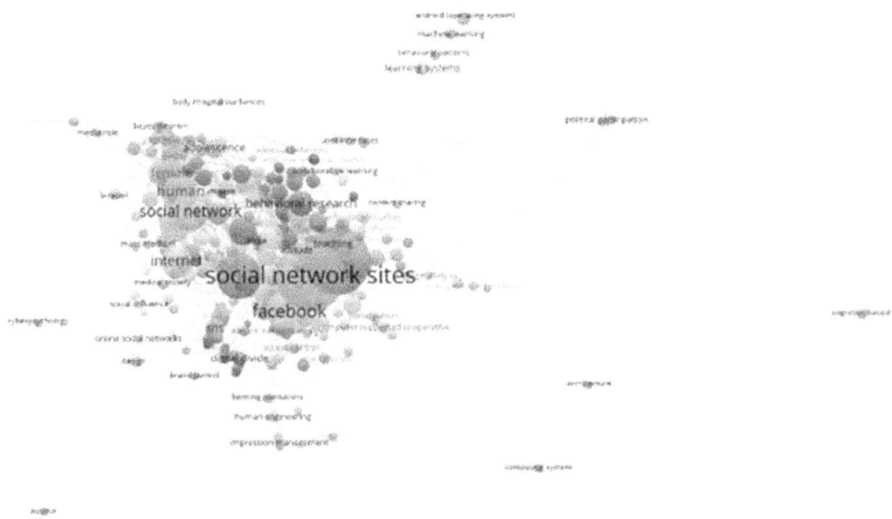

Figure 5. Countries and no of citations (Scopus Analyze)

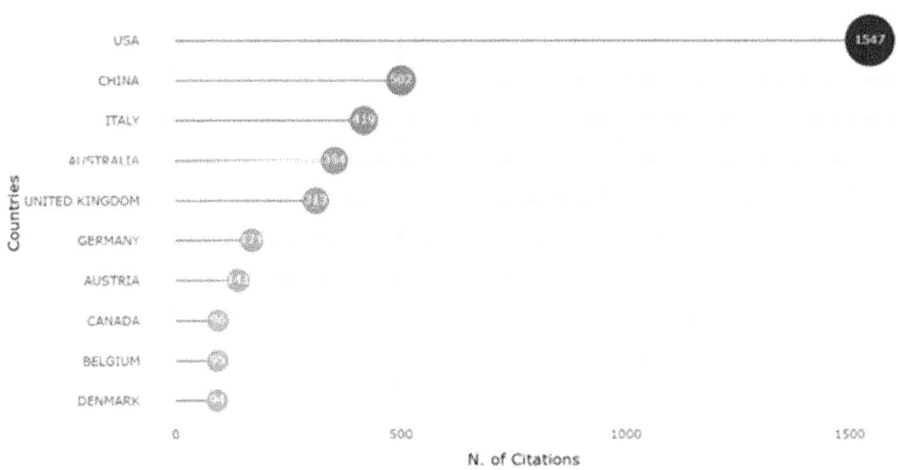

Table 4. Total and average article citation

Country	TC	Average Article Citations
USA	1547	57.30
CHINA	502	27.90
ITALY	419	52.40
AUSTRALIA	354	88.50
UNITED KINGDOM	313	62.60
GERMANY	171	57.00
AUSTRIA	141	35.20
CANADA	96	19.20
BELGIUM	95	23.80
DENMARK	94	94.00

(Source- R studio edited by Authors)

The dataset, which is based on average article citations and total citations (TC), identifies the most significant nations in social network site research. With 1547 total citations and an average of 57.30 citations per piece, the USA dominates the field and is the dominant force. China comes in second with 502 total citations, averaging 27.90 citations per piece, indicating a significant but relatively lesser impact. With a high average of 52.40 citations per article, Italy has 419 total citations, indicating noteworthy contributions. Australia has the highest average number of citations per article (88.50), indicating very influential research, with 354 total citations. With 313 and 171 total citations, respectively, and averages of 62.60 and 57.00 citations per piece, the UK and Germany both demonstrate a significant amount of influence. Denmark stands out for having a high average of 94.00 citations per article, indicating exceptionally influential contributions despite the lower overall citation count. Austria, Canada, Belgium, and Denmark have varying average citation counts but less total citation counts (141, 96, 95, and 94, respectively). This analysis shows how influential research in the field is distributed globally, with both Western and Asian nations making major contributions.

Figure 6. Word cloud

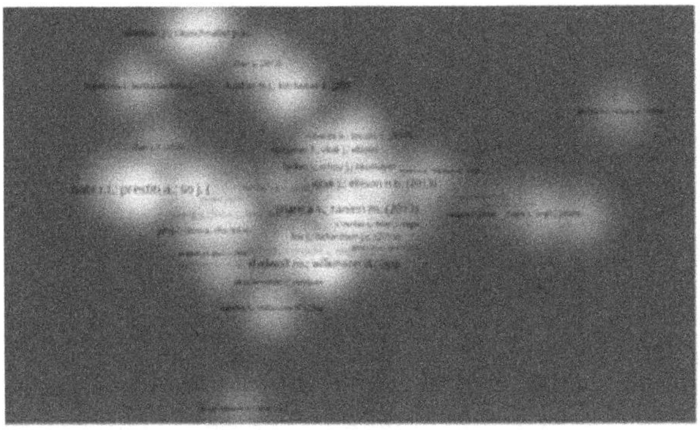

Table 5. Word occurrence and years

Year	SOCIAL NETWORKING (ONLINE)	SOCIAL NETWORK SITES	SOCIAL MEDIA	SOCIAL NETWORK	HUMAN	FACEBOOK	FEMALE	MALE	INTERNET	ADULT
2017	46	35	18	9	10	13	8	8	13	5
2018	51	38	19	9	10	15	8	8	13	5
2019	56	42	23	10	12	16	10	10	13	7
2020	60	44	23	10	12	17	10	10	13	7
2021	60	44	25	12	13	17	11	11	13	8
2022	65	48	26	19	18	17	15	15	14	11
2023	66	49	26	20	19	17	16	16	14	11

(Source- R studio edited by Authors)

The dataset shows developments in the focus of scholarly literature by tracking the frequency of key phrases associated with social network site studies from 2017 to 2023. There is a constant growth in the term "Social Networking (Online)" from 46 mentions in 2017 to 66 in 2023, suggesting that the idea of online social interactions is becoming more and more popular. A consistent increase in "Social Network Sites" is also observed, rising from 35 mentions in 2017 to 49 in 2023, indicating a continued interest in certain platforms. Mentions of "Social Media" rose from 18 to 26, indicating the growing significance of this topic in the study. The number of mentions of the term "Social Network" increased moderately, from 9 in 2017 to 20 in 2023. Terms that are particular to gender, such as "Female" and "Male," both show an increase: from 8 to 16, "Female" increased, and from 8 to 16, "Male" increased. Over time, "Internet" references stay consistent at 13–14, but

"Adult" mentions slightly rise from 5 to 11. These patterns point to a widening field of study, with a persistent focus on large social media platforms and their effects on people as well as a growing emphasis on gender-specific studies.

5. CONCLUSION

To sum up, this bibliometric analysis offers a thorough summary of the state of the research on social network sites (SNS) from 2007 to 2024. After reviewing 188 research articles from several disciplines, we were able to pinpoint important study issues, prominent writers, and important trends. The results show that SNS is becoming more and more popular among academics, with notable contributions from disciplines including business management, social science, and computer science. Trends to watch out for are the psychological effects of social media use, concerns about data security and privacy, the dissemination of false information, and the use of social media for political and commercial purposes. Even with the large amount of research, there are still gaps and new areas that need to be looked at, such as how advanced technology like AI and AR/VR affect social interactions.

This study emphasizes the necessity for ongoing interdisciplinary efforts to properly comprehend the complex effects of social network sites on society. It also illustrates the evolution and current condition of SNS research and offers strategic recommendations for future research areas.

6. IMPLICATIONS

This thorough bibliometric examination of Social Network Site (SNS) research has important ramifications for academics, corporations, and policymakers. This study aims to identify important discoveries that will influence the future direction of research in this topic by methodically mapping the scholarly landscape.

6.1 Recognizing New Themes and Trends:

The analysis shows how the field of SNS research has dynamically evolved, bringing to light new subjects like the psychological impacts of social media use, the influence of algorithms on user behavior, and the moral implications of data privacy. These patterns point to a move toward more interdisciplinary methods that combine knowledge from communication studies, psychology, sociology, and computer science. To improve our comprehension of the intricate relationships that exist within social networking spaces, future studies should carry out more investigation into these developing themes.

6.2 Taking Care of Research Opportunities and Knowledge Gaps:

In several domains, the research reveals continuing gaps in knowledge despite the expanding volume of literature. For example, although a great deal of study has been done on the psychological consequences of social networking sites, more in-depth studies are required to comprehend the varying effects in different demographic groups and cultural contexts. Furthermore, studies examining the long-term effects of SNS use on cultural norms, political participation, and economic habits are noticeably lacking. Closing these gaps offers important avenues for future research efforts.

6.3 Increasing Methodological Innovation and Rigor:

The significance of methodological rigor in mapping and assessing the scholarly environment of SNS research is highlighted by the application of sophisticated bibliometric tools and techniques, such as VOSviewer and R Studio. Researchers are urged to use cutting-edge strategies going forward, such as mixed-methods designs and longitudinal studies, in order to fully capture the complex character of the social networking phenomena. These methodologies not only augment the validity and reliability of results but also cultivate a more all-encompassing comprehension of the dynamic interplay among users, platforms, and societal surroundings.

6.4 Encouraging Ethical Deliberations and Their Policy Consequences:

The investigation draws attention to important ethical issues with regard to algorithmic bias, data privacy, and the spread of false information in SNS environments. These results highlight the necessity of strong legislative frameworks that protect user rights while encouraging digital literacy and social responsibility.

Together with researchers, policymakers and platform developers should put into practice evidence-based regulations that reduce possible risks and maximize the benefits of social networking sites for society.

6.5 Encouraging International Collaboration and Knowledge Exchange:

The analysis's findings about the research contributions' global distribution highlight how crucial it is to encourage international cooperation between scholars, organizations, and decision-makers. Through the exchange of best practices and insights among various cultural and geographical contexts, international collaboration helps hasten the diffusion of knowledge and innovation in SNS research. Furthermore, cooperative efforts can aid in the creation of contextually appropriate answers to worldwide problems related to social networking platforms.

6.6 Encouraging Public Awareness Campaigns and Educational Initiatives:

The widespread impact of social media on daily life underscores the importance of educational programs that foster critical thinking and digital literacy. The results of this bibliometric research can help shape educational initiatives that give users the information and abilities they need to responsibly and safely navigate digital settings. Additionally, educating the public about the possible advantages and disadvantages of SNS will help users make more informed decisions, which will encourage better online habits and lessen detrimental effects on society.

This study's bibliometric analysis of research on social network sites offers important new perspectives on the changing scholarly conversation and its consequences for further study, practice, and policy. Stakeholders can work together to advance knowledge and promote positive outcomes in the quickly changing field of social science by recognizing emerging trends, filling in knowledge gaps, strengthening methodological rigor, encouraging ethical considerations, facilitating international collaboration, and supporting educational initiatives.

7. LIMITATIONS

First off, depending just on Scopus as a database could lead to bias towards English-language publications and those included in Scopus's index, thereby omitting pertinent studies that have been published in other languages or databases. This could result in a portrayal of global SNS research that is insufficient.

Second, the search term that concentrates on “Exploring” and “Social Network Sites” can ignore research that employ different language or concentrate on particular SNS features that these terms do not cover. This constraint may limit the analysis's scope and obscure new trends or specialized subjects.

Thirdly, the bibliometric approach may ignore qualitative components of the research, such as theoretical breakthroughs or methodological innovations, because it mainly depends on quantitative indicators like citation counts and keyword co-occurrence. This quantitative bias may cause important studies with low citation counts to be undervalued.

Fourthly, even if the study features important writers and works, the collaborative dynamics and multidisciplinary character of modern SNS research might not be adequately captured. Contributions from interdisciplinary fields and co-authorship patterns may offer deeper insights into the development of ideas within the discipline.

Finally, because the study only included studies that were published between 2007 and 2024, it's possible that certain recent advances in SNS research—especially those that came about after 2024—were not sufficiently covered. The findings' applicability to both present and future research areas may be impacted by this time restriction.

Conclusively, "Unveiling the Web" offers an extensive synopsis of SNS research via bibliometric analysis; yet these constraints indicate directions for additional improvement and enlargement in subsequent investigations to attain a fuller comprehension of the domain.

REFERENCES

Abbas, A. F., Jusoh, A., Mas'od, A., Alsharif, A. H., & Ali, J. (2022). Bibliometrix analysis of information sharing in social media. *Cogent Business and Management*, 9(1), 2016556. Advance online publication. DOI: 10.1080/23311975.2021.2016556

Bakshy, E., Messing, S., & Adamic, L. A. (2015). Exposure to ideologically diverse news and opinion on Facebook. *Science*, 348(6239), 1130–1132. DOI: 10.1126/science.aaa1160 PMID: 25953820

Boulianne, S. (2020). Social media use and participation: A meta-analysis of current research. *Information Communication and Society*, 23(2), 248–266.

Boyd, D. M., & Ellison, N. B. (2007). Social network sites: Definition, history, and scholarship. *Journal of Computer-Mediated Communication*, 13(1), 210–230. DOI: 10.1111/j.1083-6101.2007.00393.x

Brooks, S., & Hogan, B. (2021). Professional networking on LinkedIn: The role of social capital. *Journal of Social Media in Society*, 10(1), 45–63.

Cadwalladr, C., & Graham-Harrison, E. (2018). The Cambridge Analytica files. The Guardian. Retrieved from https://www.theguardian.com/news/series/cambridge-analytica-files

Cao, Y., & Smith, P. (2021). LinkedIn as a platform for professional networking and career development. *Journal of Career Development*, 48(2), 150–165.

Chen, J., Fay, S., & Wang, Q. (2021). The impact of influencer marketing on consumer behavior. *JMR, Journal of Marketing Research*, 58(1), 90–110.

Ellison, N. B., Steinfield, C., & Lampe, C. (2007). The benefits of Facebook "friends": Social capital and college students' use of online social network sites. *Journal of Computer-Mediated Communication*, 12(4), 1143–1168. DOI: 10.1111/j.1083-6101.2007.00367.x

Ellison, N. B., Vitak, J., Gray, R., & Lampe, C. (2022). Cultivating social resources on social network sites: Facebook relationship maintenance behaviors and their implications for social capital. *New Media & Society*, 24(1), 15–37.

Freelon, D., McIlwain, C. D., & Clark, M. D. (2018). Beyond the hashtags: #Ferguson, #Blacklivesmatter, and the online struggle for offline justice. *New Media & Society*, 20(4), 1025–1045.

Gillespie, T. (2018). *Custodians of the Internet: Platforms, content moderation, and the hidden decisions that shape social media*. Yale University Press.

Grover, P., Kar, A. K., & Dwivedi, Y. (2022). The evolution of social media influence - A literature review and research agenda. *International Journal of Information Management Data Insights*, 2(2), 100116. DOI: 10.1016/j.jjimei.2022.100116

Hartman, R., & Simova, T. (2021). How changing API terms changed Instagram's domain? A bibliometric analysis. *7th International Conference on Computer Technology Applications, ICCTA 2021*, 73–79. https://doi.org/DOI: 10.1145/3477911.3477923

Howard, P. N., & Hussain, M. M. (2011). The role of digital media. *Journal of Democracy*, 22(3), 35–48. DOI: 10.1353/jod.2011.0041

Huang, C. (2022). Time spent on social network sites and psychological well-being: A meta-analysis. *Cyberpsychology, Behavior, and Social Networking*, 25(1), 13–19. PMID: 28622031

Javid, E. T., Nazari, M., & Ghaeli, M. R. (2019). Social media and e-commerce: A scientometrics analysis. *International Journal of Data and Network Science*, 3(3), 269–290. DOI: 10.5267/j.ijdns.2019.2.001

Kaplan, A. M., & Haenlein, M. (2010). Users of the world, unite! The challenges and opportunities of Social Media. *Business Horizons*, 53(1), 59–68. DOI: 10.1016/j.bushor.2009.09.003

Kross, E., Verduyn, P., Demiralp, E., Park, J., Lee, D. S., Lin, N., & Ybarra, O. (2022). Social media and well-being: Pitfalls, progress, and next steps. *Trends in Cognitive Sciences*, 26(4), 293–306. PMID: 33187873

Levy, R. (2022). Algorithmic content curation in online platforms: An examination of echo chambers and filter bubbles. *Digital Journalism (Abingdon, England)*, 8(2), 193–211.

Lohtia, R., Donthu, N., & Guillory, M. D. (2013). The impact of advertising, trustworthiness, and valence on the effectiveness of blogs. *International Journal of Electronic Marketing and Retailing*, 5(4), 317–339. DOI: 10.1504/IJEMR.2013.060264

Pennycook, G., & Rand, D. G. (2021). The Implied Truth Effect: Attaching warnings to a subset of fake news stories increases perceived accuracy of stories without warnings. *Management Science*, 67(1), 508–527.

Sağkaya Güngör, A., & Ozansoy Çadırcı, T. (2022). Understanding digital consumer: A review, synthesis, and future research agenda. *International Journal of Consumer Studies*, 46(5), 1829–1858. DOI: 10.1111/ijcs.12809

Shin, D. H., & Biocca, F. (2020). The role of privacy concerns in shaping users' social media behavior. *Computers in Human Behavior*, 102, 139–147.

Statista. (2023). Leading social networks worldwide as of January 2023, ranked by number of monthly active users. Retrieved from https://www.statista.com/statistics/272014/global-social-networks-ranked-by-number-of-users/

Studies, A., Relations, P., Andreea, M., Studies, A., & Relations, P. (2012). Social media and marketing of the "Popcorn" music wave: The success of Romanian commercial musicians analysed through their perceived image on. 5(2), 125-139.

Valkenburg, P. M., Beyens, I., Pouwels, J. L., van Driel, I. I., & Keijsers, L. (2022). Social media use and adolescents' well-being: Developing a typology of person-specific effects. *Child Development*, 93(5), e322–e338.

Van Esch, P., & Black, J. S. (2023). Virtual reality and social presence: The potential of VR to enhance social media engagement. *JMR, Journal of Marketing Research*, 60(1), 45–58.

Verduyn, P., Ybarra, O., Résibois, M., Jonides, J., & Kross, E. (2020). Do social network sites enhance or undermine subjective well-being? A critical review. *Social Issues and Policy Review*, 14(1), 274–302. DOI: 10.1111/sipr.12033

Vosoughi, S., Roy, D., & Aral, S. (2018). The spread of true and false news online. *Science*, 359(6380), 1146–1151. DOI: 10.1126/science.aap9559 PMID: 29590045

Zarei, E., & Jabbarzadeh, A. (2019). Knowledge management and social media: A scientometrics survey. International Journal of Data and Network Science, 3(4), 359-378. https://doi.org/Top of FormDOI: 10.5267/j.ijdns.2019.2.008

KEY TERMS AND DEFINITIONS

Social Networking Sites (SNS): Social networking sites are online platforms that enable users to create public or semi-public profiles, interact with other users, and share content such as text, images, and videos. Examples include Facebook, LinkedIn, and Twitter. SNS often serve as a medium for building social connections, engaging in community discussions, and forming online communities based on shared interests or goals.

Social Media: Social media refers to the collective online communication channels dedicated to community-based input, interaction, content-sharing, and collaboration. Social media platforms facilitate the creation and sharing of information, ideas, career interests, and other forms of expression through virtual communities and networks. Examples include Instagram, YouTube, and Snapchat.

Social Networks: Social networks are structures of interconnected individuals or organizations that facilitate the exchange of information, ideas, and resources. These networks can exist online, such as on social media platforms, or offline, in the form of personal or professional relationships. Social networks are often analyzed to understand the dynamics of influence, communication, and behavior within groups.

Social Activism: Social activism is the practice of advocating for, promoting, or striving to enact social, political, or environmental change through various forms of protest, advocacy, and public engagement. Social activism can involve organizing campaigns, raising awareness, lobbying for policy changes, and using both online and offline platforms to mobilize people and influence public opinion.

Bibliometric: Bibliometric is a quantitative analysis method used to measure the impact, dissemination, and productivity of scholarly literature. It involves the use of statistical tools to analyze patterns in citations, authorship, publication sources, and research trends. Bibliometric analysis is often employed to evaluate the influence of research articles, journals, institutions, and researchers within a particular field or discipline.

Chapter 6
The Impact of Instagram on Consumer Behavior of Football Supporters: The Case of Sport Lisboa e Benfica

Alexandre Duarte
https://orcid.org/0000-0002-2665-864X
FCSH, Universidade Nova de Lisboa, Portugal

Marta Araújo
FCH, Universidade Católica Portuguesa, Portugal

ABSTRACT

Brands need to be where their consumers are. Social networks, by providing the possibility of interaction in real time, have become excellent communication and relationship tools between organizations and their stakeholders. Football clubs, highly complex sports and social organizations cannot stay out of this new reality. This chapter aims to understand the impact that the relationship quality and the communication and engagement on Instagram have on the consumption behaviors of supporters of the football club Sport Lisboa e Benfica (SLB). To this end, a mixed data collection method was applied, with exploratory interviews to some directors of the club, analysis of the club's Instagram publications, and a questionnaire survey to supporters (n= 361). The results confirm that there is a significant relationship quality between the supporters and the club, and that the communication and engagement on Instagram stimulates the consumption of the club's products and services, which generates significant financial returns.

DOI: 10.4018/979-8-3693-3868-1.ch006

INTRODUCTION

Over the last few years, the relationship between social networks and football has gained considerable prominence (Nisar, Prabhakar, & Patil, 2018; Kharmalki & Raizada, 2020; Koronios, Travlos, Douvis & Papadopoulos, 2020; Kim, Qian, Lee, Mastromartino & Zhang, 2020; Fenton, Keegann & Parry, 2021). On one hand, social networks are virtual platforms that connects millions of people, regardless of the country they are in (Fenton, Keegann & Parry, 2021). Instagram, the focus of this investigation, prioritizes communication between users through the sharing of photographs and videos (Abeza, O'Reilly, Sanderson & Frederick, 2021). This platform also encourages supporters to become more and more involved with football clubs (Kuzma, Bell & Logue, 2014), and it is the one they most value for their interaction (Kharmalki & Raizada, 2020; Mahmoudian, Boroujerdi, Siyani & Mahmoud, 2021). On the other hand, football clubs recognize the increasing importance and impact of new media and social networks, in the detriment of the so-called traditional media, to obtain high levels of engagement with supporters, whose feeling of passion for clubs goes beyond logic and reason (Giulianotti, 2002), creating a strong relationship of commitment and loyalty to them (Kim & Trail, 2011). Moreover, the impact of Instagram on sport club fans' engagement and consumer behavior is related to Web 3.0 in the following ways:

a) As Instagram is a image-centric platform, its influence on consumer behavior lies in the power of visual content. People are often drawn to aesthetically pleasing images and videos, impacting their purchasing decisions. With the growing emphasis on immersive and interactive experiences in web 3.0, the use of integrated visual content in innovative ways such as VR or AR (among others) can therefore enhance consumer engagement.
b) Also, in the last years, Instagram has been a major platform for influencer marketing, where individuals and/or organizations with a significant number of followers promote products or services. This can shape consumer's opinions and decisions, as we can see in this study.
c) Finally, Instagram fosters community building through features like hashtags, comments, shares and direct messages. Building a brand community can influence brand perception and consumer loyalty (Duarte, 2023). Once Web 3.0 emphasizes decentralized and community-driven platforms, organizations (like football clubs in this case) can explore decentralized social networks or community-driven initiatives where users have more active participation and ownership to foster the relation and engagement with their fans.

1. THEORETICAL FRAMEWORK

1.1. A Phenomenon Called Football

The origin of this sport is not universally recognized, but it is commonly accepted that modern football, as well as its first regulatory institution - the International Football Association Board (IFAB) whose 1863 rules are the basis of the sport today, have emerged in England, around the 1980s (Godói & Cardoso, 1989; Sousa & Vieira, 2018). Considered the "sports king" (Sousa & Vieira, 2018; Quintela, 2020) and the most popular sport ever (Cruz, Schregel & Zülch, 2021; Nielsen Sports, 2018), football is responsible for generating millions of dollars every year (Quintela, 2020), and exerts a direct influence on various sectors such as social, cultural, economic, educational and tourism (Sousa & Vieira, 2018). Much more than a simple game played between the four lines (Giulianotti & Robertson, 2012; Penn, 2016), football is an official global spectacle that unites (or divides) people from all over the world (Gantz, 2013), regardless of color, race, or religion (Sousa & Vieira, 2018).

Its rapid evolution spurred the creation of distinct regulatory institutions at an international level, such as the Féderation Internacionale de Football Association (FIFA) in 1904 (Sousa & Vieira, 2018), and the Union of European Football Associations (UEFA), in 1954 (UEFA, 2022). At a national level, the Portuguese Football Federation (FPF) emerged in 1914 and, in 1978, the Professional Football Portuguese League (LPFP) was founded (Federação Portuguesa de Futebol, 2021). In the mid-1990s, the concept of "brand"[1] began to be associated with the sports industry. Football clubs are no longer recognized as "non-profit" organizations and are now recognized as "for-profit" organizations (Sousa & Vieira, 2018), offering a set of services to their supporters, who in this way become customers and consume the products that are offered to them (McLean & Wainwright, 2009; Tapp, 2004; Lucena & Casaca, 2013). Recently, the emergence of the COVID-19 pandemic has imposed serious challenges on this activity, such as playing games behind closed doors, declining revenues, uncertainty in the relationships between current and potential partners in the transmission and commercialization of television rights, among others (Deloitte, 2021). Consequently, communication on social networks has allowed clubs the opportunity not only to consolidate their brand power, but also to enhance their relationship with supporters, and stimulate their consumption behaviors.

1.2. Supporters: Characteristics and Relationship with Football Clubs

"The supporters are the main fuel to keep the clubs alive" (Sousa & Vieira, 2018:297) and, depending on victories or defeats, they can positively or negatively influence the environment experienced inside and outside the stadiums (Abosag, Roper & Hind, 2010). The big difference between a football supporter and a consumer of other products categories is that the former remains loyal, even when their expectations are unrequited (Kuzma, Bell & Logue, 2014; Balliauw, Onghena & Mulkens, 2020; Aichner, 2019). Commonly associated with tribalism (Diário de Notícias, March 20, 2017) and even with religion, supporters engage with football clubs through their commitment, passion, attachment, and loyalty (McCarthy, Rowley, Ashworth & Pioch, 2014; Dionísio, Leal & Moutinho, 2008; Hunt, Bristol & Bashaw, 1999). In addition to the direct relationship between the sporting event, the state of mind and sense of humor (Kim, James & Kim, 2013), supporters invest their financial, emotional, and temporal resources (Vale & Fernandes, 2018; Balliauw, Onghena & Mulkens, 2020), act as true brand ambassadors and, consequently, help to strengthen and expand them (Salmi, Benar & Honari, 2019). Their dedication translates into a relationship with football clubs, which can be enhanced through its quality.

By relationship quality we understand the strength of a given relationship (Kim & Trail, 2011) and, in the sports field, this allows the understanding of the relationship between sports organizations and supporters in order to develop more comprehensive relationships, to obtain information about relational assessments, and diagnose and/or resolve any problems that may arise more easily (Lee, Kunkel, Funk, Karg & McDonald, 2020). According to Kim and Trail (2011), it is necessary to observe five constructs in order to consider that there is a significant relationship quality between football clubs and supporters: 1. Trust, which means the conviction that the needs of a person are fulfilled by others, and where there is a willingness to trust in those who they believe; 2. Commitment, which symbolizes the belief that the relationship is important, and that efforts by the parties to maintain it are accepted; 3. Self-connection, which reflects the degree of concern that brands have with defining people's identity; 4. Intimacy, which represents familiarity and proximity between people; 5. Reciprocity, which means the existence of a balance in relationships that have feelings of indebtedness and obligations, and that exchange favors with each other.

1.3. Communication and Football

The relationship between communication and sports began to be highlighted in the 1990s (Pedersen, 2017; Kharmalki & Raizada, 2020), essentially due to the increase in academic studies, the mass dissemination of events such as the UEFA Champions League, the multimillion contracts with the media, the creation of sports-related industries such as online betting or fantasy games, among others (Abeza, 2021; Mastromartino, Ross, Wear & Naraine, 2020; Butterworth, 2021; Kim et al., 2020; Frandsen, 2016). Communication, indispensable in any organization, is increasingly related to several other areas, such as finance, with millionaire television rights contracts, technology, with streaming services or artificial intelligence, promotional, with for instance the use of hashtags, the personal one, with the mediatization of interactions with consumers, or the organizational one, with information obtained through big data (Pedersen, Laucella, Kian & Geurin, 2020). Consequently, the demand for the amount and qualification of communication professionals in sports increases progressively. This fact is evidenced by the number of training courses specialized in the area (Pedersen et al., 2020), by empowering sports organizations that create their own departments of communication, marketing, public relations, etc. (Herencia, 2021; Mahan, 2011; Koronios et al., 2020), and for the media prominence of professions such as Communication Directors (Quintela, 2020). As a result, football clubs are becoming true media organizations, offering exclusive content, creating advertising content with them, selling them to sponsors and being financed directly by the public, with subscription fees (Borges, 2019).

1.4. New Media, Social Networks, and Engagement in Football

The emergence of the internet allowed an increase in the independence of communication systems, and the appearance of a bottow-up culture. As a result of this evolution, social media emerged, which translates into internet applications, whose main characteristic are the creation and exchange of content between users. Easy accessibility, through personal devices such as smartphones, for example, contributed to their worldwide proliferation without once decisive restrictions such as location or time (Mastromartino et al., 2020; Balliauw, Onghena & Mulkens, 2020; Popp, Germelmann & Jung, 2016). In the context of social media, social networks arised, which are electronic platforms that allows consumers to disseminate and share their thoughts and experiences about any type of subject through written, visual, or audiovisual forms (Hussain, Naz, Shahzad & Bajwa, 2021; Ozora & Susanto, 2021; Boyd & Ellison, 2007). In addition, they have several benefits for organizations, such as: reduction of marketing costs by acquiring detailed information; building customer loyalty and commitment; obtaining immediate feedback on services or products; strengthening the brand image and opportunity to act proactively (Mabić, Lasić & Zovko, 2019; Balliauw, Onghena & Mulkens, 2020).

Instagram is a social network founded on October 6th, 2010, by Kevin Systrom and Mike Krieger. This platform allows the sharing of photographs and videos, accompanied by descriptions with unlimited characters (Aragão, Farias, Mota & Freitas, 2016; Kharmalki & Raizada, 2020; Ozora & Susanto, 2021), and it is increasingly used by global brands to achieve brand recognition and image goals (Anagnostopoulos, Parganas, Chadwick & Fenton, 2018). Instagram is currently the third most used social network in the world (Hussain et al., 2021) — excluding exclusive conversation platforms such as Whatsapp and Facebook Messenger — and has more than 830 million users (Hootsuite, 2021).

Supporters use this social network to follow their clubs, which in turn is responsible for most of the engagement between this parties (1.5 billion engagement), compared to other social networks such as Facebook (140 million) or Twitter (41 million) (Nielsen Sports, 2018). Overall, supporters engage with brands four times more on Instagram than on Facebook (Price, 2017) because they prefer visual and instant interactions to written information (Kharmalki & Raizada, 2020; Hussain et al., 2021; Teo, Leng & Phua, 2019; Clavio, 2013).

Engagement contributes to the success of football clubs' strategies, as they can develop solutions that meet the demands and expectations created by the supporters (Aichner, 2019; Alonso-Dos-Santos, Rejón Guardia, Pérez Campos, Calabuig-Moreno, & Ko, 2018; Stander, Llewellyn & Kemiso, 2016; van Doorn, Lemon, Mittal, Nass, Pick, Pirner & Verhoef, 2010). In addition, it allows to determine the level of interaction, intimacy, influence, and involvement that consumers have with organizations (Nisar, Prabhakar, & Patil, 2018; Obradović, Alčaković, Vyugina & Tasevski, 2019; McCarthy et al., 2014). Thus, when supporters' consumption motives and the degree of satisfaction that clubs provide them are congruent, engagement levels are significant and rewarding, as loyalty between parties increases significantly (Alonso-Dos-Santos et al., 2018).

1.5. Relationship Quality, Communication, Engagement on Instagram and Consumption Behaviors

Relationship quality has a strong influence on the performance of consumption behaviors, with a direct correlation between the emotional and relational connection of supporters with a football brand and their willingness to demonstrate behaviors that value it (Kim & Trail, 2011). The five relational constructs mentioned above — trust, commitment, self-connection, intimacy, and reciprocity — become dimensions of consumption triggered by yearning, preferences, and decision-making power (Albert, Merunka & Valette-Florence, 2009).

The result of the relationship quality between supporters and football clubs translates into consumption behaviors such as word of mouth, media consumption, purchase of merchandising and presence in club activities (Kim & Trail, 2011), as can be seen in the following Figure 1:

Figure 1. Conceptual structure proposed for the effects of the relationship quality between sports organizations and supporters (Kim e Trail, 2011)

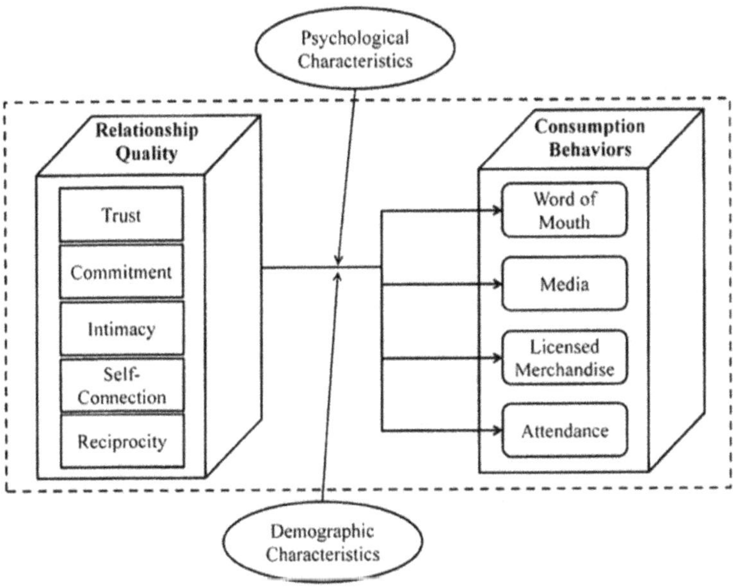

In its turn, Instagram allows supporters to benefit from a more active role in their relationship with the clubs, as they have the opportunity to express their love, belonging and, in some cases, criticize the behavior of their constituents both within and off the field (Anagnostopoulos et al., 2018; Mastromartino et al., 2020). For clubs, Instagram allows, through communication, the ability to engage and persuade current and potential supporters, while building a relationship of trust in real time (Nisar, Prabhakar, & Patil, 2018). Thus, the greater the involvement of supporters on Instagram, the greater is the demonstration of their loyalty and attachment to the clubs that they choose to "follow" on this platform (Mahmoudian et al., 2021).

The relationship quality between supporters and clubs, combined with the communication and engagement generated on social networks, can lead to win-win results: supporters can express their needs, and clubs have the opportunity to understand

and satisfy them (Williams & Chinn, 2010; Stavros, Meng, Westberg & Farrelly, 2014). Consequently, supporters are satisfied, more committed, and develop more consumption behaviors of the clubs' products/services (Kim & Trail, 2011). On the other hand, clubs can achieve significant financial profits, in the most varied areas of activity (Yoshida, Gordon, Nakazawa, Shibuya, & Fujiwara 2018; Maderer & Parganas, 2018; Thompson, Martin, Gee & Geurin, 2018).

2. METHODOLOGY

2.1 Research Hypothesis

Based on the literature review and on the object of study, the following research hypotheses were formulated:

H1 — SLB has a defined communication strategy for the development of engagement on Instagram;

H2 — There is a direct and positive effect of the relationship quality on the consumption behaviors of SLB supporters;

H3 — There is a direct and positive effect of the relationship quality on the engagement on Instagram;

H4 — There is a direct and positive effect of the engagement on Instagram on the consumption behaviors of SLB supporters;

H5 — Engagement on Instagram plays a mediating role in the effect that the relationship quality has on the consumption behaviors of SLB supporters.

2.2 Research Model

Figure 2. Proposed investigation model (Authors Self elaboration)

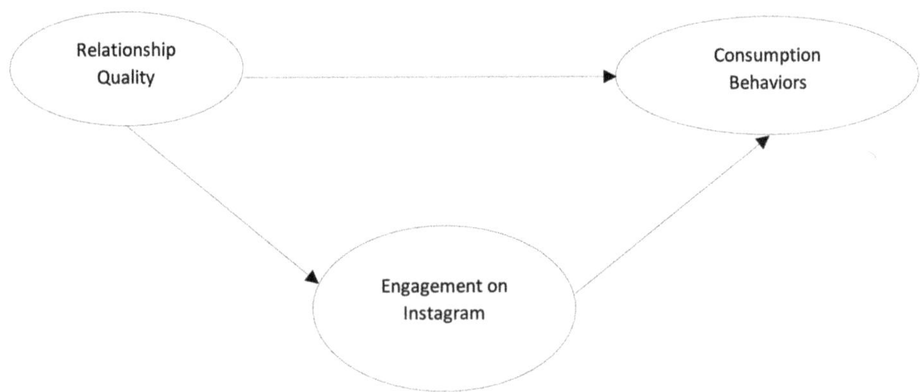

In this research model, it is assumed that there is a mediating effect of the variable "engagement on Instagram", in the association between the variables "relationship quality" and "consumption behaviors".

2.3 Methodological Strategy

A mixed methodological strategy was chosen, using a combination of qualitative and quantitative research (Creswell, 2009).

2.3.1 Exploratory Data

For primary data collection and analysis, two techniques were used: exploratory interviews and documents analysis. The exploratory interviews had a semi-structured character, with a guiding script, but without a specific order and with open questions. The documental analysis allowed the obtaining of more and better information and knowledge about the study object, by identifying various communication elements that the club prioritizes on Instagram and which type of content supporters most value and interact with, that consequently results in greater engagement.

2.3.2 Primary Data

A questionnaire survey was applied for ten days (from April 5 to April 15, 2022), with a non-probabilistic convenience sample. The link was shared in supporter's groups and pages on both Facebook and Instagram, and the aim was to understand their perception about the variables of the study and their connection.

3. RESULTS

3.1 Exploratory Interviews

The exploratory interviews provided valuable insights that allowed not only to discover SLB's "communication backstage" on Instagram, but also to understand the Directors' perspectives regarding the relationship between the club and the supporters, and the behaviors that they adopt/may adopt. The Communication Director, Pedro Pinto, stated that there is a growing investment in the management of the platform's human resources and that the most used tones of communication are informative and informal.

The Social Networks Director, Diogo Canas, confirmed that there is a defined communication strategy to achieve greater engagement with supporters and increase the relationship quality with them. He also stated that Instagram is the club's best social network, as it offers advantages such as reaching a younger audience and more interactions than any other platform. The Corporate Communication Director, Ricardo Maia, reinforced the advantages of Instagram and added the flexibility in publishing content and the possibility to communicating in different languages. Both the Directors of Social Networks and Corporate Communication recognized the importance of the connection between the investigated variables — relationship quality, communication, engagement on Instagram, and consumption behaviors — for the success of the various areas of activity of the club. However, they also mentioned that this success will always depend on the results and on the performance of the team's club, because these factors have great influence in the state of mind of the supporters.

3.2 Documental Analysis

The publications observed on SLB's Instagram allowed a general understanding of the contents that the club publishes in the various competitions and sporting phases, as well as the contents that the supporters most value and interact with. Game days are the ones that generate more publications and greater engagement, with a special focus on supporters, games results, the "men of the match", and player debuts. On the other hand, there is less engagement in contents like goals celebrations, extra game information, warm-up moments and team backstage. The defeats with the most direct rivals, such as Sporting Clube de Portugal (SCP) and Futebol Clube do Porto (FCP), influences the lower influx of publications by the club and even a minor supporter's engagement. It should be noted that factors such as different competitions, coach changes, among other adversities that may occur in the club's environment, do not affect its form of communication which remains cohesive throughout the entire season.

3.3 Questionnaire Survey

The present study is composed by a sample of 361 individuals (Table 1), of which 60.1% are male and 39.6% are female. As for ages, the age group from 19 to 25 years old (45.7%) is predominant, followed by the age group from 36 to 59 years old (28.8%), from 26 to 35 years old (14.4%), higher over 60 years old (8%) and under 18 years old (3.0%). Education with a degree/bachelor's degree is the one with the highest percentage among respondents (41.3%), followed by secondary (25.8%), master's/doctoral (15%), postgraduate (7.2%), 3rd cycle (5%) and non-higher post-secondary (4.4%). The remaining respondents have primary education and the 2nd cycle (1.4%). In terms of region, most come from Lisbon and the Tagus Valley (74%), followed by the Center (10.2%), North (5.5%), Algarve (4.7%), Alentejo (3.6%). The remaining surveys came from the archipelagos of Madeira and the Azores, as well as from other regions (2.0%). The vast majority considers being an SLB supporter due to family influence (87.9%) and since childhood (87%). As for the fact of being a club member, the respondents are divided with 52.4% saying that they are and 47.6% saying that they are not.

Table 1. Sociodemographic profile of the sample – frequencies

	Absolute Frequency (n=361)	Relative Frequency (%)
Gender		
Masculine	217	60,1
Feminine	143	39,6
Omitted	1	0,3
Age		
<18	11	3,0
19-25	165	45,7

continued on following page

Table 1. Continued

	Absolute Frequency (n=361)	Relative Frequency (%)
26-35	52	14,4
36-59	104	28,8
>60	29	8,0
Education		
Primary	2	0,6
2º Cycle	3	0,8
3º Cycle	18	5,0
Secondary	93	25,8
Non Higher Secundary Post	16	4,4
Degree/Bachelor's Degree	149	41,3
Post-Graduation	26	7,2
Masters/Doctoral	54	15
Region		
Lisbon and the Tagus Valley	267	74,0
Center	37	10,2
North	20	5,5
Alentejo	13	3,6
Algarve	17	4,7
Madeira	2	0,6
Açores	2	0,6
Other	3	0,8
How long are you a SLB supporter		
Since little	315	87
Many years ago	43	12
Recent time	4	1
Are you a club member		
Yes	189	52,4
No	172	47,6

3.4 Internal Consistency and Descriptive Analysis of the Scales

Synthetic indices were created with the respective scales and their internal consistency was evaluated using Cronbach's Alpha, as shown in Table 2. According to Pestana and Gageiro (2005), coefficients above 0.9 have very good internal consistency; between 0.8 and 0.9 good; between 0.7 and 0.8 reasonable; between 0.6 and

0.7 weak; and below 0.6 inadmissible. Thus, it is observed that the synthetic indices "relationship quality" and "consumption behaviors" present a very good internal consistencies and the index "engagement on Instagram" a reasonable internal consistency. The item "likes" was removed from this last scale, having substantially improved its internal consistency.

Analyzing Table 2 it is observed that the respondents have very positive perceptions regarding the relationship quality that they have with the club. This index has an average well above the midpoint of the scale (M=478, SD=0.97), with special emphasis on the perceptions "I treat SLB as my club" (M=5.56; SD=0, 99), "I am eternally loyal to SLB" (M=5.50, SD=1.41) and "I support SLB whatever the sporting situation in which it finds itself" (M=5.42, SD=1, 09). Far from these averages, the item with the lowest score is presented: "I feel that the club rewards me for what I give it" (M=3.72; SD=1.40). Regarding the engagement with the club's communication on Instagram, it is observed that it presents an average above the midpoint of the scale (M=3.74; SD=1.44), suggesting that respondents interact with the club in this platform essentially through shares (M=3.75; SD=1.56) and comments (M=3.73; SD=1.60). Regarding consumption behaviors, they are quite positive, with the average of the index above the midpoint of the scale (M=3.94; SD=1.22). The items "I am more interested in the activities and initiatives undertaken by the club" (M=4.45, SD=1.29), "I want to get more involved with the club" (M=4,42, DP=1,37), "I support my club more" (M=4.19, SD=1.54), and "I want to become or remain a member" (M=4.10, SD=1.61) stand out. With the lowest average in this index, we have the item "I participate in more online debates about the club" (M=3.28; SD=1.56).

Table 2. Descriptive analysis of the scales

Item (n=361)	**M**	**DP**	*Cronbach Alpha*	**M**	**DP**
Relationship Quality			0,913	4,78	0,97
- I have a high degree of confidence in the club.	4,63	1,29			
- I am eternally loyal to SLB.	5,50	1,41			
- I support SLB, whatever the sporting situation.	5,42	1,09			
- I treat SLB as "my club".	5,56	0,99			
- I feel that I belong to the SLB universe.	5,05	1,23			
- I defend the club as if it were a family member.	4,64	1,47			
- SLB can stir my state of mind	4,97	1,30			
- I use the name and emblem of the club as a way to represent myself.	4,14	1,48			

continued on following page

Table 2. Continued

Item (n=361)	M	DP	*Cronbach Alpha*	M	DP
- I dedicate financial, emotional, and temporal resources to support the club.	4,16	1,51			
-I feel that the club rewards me for what I give.	3,72	1,40			
Engagement on Instagram			0,797	3,74	1,44
- Shares.	3,75	1,56			
- Comments.	3,73	1,60			
Consumption behaviors			0,919	3,94	1,22
- I have more interest in the activities and initiatives done by the club.	4,45	1,29			
- I am willing to get more involved with the club.	4,42	1,37			
- I participate in more online discussions about the club.	3,28	1,56			
- I post more pictures and/or videos of the club.	3,55	1,62			
- I support the club more.	4,19	1,54			
- I go to more games.	3,98	1,62			
- I buy more merchandising of the club.	3,50	1,57			
- I have a desire to become or remain a member.	4,10	1,61			

1=Strongly Disagree; 6=Strongly Agree; M: Mean; SD: Standard Deviation.

3.5 Correlations Between Variables

Table 3 presents the data referring to the correlations among the variables. According to Pestana and Gageiro (2005), correlations below 0.2 are considered very weak; between 0.2 and 0.39 weak; between 0.4 and 0.69 moderate; between 0.7 and 0.89 high; and between 0.9 and 1 very high. It can be seen from the analysis of Table 3 that, for the total sample (n=361), relationship quality ($r=0.458$; $p<0.01$) and engagement ($r=0.553$; $p<0.01$) show statistically significant correlations with behaviors. These correlations are positive and moderate. Regarding the sample of Instagram users (n=217), the variables "relationship quality" ($r=0.345$, $p<0.01$) and "engagement" ($r=0.456$; $p<0.01$) shows statistically significant correlations with behaviors. The correlation between relationship quality and consumption behaviors is positive and weak. The correlation between engagement and consumption behaviors is positive and moderate. Thus, the higher the relationship quality and the engagement on Instagram, the more pronounced the consumption behaviors of SLB supporters.

Table 3. Pearson's linear correlations

	Total Sample (n=361)		Instagram (n=217)	
Variables	**RQ**	**EN**	**RQ**	**EN**
Engagement	0,334**		0,220**	
Consumption Behaviors	0,458**	0,553**	0,345**	0,456**

RQ: Relationship Quality EN: *Engagement*; **p<0,01

3.6 Mediation Model

To verify the hypotheses, the mediating role of engagement on Instagram on the effect that the relationship quality has on supporters' consumption behaviors was tested for the subsample of supporters who follow the club on Instagram, using the PROCESS macro for SPSS (Hayes, 2017). The assumption of normality of the residuals was validated by the Kolmogorov-Smirnov test (Table 4), that of homoscedasticity of the residuals by the graph output (Figure 3), and that of multicollinearity by the Tolerance and VIF statistics (Table 5). Table 4 shows that the model is globally significant (F=39.756; p<0.01). Through the analysis of the adjusted R2, it is concluded that 27% of the variability of the supporters' consumption behaviors is explained by the two predictors: relationship quality and engagement on Instagram. In fact, both relationship quality (ß=0.471; p<0.01) and engagement on Instagram (ß=0.336; p<0.01) exert a direct and positive effect on consumption behaviors. Relationship quality (ß=0.358; p<0.01) was also found to have a direct and positive effect on engagement on Instagram.

To test the mediating effect of engagement on Instagram, we used the bootstrapping method for a 95% confidence interval and 5000 subsamples (Hayes, 2017). The results confirm that there is a mediating effect of engagement on Instagram on the relationship between the variables "relationship quality" and "consumption behaviors" (ß=0.120; CI=0.029 and CI=0.249). In fact, we find that the direct effect of relationship quality (ß=0.351; p<0.01) on consumption behaviors is smaller when controlled by the engagement on Instagram variable, suggesting a partial mediation effect (Figure 4). Thus, hypotheses H2, H3, H4 and H5 are accepted.

Table 4. Kolmogorov-Smirnov test for normality of residuals

Variable	Statistic	gl	p *value*
Standardized waste	0,046	217	0,200

Figure 3. Homoscedasticity of the residuals

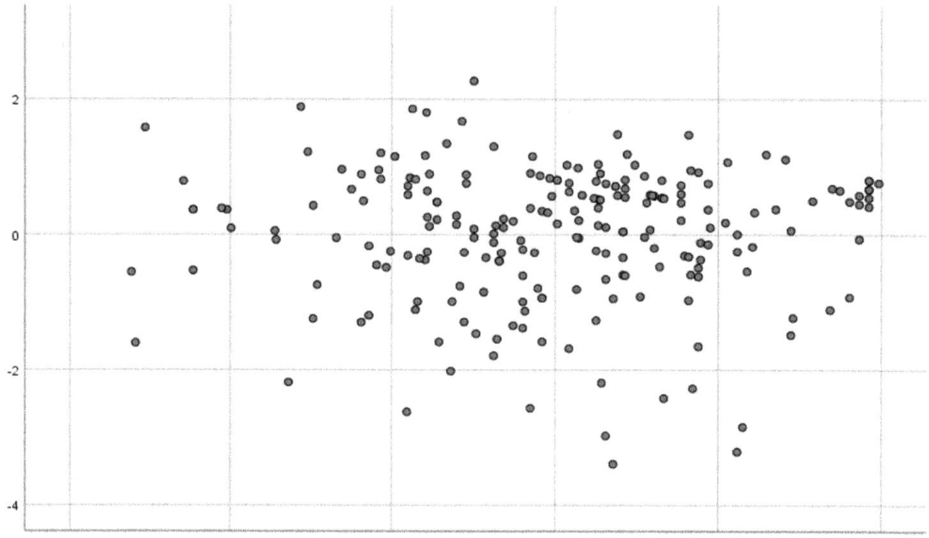

Table 5. Multicollinearity

Variable	Tolerance	VIF
Relationship Quality	.952	1.051
Engagement	.952	1.051

Table 6. Effects of relationship quality and engagement on instagram on consumption behaviors

Steps	*ß*	**SE**	*t*	*p*
Effect of Relationship Quality on Consumption Behaviors (c *path*)	0,471	0,088	5,388	0,000
Effect of Relationship Quality on Engagement (a *path*)	0,358	0,108	3,307	0,001
Effect of Engagement on Consumption Behaviors (b *path*)	0,336	0,050	6,678	0,000
Effect of Relationship Quality on Consumption Behaviors controlled by Engagement (c´*path*)	0,351	0,082	4,295	0,000

continued on following page

Table 6. Continued

Steps	β	SE	t	p
			LL95%CI	UL95%CI
Bootstrap results for the indirect effect	0,120	0,055	0,029	0,249

Total and Direct Effect: Adjusted R2=0.2709; F(39.756); p=0.000

Figure 4. Mediation model

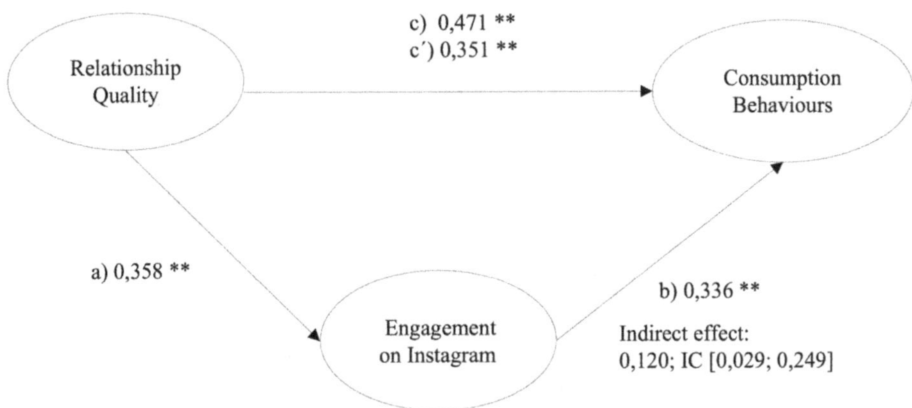

CONCLUSIONS

Despite the increasing number of publications on the relationship between social media and soccer clubs, this phenomenon is still relatively recent, and mostly focused on international soccer clubs (Mahmoudian et al., 2021; Hussain et al., 2021; Ozora & Susanto, 2021; Herencia, 2021; Kuzma, Bell & Logue, 2014). The authors found no research on the role of the relationship quality, and of the communication and consequent engagement on Instagram on SLB supporter's consumption behaviors. This study also contributed to adding to the existing body of theory on the topic by bringing new data on the relationship of these variables. Finally, it provided valuable insights to the analyzed club, as it is now able to use the results to solidify the relationship quality with its supporters and, through communication, generate greater engagement. Consequently, supporters can develop more consumption behaviors for their products and services, resulting in a positive financial return.

Limitations and Future Research

The main limitations felt during this research were the short bibliography available on the subject, both in the specific scope of the analysis and on the targeted club. Another limitation was the impossibility of analyzing all the publications made by SLB on Instagram (concerning the "2021/2022" sports season), since they are extraordinarily numerous and could make the research exhaustive. The relatively low adherence to the questionnaire survey was another difficulty, despite the thousands of members in the various Facebook groups and Instagram pages that helped in the sharing. This finding seems to indicate that most supporters who belong to groups and/or follow online pages about the club do not interact with them, maintaining a passive posture. Finally, it was impossible to access to all the statistics of SLB's Instagram posts (e.g., the number of views on photos or on photo sequences), since these data are only available on videos.

Regarding future research, the authors suggest extending the study to other social networks, such as Facebook, since the answers to the questionnaire indicated that it is the second most used social network by respondents (29.1%). Another interesting line of research would be to compare the results obtained between different social networks, to identify which ones are more significant. It would also be pertinent to deepen the issues mentioned by respondents regarding performance and sports results, which would allow the measuring of their influence and the identifying of their impact on the correlation between the different variables. It would also be interesting to deepen the study of the people who said they were not paying attention to the communications made by the club on social networks to identify their characteristics and, on the other hand, to understand their motives and find what resources are necessary to eventually change their behavior. Finally, this study could be adapted to any other national or international football club that wants to explore the importance of the mentioned variables, their effects, their connection, and consequences.

REFERENCES

Abeza, G. (2021). Sport Communication. *Sport Management Digest (1),* 1, 1-8. https://digestsm.com/digest/sport-communication/

Abeza, G., O'Reilly, N., Sanderson, J., & Frederick, E. (2021). *Social media in sport: Theory and practice*. World Scientific Publishing Co. Pte. Ltd., https://books.google.pt/books?id=loM8EAAAQBAJ&pg=PR4&dq=Abeza,+Gashaw,+O'Reilly,+Norman,+Sanderson,+Jimmy+%26+Frederick,+Evan.+(2021).+Social+media+in+sport:+Theory+and+practice.+London:+World+Scientific+Publishing+Co.+Pte.+Ltd.&hl=pt-PT&sa=X&ved=2ahUKEwij3bX_3er8AhXaTaQEHSqFDB0Q6AF6BAgHEAI#v=onepage&q=Abeza%2C%20Gashaw%2C%20O'Reilly%2C%20Norman%2C%20Sanderson%2C%20Jimmy%20%26%20Frederick%2C%20Evan.%20(2021).%20Social%20media%20in%20sport%3A%20Theory%20and%20practice.%20London%3A%20World%20Scientific%20Publishing%20Co.%20Pte.%20Ltd.&f=false DOI: 10.1142/12299

Abosag, I., Roper, S., & Hind, D. (2010). Examining the relationship between brand emotion and brand extension among supporters of professional football clubs. *European Journal of Marketing*, (46), 9, 1233–1251. https://www.emerald.com/insight/content/doi/10.1108/03090561211247810/full/html

Aichner, T., Grünfelder, M., Maurer, O., & Jegeni, D. (2021). Twenty-Five Years of Social Media: A Review of Social Media Applications and Definitions from 1994 to 2019. *Cyberpsychology, Behavior, and Social Networking*, 24(4), 4, 215–222. https://www.liebertpub.com/doi/10.1089/cyber.2020.0134. DOI: 10.1089/cyber.2020.0134 PMID: 33847527

Albert, N., Merunka, D., & Valette-Florence, P. (2009). The feeling of love toward a brand: Concept and measurement. *Advances in Consumer Research. Association for Consumer Research (U. S.)*, 36, 300–307. https://www.researchgate.net/publication/49136328_The_Feeling_of_Love_Toward_a_Brand_Concept_and_Measurement

Alonso-Dos-Santos, M., Rejón Guardia, F., Pérez Campos, C., Calabuig-Moreno, F., & Ko, Y. J. (2018). Engagement in sports virtual brand communities. *Journal of Business Research*, 89, 273–279. DOI: 10.1016/j.jbusres.2017.12.053

Anagnostopoulos, C., Parganas, P., Chadwick, S., & Fenton, A. (2018). Branding in pictures: Using Instagram as a brand management tool in professional team sport organisations. *European Sport Management Quarterly*, 18(4), 4, 413–438. DOI: 10.1080/16184742.2017.1410202

Aragão, F., Farias, F., Mota, M., & Freitas, A. (2016). Curtiu, comentou, comprou. A mídia social digital Instagram e o consumo. *Revista Ciências Administrativas (22),* 1, 130-161. https://www.redalyc.org/articulo.oa?id=475655250006

Balliauw, M., Onghena, E., & Mulkens, S. (2020). Identifying factors affecting the value of advertisements on football clubs' and players' social media: A discrete choice analysis. *International Journal of Sports Marketing & Sponsorship*, •••, 1–25. DOI: 10.1108/IJSMS-12-2019-0138

Borges, F. (2019). Soccer Clubs as Media Organizations: A Case Study of Benfica TV and PSG TV. *International Journal of Sport Communication*, 12(12), 275–294. DOI: 10.1123/ijsc.2019-0001

Boyd, D. M., & Ellison, M. B. (2007). Social network sites: Definition, history, and scholarship. *Journal of Computer-Mediated Communication*, 13(1), 210–230. DOI: 10.1111/j.1083-6101.2007.00393.x

Butterworth, M. (2021). *Communication and Sport* (Volume 28). Germany: Walter de Gruyter GmbH & Co KG. https://books.google.pt/books?id=nls8EAAAQBAJ&pg=PT112&dq=Communication+and+sport&hl=pt-PT&sa=X&ved=2ahUKEwiIyJev4ur8AhWMr6QKHbxrAxEQ6AF6BAgIEAI#v=onepage&q=Communication%20and%20sport&f=false

Clavio, G. (2013). Emerging social media and applications in sport. In Pedersen, P. (Ed.), *Handbook of sport communication* (pp. 259–268). Routledge., DOI: 10.4324/9780203123485.ch26

Creswell, J. (2009). *Research Design: Qualitative, quantitative and mixed methods approaches.* California: Sage Publications, 3, 1-173. https://www.ucg.ac.me/skladiste/blog_609332/objava_105202/fajlovi/Creswell.pdf

Cruz, J. M., Schregel, J. P., & Zülch, H. (2021). Measuring robustness: Sustainable success factors affecting professional football clubs. *Sport, Business and Management*, 3(12), 1–19. DOI: 10.1108/SBM-03-2021-0041

Deloitte. (2021). *Deloitte Football Money League 2021*. Deloitte. Consultado em: 15 de novembro de 2021. https://www2.deloitte.com/uk/en/pages/sports-business-group/articles/deloitte-football-money-league.html

Diário de Notícias. (20 de março de 2017). *Paixão pelo futebol é "uma forma de amor tribal", conclui estudo.* Diário de Notícias. Consultado em: 26 de novembro de 2021. https://www.dn.pt/sociedade/paixao-pelo-futebol-e-uma-forma-de-amor-tribal-conclui-estudo-5735943.html

Dionísio, P., Leal, C., & Moutinho, L. (2008). Fandom affiliation and tribal behaviour: A sports marketing application. *Qualitative Market Research*, 11(1), 17–39. DOI: 10.1108/13522750810845531

Duarte, A. (2023). The relationship between Brands and Consumers. In *Social Brand Management in a Post Covid-19 Era* (pp. 3–16). Routledge., DOI: 10.4324/9781003382331-2

Federação Portuguesa de Futebol. (2021). Sobre a FPF. Consultado em: 20 de novembro de 2021. https://www.fpf.pt/Institucional/Sobre-a-FPF/História-FPF

Fenton, A., Keegan, B.J. & Parry, K.D. (2021). Understanding Sporting Social Media Brand Communities, Place and Social Capital: A Netnography of Football Fans. *Sage Journals,* 1-21. https://doi.org/DOI: 10.1177/216747952098614

Frandsen, K. (2016). Sports organizations in a new wave of mediatization. *Communication & Sport*, 4(4), 385–400. DOI: 10.1177/2167479515588185

Gantz, W. (2013). Reflections on communication and sport: On fanship and social relationships. *Communication & Sport*, 1(1), 176–187. DOI: 10.1177/2167479512467446

Giulianotti, R. (2002). Supporters, Followers, Fans, and Flaneurs: A Taxonomy of Spectator Identities in Football. *Journal of Sport and Social Issues*, 26(1), 25–46. DOI: 10.1177/0193723502261003

Giulianotti, R., & Robertson, R. (2012). Mapping the global football field: A sociological model of transnational forces within the world game. *The British Journal of Sociology*, 63(2), 216–240. DOI: 10.1111/j.1468-4446.2012.01407.x PMID: 22670645

Herencia, C. A. B. (2021). La narrativa digital del fútbol. Desintermediación de la agenda a través de las redes sociales de los clubes [The digital narrative of soccer. Disintermediation of the agenda through the social networks of the clubs]. *Revista Académica sobre Documentación Digital y Comunicación Interactiva, (22),* 85-96. https://orcid.org/0000-0002-8990-7949

Hootsuite. (2021). *Digital 2021: Global Overview Report*. Data Reportal. Consultado em: 3 de janeiro de 2022. https://datareportal.com/reports/digital-2021-global-overview-report

Hunt, K. A., Bristol, T., & Bashaw, R. E. (1999). A conceptual approach to classifying sports fans. *Journal of Services Marketing*, 13(6), 6, 439–452. DOI: 10.1108/08876049910298720

Hussain, G., Naz, T., Shahzad, N., & Bajwa, M. J. (2021). Social Media Marketing in Sports and using social media platforms for sports fan engagement. *Journal of Contemporary Issues in Business and Government*, (27), 6, 1460–1474. DOI: 10.47750/cibg.2021.27.05.145

Kharmalki, G. W., & Raizada, S. (2020). Social media marketing in sports: The rise of fan engagement through Instagram. *Annals of Tropical Medicine and Public Health*, 17(23), 1–8. DOI: 10.36295/ASRO.2020.231721

Kim, A., Qian, Y., Lee, H-W., Mastromartino, B. & Zhang, J.J. (2020). Growth in Sport Media and the rise of new sport fandom. *Multidisciplinary Perspectives on Media Fandom*, 150-171. DOI: 10.4018/978-1-7998-3323-9.ch009

Kim, J., James, J., & Kim, Y. (2013). A model of the relationship among sport consumer motives, spectator commitment, and behavioral intentions. *Sport Management Review*, 16(2), 173–185. DOI: 10.1016/j.smr.2012.08.004

Kim, K., & Trail, G. (2011). A Conceptual Framework for Understanding Relationships Between Sport Consumers and Sport Organizations: A Relationship Quality Approach. *Journal of Sport Management*, 25(1), 57–69. DOI: 10.1123/jsm.25.1.57

Koronios, K., Travlos, A., Douvis, J., & Papadopoulos, A. (2020). Sport, media and actual consumption behavior: An examination of spectator motives and constraints for sport media consumption. *EuroMed Journal of Business*, 15(2), 151–166. DOI: 10.1108/EMJB-10-2019-0130

Kuzma, J., Bell, V., & Logue, C. (2014). A Study of the Use of Social Media Marketing in the Football Industry. *Journal of Emerging Trends in Computing and Information. The Sciences*, 10(5), 728–738. https://eprints.worc.ac.uk/3460/1/kuzmacisoct2014paper.pdf

Lee, M. A., Kunkel, T., Funk, D. C., Karg, A., & McDonald, H. (2020). Built to last: Relationship quality management for season ticket holders. *European Sport Management Quarterly*, 20(3), 364–384. DOI: 10.1080/16184742.2019.1613438

Lucena, J., & Casaca, J. (2013). Branding no futebol: O valor económico das marcas dos três grandes do futebol português. *Revista Portuguesa e Brasileira de Gestão*, •••, 33–46. https://www.redalyc.org/articulo.oa?id=388539138005

Mabić, M., Lasić, M., & Zovko, J. (2019). Web 2.0 technologies in business: Why not? *Interdisciplinary Description of Complex Systems*, 17(2, 2-B), 304–314. DOI: 10.7906/indecs.17.2.7

Maderer, D., Parganas, P., & Anagnostopoulos, C. (2018). Brand-Image Communication Through Social Media: The Case of European Professional Football Clubs. *International Journal of Sport Communication*, 3(11), 1–20. DOI: 10.1123/ijsc.2018-0086

Mahan, J. (2011). Examining the predictors of consumer response to sport marketing via digital social media. *International Journal of Sport Management and Marketing*, 9, 254–267. DOI: 10.1504/IJSMM.2011.041575

Mahmoudian, A., Boroujerdi, S. S., Siyani, M. G., & Mahmoud, A. I. F. (2021). Moderating Role of Using Instagram in Relation between Involvement with the Team, Attachment and Fan Loyalty (Case Study: Persepolis Football Team). *Communication Mangagement in Sports Media*, 2(8), 103–115. DOI: 10.30473/jsm.2020.50380.1370

Mastromartino, B., Ross, W. J., Wear, H., & Naraine, M. L. (2020). Thinking outside the 'box': A discussion of sports fans, teams, and the environment in the context of COVID- 19. *Sport in Society*, 11(23), 1–17. DOI: 10.1080/17430437.2020.1804108

McCarthy, J., Rowley, J., Ashworth, C., & Pioch, E. (2014). Managing brand presence through social media: The case of UK football clubs. *Internet Research*, 24(2), 181–204. DOI: 10.1108/IntR-08-2012-0154

McLean, R., & Wainwright, D. (2009). Social networks, football fans, fantasy and reality: How corporate and media interests are invading our life world. *Journal of Information. Communication and Ethics in Society*, 7(1), 54–71. DOI: 10.1108/14779960910938098

Nisar, T. M. N., Prabhakar, G., & Patil, P. P. (2018). Sports clubs' use of social media to increase spectator interest. *International Journal of Information Management*, 43, 188–195. DOI: 10.1016/j.ijinfomgt.2018.08.003

Obradović, M., Alčaković, S., Vyugina, D., & Tasevski, S. (2019). Use of social media in communication strategies of premier league football clubs. *International scientific conference on information technology and data related research,* 244-249. DOI: 10.15308/Sinteza-2019-244-249

Ozora, S., & Susanto, E. H. (2021). The Use of Instagram in an Effort to Attract Fans of the PSIM Jogja Soccer Club. *Advances in Social Science, Education and Humanities Research*, (570), 818–823. DOI: 10.2991/assehr.k.210805.129

Pedersen, P. M. (2017). *Routledge handbook of sport communication.* Routledege Taylor & Francis Group., https://api.taylorfrancis.com/content/books/mono/download?identifierName=doi&identifierValue=10.4324/9780203123485&type=googlepdf DOI: 10.4324/9781315088556

Pedersen, P. M., Laucella, P. C., Kian, E. M., & Geurin, A. N. (2020). *Strategic Sport Communication* (3a Edição). United States of America: Human Kinetics. https://books.google.com/books?hl=pt-PT&lr=&id=LObsDwAAQBAJ&oi=fnd&pg=PP2&dq=Pedersen,+Paul+M.,+Laucella,+Pamela+C.,+Kian,+Edward+M.+%26+Geurin,+Andrea.+N.+(2020).+Strategic+Sport+Communication+(3a+Edição).+United+States+of+America:+Human+Kinetics.+&ots=FkOzivaSRv&sig=cRVSdGOwovzqTir24hp2nUgaFjE

Penn, R. (2016). Football talk: Sociological reflections on the dialectics of language. *EJSS European Journal for Sport and Society*, 13(2), 154–166. DOI: 10.1080/16138171.2016.1183931

Popp, B., Germelmann, C., & Jung, B. (2016). We love to hate them! Social media-based anti-brand communities in professional football. *International Journal of Sports Marketing & Sponsorship*, 17(4), 349–367. DOI: 10.1108/IJSMS-11-2016-018

Price, W. (2017). *The Evolution of Instagram* Ads [Infographic]. Sovial Media Today. Consultado em: 4 de janeiro de 2022. https://www.socialmediatoday.com/news/the-evolution-of-instagram-ads-infographic/507628/

Quintela, J. (2020). O diretor de comunicação no futebol: perfis e tendências nos "três grandes" clubes portugueses. *PODIUM Sport, Leisure and Tourism Review, 9 (1),* 21- 41. https://periodicos.uninove.br/podium/article/view/13748

Salmi, T. S., Benar, N., & Honari, H. (2019). Identifying value creation strategies in the brand communities of sport clubs based on the use of social media. *Annals of Applied Sport Science*, 7(2), 55–61. http://aassjournal.com/article-1-718-en.html. DOI: 10.29252/aassjournal.7.2.55

Sousa, B., & Vieira, C. (2018). Um Estudo Sobre a Afetividade Aplicada ao Fenómeno do Futebol: Abordagemn na Ótica dos Consumidores. *PODIUM Sport, Leisure And. Podium (São Paulo)*, 7(2), 293–312. DOI: 10.5585/podium.v7i2.282

Sports, N. (2018). *World Football Report.* Nielsen Sports. Consultado em: 16 de novembro de 2021. https://www.nielsen.com/wp-content/uploads/sites/3/2019/04/world- football-report-2018.pdf

Stander, F. W., Llewellyn, E. V. Z., & Kemiso, M. (2016). Promoting fan engagement: An exploration of the fundamental motives for sport consumption amongst premier league football spectators. *Journal of Psychology in Africa*, 26(4), 309–315. DOI: 10.1080/14330237.2016.1208920

Stavros, C., Meng, M., Westberg, K., & Farrelly, F. (2014). Understanding fan motivation for interacting on social media. *Sport Management Review*, 17(4), 455–469. DOI: 10.1016/j.smr.2013.11.004

Tapp, A. (2004). The loyalty of football fans – we'll support you ever more? *The Journal of Database Marketing & Customer Strategy Management*, 11(3), 225–246. DOI: 10.1057/palgrave.dbm.3240221

Teo, L. X., Leng, H. K., & Phua, Y. X. P. (2019). Marketing on Instagram. *International Journal of Sports Marketing & Sponsorship*, 2(20), 321–332. DOI: 10.1108/IJSMS-04-2018-0028

Thompson, A.-J., Martin, A., Gee, S., & Geurin, A. N. (2018). Building brand and fan relationships through social media. *Sport, Business and Management*, 8(3), 235–256. DOI: 10.1108/SBM-04-2017-0024

UEFA. (2022). *History: Seasons*. UEFA. Consultado em: 15 de novembro de 2021. https://pt.uefa.com/uefaeuro/history/seasons/1980/

Vale, L., & Fernandes, T. (2018). Social media and sports: Driving fan engagement with football clubs on Facebook. *Journal of Strategic Marketing*, 26(1), 1, 37–55. DOI: 10.1080/0965254X.2017.1359655

van Doorn, J., Lemon, K. N., Mittal, V., Nass, S., Pick, D., Pirner, P., & Verhoef, P. C. (2010). Customer Engagement Behavior: Theoretical Foundations and Research Directions. *Journal of Service Research*, 13(3), 253–266. DOI: 10.1177/1094670510375599

William, J., & Chinn, S. (2010). Meeting Relationship-Marketing Goals Through Social Media: A Conceptual Model for Sport Marketers. *International Journal of Sport Communication*, 3(4), 422–437. DOI: 10.1123/ijsc.3.4.422

Yoshida, M., Gordon, B. S., Nakazawa, M., Shibuya, S., & Fujiwara, N. (2018). Bridging the gap between social media and behavioral brand loyalty. *Electronic Commerce Research and Applications*, 28, 208–218. DOI: 10.1016/j.elerap.2018.02.005

ENDNOTE

1 "(...) a name, term, sign, symbol, design, or a combination thereof, intended to identify the goods and services of a seller/group of sellers and to differentiate them from other competitors" (Pinho, 1996:14).

Chapter 7
Implicit Virtual Communities in Social Networks

Shyam Sundar Meena
Shri Vaishnav Vidyapeeth Vishwavidyalaya, Indore, India

Vrinda Tokekar
Devi Ahilya Vishwavidyalaya, Indore, India

ABSTRACT

This chapter explores the topic of virtual community discovery in social networks. It starts with defining virtual communities. After that, the chapter goes over several network modelling strategies and community identification techniques. The significance of standardised datasets in evaluating algorithm performance is shown by a thorough analysis of benchmark networks used to test community detection techniques. The accuracy indices for assessing virtual community identification algorithms are also covered. The chapter offers common datasets needed to evaluate virtual community discovery techniques. Next, it explores community discovery using the Girvan-Newman and Louvain algorithms, two well-known techniques, to demonstrate practical applications. These illustrations explain how theoretical ideas can be applied in practical settings. Finally, this chapter provides a thorough overview of the concepts and assessment criteria for virtual community discovery in social networks, providing insightful information for both scholars and industry professionals.

DOI: 10.4018/979-8-3693-3868-1.ch007

1. INTRODUCTION

In recent years, interest in the modelling and mining of social networks has grown tremendously. These networks are usually modelled using a graph structure in the literature. Entities and relationships between them in graph-based modelling of social networks are depicted by nodes or vertices (often denoted by a set V) and links or edges (often denoted by a set E). The edges in graph modelling of these networks can be depicted as directed or undirected, labelled or unlabeled and weighted or un-weighted (Meena & Tokekar, 2021).

In a network social network, friendship between persons is developed due to mutual affection. This relationship builds a strong connection than an association. An individual is depicted as a node in the graph modelling these networks, and the association between them is shown as an edge. Undirected and unweighted graphs are typically utilised in the modelling process for these sorts of networks. Weighted edges can be helpful when attempting to provide a more in-depth comprehension of relationships. Networks that fall within this category include Facebook, LinkedIn, and Twitter, among others.

Entities having the same values of some features generally form virtual communities (communities) in these networks. The term "community" in the context of networks refers to a group or cluster of closely interconnected nodes. From various points of view, people have defined a community (virtual community) in a variety of ways. These comprise definitions based on node similarity, global definition based on network modularity, local definition based on subgraphs and definition based on their formation, detection, and member engagement (Meena & Tokekar, 2020).

(i) Local Definition Based on Subgraph

A community structure in a network is represented by many strongly linked groupings of nodes. These groupings frequently stand for individual qualities or functions inside the network. Thus, we may use the characteristics of the local network connections to determine the community structure. As of right now, researchers from many disciplines agree on a single concept of community structure. The basis for this concept is a subgraph. According to this, a complex network's community structures are made up of multiple smaller node groupings. Each group's nodes are intimately linked to one another, although connections between nodes in other groups are less common. Figure 1 depicts the network's twenty nodes divided into three community structures, each represented by a dotted circle. The nodes in these three communities are extremely linked, whereas there are less connections between nodes in other groups (Meena & Tokekar, 2020).

Figure 1. A small network with virtual community structure

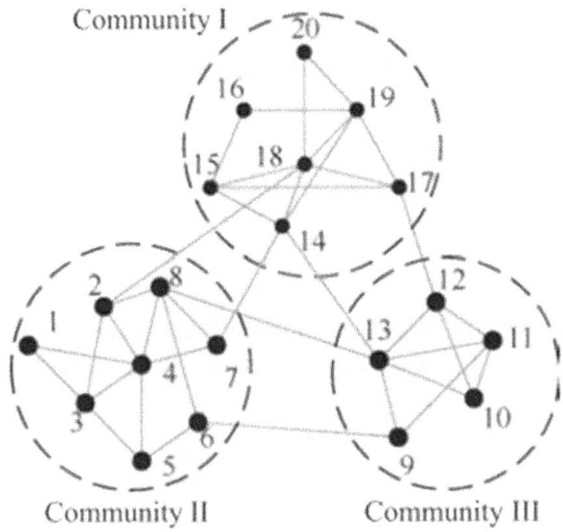

(ii) Global Definition Based on the Network Modularity

Newman and others introduced the idea of modularity to assess community structure. Between a network's actual connections and the connections, you would anticipate in a random network, modularity quantifies the difference. In contrast to how many connections there would be if the nodes were assigned at random, it examines how many edges link nodes within the same community. An improved community structure results from higher modularity. This metric gauges how successfully the communities are built by utilizing global topological knowledge about the network. In order to evaluate the structure of the community or determine whether to halt the process, community identification methods frequently make use of modularity.

(iii) Definition Based on the Similarity Between Nodes

Communities, in the physical sense, are often groups of components that share or are similar to each other in complex systems or networks. These components cooperate or communicate with one another to carry out certain tasks or create unique organizational structures. As a result, node similarities may be used to define communities. According to this definition, nodes in the same community are assumed to be similar, but nodes in separate communities are assumed to be less similar. In order to better characterize community structure, some metrics for comparing network node similarity should be applied (Meena & Tokekar, 2021).

From the perspective of essential meaning, all current definitions of community (or virtual community) are generally consistent in that, for a subset of the set made up of all individuals in networks, the individuals within the subset have sparse connections with individuals outside the subset and are closely connected to each other based on specific properties.

Detection of communities can reveal various facts about networks. Community detection can be helpful in many situations. First, groups provide a clear global view of networks. Second, sometimes group behaviors offer more information about the networks. For example, people frequently form groupings based on shared interests on social media. The online bookseller may utilize groups of individuals with comparable reading choices to make book recommendations. The analysis of protein networks may be investigated to understand the structural connections between proteins and the functionality prediction of proteins, and topic identification in webpage networks may be achieved networks (Shang et al., 2016).

(iv) Definition Based on Formation, Detection, and Member Engagement

The virtual communities in social networks can be classified into Implicit Virtual Community (IVC) and Explicit Virtual Community (EVC) based on formation, detection, and member engagement.

a) Implicit Virtual Community

- *Definition*: Implicit virtual communities are associations that develop organically among members without their express consent. These communities are recognized by common interests, patterns of engagement, or behaviors deduced from data.
- *Formation*: Rather than being consciously joined or identified, these communities are found by algorithms that look for certain online behaviors, such sharing material, having similar interests, or interacting often.
- *Examples* include groups of individuals that like and share similar content regularly, followers of a certain set of influencers, and users who frequently comment on related issues.
- *Detection*: Based on trends in data, community detection algorithms—like clustering strategies or social network analysis tools—are frequently employed to find these groups.

- *Benefits*: Identifies innate clusters and latent relationships. beneficial for studying user behavior, making tailored suggestions, and focusing marketing efforts.

b) Explicit Virtual Community

- Explicit virtual communities are defined as organizations whose members consciously built them with a specific goal in mind. Participants voluntarily join and participate, and they acknowledge this.
- Formation: People actively participate in these communities by enrolling, signing up, or showing interest in a particular social media page, forum, or group.
- *Examples:* include Reddit communities, Facebook groups, online forums, and any other online community that requires a membership procedure.
- *Detection*: These communities are readily recognized since they have member lists, distinct boundaries, and frequently official participation rules or norms.
- *Benefits: include* a well-defined goal that makes them simpler to interact with and manage. Participants can actively participate and are aware of their membership.

2. FRAMEWORK OF VIRTUAL COMMUNITY DETECTION

The first step in community discovery in social networks is data modelling. This section examines many models that have been suggested in the literature along with the most popular community detection techniques.

2.1 Network Modelling

Following the discovery of scale-free and small-world networks (Watts & Strogatz, 1998), academics' interest in modelling complex networks has grown. These networks include social, biological, and co-authorship. Lots of users can be part of real-world social media networks. Models provide details about the structure and the underlying formation process. Modelling is also needed to assess the precision of the community detection techniques (Pasta & Zaidi, 2016a). When real-world networks are unavailable, they could provide mathematical explanations for studies conducted on artificial networks. These models need to simulate the characteristics and attributes of actual network structures.

(i) **Random Graphs Model:** Erds-Rnyi (ER) and Gilbert have studied the random network theory in 1959. Their findings suggest that in the graph generation process, connections between the disconnected set of nodes grow randomly (ERDdS & R&wi, 1959). The most basic Model is known as the *G(n,m)* Model. *G(n,m)* represents a group of graphs, where n and m represent a set of nodes and a set of edges, respectively. The *G(n,p)* Model presented by Edgar Gilbert, on the other hand, is the one that is most frequently studied. In *G(n,p)*, the probability (p) of the appearance of edges in the graph falls between 0 to 1. The *G(n,p)* defines a group of graphs, where the construction of the graph start n disconnected set of nodes. The insertion of an edge between each precise node couples with likelihood p. In the *G(n,p)* Model, the likelihood of getting any one random graph with m edges is represented by $p^m(1-P)^{N-m}$, where N is equal to $\binom{n}{2}$. As a result, *G(n,p)* describes a more prominent family than *G(n,m)*. However, two crucial characteristics seen in a lot of real-world networks are absent from Erdos-Renyi graphs:

- Local clustering and triadic closures generally do not present the resultant graphs
- They do not consider hub construction (In contrast to the power law distribution of nodes' degree that may be found in many networks, the distribution of the degree of nodes in ER graphs belongs to a Poisson distribution).

(ii) **Small-World Models:** Based on the computation of the transitivity C and the path length l, Watts and Strogatz (WS) have concluded from their analysis of network topologies that most networks belong to the class of small-world. They discovered that real-world networks have a short average path length and a high value of transitivity (Watts & Strogatz, 1998). By switching from a uniform grid to a random one, the objective is to produce a graph representing the little world's characteristics. Edges are rewired according to probability p (see Figure 2). The original Model of the WS has several issues. The small-world Model can produce networks with transitivity and a small average path length. However, the simulated graph does not produce a realistic degree distribution. Many variants of the WS model are suggested in the literature. Between them, the Model proposed in (Newman et al., 2000) by Newman, Moore and Watts produces almost the same Model with the only difference that here it does not replace the existing edges but adds new edges between two nodes with a probability of *p*.

Figure 2. Rewiring procedure of Small-World models (Watts & Strogatz, 1998)

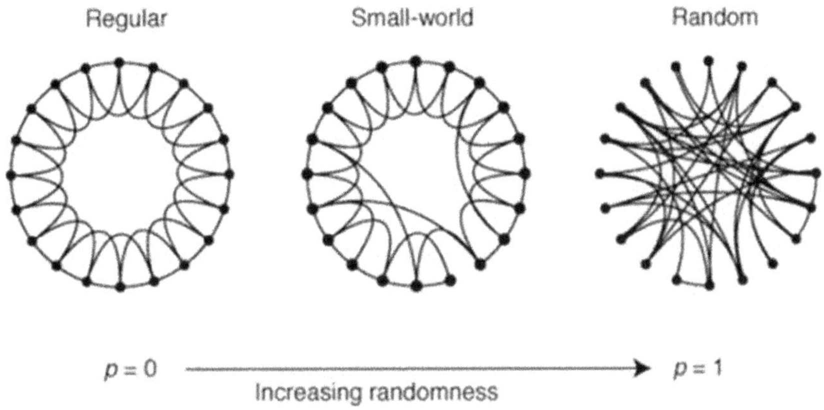

(iii) **Scale-free Networks:** Derek de Solla Price's 1965 study of scale-free networks mainly worked on scientific paper networks and shows that the scientific article citations network exhibits power-law distribution (Price, 1966). In this analysis, he finds that while the network increases the node degree, the number of more connected nodes becomes higher than less connected nodes: he calls the cumulative advantage to this event. Nowadays, this concept is known as the preferential attachment introduced by Barabási and Albert (BA) (Barabási & Albert, 1999). Barabási and Albert analyzed the World Wide Web based on two fundamental rules: preferential attachment and growth. These two basic rules are used to generate a $G^{BA}_{(N,E)}$ undirected graph from a set of vertices with initial size m0. A new vertex j with edges of $m \leq m_0$ is introduced to the network in each step $t = \{1, 2 \ldots, N - m_0\}$ of the algorithm. The probability of a j vertex connecting with an existing i

$$\Pi_{j \to i} = \frac{k_i}{\sum_l k_l}$$

vertex is linearly proportional to the degree of i.

The network will have a set of vertices of N = t + m0 per moment and a set of edges of E = mt with a mean degree of (k) = 2m. Numerical simulations suggest that the BA model randomly forms a $P(k) \sim k^{-\lambda}$ distribution of power law.

(iv) **Configuration Model:** A configuration model (CM) generates networks beginning with a predecided degree sequence (Molloy & Reed, 1995a). The ability to incorporate different degree distributions makes it a popular starting point for simulating real-world social networks. The configuration model does not use a probability distribution to determine each vertex's degree; instead, the degree is explicitly defined for each vertex. The configuration model differs from the Erds-Renyi model (Erdos et al., 1960) in that a Poisson distribution is unnecessary for the degree sequence.

As a bonus, the Model lets users implement a degree distribution into the network however they see fit. Detailed below are the building blocks of the CM model.

(i) Take a degree sequence, which means you should give each vertex a degree value of ki. The degrees at each vertex are shown as stubs or half-links in the representation of the graph. To build a graph, the sum of the stubs must be even ($\sum$ ki = 2m). The degree sequence may be selected from a theoretical distribution or represent an entire network (determined from the network's adjacency matrix).
(ii) A random pair of stubs is chosen and joined together to form a new edge. Pick another two 2m−2 pieces to join from the collection. Keep going until there are no more stubs.
(iii) A network with a specified order of degrees is the end result.

Various new models have been developed after the finding of the scale-free (Albert & Barabási, 2002) and small-world (Watts & Strogatz, 1998) network-generating models. These new models either use versions, modify the existing models, or take an entirely different approach. Previous models produced networks with characteristics such as short average path lengths, transitivity, and power-law degree distributions. Other network structural aspects have also received attention over time thanks to developments that have been made, resulting in newer models being presented. The following paragraphs will review several models that can produce networks with community structures. There have been some ideas about making an artificial network with a community in the literature. The model that Girvan and Newman (GN) came up with is the first step in this direction. GN is a simple model that generates an empty network (i.e. without any edge), randomly assigns community to nodes, and adds intra- and inter-community edges between the nodes. Several advancements have been developed in order to make it possible to generate weighted or directed relationships in addition to hierarchical or overlapping communities. The community detection techniques have been evaluated on the artificial networks constructed using the GN model. However, there are a few drawbacks to it (Lancichinetti et al., 2008):

- It can only produce networks of a somewhat relatively small scale.
- Every network node adheres to the same degree when it is built. On the other hand, most of the networks generally follow a power-law distribution of nodes' degrees.
- It results in networks where communities of the same size are produced.

Bagrow, J. P. uses the BA model to construct the initial network (Barabási & Albert, 1999). The generated networks follow the power-law distribution of degrees. However, this results in relatively small networks with communities of similar sizes (Bagrow, 2008). Most studies generated artificial benchmark networks using LancichinettiFortunato- Radicchi(LFR) model (Lancichinetti et al., 2008). LFR model builds networks with a power-law distribution of degrees. LFR model does not impose any restrictions on the network size, in contrast to Bagrow's. However, it fails to generate realistic networks because of the following reasons. The possible causes identified in this study are:

- LFR utilized configuration model (CM) for the generation of initial structure which does not include preferential attachment feature (Molloy & Reed, 1995b),
- Nodes have a similar connectivity pattern, whereas connectivity patterns in real-world networks may differ for each node.
- LFR-generated networks have a low value of transitivity, which causes random connectivity patterns between the nodes in a network. Newman has ob served a quite high value of transitivity in the study of real-world networks (Newman, 2003).

Lancichinetti and Fortunato presented a model for generating networks of different sizes (Lancichinetti & Fortunato, 2009). On the other hand, this Model does not adhere to some dynamic principles, like preferential attachment (Pasta & Zaidi, 2016b). The scale-free Model is expanded upon in the Model put forth by Xu et al. Three processes—the development of new nodes inside a community and new links within or between communities—are combined in this Model. Growing and preferred attachment processes are used in the Model. Nonetheless, it can produce networks with a decent right-skewed distribution of the degrees of the nodes (Xu et al., 2009). Xie et al. suggested a preferential-based strategy for building networks with a community structure. Larger communities are preferred when choosing a community, and hub nodes are preferred for picking neighbors to make inter-cluster edges. The concept followed was based on real-life situations, such as more people are likely to live in larger towns. The proposed Model is empirically investigated for the small-world pattern and the hierarchical feature. It can create complex networks that cut across the social and technological domains (Xie et al., 2007). The self-organization of communities in developing weighted networks is modelled and described by Zhou et al. The work presented here offers a favored community and node-level mechanism. It demonstrates power-law distributions of the sizes of communities, the strengths of their nodes, and the weights of their links. In addition, the Model's efficiency is demonstrated by using a social network as an example, specifically the networks of scientific co-authorship (Zhou et al., 2008). The Model proposed by Kumpula at al. generate networks with medium size communities. This network adheres to microscopic sociological laws. Sociology's focal and cyclic closure serve as the Model's main molecular principles. Sociology's cyclic and focal closure mechanisms make new friends on social media platforms. A random walk is utilized to create cyclic closures, and focal closure is obtained by introducing the arbitrary connection between nodes in the network (Kumpula et al., 2009). Zaidi investigated how randomness contributes to the formation of community structures in networks (Zaidi, 2013). This Model substitutes cliques of varying sizes for each node in the random graph produced by the ER model (Erdos et al., 1960). The transitivity rises to the appropriate level in this Model even though the links between the cliques are random. This Model has been expanded further to incorporate the characteristics of social, biological, and technological networks and other real-world networks that contain community structures. According to the study, clustered networks can be produced by giving random networks minimal organization. However, unlike many networks worldwide, networks created using this method do not have the scale-free feature. The concept suggested by A. Sallaberry, F. Zaidi, and G. Melanç is very much like the Generalized Random Graph. The overall process works in three steps. Here in the place of inserting a node, it inserts a clique. The size of cliques may also vary. Because of this, the resultant networks have a high transitivity value. In the second step, establishes a connection between a possible connectivity attribute. The power-law distribution of degrees is also followed in the creation of networks. The above step ensures that resultant networks have a scale-free property that is basically followed by real-world networks. The last step, generate a tree of clusters to achieve the community structure. The connectedness characteristic and the distances between nodes in the cluster tree are considered when merging nodes within cliques. This process of merging produces dense node clusters. This model generates static networks with fixed nodes (Sallaberry et al., 2013). Pasta et al. consider that networks have a small world, scale-free features, and the existence of community structures (Pasta et al., 2013). This concept is consistent with the presence of three key traits that are observed in community-based systems. The first discovery is that the distribution of node degrees within a community may follow a power-law behavior. This behavior can be seen by looking at the degrees of individual nodes. The second discovery is that the transitivity observed within communities is relatively high. The third discovery is that community structure may be hierarchical. The Model is highly elastic and durable and can be utilized to develop various network configurations to fulfil the needs of various scenarios. These features might come in handy when constructing benchmark and test datasets for experimental study at some point. However, it does not incorporate any knowledge exclusive to the domain. Because of the above rationale, we cannot utilize this model to construct networks with realistic characteristics(Meena & Tokekar, 2023).

2.2 Community Detection Algorithms

The technique of defining virtual communities in online social networks requires dividing network nodes into many subgraphs based on their degree of connectedness within the network structure. The term "graph partitioning issue" refers to this in computer science. Studies on this topic date back to the twentieth century, and two of the most important approaches are the spectral bisection algorithm (Fiedler, 1975) and the Kernighan-Lin algorithm (Kernighan & Lin, 1970)

The Kernighan-Lin algorithm employs a greedy optimization approach to specify an objective revenue function and then conducts a greedy search to identify the optimal partitioning that will allow the objective revenue function to achieve its maximum value. In addition to defining the network's allowable partition, Kernighan-Lin's tree diagram approach for visualizing community structure indicates a hierarchical community structure. The spectral bisection approach, which begins with the Laplacian matrix, applies dichotomy to the network's topological structure by studying the matrix's eigenvalue and eigenvector.

Applying the process repeatedly results in a community division with more than two communities. As complex network science evolves, researchers from several disciplines are becoming increasingly interested in the problem of identifying network community structures in the twenty-first century.

In recent years, researchers' attention has shifted to real-world network analysis. Complex networks are commonly employed to model these real-world networks. Real-world networks, such as biological networks, social networks, etc., can be represented using complex networks (Girvan & Newman, 2002a). Examining the network at different levels is necessarily better for comprehending the operation and structure of complex networks. Component-level study of these networks can provide details about the structure and connectivity pattern within the group of nodes. The methods used to find the network component are generally called community detection techniques. A community in these networks is described as any cohesive cluster of nodes. The community has a high density of internal links compared to the connections in the rest of the network (Newman & Girvan, 2004). Community detection has a wide range of applications, such as the detected community structure may provide a clear global view of networks. Sometimes group behaviors offer more information about the networks. On social media, for example, individuals commonly form groups based on mutual interests. The online retailer may interact with groups of individuals with similar reading tastes to make reading recommendations. Community structure may be investigated in protein networks to understand the connections between proteins. We can utilize community detection to identify topics in web page networks. Therefore, identifying communities is essential in the various type of networks.

The researchers have developed several approaches for community detection based on diverse theories. As an example, there are algorithms based on random walks (Van Dongen, 2000), spectral algorithms (Ng et al., 2001), and optimization algorithms based on an objective function (Blondel et al., 2008). Modularity was first presented as a quality function by M. Girvan, M. E. J. Newman (Girvan & Newman, 2002b), and it has since become one of the most prominent quality functions in community detection.

Modularity is a well-known and most-used measure of quality. The central concept it relies on is that a random network has no clear community structure. Consequently, the modularity of the community is calculated by comparing the cluster's edge count to the number of edges expected to have in the cluster when nodes are connected randomly. The expected number of connections within the group depends on the selected null Model. The null Model is generated by duplicating the original network. Most of the properties between both remain the same except for community structure.

In networks with high modularity, the links inside modules will be dense, while the links between nodes of different modules will be sparse, as is the case in most networks. High modularity ratings are indicative of excellent partitions. The following section categorizes community detection algorithms that need some level of modularity in their strategy.

Using a greedy approach to maximize modularity, Newman developed the first successful community detection method (Newman, 2004). As a result of the joining process, the system's modularity rises due to the agglomerative hierarchical clustering strategy. Clauset et al. made Newman's algorithm more efficient by introducing more efficient data structures, such as max heaps (Clauset et al., 2004). Danon et al. argue that the fraction of edges between the communities should be used to normalize the modularity gain ΔQ caused by the merger of communities to encourage tiny communities (Danon et al., 2006).

Wakita and Tsurumi found that the rapid technique created by Clauset et al. could be more efficient since it produces excessively imbalanced dendrograms due to the bias towards large communities (Wakita & Tsurumi, 2007). They concluded that this technique should be abandoned. According to Schuetz and Caflisch, there is yet another approach to avoiding the formation of large communities that might be employed (Schuetz & Caflisch, 2008).

A novel greedy approach for the generalized form of weighted graphs was developed by Blondel et al. and is now recognized as the Louvain algorithm. It is based on a greedy strategy (Blondel et al., 2008). It is divided into two stages: The initial stage is to optimize local modularity to find "small" communities. It then uses the same community's nodes to create a brand-new network, whose nodes are the communities created in the first stage. Then build a new network by representing each community as a node. The above steps are iterated multiple times until positive modularity improvements are found. The modularity maximization approaches delivered superior performance compared to those developed by Clauset et al.(Clauset et al., 2004) and Wakita and Tsurumi (Wakita & Tsurumi, 2007). The first step of Louvain takes up most of the total computing time, and the resultant community structure is impacted by the node selection mechanism (Chakraborty et al., 2013). O. Gach and J.-K. Hao included an uncoarsening phase in the process followed by the Louvain. The modified multi-level approach is named "Louvain+". Vertices are enlarged during the non-coarsening stage. The refinement (optimization) process then takes place. Louvain's approach to identifying communities uses a "coarsening phase." The coarsening process is left out of this analysis. The un-coarsening enhances the quality of the result if we are concerned with optimization. Additionally, the experimental outcome demonstrated in their study concluded that adding coarsening isn't elevating the computing cost (Gach & Hao, 2014).

A parallel variation of the Louvain method was released in (Que et al., 2015). It requires very little processing power. Large, complicated, and ever-changing networks can now be processed and stored using an efficient new hash-based method. The proposed algorithm can obtain comparable results to the classic Louvain sequential technique. HU at al. developed a hybrid approach to overcome the classical Louvain'limitations (Hu et al., 2016). The offered technique improved an effective mechanism for the detection of groups. The hybrid approach integrated Louvain with the LPA (Label Propagation Algorithm) (Raghavan et al., 2007).

R. Forster presented a method for identifying communities based on GPUs (Forster, 2016). The Louvain technique and parallelization heuristics are utilized in community detection. They found that employing a graphics processor achieves a total of twelve times higher acceleration as compared to the parallel processor-based algorithms. Both strategies employ the same heuristics to make decisions. R. Forster, in another study, also developed a GPU-based parallel variant of the Louvain approach using CUDA (Compute Unified Device Architecture). The approach achieved a good speedup as per experiments and a theoretically achieved 31-time higher speed as compared to the CPU-based parallel variant of the Louvain (Forster, 2018). In addition to the above findings, the studies conclude that the effective use of GPUs can be done if the data are sufficiently vast. Another modified version of Louvain was presented in (Ryu & Kim, 2016); authors suggested restrictions on the internal search process. It helps eliminate candidate nodes that do not impact the community detection process. The findings provide impressive accelerations across a range of weighted and unweighted networks of various sizes. M. Fazlali, E. Moradi, and H. T. Malazi developed a parallel method for community detection. The algorithm starts out by treating every node in the input graph as a part of the same Community. After that, it randomly selects a community and utilizes an adaptive mechanism to distribute threads among its neighbors while accounting for all of the system's unused cores. The threads account for the chance that the neighbor will join the Community when determining modularity. Following that, the algorithm can decide whether or not to incorporate the selected nodes in the Community. The process will continue until every node has been shut down (Fazlali et al., n.d.).

Ghosh et al. presented an algorithm that employs the distributed memory notion and uses Louvain as its foundation to locate a community. In addition to it, they provided several heuristics. It has been determined that inclusion heuristics are essential for enhancing performance and scalability. Compared to the standard version, this parallel implementation demonstrated significant acceleration improvements over various real-world networks (Ghosh et al., 2018).

V.A. Traag's Random Neighbor Louvain Algorithm aids in reducing the time required to determine modularity change (ΔQ). In this method, a neighbor node is picked randomly to determine the inclusion of the node in a community in the first phase of Louvain, and the gain ΔQ is computed. ΔQ decides the node's movement; it determines whether the node would migrate to the neighborhood community or remain in the present Community. The results show that this new strategy can significantly accelerate the original processing while reducing the modularity of the prior algorithm.

Because the method cannot ensure that the chosen Community of neighbors is the best suitable Community to which it can transfer a node, random selection yields inconsistent results. This leads to random selection producing inconsistent results (Traag, 2015). In 2018, the authors offered an improved iteration of the Louvain algorithm.

The term for this methodology is Random Self-adaptive Neighbor. In this scenario, neighbors are selected randomly by applying the low likelihood of an event principle (Zhang et al., 2018).

The V. A. Traag, L. Waltman, and N. J. Van Eck presents a community detection algorithm. They named it the Leiden (Forster, 2016). The Leiden algorithm somewhat emanates from the smart local move algorithm (Waltman & Van Eck, 2013), which suggested modification in the Louvain algorithm. To put it another way, the Leiden algorithm is a modified and improved form of the Louvain. The Leiden algorithm further utilizes the speeding up of the local moving of node (Ozaki et al., 2016) and the idea of moving nodes to arbitrary neighbors (Traag, 2015) to optimize its performance. These proposals represent the most promising future directions for the Louvain algorithm. The Leiden algorithm is divided into three parts:

- It applies the movement of nodes locally
- second is the refinement process
- At the last phase of the procedure, the non-refined partition is employed to generate a starting partition for the aggregated network based on the refined partition.

The complexity of the Leiden method is relatively higher than that of the Louvain algorithm.

3. TYPICAL DATASETS NEEDED FOR TESTING VIRTUAL COMMUNITY DETECTION ALGORITHMS

Several academics from a range of disciplines, notably sociology, have modelled and abstracted complex systems from several areas to evaluate the effectiveness of community identification algorithms. As a result of these efforts, various topological reference networks with typical community structure have been identified. Typical datasets may be classified into two categories depending on the community structure detection problem: manufactured reference networks and real reference networks.

(i) Real Reference Network

A genuine reference network is an abstraction of real social networks with visible community structure, and the community structure there often has a specific practical purpose. All these networks are also available free for experimental purposes.

Figure 3. Community Structures in real-world networks

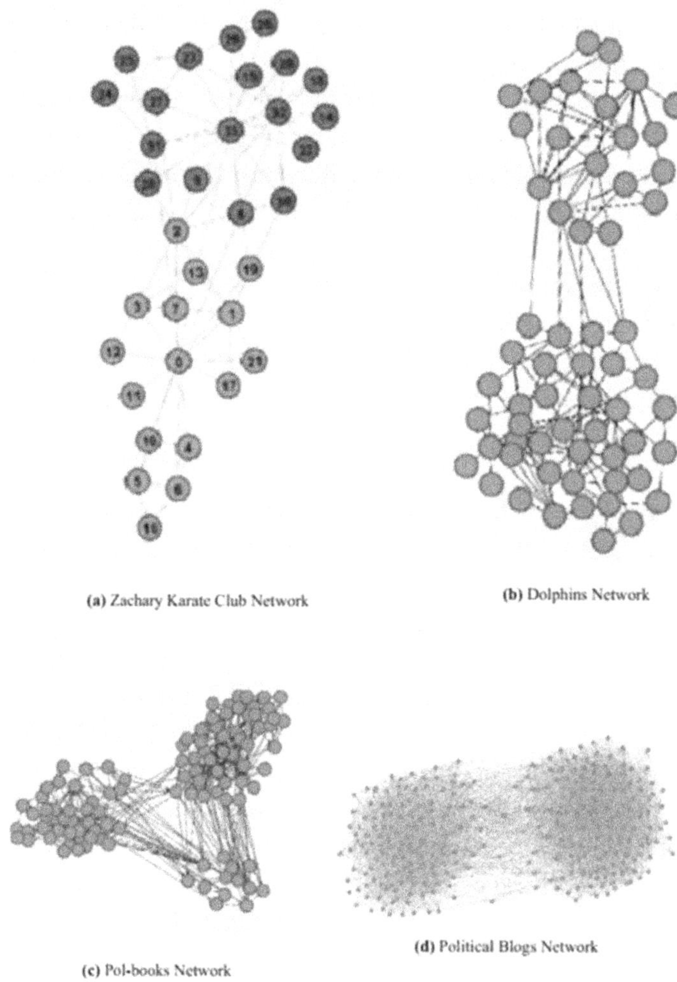

(a) Zachary Karate Club Network

(b) Dolphins Network

(c) Pol-books Network

(d) Political Blogs Network

In this study, four such networks are chosen that are named as Zachary karate network (ZKN) (Zachary, 1977), Dolphins network (Lusseau et al., 2003), Pol-books network (Newman, 2006) and Political blog network (PBN)(Adamic & Glance, 2005). The graphical representation of these networks are shown in Figure 3 and detail description is given as follows:

(i) **Zachary Karate Network (ZKN):** It is a network having 34 nodes and 78 links. Data from a university karate club was acquired in 1977 by Wayne Zachary. He was the one who collected it. Each node in the graph denotes a different member of the club, and each edge depicts a relationship between two of those members. An undirected graph generally models this network. After a disagreement between two instructors at a karate club, two groups of people within the club was formed.

(ii) **Polbooks Network:** A collection of political books pertaining to the United States that were released in 2004 and were offered through the digital bookstore Amazon.com. The links connecting books are a visual representation of the fact that the same purchasers frequently purchased multiple copies of the same book.

(iii) **Dolphins Network:** This is a network that Lusseau et al. (Lusseau et al., 2003) has created that is undirected. It illustrates the family ties of 62 different dolphin species. The network consists of 62 nodes (vertices) and 159 linkages (edges).

(iv) **Political Blogs Network (PBN):** It is a connected web with a predetermined structure. The interconnections seen between blogs are represented by the hyperlinks. The system is divided into two different assemblies: liberal and conservative. There are a total of 1490 nodes and 19090 linkages within the blogsite network.

(ii) Artificial Reference Network

Real reference networks are abstractions of real-world systems, and the communities contained within them typically have a specific background meaning. Systems are frequently influenced by a variety of events in the real world, therefore the community structure inside them does not fully adhere to the concept of community. Experts and researchers in complex science and sociology developed an artificial network reference graph model based on the power-law distribution of node degree and the small-world phenomena in complex networks. Artificial networks offer a more unique and realistic community structure, making them effective for assessing community detection techniques. Newman et al. suggested the GN network, whereas Lancichinetti et al. proposed the LFR network (Pasta & Zaidi, 2016a). These are two well-known artificial reference network models.

These two artificial networks build networks with a specific node scale and community structure using complicated network topology and node number as a parameter. As a result, they are suited for developing large-scale online social networks. Mark Newman introduced the GN artificial network, which divides nodes into communities based on network size, number of communities, and edge distribution. The degree of every node, the number of edges inside a community, and additional data determine which community a node is a part of and how clearly the network's community structure is organized overall. A network topological structure graph with 128 nodes is shown in Figure 4. It was created using the GN artificial network and is divided into 4 communities, each of which has 32 nodes and a degree of 16.

The uniform partitioning of nodes into designated communities results in an equal number of nodes in each community, even though GN artificial networks can approximate networks with community structure to some extent. The topological characteristics of networks created from GN artificial networks and actual complex networks differ significantly because of this defect. Lancichinetti et al. suggested the LFR reference network model as a solution to this issue.

Figure 4. Topological structure of GN network of 128 nodes and 4 communities

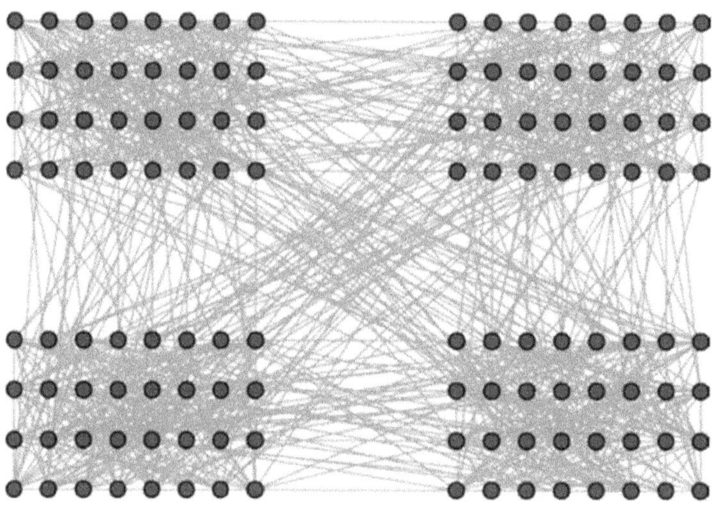

Due to the greater flexibility of the topological structure reference network, it constructs, the LFR artificial network requires more input parameters than the GN artificial network and more closely resembles genuine online social networks in terms of topological features. Users may adjust parameters in an LFR artificial network to manage the topological characteristics of individual communities as well as the network. These features include the degree distribution of nodes, the community scale, and the ratio of edges to nodes within a community. An artificial network with five communities created using LFR is seen in Figure 5.

Figure 5. LFR artificial networks with 5 communities

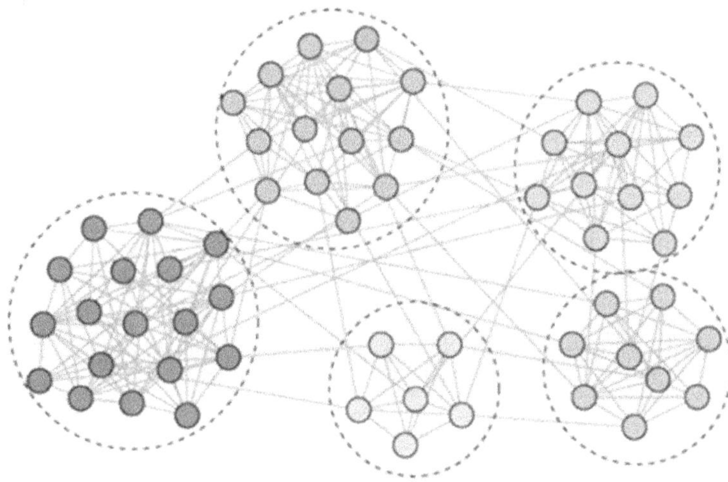

In contrast to the GN artificial network, this network more clearly resembles the topological structural features of actual networks since each community has a varied number of nodes, and the node degree is distributed according to a power-law distribution. Users may also adjust the number of overlapping nodes in LFR artificial networks to provide communities with an overlapping structure for detection methods, simulating the features of overlapping community structure in actual networks. In light of Numerous academics have analyzed different property indexes of virtual community recognition algorithms in online social networks and employed LFR artificial networks to simulate large-scale online social networks based on the properties.

4. VIRTUAL COMMUNITY DETECTION

Detecting communities in social networks is an important step towards understanding network structure and behavior. Several techniques have been created to detect communities (groups of nodes that are more densely linked to one another than the rest of the network). The **Girvan-Newman Algorithm** and Louvain are wel-known algorithms for community detection. How these algorithms process the networks for the detection of communities are discussed here.

a) **Girvan-Newman Algorithm**: Girvan-Newman iteratively eliminates edges with the highest betweenness centrality to identify communities. Since many shortest routes cross through edges linking various communities, the theory goes that these edges will have higher betweenness centrality.

Algorithm:

(i) Calculate betweenness centrality of each edge's of network.
(ii) Eliminate the edge with the highest centrality betweenness.
(iii) Compute the betweenness centrality once again for each edge that was impacted by the removal.
(iv) Until the network is divided into the necessary number of communities, repeat steps 2-3.

Example:
Consider a simple network (see Figure 6):

Figure 6. Example network

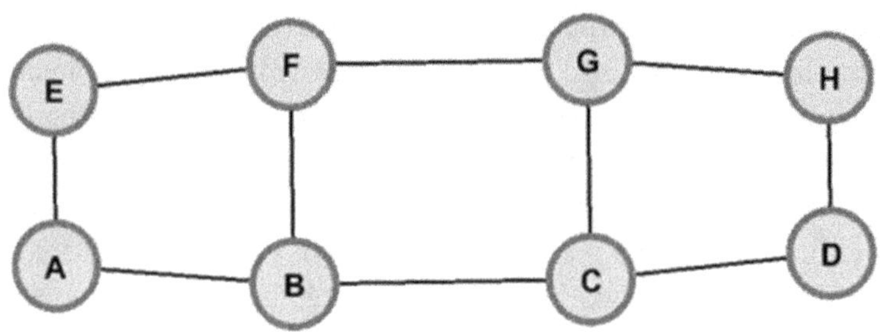

Calculate edge betweenness centrality. Assume A-B, B-C, C-D, etc., have high betweenness.

Remove edge A-B. Recalculate betweenness and remove the next highest edge. Repeat until the network is divided into two communities, say {A, E, F} and {B, C, D, G, H}.

b) **Louvain Method:** An optimization technique called the Louvain Method is used to increase a network partition's modularity. It operates in two stages: network aggregation and local modularity optimization.

Algorithm: Put every node in a community of its own.

(i) Determine the modularity gain for each node by shifting it to each neighbor's community.
(ii) If the gain is positive, move the node to the community where it is greatest.
(iii) For each node, repeat steps 2-3 until there is no more modularity gain.
(iv) Combine all of the nodes in a community into a single node.
(v) On the aggregated network, repeat steps 1 through 5 until the maximum modularity is reached.

Example:
Consider the same network given in Figure 6:

(i) Every node in its own community should come first.
(ii) Determine the increase in modularity by shifting nodes. As an example, if moving A to the community of B promotes modularity.
(iii) Combine nodes within the same group.
(iv) Continue till the modularity reaches its maximum. {A, B, E, F} and {C, D, G, H} might be the final communities.

CONCLUSION

Online social networks have been a key area of study interest in recent times due to the emergence of social network services such as Facebook, Twitter, and Sina Weibo. For social network analysis, virtual community discovery in these networks is essential. Studying social networks' topology, determining user clustering and impact factors, and enhancing information indexing, recommendation, propagation, control, and public security are all made easier with an understanding of their community structures. Research on community detection algorithms is therefore very valuable in both social and practical contexts.

The notion of community structure is condensed in this chapter, and popular community identification techniques are included. Related research on virtual community discovery techniques is also included. Even though community detection algorithms are effective, further study is still required in a number of areas: The majority of existing algorithms target static social networks, meaning that their structure does not alter over time. On the other hand, social networks on the internet are dynamic, constantly adding new edges and nodes. It is difficult to identify community structures in these dynamic networks. One option is to use snapshots transferred to static structures at predefined times, however this approach is not ideal for real-time detection due to its high temporal complexity and sensitivity to noise. For dynamic networks based on "incremental" data, efficient algorithms are required. The majority of current algorithms are limited to homogeneous networks with a single kind of nodes and edges and are modifications of classical complex network methods. Real-world social networks and internet technologies are combined to create online social networks, which frequently have a variety of node and edge kinds. One important area of study continues to be the development of effective community identification methods for these complex, dynamic, and varied network architectures.

REFERENCES

Adamic, L. A., & Glance, N. (2005). The political blogosphere and the 2004 US election: divided they blog. *Proceedings of the 3rd International Workshop on Link Discovery*, 36–43. DOI: 10.1145/1134271.1134277

Albert, R., & Barabási, A.-L. (2002). Statistical mechanics of complex networks. *Reviews of Modern Physics*, 74(1), 47–97. DOI: 10.1103/RevModPhys.74.47

Bagrow, J. P. (2008). Evaluating local community methods in networks. *Journal of Statistical Mechanics*, 2008(05), P05001. Advance online publication. DOI: 10.1088/1742-5468/2008/05/P05001

Barabási, A.-L., & Albert, R. (1999). Emergence of scaling in random networks. *Science*, 286(5439), 509–512. DOI: 10.1126/science.286.5439.509 PMID: 10521342

Blondel, V. D., Guillaume, J.-L., Lambiotte, R., & Lefebvre, E. (2008). Fast unfolding of communities in large networks. *Journal of Statistical Mechanics*, 2008(10), P10008. Advance online publication. DOI: 10.1088/1742-5468/2008/10/P10008

Chakraborty, T., Srinivasan, S., Ganguly, N., Bhowmick, S., & Mukherjee, A. (2013). Constant Communities in Complex Networks. *Scientific Reports*, 3(1), 1825. DOI: 10.1038/srep01825 PMID: 23661107

Clauset, A., Newman, M. E. J., & Moore, C. (2004). Finding community structure in very large networks. *Physical Review. E*, 70(6), 066111. DOI: 10.1103/PhysRevE.70.066111 PMID: 15697438

Danon, L., Díaz-Guilera, A., & Arenas, A. (2006). The effect of size heterogeneity on community identification in complex networks. *Journal of Statistical Mechanics*, 2006(11), 11010–P11010. DOI: 10.1088/1742-5468/2006/11/P11010

ERDdS, P., & R&wi, A. (1959). On random graphs I. *Publ. Math. Debrecen, 6*(290–297), 18.

Erdos, P., & Rényi, A. (1960). On the evolution of random graphs. *Publ. Math. Inst. Hung. Acad. Sci*, 5(1), 17–60.

Fazlali, M., Moradi, E., & Tabatabaee Malazi, H. (n.d.). *Adaptive Parallel Louvain Community Detection on a Multicore Platform*.

Fiedler, M. (1975). A property of eigenvectors of nonnegative symmetric matrices and its application to graph theory. *Czechoslovak Mathematical Journal*, 25(4), 619–633. DOI: 10.21136/CMJ.1975.101357

Forster, R. (2016). Louvain community detection with parallel heuristics on GPUs. *2016 IEEE 20th Jubilee International Conference on Intelligent Engineering Systems (INES)*, 227–232. DOI: 10.1109/INES.2016.7555126

Forster, R. (2018). *Parallel Louvain Community Detection Optimized for GPUs*. http://arxiv.org/abs/1805.10904

Gach, O., & Hao, J.-K. (2014). *Improving the Louvain Algorithm for Community Detection with Modularity Maximization.*, DOI: 10.1007/978-3-319-11683-9_12

Ghosh, S., Halappanavar, M., Tumeo, A., Kalyanaraman, A., Lu, H., Chavarria-Miranda, D., Khan, A., & Gebremedhin, A. (2018). Distributed louvain algorithm for graph community detection. *Proceedings - 2018 IEEE 32nd International Parallel and Distributed Processing Symposium, IPDPS 2018*, 885–895. DOI: 10.1109/IPDPS.2018.00098

Girvan, M., & Newman, M. E. J. (2002a). Community structure in social and biological networks. *Proceedings of the National Academy of Sciences of the United States of America*, 99(12), 7821–7826. DOI: 10.1073/pnas.122653799 PMID: 12060727

Girvan, M., & Newman, M. E. J. (2002b). Community structure in social and biological networks. *Proceedings of the National Academy of Sciences of the United States of America*, 99(12), 7821–7826. DOI: 10.1073/pnas.122653799 PMID: 12060727

Hu, B., Li, W., Huo, X., Liang, Y., Gao, M., & Pei, P. (2016). Improving Louvain Algorithm for Community Detection. *Proceedings of the 2016 International Conference on Artificial Intelligence and Engineering Applications*. DOI: 10.2991/aiea-16.2016.20

Kernighan, B. W., & Lin, S. (1970). An efficient heuristic procedure for partitioning graphs. *The Bell System Technical Journal*, 49(2), 291–307. DOI: 10.1002/j.1538-7305.1970.tb01770.x

Kumpula, J. M., Onnela, J.-P., Saramäki, J., Kertész, J., & Kaski, K. (2009). Model of community emergence in weighted social networks. *Computer Physics Communications*, 180(4), 517–522. DOI: 10.1016/j.cpc.2008.12.016

Lancichinetti, A., & Fortunato, S. (2009). Benchmarks for testing community detection algorithms on directed and weighted graphs with overlapping communities. *Physical Review. E*, 80(1), 016118. DOI: 10.1103/PhysRevE.80.016118 PMID: 19658785

Lancichinetti, A., Fortunato, S., & Radicchi, F. (2008). Benchmark graphs for testing community detection algorithms. *Physical Review. E*, 78(4), 046110. DOI: 10.1103/PhysRevE.78.046110 PMID: 18999496

Lusseau, D., Schneider, K., Boisseau, O. J., Haase, P., Slooten, E., & Dawson, S. M. (2003). The bottlenose dolphin community of doubtful sound features a large proportion of long-lasting associations: Can geographic isolation explain this unique trait? *Behavioral Ecology and Sociobiology*, 54(4), 396–405. DOI: 10.1007/s00265-003-0651-y

Meena, S. S., & Tokekar, D. V. (2021). Community detection in social networks by incorporating the preferential selection. *Journal of Complex Networks*, 9(6), cnab040. Advance online publication. DOI: 10.1093/comnet/cnab040

Meena, S. S., & Tokekar, V. (2020). Modularity based Community Detection in Social Networks. *International Journal of Engineering and Advanced Technology*, 9(3), 564–569. DOI: 10.35940/ijeat.B3382.029320

Meena, S. S., & Tokekar, V. (2023). *A Model to Generate Benchmark Network with Community Structure.*, DOI: 10.1007/978-981-16-9967-2_23

Molloy, M., & Reed, B. (1995a). A critical point for random graphs with a given degree sequence. *Random Structures and Algorithms*, 6(2–3), 161–180. DOI: 10.1002/rsa.3240060204

Molloy, M., & Reed, B. (1995b). A critical point for random graphs with a given degree sequence. *Random Structures and Algorithms*, 6(2–3), 161–180. DOI: 10.1002/rsa.3240060204

Newman, M. E. J. (2003). The structure and function of complex networks. *SIAM Review*, 45(2), 167–256. DOI: 10.1137/S003614450342480

Newman, M. E. J. (2004). Fast algorithm for detecting community structure in networks. *Physical Review. E*, 69(6), 066133. DOI: 10.1103/PhysRevE.69.066133 PMID: 15244693

Newman, M. E. J. (2006). Modularity and community structure in networks. *Proceedings of the National Academy of Sciences of the United States of America*, 103(23), 8577–8582. DOI: 10.1073/pnas.0601602103 PMID: 16723398

Newman, M. E. J., & Girvan, M. (2004). Finding and evaluating community structure in networks. *Physical Review. E*, 69(2), 026113. DOI: 10.1103/PhysRevE.69.026113 PMID: 14995526

Newman, M. E. J., Moore, C., & Watts, D. J. (2000). Mean-Field Solution of the Small-World Nctwork Modcl. *Physical Review Letters*, 84(14), 3201–3204. DOI: 10.1103/PhysRevLett.84.3201 PMID: 11019047

Ng, A., Jordan, M., & Weiss, Y. (2001). On Spectral Clustering: Analysis and an algorithm. In T. Dietterich, S. Becker, & Z. Ghahramani (Eds.), *Advances in Neural Information Processing Systems* (Vol. 14). MIT Press. https://proceedings.neurips.cc/paper_files/paper/2001/file/801272ee79cfde7fa5960571fee36b9b-Paper.pdf

Ozaki, N., Tezuka, H., & Inaba, M. (2016). A Simple Acceleration Method for the Louvain Algorithm. *International Journal of Computer and Electrical Engineering*, 8(3), 207–218. DOI: 10.17706/IJCEE.2016.8.3.207-218

Pasta, M. Q., Jan, Z., Sallaberry, A., & Zaidi, F. (2013). Tunable and Growing Network Generation Model with Community Structures. *2013 International Conference on Cloud and Green Computing*, 233–240. DOI: 10.1109/CGC.2013.44

Pasta, M. Q., & Zaidi, F. (2016a). Leveraging evolution dynamics to generate benchmark complex networks with community structures. *ArXiv Preprint ArXiv:1606.01169.*

Pasta, M. Q., & Zaidi, F. (2016b). Leveraging evolution dynamics to generate benchmark complex networks with community structures. *ArXiv Preprint ArXiv:1606.01169.*

Price, D. J. (1966). *NETWORKS OF SCIENTIFIC PAPERS.*

Que, X., Checconi, F., Petrini, F., & Gunnels, J. A. (2015). Scalable Community Detection with the Louvain Algorithm. *2015 IEEE International Parallel and Distributed Processing Symposium*, 28–37. DOI: 10.1109/IPDPS.2015.59

Raghavan, U. N., Albert, R., & Kumara, S. (2007). Near linear time algorithm to detect community structures in large-scale networks. *Physical Review E: Statistical, Nonlinear, and Soft Matter Physics*, 76(3), 036106. Advance online publication. DOI: 10.1103/PhysRevE.76.036106 PMID: 17930305

Ryu, S., & Kim, D. (2016). *Quick Community Detection of Big Graph Data Using Modified Louvain Algorithm.* https://doi.org/DOI: 10.1109/HPCC-SmartCity-DSS.2016.167

Sallaberry, A., Zaidi, F., & Melançon, G. (2013). Model for generating artificial social networks having community structures with small-world and scale-free properties. *Social Network Analysis and Mining*, 3(3), 597–609. DOI: 10.1007/s13278-013-0105-0

Schuetz, P., & Caflisch, A. (2008). Efficient modularity optimization by multistep greedy algorithm and vertex mover refinement. *Physical Review. E*, 77(4), 046112. DOI: 10.1103/PhysRevE.77.046112 PMID: 18517695

Shang, J., Liu, L., Li, X., Xie, F., & Wu, C. (2016). Targeted revision: A learning-based approach for incremental community detection in dynamic networks. *Physica A*, 443, 70–85. DOI: 10.1016/j.physa.2015.09.072

Traag, V. A. (2015). *Faster unfolding of communities: speeding up the Louvain algorithm*. DOI: 10.1103/PhysRevE.92.032801

Van Dongen, S. (2000). Graph clustering by flow simulation. *PhD Thesis, University of Utrecht.*

Wakita, K., & Tsurumi, T. (2007). Finding community structure in mega-scale social networks. *Proceedings of the 16th International Conference on World Wide Web*, 1275–1276. DOI: 10.1145/1242572.1242805

Waltman, L., & Van Eck, N. J. (2013). A smart local moving algorithm for large-scale modularity-based community detection. *The European Physical Journal B*, 86(11), 471. Advance online publication. DOI: 10.1140/epjb/e2013-40829-0

Watts, D. J., & Strogatz, S. H. (1998). Collective dynamics of 'small-world' networks. *Nature*, 393(6684), 440–442. DOI: 10.1038/30918 PMID: 9623998

Xie, Z., Li, X., & Wang, X. (2007). A new community-based evolving network model. *Physica A*, 384(2), 725–732. DOI: 10.1016/j.physa.2007.05.031

Xu, X.-J., Zhang, X., & Mendes, J. F. F. (2009). Growing community networks with local events. *Physica A*, 388(7), 1273–1278. DOI: 10.1016/j.physa.2008.12.022

Zachary, W. W. (1977). An information flow model for conflict and fission in small groups. *Journal of Anthropological Research*, 33(4), 452–473. DOI: 10.1086/jar.33.4.3629752

Zaidi, F. (2013). Small world networks and clustered small world networks with random connectivity. *Social Network Analysis and Mining*, 3(1), 51–63. DOI: 10.1007/s13278-012-0052-1

Zhang, Z., Pu, P., Han, D., & Tang, M. (2018). Self-adaptive Louvain algorithm: Fast and stable community detection algorithm based on the principle of small probability event. *Physica A*, 506, 975–986. DOI: 10.1016/j.physa.2018.04.036

Zhou, X., Xiang, L., & Xiao-Fan, W. (2008). Weighted Evolving Nctworks with Self organized Communities. *Communications in Theoretical Physics*, 50(1), 261–266. DOI: 10.1088/0253-6102/50/1/50

Chapter 8
Grid Management and Privacy Concerns

Sunita Kumar
https://orcid.org/0000-0002-0628-1873
Christ University, India

Nabanita Ghosh
https://orcid.org/0000-0001-5176-7314
Christ University, India

Shivi Khanna
https://orcid.org/0000-0002-4410-5694
Christ University, India

A. Sridharan
https://orcid.org/0000-0002-0753-3585
NSB, Bangalore, India

ABSTRACT

The integration of advanced technologies and data analytics in smart grid management brings numerous benefits, but it also raises privacy concerns. One major issue is the collection and use of granular energy consumption data, which can reveal sensitive information about individuals' activities and behavior patterns. The interconnectivity of the smart grid with other systems and devices further increases the potential for unauthorized data collection and surveillance. Additionally, data security and protection are essential to safeguarding personal information against cyber threats and un-authorized access. To address these privacy issues, robust privacy protec-tion measures should be implemented, including clear guidelines on data collection, usage, and retention, informed consent mechanisms, strong en-cryption and authentication protocols, and regulatory frameworks. Collabo-ration

DOI: 10.4018/979-8-3693-3868-1.ch008

among policymakers, industry stakeholders, and privacy advocates is necessary to balancing the merits of smart grid technology and individual privacy rights, ensuring that the potential of the smart grid

INTRODUCTION

Rome is not built in a day," this proverb reiterates, pointing to today's competitive technological developments conceived hundreds of years ago. Limited use of resources, limited wants and needs, and limited exposures of bygone days went to oblivion as modern civilians are standing on the verge of expansion and diversification, and their growing demands compelled the implementation of technological frameworks and systems. Today's smart grid system was the fruit of the historic think tanks. Looking back, the needs were limited; power was made within the local limits, around the borders of dwelling. Most domestic usage primarily rested on small energy domains. However, the grid was there for utilities to deliver the electricity to consumer homes, and they are about to pay for their usage every month. This restricted and singular interaction makes it difficult for the grid system to react to the dynamic and upsurging power demands of the 21st century.

Figure 1. Comparison between traditional vs smart grid

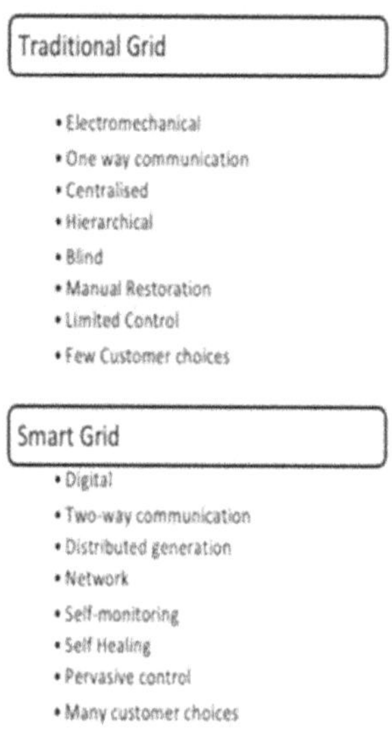

Figure 1 shows how the traditional smart grid functions differently. The traditional grid and smart grid are two distinct approaches to electricity distribution. The traditional grid operates on a one-way system with centralized power generation and limited visibility into consumer energy usage. It needs advanced communication and control capabilities, resulting in efficient resource management. In contrast, the intelligent grid incorporates modern technology, bidirectional communication, and real-time data analysis to enhance grid efficiency, reliability, and sustainability. It enables proactive management of energy consumption, empowers consumers to make informed decisions, and facilitates the integration of renewable energy sources. The smart grid's advanced capabilities improve overall grid performance and support the transition towards a more sustainable and resilient energy future ((Liu & Zhang, 2012)

Figure 2. Application of smart grid

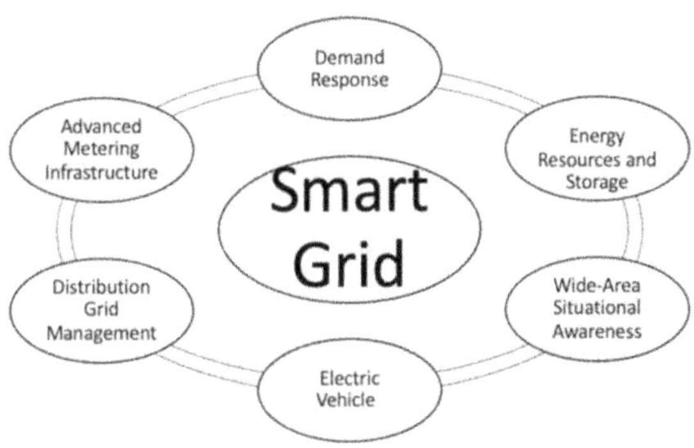

1.APPLICATION OF SMART GRID

Figure 2 reveals the application of the intelligent grid mechanism. The smart grid is an advanced electrical grid system incorporating modern technology to enhance power distribution efficiency, reliability, and continuity. It fetches bidirectional transmission between utilities and customers, enabling real-time supervision and control of energy consumption. Through the integration of sensors, smart meters, and automation systems, the smart grid enables utilities to obtain detailed insights into energy usage patterns, identify areas of high demand, and implement load-balancing strategies. This two-way exchange also empowers consumers to participate actively in energy management, enabling them to understand consumption based on real-time data. The ability of the smart grid to optimize energy distribution and bring up a more responsive and interactive relationship between utilities and consumers has a distinguished role in achieving a sustainable, resilient energy future (Khatib et al., 2015).

The innovative grid technology, today's invention, evolved as a way of communication where both the providers and users of electricity believe in information exchange. Today's intelligent grid framework has become more innovative, greener, robust, and effective due to modern technology automation and communication systems. Today's smart grid also supports vehicle charging. The age-old concept of power generation shifted to the modern-day efficient power transmission system. Consumers also supported the change, and a new power distribution methodology in an intelligent grid framework helped optimize the power requirements. Smart homes interact with the grid and enable consumers to customize their electricity needs by judiciously measuring consumption through intelligent meter devices, which, in other words, would support reducing electricity bills. A Home Area Network (HAN) connects the home appliances to the electricity management system. The primary responsibility of HAN is to reduce the electricity bills by technically modulating energy consumption, keeping in mind not to compromise with the actual requirement. Modern grid systems respond to the complications generated by renewable energy sources. Smart grid, as the modern name goes, removes the traditional feature of erroneous power management.

Cost to customers is also ascertained based on the dissemination of power at a specific period; cost is not uniformly charged to customers throughout the day for the use of power. During the peak hours of the day, since additional power plants are to be utilized to manage more considerable power demand, the cost becomes dearer during the peak use hours. To manage the cost and ensure seamless power distribution to the customers, both the utility and the consumers need to strategize their plan to release power and use the received power. This will subdue the outages and curb the control room's peak-hour power requirement. This, in turn, will also help the engineers. The distribution channels take the supply from the route named as utility and transmit the same to the residential and commercial blocks looking for the power source. The utility still believes in using the traditional system of power distribution. Any catastrophic and calamitous issue would severely damage the power distribution system. These disasters also bring in some interruptions in the smooth flow of power distribution, which might be attributed to the cause of energy fluctuations, and the intelligent grid here plays a significant role in locating the inconsistencies in power and thereby restoring—the power. The distribution methodology, accompanied by the customers' cooperation, can only lead to flawless and uninterrupted power flow cost-effectively. HAN aids in charging an electric vehicle, which consumes considerable energy. Consumers can charge such vehicles during non-peak hours to avoid significant power disruption. Moreover, this will also make the cost affordable to the customers. The transformation from the traditional fuel-based era to the modern electric and green vehicle will pollute society less and contribute to greenhouse gas emissions.

Figure 3. Working of HAN

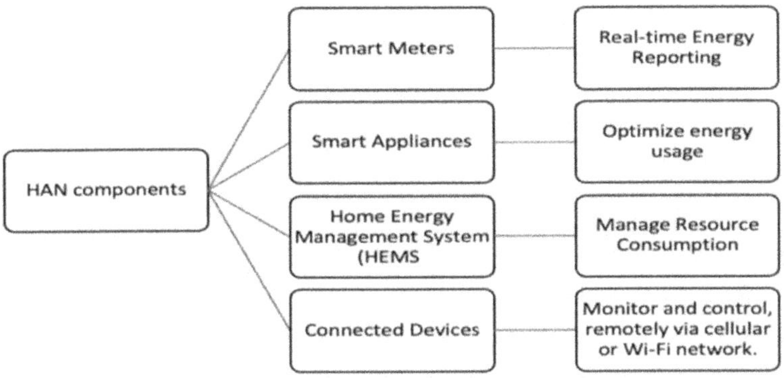

2. CONCEPT OF PRIVACY AND PRIVACY STANDARDS IN SMART GRID MANAGEMENT:

Smart grids have emerged as advanced electricity distribution systems incorporating communication and information technologies to improve energy efficiency and reliability. The most essential component of an intelligent grid is energy consumption monitoring, which provides running information about energy usage patterns to both utility providers and consumers. In today's scenario, smart grids are the future of energy dissemination, and they also promise to revamp the methods of production, distribution, and, finally, the consumption of electricity. Smart grids utilize advanced technologies such as sensors, data analytics, and automation to make the grid more strengthened, trustworthy, and sustainable. However, smart grids also pose significant privacy risks, as they collect vast amounts of data about consumers' energy usage patterns. However, as intelligent grids gather and transmit vast amounts of sensitive data, privacy concerns have become a significant challenge.

Technology leads to innovation, and the implementation of modern tools and strategies are the fruits of technology. Similarly, technology is instrumental in the success of smart grid management. Looking at the traditional days with limited wants and limited usage, the technology was in mothers' wombs. However, with the rapidity of transformation and the emergent need to address climate change issues to gear up the prioritization of implementing a carbon-neutral society for safety and hygiene, efficient power management has gained significant importance. However, the transmission of power under the framework of the intelligent grid technique also needs to adopt the privacy aspect and bear in mind the upkeeping of the privacy standards (Leszczyna, 2018). The bidirectional movement of information from electricity users to providers of services entails various probabilities of mismanagement like other data processing mechanisms. The massive use of intelligent meters where energy consumption-related information is trapped leads to significant public discomfort about the technological operation. So, a seamless switchover from the age-old method to the intelligent grid systems needs to keep the fears and doubts of power users in abeyance. In addition, their personal and private matters must be explicitly protected (Uludag et al., 2015).

Intelligent metering infrastructure (SMI) significantly influences innovative grid management. It enables the smart grid to control, monitor, and manage different domains. Still, security concerns prevail in the smart grid technique in contrast with the traditional technique. Multiple heterogeneous appliances need to be coordinated across a public communication network. Due to the internet and wireless network problems, smart grid systems are vulnerable to security assaults. This persisting problem can be reasonably arrested. by introducing a policy of protecting the privacy issues of the users (Rao et al., 2022)

3 APPLICATION OF SMART METERS

With the spreading of smart meters in households, consumers are directly affected by the technology. Personal data is collected, and therefore, the habits of the consumers are being vigilled by the electricity providers (Petrlic, 2010). There are both functional and non-functional requirements for an intelligent grid system.

3.1 Functional Requirements:

Besides data collection and processing, care should be given to communicating the intelligent meters with various parties, namely ESP, grid operator, and electricity user. Periodical consumption of electricity-related data for ESP is a major functional step for smart meters. Another essential requirement is the updated information provided by ESP. Customers' appliances must be capable of capturing the commands provided by the ESP.

The grid operator needs the consumption data from the users to charge the ESP for the provisioning of the infrastructure. Updating the smart meters software by the grid operator is also a must.

The power meter introduced by Google is already in vogue. Customers can send their data on electricity consumption to Google, which can present it in a graphical form to enable the visualization of data, which allows the consumers to keep track of the present electricity utilization of devices. This eliminates the interrogation and involvement of third parties.

3.2 Non-functional Requirements:

The availability and reliability of the smart meters are needed as the ESP is significantly dependent on the updated electricity utilization data and the correct computation of the monthly bill. In addition, scalability is an essential feature of intelligent grids.

3.3 Merits and demerits of smart meters:

The principal merit of using smart meters is the process of billing the consumers accurately; again, the increased rate of capturing the private consumption-related inputs of the power user with the utility also brings the concern of leakage and non-confidentiality of information. Again, every user needs smart billing and wants to minimize their vital day-to-day expenses concerning electricity and power consumption, so to protect the billing information technique, battery management, zero knowledge, and homomorphic encryption techniques can be an option. In the innovative grid framework, the communication between the user of the power and the intelligent meter device is handled correctly by using insecure channels to manage the demand responses during peak hours. This poses genuine threats to the confidentiality of the power consumption-related information of the users (Ali et al., 2022)

3.4 Privacy Goals:

Regular and irregular power behavior can easily be traced with an adversary's involvement in the smart home's energy consumption. In order to restore security and privacy, energy consumption undergoes encryption either at the appliance level or before it leaves the HAN. The details of the consumers' energy consumption captured by HAN are further processed, and CC receives the same from various intelligent meter devices. CC continuously collects consumption details from different devices. The information received is fully encrypted and then aggregated to keep the information safe and untampered; if an intruder peeps into and changes the information, then the purpose is defeated.

Specific new schemes exist for HAN to ensure confidentiality. The schemes are homomorphic encryption, blind signature, and in-network aggregation.

Integrity in competent grid management means the message sent by the sender and that same message when received by the receiver on the other side without alteration. For the integrity of HAN data, some schemes were introduced: message digest, MAC, digital signature and H-MAC.

Anonymity in competent grid management means protecting one's identity from one appliance to another, appliance to smart meters, smart meters to SP, and SP to the appliance. On the other hand, some vital strategies maintained for anonymity are PLAK, ASF, and TAI.

Availability in competent grid management means making the data, applications, appliances, and systems available to users whenever needed. Availability is defeated when someone attempts to make unethical access to the system, thereby keeping the network busy.

4. CYBERSECURITY IN SMART GRID SYSTEM:

Cyber security needs an appropriate application to the integrated system of power, Internet technology, communication, and network domains to maintain the reliability of the intelligent grid system and, on the other hand, consumers' security. So, cybersecurity in an intelligent grid attempts to balance power and cyber system technologies and processes, power system operations and governance. Whatever the cyber security system, it should in no way be able to impede the safety and reliability of power system operations.

4.1 Cybersecurity principles in smart grid

The prominent drawback of the intelligent grid system is the cyber security that has crept into it. It makes the progress of innovative grid applications much slower and faster. Generation, transmission, distribution, and consumption are vital areas of the intelligent grid framework. Privacy, confidentiality, and data authentication are needed to maintain reliability and efficiency so that strange alterations throughout the infrastructure can be arrested. Therefore, distributed cyber security systems must exist to maintain data integrity and monitor the architecture.

4.2 Types of cyber-attacks:

An adversary would search for an entry point to enter the network and constitute an attack. The types of the attacks are:

Impersonation attack: An appliance impersonates the intelligent meters and requests the other appliance to a summary of consumption report every 15 minutes. This brings the possibility of electricity tampering.

Eavesdropping: When an adversary eavesdrops on the smart meters, it can easily trace every inch of the users' movement, leading to a significant compromise of the users' privacy and possibilities for other thefts and malpractices.

Replay attack: In case of the need for additional power or if an appliance is set up for a non-peak hour, a replay attack can change the demand, or the appliance can be set on immediately, and that leads to disaster.

Alteration attack: An alternation attack occurs when a HAN, appliance and intelligent meters are compromised due to the unethical entry of the adversary into the consumption report or when the adversary makes a forgery.

Message modification attack: When an adversary exists between the smart grid and HAN and alternates the messages, there is a probability of danger and damage to the parties concerned.

Energy import/export attack: An intelligent grid enables distributed power generation where a consumer can fix some renewable sources of power generation, such as if an electric vehicle is in the mode of extracting from the smart grid at a peak hour load a significant quantum of power which is avoidable that leads to load shedding and power falls.

4.3 Framework for smart grid security analysis:

Some necessary countermeasures to avoid the aforementioned typical cyber-attacks are as follows:

- Firewall
- Encryption
- VPN
- Early warning systems
- Antivirus software
- Dynamic reconfiguration system
- Access control
- IDS
- Demilitarized zones for technical solutions

5 PRIVACY IMPACT ASSESSMENT IN SMART GRIDS

Many templates and tools have been developed to support the implementation of a Data Protection Impact Assessment (DIPA). Recently, they have been developed as a web-based application to make intelligent grids with user-friendly interfaces and enable teamwork. One assessment tool explained here is developed using the Django Python framework to develop web-based applications rapidly (Piatkowska et al., 2017). Initially, a risk assessment exercise was performed to have three main sub-parts. Firstly, smart grid configured assets were analyzed for cyber risk that external threats could exploit. Besides this, threats relevant to each asset were identified based on historical experiences. Secondly, the probability for each threat manifesting was identified using two indicators: (i) a level of unfortified and (ii) the aptness of a source of danger (threat actor). Lastly, the impact assessment of primary assets which might be impacted due to cyber-attacks on supporting assets is measured. The impact is determined by outlining an inimical effect and the level of the identification of the data subject. The risk level is calculated as the sum of the probability of a threat to a supporting asset and the impact of a compromise of a primary asset on a data subject. The relationships between threats associated with various assets configured to the smart grid and their impact assessment are used to determine a risk level. This data was saved in the tool 4 (Tariq et al., 2021). These data-driven risk measurements can be presented to the users and ranked by their level to support risk summarizing and treatment. This step is an upgrade of the previous techniques, which merely focused on dealing with the current cyber-attack. This step is intended to determine whether an organization is operating an intelligent grid service in a manner that preserves privacy. The user can choose self-privacy targets relevant to them under scrutiny from a catalogue provided by the DPIA template. Subsequently, they are asked to pinpoint all the possible privacy threats that could disturb the selected privacy targets and provide methods to ensure the implementation of these targets, e.g., developing a privacy framework or attesting the data processing systems in place to be glassier. Finally, the tool could generate a report in PDF format that can be downloaded. The report summarizes the service description, the risk assessment results, and proposed risk treatment strategies (Tariq et al., 2021). It is intended that this report can be submitted to a national data protection authority to support compliance with the General Data Protection Regulation (GDPR) (Information Commissioner's Office, 2009).

In recent times, many new types of Smart Grids have been introduced, such as neighborhood area networks (NANs), home area networks (HANs) and vehicle-to-grid (V2G) networks. Moreover, the scope and coverage of the vast area network (WAN) have also spread out. It is now being used in various other networks. HAN is a link between intelligent household appliances and the house smart meter; thus, the smart meter takes the reading of the appliances and sends data to the utility company (Kloza et al., 2015). The industrial area networks (IANs) and the building area networks (BANs) are types of HANs which connect many HANs in the same industrial or residual area to a local substation. NAN forwards the report for the region in its vicinity to the control center (CC) of the utility grid through the existing WAN (Islam et al., 2023).

6 PRIVACY REGULATIONS AND LEGAL CONSIDERATIONS IN SMART GRIDS

Smart grids have revolutionized distribution systems' functioning, the associated job demands, and the dynamics among users, operators, and emerging stakeholders. Consequently, it becomes crucial to comprehend the legal aspects connected to smart grids. Traditionally, distribution systems were solely responsible for delivering electricity, entailing power transfer from the transmission system and subsequent transformer stations through the distribution grid to end users for diverse purposes. Consumers were passive in electricity consumption, adhering to mostly predictable consumption patterns (He et al., 2012). Over the period, the smart grids have been upgraded, leading to the extension of responsibilities for the distribution system. While they were earlier only transporting electricity, they now also work as communication networks for transferring data and information (often susceptible information of its users). This leads to an obvious research question as to whether the distribution system and its operators can engelectricity distribution of electricity and the operation of a communication network, which carries confidential information of its customers. A liberalized market setting is based on the principle of independent network operation. In essence, it provides all its operators equal access to its system, thus creating a perfect market situation wherein anyone can be a producer or consumer in its structure. In a liberalized market environment, the core principle is the independent operation of the network. This means that all operators have equal access to the system, creating an ideal market where anyone can participate as a producer or consumer. Since communication networks and data play essential roles in smart grids, it is crucial to ensure that various operators and related systems can access them. To establish a liberalized market framework for smart grids, lawmakers must carefully evaluate whether Distribution System Operators should take on new responsibilities in managing the (intelligent) grid system or if doing so would hinder potential markets. This evaluation should balance the need for coordination for system operation purposes and fostering competition for flexibility services system users offer (Diestelmeier, 2021).

6.1 Legal framework in India

Digital India is an ambitious program of this nation to make its people match with global technological upgrades. Additionally, this development has opened the door for a significant influx of digital data nationwide. It represents a thoughtfully designed digital framework that guarantees robust connectivity and seamless integration of services, particularly in trendy urban areas. The intelligent grid is a promising electricity delivery infrastructure that incorporates communication and information technologies, enabling awareness, prediction, and efficient utilization of energy consumption.

In 2013, the Ministry of Power (MoP) collaborated with the India Smart Grid Forum and India Smart Grid Task Force to publish a bright grid vision and roadmap for India. This policy document, in line with MoP's objective of ensuring accessible and affordable electricity for all, outlines a framework to address cybersecurity issues in smart grids.

Although intelligent grids are an integral part of the development of any digital nation, they come with specific cyber security threats and concerns, particularly to a nation's cyber structure. Increased propinquity of data and information on digital technologies may render the grids vulnerable to cyber threats, putting stored data and its systems at significant risk. A modern power system needs to be more efficient and reliable, with policies and frameworks in place. Like other developed and developing nations, India also finds data privacy and cyber security to be key challenges in Smart Grid Management (Diestelmeier, 2019). There is always a very high risk of malicious attacks by hackers on the smart grid, which may compromise the private information of its consumers; attackers may break the security network and get illegal access to user-based software and edit load conditions, destabilizing the grid. Hackers who compromise a smart meter reduce energy costs by altering data stored using remote systems. This incorporation of wrong information can provide misleading information on energy consumption in a local area (Anaya & Pollitt, 2021).

The release of the National Cyber Security Policy 2013 introduced a framework that offers guidance on actions concerning the security of cyberspace. The group responsible for this initiative, operating under the guidance of the Planning Commission, also published an IT development plan for India. This plan includes a roadmap for cyber security, highlighting six key areas of priority and focus: the establishment of a legal structure, policies to ensure a secure cyberspace, compliance and assurance measures, the development of a secure research and development environment, early identification of security threats and the creation of protocols for timely responses, awareness of security issues, and training and development programs in the field of cyber security. Collaboration among relevant stakeholders is also emphasized in this plan (Rakesh & Hickok, 2023).

7 CRYPTOGRAPHIC TECHNIQUES FOR PRIVACY PROTECTION IN SMART GRIDS

Cryptography is a method to secure and verify data transfer between secure and insecure communication channels. It enables storing or transmitting sensitive information over unsecured networks, ensuring that only authorized individuals can access it while preventing unauthorized access. Cryptography is vital in safeguarding confidential and sensitive data across different systems. Cryptography makes the data unreachable to unrelated parties by various transformations (Rasheed, 2011). Data cryptography works by converting readable text, visual images, and audio content scrambles for strangers, thus protecting them from getting into the hands of cyber attackers or any other threats.

The primary objective of cryptography is to protect data from unauthorized individuals. When information is in a format that can be easily read and understood, it is referred to as plaintext or clear text. Encryption transforms the plaintext into a form that can only be comprehended with proper access. This transformation results in unreadable information known as ciphertext. Decrypting ciphertext involves converting it back to its original form. Cryptosystems are technologies that enable encryption and decryption for users. The algorithm and software utilized to do encryption determine the complexity and security standard of encryption. Therefore, algorithms play an essential role in this process.

The security of any encryption system is contingent upon the security principle put forth by Kirchhoff. Kirchhoff's principle states that the security of an encryption system should rely on the secrecy of the encryption/decryption key rather than the encryption algorithm itself (Mandal et al., 2012). A research study examining cryptography algorithms utilized for securing and protecting privacy in smart grids has compared various algorithms such as Data Encryption Standard (DES), Advanced Encryption Standard (AES), Triple Data Encryption Standard (3DES), Educational Data Encryption Standard (E-DES), RSA, and Blowfish Encryption. The study indicates that some algorithms exhibit similar encryption and decryption times to AES. However, AES outperforms all other algorithms when considering security, flexibility, and encryption performance. Therefore, symmetric algorithms are preferable to asymmetric algorithms. AES algorithms are recommended to ensure data security in smart grids (Abood et al., 2017).

8 IMPORTANCE OF PRIVACY FOR SMART GRID MANAGEMENT:

Several measures can be taken to protect consumers' privacy in smart grid management. Firstly, data should be collected on a need-to-know basis, and consumers should be informed about the data being collected, how it will be used, and who will have access to it. Secondly, data should be stored securely, with robust encryption and access controls, to prevent unauthorized access and data breaches. Thirdly, data should be anonymized wherever possible so that it cannot be traced back to individual consumers. Fourthly, consumers should have control over their data, including the ability to view, correct, and delete it and opt out of data collection altogether. Lastly, regulatory frameworks should be put in place to govern data collection, use, and sharing, with strict penalties for non-compliance (Farhangi, 2010).

Privacy is essential for smart grid management, protecting consumers' personal and sensitive data from misuse and abuse. Measures should be taken to protect privacy in smart grid management, including data minimization, secure storage, anonymization, consumer control, and regulatory frameworks. These measures will protect consumers' privacy and increase their trust and confidence in innovative grid technology, leading to increased adoption and uptake and a more sustainable and efficient grid.

It was found that privacy and security were consumers' top concerns regarding intelligent grid technology. The study revealed that consumers were worried about the collection and use of their data and the risk of cyber-attacks. Implementing privacy and security measures, such as data encryption and access controls, could increase consumer trust in smart grid technology and promote its adoption. Similarly, a review (Baiden & Chen, 2017) noted that intelligent grids were vulnerable to cyber-attacks and that privacy and security concerns could hinder their development and sustainability. Adopting cybersecurity measures, such as intrusion detection systems and regular software updates, could help mitigate these risks.

In contrast, a study by (Xu et al., 2021) found that the benefits of innovative grid technology, such as improved efficiency and sustainability, outweighed the privacy and security risks. The authors argued that implementing privacy and security measures was necessary but insufficient and that a balance needed to be struck between security and functionality.

Privacy and security are essential aspects of smart grid management, as they protect consumers' personal and sensitive data from misuse and abuse and ensure the reliability and sustainability of the grid (Gong et al., 2021). Measures should address privacy and security concerns in innovative grid management, including data minimization, secure storage, anonymization, consumer control, regulatory frameworks, and cybersecurity measures. By implementing these measures, we can ensure the long-term viability of smart grid technology and promote its adoption (Li & Ma, 2020).

The rapid development of smart grid technologies has enabled precise energy consumption monitoring, which can improve energy management, grid stability, and demand response. However, collecting and analyzing detailed energy consumption data raises significant privacy concerns for consumers. This literature review explores the state-of-the-art approaches and techniques proposed to tackle the privacy challenges associated with energy consumption monitoring in smart grids. Different privacy concerns and challenges in the context of data analytics highlight key research directions and prospects for privacy-preserving techniques in innovative grid applications. This comprehensive survey offers valuable insights into the efforts and advancements in ensuring privacy protection while leveraging big data analytics for intelligent grid operations (Kumar et al., 2017).

9 PRIVACY CHALLENGES IN SMART METERING AND METER DATA MANAGEMENT:

The key challenges identified are as follows:

9.1 Granularity of Data:

Smart meters generate highly granular data, often collected at short time intervals, which can reveal detailed information about consumers' daily routines, occupancy patterns, and appliance usage. This fine-grained data poses privacy risks, as it can potentially disclose sensitive information, including behavior patterns and lifestyle preferences (Zhang et al., 2018).

9.2 Inference Attacks:

The analysis of aggregated meter data can lead to inference attacks, where an adversary can deduce specific details about individuals' activities, habits, and appliances (Khoei et al., 2022). Through sophisticated techniques such as load disaggregation and pattern recognition, adversaries can infer sensitive information from seemingly anonymous meter data (Zeadally et al., 2012).

9.3 Third-Party Access:

Meter data is typically accessed by multiple entities, including utilities, third-party service providers, and researchers. The sharing of data with third parties increases the risk of unauthorized access, data breaches, and potential misuse of sensitive consumer information (Faisal et al., 2015).

9.4 Likability and Correlation:

The integration of smart meter data with other datasets, such as demographic or geolocation data, can enable link ability and correlation attacks. Adversaries can exploit the combined datasets to re-identify individuals and derive sensitive information that was not initially disclosed (Rong et al., 2023).

10 PRIVACY-AWARE ENERGY CONSUMPTION MONITORING TECHNIQUES

The reviewed articles presented a range of techniques and methodologies to address privacy concerns in energy consumption monitoring. These techniques can be broadly categorized into the following areas:

10.1 Data Aggregation and Anonymization:

Several studies proposed data aggregation and anonymization techniques to preserve privacy. Aggregating energy consumption data at different levels (e.g., households, neighborhoods) helps obfuscate individual consumer behavior, reducing the risk of privacy breaches. Anonymization techniques, such as k-anonymity and l-diversity, were explored to ensure the privacy of consumers' identities while maintaining data utility (Cao et al., 2017).

10.2 Differential Privacy:

Differential privacy emerged as a promising approach to protect individual privacy in smart grid environments. By adding noise to the energy consumption data, differential privacy mechanisms achieve a trade-off between privacy and data accuracy (Winanda et al., 2014). Several studies discussed the application of differential privacy in energy consumption monitoring, considering factors such as privacy budget allocation and utility optimization.

10.3 Secure Data Transmission and Storage:

To safeguard energy consumption data during transmission and storage, cryptographic techniques, including homomorphic encryption, secure multi-party computation, and secure data aggregation, were proposed. These techniques ensure that the data remains confidential and secure against eavesdropping and unauthorized access (He et al., 2023).

10.4 Privacy-Preserving Load Forecasting:

Load forecasting is crucial for efficient grid management but may expose sensitive information. Various privacy-preserving load forecasting methods were explored, including federated learning, secure aggregation, and privacy-preserving machine learning techniques. These methods enable accurate forecasting while protecting consumer privacy.

The reviewed studies emphasize the significance of balancing privacy and data utility, enabling efficient energy management while safeguarding consumer privacy. Data aggregation, anonymization, differential privacy, secure data transmission, and privacy-preserving load forecasting techniques emerged as effective means to address privacy concerns. Future research should focus on evaluating the practical implementation and scalability of these techniques to ensure their effectiveness in real-world smart grid deployments (Herold & Hertzog, 2015).

11 PRIVACY-PRESERVING TECHNIQUES

To address the privacy challenges associated with demand response programs, several techniques have been developed to ensure the confidentiality of consumer data while maintaining the effectiveness of these programs. Some prominent privacy-preserving techniques include:

11.1 Data Aggregation:

Instead of sharing individual energy consumption data, aggregation techniques can be employed to summarize and anonymize the information. Aggregated data can still provide insights into energy usage patterns without compromising individual privacy.

11.2 Differential Privacy:

Differential privacy adds noise to individual energy consumption data to prevent re-identification of specific users. By introducing controlled randomness, this technique ensures that no single individual's data can be distinguished from others, thereby preserving privacy.

11.3 Homomorphic Encryption:

Homomorphic encryption allows computations to be performed on encrypted data without decrypting it. This technique enables data analysis on encrypted energy consumption data, ensuring privacy while extracting necessary information.

11.4 Privacy-Preserving Data Mining:

Various privacy-preserving data mining algorithms, such as secure multiparty computation and secure sum aggregation, can be employed to extract useful information from energy consumption data without revealing sensitive details about individuals.

11.5 User-Controlled Privacy Settings:

Empowering consumers with control over their privacy settings is vital. Users should have the ability to choose the level of data sharing and the types of information disclosed. Transparent privacy policies and user-friendly interfaces can enhance consumer trust and participation in demand response programs.

Demand response programs play a crucial role in optimizing energy consumption and ensuring grid stability in smart grids. However, privacy concerns associated with the collection and utilization of consumer data must be addressed to foster trust and participation (Saputro & Akkaya, 2013). By implementing privacy-preserving techniques such as data aggregation, differential privacy, homomorphic encryption, privacy-preserving data mining, and user-controlled privacy settings, it is possible to strike a balance between effective demand response programs and the protection of individual privacy rights. The development and adoption of robust privacy frameworks are essential to promote the widespread implementation of demand response programs in smart grids, leading to a sustainable and privacy-preserving energy future (Herold & Hertzog, 2015)

The Privacy and security issues for smart grid management, as they protect consumers' personal and sensitive data from misuse and abuse and ensure the reliability and sustainability of the grid. Measures should be taken to address privacy and security concerns in smart grid management, including data minimization, secure storage, anonymization, consumer control, regulatory frameworks, and cybersecurity measures. By implementing these measures, we can ensure the long-term viability of smart grid technology and promote its adoption (Herold & Hertzog, 2015).

12 PRIVACY-ENHANCING TECHNOLOGIES FOR SMART GRID DATA ANALYTICS

To mitigate privacy risks and protect sensitive information, various privacy-enhancing technologies can be employed in smart grid data analytics:

12.1 Anonymization and Pseudonymization:

Anonymization techniques remove or modify personally identifiable information from datasets, making it impossible to directly identify individuals (Jia et al., 2019). Pseudonymization replaces identifiable information with pseudonyms, enabling data analysis while protecting privacy. These techniques ensure that data analysts cannot directly link energy consumption data to specific individuals. (Khan et al., 2018)

12.2 Differential Privacy:

Differential privacy is a robust privacy framework that adds controlled noise or perturbation to the aggregated data. By ensuring that the noise is sufficient to prevent re-identification of individuals, differential privacy allows for accurate data analysis while safeguarding privacy. It provides a quantifiable measure of privacy protection.

12.3 Secure Multiparty Computation (SMC):

SMC allows multiple parties to jointly compute desired results while keeping their individual inputs private. In smart grid data analytics, SMC can be used to perform computations on distributed data sources without exposing the raw data, thereby protecting individual privacy while enabling collaborative analysis.

12.4 Homomorphic Encryption:

Homomorphic encryption enables computations to be performed on encrypted data without decrypting it. By applying homomorphic encryption to energy consumption data, privacy is preserved throughout the data analytics process, as the sensitive information remains encrypted (Saputro & Akkaya, 2013).

12.5 Privacy-Preserving Data Mining:

Privacy-preserving data mining techniques, such as secure sum aggregation, allow for extracting aggregate information from energy consumption data while preventing the disclosure of individual details. These techniques enable efficient analysis while preserving privacy.

As intelligent grid data analytics become increasingly vital for optimizing energy management, ensuring privacy protection is paramount. Privacy-enhancing technologies are crucial in addressing the privacy challenges associated with intelligent grid data analytics. Anonymization, pseudonymization, differential privacy, secure multiparty computation, homomorphic encryption, and privacy-preserving data mining techniques enable practical data analysis while preserving the privacy of consumers. By implementing these technologies, stakeholders in the smart grid ecosystem can strike a balance between data-driven insights and the protection of personal information, fostering trust and ensuring a secure and privacy-conscious energy future (He et al., 2023).

CONCLUSION

Intelligent grid management presents various privacy issues that need to be carefully addressed. While integrating advanced technologies and data analytics in the grid offers numerous benefits, such as improved efficiency and reliability, it also raises concerns regarding the privacy of individuals and their personal information.

One significant privacy concern in intelligent grid management is the collection and use of granular energy consumption data. Smart meters and sensors installed throughout the grid can provide detailed information about when and how much electricity is consumed by individual households or businesses. This level of data granularity can reveal sensitive information about people's activities, behavior patterns, and even their presence or absence at home. Unauthorized access to this data or its misuse can lead to privacy breaches and potential misuse of personal information.

Another privacy issue arises from the interconnectivity of the smart grid with other systems and devices. The potential for data sharing and aggregation increases as the smart grid becomes integrated with various internet-connected devices, such as home automation systems or electric vehicle chargers. This interconnectedness creates opportunities for the unauthorized collection of personal information, potentially enabling surveillance or targeted advertising.

Furthermore, the storage and transmission of intelligent grid data raise concerns about data security and protection. Safeguarding the data collected from the grid against cyber threats and unauthorized access is crucial to maintaining privacy. A data breach or hacking incident could expose sensitive information, compromising the privacy and safety of individuals and their homes.

To address these privacy issues, robust privacy protection measures must be implemented in smart grid management. These measures should include clear guidelines on data collection, usage, retention, and informed consent mechanisms for customers. Implementing strong encryption and authentication protocols for data storage and transmission can enhance data security. Additionally, regulations and standards should govern smart grid data collection, storage, and use, ensuring compliance and accountability among grid operators, utility companies, and other stakeholders.

Balancing the benefits of smart grid technology with privacy concerns requires ongoing dialogue and collaboration between policymakers, industry stakeholders, and privacy advocates. By prioritizing privacy and adopting privacy-enhancing technologies and practices, it is possible to realize the potential of the smart grid while safeguarding individual privacy rights.

Future scope

The future scope of study on grid management and privacy concerns in the era of smart grids can explore several promising areas. One key direction is the advancement of privacy-enhancing technologies (PETs) specifically tailored for smart grids. Research could focus on developing new cryptographic techniques, differential privacy, and secure multi-party computation methods to protect consumer data while maintaining grid efficiency. Another area for future investigation is the integration of machine learning and artificial intelligence into smart grids. This includes designing privacy-preserving machine learning models that operate effectively with anonymized or encrypted data. Additionally, there is a need to study the evolving regulatory and policy frameworks related to data privacy and security in smart grids. Future research could examine how new policies impact grid management practices and how these practices can adapt to better protect consumer data.

Consumer perception and trust also warrant further exploration. Understanding how privacy and trust influence the adoption and effectiveness of smart grid technologies could lead to more effective communication and transparency strategies. Research into standardized protocols for data sharing and interoperability is also crucial, as it could help balance efficiency with privacy protection. Investigating the implications of emerging technologies, such as quantum computing and blockchain, on smart grid security and privacy could provide insights into how these innovations can be integrated to enhance both aspects.

Practical implications:

In terms of practical implications, implementing advanced privacy measures can significantly build consumer trust, leading to greater adoption of smart grid technologies and improved grid management. Enhanced data security through the deployment of encryption and privacy-preserving algorithms can safeguard consumer data against unauthorized access and breaches. Findings from this research can guide policymakers in crafting regulations that balance privacy protection with the advancement of smart grid technologies. Educating and engaging consumers about privacy practices can improve user acceptance and cooperation, while standardization efforts could facilitate smoother implementation and operation of smart grids. Finally, developing adaptive grid management solutions that incorporate privacy considerations can lead to more efficient and secure grid operations.

REFERENCES

Abood, O. G., Elsadd, M. A., & Guirguis, S. K. (2017). Investigation of cryptography algorithms used for security and privacy protection in smart grid. In *2017 Nineteenth International Middle East Power Systems Conference (MEPCON)* (pp. 644–649). https://doi.org/DOI: 10.1109/MEPCON.2017.8301249

Ali, W., Din, I. U., Almogren, A., & Kim, B.-S. (2022). A novel privacy preserving scheme for smart-grid-based home area networks. *Sensors (Basel)*, 22(2269), 2269. Advance online publication. DOI: 10.3390/s22062269 PMID: 35336439

Anaya, K. L., & Pollitt, M. G. (2021). How to procure flexibility services within the electricity distribution system: Lessons from an international review of innovation projects. *Energies*, 14(4475), 4475. Advance online publication. DOI: 10.3390/en14154475

Baiden, B. K., & Chen, X. (2017). Security and privacy in smart grid: A review. *Renewable & Sustainable Energy Reviews*, 72, 698–706. DOI: 10.1016/j.rser.2017.01.069

Cao, H., Liu, S., Guan, Z., & Zhang, X. (2017). Achieving differential privacy of data disclosure from non-intrusive load monitoring in smart grid. In *Cyberspace Safety and Security* (pp. 32–42). https://doi.org/DOI: 10.1007/978-3-319-69471-9_3

Diestelmeier, L. (2019). Unlocking flexibility with law: Developing a legal framework for smart electricity systems.

Diestelmeier, L. (2021). A legal framework for smart grids. In Energy Law, Climate Change and the Environment (pp. 645–655). University of Groningen. https://doi.org/DOI: 10.4337/9781788119689.IX.54

Faisal, M., Cardenas, A. A., & Mashima, D. (2015). How the quantity and quality of training data impacts re-identification of smart meter users? In *2015 IEEE International Conference on Smart Grid Communications (SmartGridComm)*. https://doi.org/DOI: 10.1109/SmartGridComm.2015.7436272

Farhangi, H. (2010). The path of the smart grid. *IEEE Power & Energy Magazine*, 8(1), 18–28. DOI: 10.1109/MPE.2009.934876

Gong, X., Li, J., Liang, H., Yu, R., & Wu, Y. (2021). Privacy preservation in big data analytics for smart grids: A survey. *IEEE Transactions on Industrial Informatics*, 17(8), 5736–5746. DOI: 10.1109/TII.2021.3055049

He, X., Pun, M.-O., & Kuo, C.-C. J. (2012). *Secure and efficient cryptosystem for smart grid using homomorphic encryption. In 2012 IEEE PES Innovative Smart Grid Technologies.* ISGT., DOI: 10.1109/ISGT.2012.6175676

He, X., Zhang, Y., Liu, X., Huang, D., & Liu, Y. (2022). A comprehensive survey on privacy-preserving techniques in smart grid communications. *IEEE Transactions on Industrial Informatics*, 18(6), 4467–4483. DOI: 10.1109/TII.2021.3053940

He, Y., Luo, F., Sun, M., & Ranzi, G. (2023). Privacy-preserving and hierarchically federated framework for short-term residential load forecasting. *IEEE Transactions on Smart Grid*, 14(6), 1–1. DOI: 10.1109/TSG.2023.3268633

Herold, R., & Hertzog, C. (2015). The smart grid and privacy. In *Data Privacy for the Smart Grid* (pp. 1–10). https://doi.org/DOI: 10.1201/b18005-1

Information Commissioner's Office (ICO). (2009). Privacy impact assessment handbook, Version 2.0. https://www.huntonprivacyblog.com/wp-content/uploads/sites/28/2013/09/PIAhandbookV2.pdf

Islam, S., Zografopoulos, I., Hossain, M. T., Badsha, S., & Konstantinou, C. (2023). *A resource allocation scheme for energy demand management in 6G-enabled smart grid. In 2023 IEEE Power & Energy Society Innovative Smart Grid Technologies Conference (ISGT).* IEEE., DOI: 10.1109/ISGT51731.2023.10066396

Jia, Y., Xu, L., Lu, Z., & Zhang, Y. (2019). Consumers' privacy and security concerns in smart grid technology: An empirical study in China. *Energy Policy*, 131, 344–352.

Khan, S., Jabeen, F., & Hussain, M. (2018). A review on security and privacy issues in smart grid communications. *Sustainable Cities and Society*, 40, 600–612.

Khatib, T., Syed, A., Khan, U., & Alsharif, S. (2015). A comprehensive review on smart grid and its research challenges. *Renewable & Sustainable Energy Reviews*, 51, 1507–1518. DOI: 10.1016/j.rser.2015.07.123

Khoei, T. T., Slimane, H. O., & Kaabouch, N. (2022). Cyber-security of smart grids: Attacks, detection, countermeasure techniques, and future directions. *Communications and Network*, 14(4), 119–170. DOI: 10.4236/cn.2022.144009

Kloza, D., van Dijk, N., & De Hert, P. (2015). Assessing the European approach to privacy and data protection in smart grids: Lessons for emerging technologies. In Skopik, F., & Smith, P. (Eds.), *Smart Grid Security* (pp. 11–47). Syngress., DOI: 10.1016/B978-0-12-802122-4.00002-X

Kumar, P., Braeken, A., Gurtov, A., Iinatti, J., & Ha, P. H. (2017). Anonymous secure framework in connected smart home environments. *IEEE Transactions on Information Forensics and Security*, 12(4), 968–979. DOI: 10.1109/TIFS.2016.2647225

Kumar, P., Braeken, A., Gurtov, A., Iinatti, J., & Ha, P. H. (2017). Anonymous secure framework in connected smart home environments. *IEEE Transactions on Information Forensics and Security*, 12(4), 968–979. DOI: 10.1109/TIFS.2016.2647225

Leszczyna, R. (2018). Cybersecurity and privacy in standards for smart grids – A comprehensive survey. *Computer Standards & Interfaces*, 56, 62–73. DOI: 10.1016/j.csi.2017.09.005

Li, Y., & Ma, H. (2020). Blockchain-based privacy-preserving energy trading in smart grid. *IEEE Access : Practical Innovations, Open Solutions*, 8, 131180–131191.

Liu, C., & Zhang, H. (2012). A survey of demand response in smart grid: Approaches, initiatives and perspectives. *IEEE Transactions on Industrial Informatics*, 9(3), 1484–1495. DOI: 10.1109/TII.2012.2188407

Mandal, A. K., Parakash, C., & Tiwari, A. (2012). Performance evaluation of cryptographic algorithms: DES and AES. In 2012 IEEE Students' Conference on Electrical, Electronics and Computer Science (pp. 1–5). IEEE. https://doi.org/DOI: 10.1109/SCEECS.2012.6184991

Muralidhara Rao, P., Al-Turjman, F., & Deebak, B. D. (2022). Smart grid metering: Security, privacy, and open challenges. In Deebak, B. D., & Al-Turjman, F. (Eds.), *Sustainable Networks in Smart Grid* (pp. 255–272). Academic Press., DOI: 10.1016/B978-0-323-85626-3.00009-0

Naeem, M., Malik, A. W., & Aljohani, N. R. (2017). Security and privacy issues in smart grid: A comprehensive review. *Sustainable Cities and Society*, 28, 413–427.

Petrlic, R. (2010). A privacy-preserving concept for smart grids. B1-B14.

Piatkowska, E., Bajraktari, A., Chhajed, D., & Smith, P. (2017). Tool support for data protection impact assessment in the smart grid. *E&I Elektrotechnik und Informationstechnik*, 134(1), 26–29. DOI: 10.1007/s00502-017-0484-4

Rakesh, V., & Hickok, E. (2023). Cyber security of smart grids in India. https://www.dqindia.com/cyber-security-of-smart-grids-in-india/

Rasheed, S. (2011). Simulation of image encryption using AES algorithm.

Rong, J., Liu, W., Jiang, F., Cheng, Y., Li, H., & Peng, J. (2023). Privacy-aware optimal load scheduling for energy management system of smart home. *Sustainable Energy. Grids and Networks*, 34, 101039. DOI: 10.1016/j.segan.2023.101039

Saputro, N., & Akkaya, K. (2013). On preserving user privacy in smart grid advanced metering infrastructure applications. *Security and Communication Networks*, 7(1), 206–220. DOI: 10.1002/sec.706

Tariq, M., Ali, M., Naeem, F., & Poor, H. V. (2021). Vulnerability assessment of 6G-enabled smart grid cyber–physical systems. *IEEE Internet of Things Journal*, 8(7), 5468–5475. DOI: 10.1109/JIOT.2020.3042090

Uludag, S., Zeadally, S., & Badra, M. (2015). Techniques, taxonomy, and challenges of privacy protection in the smart grid. In Zeadally, S., & Badra, M. (Eds.), *Privacy in a Digital, Networked World. Computer Communications and Networks*. Springer., DOI: 10.1007/978-3-319-08470-1_15

Winanda, M., Satriawan, A., & Gondokaryono, Y. S. (2014). Smart grid secure data transmission for high voltage grid. In *2014 International Conference on Information Technology Systems and Innovation (ICITSI)*. https://doi.org/DOI: 10.1109/ICITSI.2014.7048240

Xu, Y., An, Z., Jin, D., Liang, W., & Hu, W. (2021). Privacy-preserving data aggregation in smart grids: A survey. *IEEE Access : Practical Innovations, Open Solutions*, 9, 57122–57133. DOI: 10.1109/ACCESS.2021.3068951

Zeadally, S., Pathan, A.-S. K., Alcaraz, C., & Badra, M. (2012). Towards privacy protection in smart grid. *Wireless Personal Communications*, 73(1), 23–50. DOI: 10.1007/s11277-012-0939-1

Zhang, H., Zhang, Y., Zhang, Q., & Tian, D. (2018). Inference attacks on privacy-preserving data publishing: A survey. *IEEE Access : Practical Innovations, Open Solutions*, 6, 29920–29936. DOI: 10.1109/ACCESS.2018.2849282

ADDITIONAL READING

Kannan, N. (2020). *Microgrid*. Research Trends and Challenges in Smart Grids., DOI: 10.5772/intechopen.88812

Ohanu, C. P., Rufai, S. A., & Oluchi, U. C. (2024). A comprehensive review of recent developments in smart grid through Renewable Energy Resources Integration. *Heliyon*, 10(3), e25705. Advance online publication. DOI: 10.1016/j.heliyon.2024.e25705 PMID: 38327483

Powell, J., McCafferty-Leroux, A., Hilal, W., & Gadsden, S. A. (2024). Smart grids: A comprehensive survey of challenges, industry applications, and future trends. *Energy Reports*, 11, 5760–5785. DOI: 10.1016/j.egyr.2024.05.051

KEY TERMS AND DEFINITIONS

Smart Grid: An advanced electrical grid that uses digital communication technology to detect and react to local changes in electricity usage, improving the efficiency, reliability, and sustainability of energy distribution.

Granular Energy: The concept of monitoring, managing, and optimizing energy consumption at a highly detailed level, often at the individual appliance or device level, to enhance energy efficiency and reduce waste.

Surveillance: The monitoring and collection of data, often in real-time, through various technologies, such as cameras or sensors, to track behavior, activities, or environmental conditions for security or regulatory purposes.

Interconnectivity: The ability of different systems, devices, or networks to communicate and work together seamlessly, often through the Internet of Things (IoT) or other digital networks, enabling data sharing and coordinated operations.

Data Security: The protection of data from unauthorized access, corruption, or theft, ensuring the confidentiality, integrity, and availability of data through various technological and organizational measures.

Cyber Threats: Malicious activities aimed at exploiting vulnerabilities in digital systems or networks, potentially causing damage, data breaches, or unauthorized access to sensitive information.

Encryption: The process of converting data into a coded format that can only be accessed or deciphered by those with the correct decryption key, used to protect information during transmission or storage.

Authentication: The process of verifying the identity of a user or system, typically through credentials like passwords, biometric data, or security tokens, to grant access to secure systems or data.

Regulatory Frameworks: The set of laws, guidelines, and standards established by governing bodies to regulate the operation, security, and privacy of digital systems, ensuring compliance and protecting public interests.

Informed Consent: The process by which individuals are fully informed about the collection, use, and sharing of their personal data and voluntarily agree to it, often required by law or ethical standards.

Privacy Protection: Measures and practices designed to safeguard personal information from unauthorized access, use, or disclosure, ensuring individuals' rights to control their own data and maintain confidentiality.

Chapter 9
Navigating the Digital Landscape: The Evolution and Challenges of Online Mapping Communities

Munir Ahmad
https://orcid.org/0000-0003-4836-6151
Survey of Pakistan, Pakistan

ABSTRACT

This chapter traces the evolution of online mapping from the 1990s to today, highlighting its transformation from basic digital maps to sophisticated, interactive applications. These advancements have democratized access to spatial information, challenged traditional cartographic methods, and shifted the focus from static maps to dynamic, user-interactive experiences. Online mapping platforms have revolutionized transportation, urban planning, and personal navigation. User participation has been pivotal, with collective intelligence enhancing map quality and utility. Despite challenges like data accuracy and misuse, robust moderation and user education can mitigate risks, ensuring reliable online mapping platforms that democratize geographic information and foster a more informed global community.

INTRODUCTION

Maps have been great tools for navigation in reality for many centuries and the definition still stands true even in the contemporary world. Not merely used to navigate the voyages, initially scribed on rolled-out skins and papyrus, later inked on manually compiled parchment scrolls, and finally drawn on elaborate atlas, these maps of real and artificial features have nurtured the spirit of discovery. The

DOI: 10.4018/979-8-3693-3868-1.ch009

application of computer techniques in cartography has opened up a new era in the mapping technique. The rise of the internet has significantly formed dynamic online mapping communities and revolutionized how people interact with spatial information (Herfort et al., 2021; Nagaraj, 2021). Today, digital maps are no longer a tool to guide one from Point A to point B, they are web-based encyclopedias or news feeds, which aggregate information at the touch of a button or input from other users. These platforms allow people to input data into the system, tag the location, and even participate in the creation of maps around the world. Modernization of such cartographic tools has increased availability and practicality, making them suitable for use across various disciplines, including land use planning, disaster management, endangered species mapping, and historical site mapping (Ahmad & Ali, 2023; Brown et al., 2018; Hilburn et al., 2021; Kantola et al., 2023).

Furthermore, improvements in telecommunication and locational technologies such as satellite imagery, GPS, and state-of-the-art analytic tools have been introduced to enhance the map quality and utility. Digital maps do more than show topographical features; instead, they represent spatial content, changed pattern prediction, and dynamic decision-making contexts in different fields. This complementarity of technology and cartography highlights the centrality of the two in meeting contemporaneous concerns and venturing into the next horizon (Murad et al., 2024; Santos et al., 2024; Taouktsis & Zikopoulos, 2024). It is crucial to know the trends of online maps as something that has developed from a specialized area to a more pervasive characteristic of our everyday lives. Such virtual cartographic spaces now exert a substantial impact over seemingly numerous facets of our lives. Not only to assist us with commuting but also to govern our leisure time, and determine how we perceive our surroundings. Essentially, these serve as digital frameworks that enable massive sharing of knowledge and ideas, allowing individuals to contribute localized information in an attempt to build a global networked informational architecture to provide an accurate understanding of the global situation (Fraisl et al., 2020; Petzold et al., 2020; Skaalsveen et al., 2020).

Nevertheless, this change harbours great opportunities concerning various aspects of human life, even though various threatening issues arise hand in hand with the change. Among such challenges, the first and the most crucial one is the matter of data accuracy. Digital maps come with features such as updates and user content; nevertheless, the authenticity of these details is still a major issue when considering digital maps powered by volunteers such as OpenStreetMap. Faulty or unreliable mapping information may result in negative consequences arising from wrong or misguided decisions that may affect people's lives and engagement in activities that are crucial to their livelihoods, such as the provision of social services (Borkowska & Pokonieczny, 2022; Foody et al., 2024; Khan & Johnson, 2020). Also, some other problems in online mapping communities might emerge, including representation bias. The information provided by the users might be coloured by demographic, cultural, or socioeconomic prejudices; merely that, this may skew the general picture of the geographical environment and deepen the disparities in terms of the distribution of opportunities and facilities.

However, the existing increased popularity and availability of new mapping technologies are becoming a problem. Malicious use and manipulation are inevitable; people's privacy is at risk, and so is the flow of accurate information due to the open use and availability of online maps. To mitigate these risks there is need for sound governance structures, code of ethics and improvement on technology controls to protect user privacy and data authenticity. In responding to these challenges there is a need to undertake critical analyses of online mapping communities. This increases the need for the involvement of the various stakeholders comprising of technology developers and designers, policymakers and regulators, academicians, and the end users which in this case are persons belonging to the society across the world in order to promote openness, responsiveness, and accessibility of these environments. In this way, threats may be minimized and opportunities maximized by providing data openness, diversification of source contributors, and stringently verifying data for online maps' proper application as conduits of powerful knowledge-sharing platforms, effective means for community mobilization, and valuable tools for the practical decision-making is the digital age.

This chapter delves into the evolution and complexities of online mapping communities. Our objective is to provide a comprehensive analysis of this phenomenon The chapter also looks at the background of these platforms and their influence on conventional cartography. We then go further and look at the collaborative nature of these communities concerning the advantages of knowledge cooperation. Finally, the chapter critically assesses the challenges posed by these digital spaces, proposing solutions and advocating for responsible online mapping practices.

THE RISE OF ONLINE MAPPING

This section explores the historical development of online mapping platforms, tracing their journey from early internet ventures to the dominant applications we use today.

Early Seeds (1990s): The foundation of modern online mapping can be traced back to the early 1990s with pioneering efforts such as the Xerox PARC Map Viewer (1993) and the National Atlas of Canada (1994). These platforms represented early experiments in using the internet to present geographical data interactively. They laid the essential groundwork by demonstrating the potential of digital maps to facilitate geographic exploration and data visualization on a global scale (Williams et al., 2003; Zentai, 2013).

The Rise of Web 2.0 (2000s): The turn of the millennium marked a significant evolution in online mapping with the advent of Web 2.0 technologies. Platforms like MapQuest (founded in 1996) (https://www.mapquest.com/) and, notably, Google Maps (launched in 2005) (https://www.google.com/maps/) transformed the landscape (Chico, 2015). Google Maps revolutionized mapping by offering intuitive user interfaces, integrated search functionalities, and groundbreaking features like satellite imagery through Google Earth. This era also witnessed the rise of OpenStreetMap (founded in 2004) (https://www.openstreetmap.org/), a community-driven initiative advocating for open data and collaborative map editing, challenging the dominance of proprietary mapping services.

Mobile Revolution and Beyond (2010s-Present): The proliferation of smartphones in the 2010s heralded a new era of mobility and convenience in online mapping. The integration of GPS technology with mapping applications enabled real-time location tracking and turn-by-turn navigation, fundamentally altering how individuals navigate their physical environments. Apple Maps (launched in 2012) (https://www.apple.com/maps/) emerged as a major competitor to Google Maps, introducing features tailored for iOS devices and pushing innovations in map design and functionality.

Today, online mapping continues to evolve rapidly, leveraging advancements in technology to enhance user experiences. The timeline of online mapping platforms is shown in Table 1. Modern platforms offer a plethora of features such as 3D cityscapes, indoor navigation for complex structures like airports and shopping malls, and real-time traffic updates to optimize route planning. The integration of augmented reality (AR) and machine learning further expands the potential of online maps, promising more immersive and personalized navigation experiences in the years to come.

Table 1. Timeline of online mapping platforms (1990s-present)

Decade	Key Milestones	Examples
1990s	Early online map viewers	Xerox PARC Map Viewer (1993), National Atlas of Canada (1994)
2000s	Rise of Web 2.0 and user-generated content	Google Maps (2005), MapQuest (1996), OpenStreetMap (2004)
2010s-Present	The mobile revolution and advanced functionalities	Apple Maps (2012), Integration with GPS and real-time navigation

Key Technological Advancements

The section provides the details on the key technological advancements that facilitated the growth of online mapping platforms.

GPS Integration

The integration of Global Positioning Systems (GPS) has been pivotal in revolutionizing online mapping. GPS technology enables devices to determine their precise geographic location anywhere on Earth, facilitating accurate mapping and real-time navigation. This integration has empowered mapping applications to offer features such as turn-by-turn navigation, location-based services, and dynamic route optimization. By leveraging GPS data, online maps can provide users with personalized and context-aware information, enhancing their utility in everyday navigation and exploration (Chen et al., 2021; Król, 2020; Lee et al., 2023).

User-Generated Content (UGC)

The rise of User-Generated Content (UGC) has significantly transformed the online mapping landscape. Platforms like OpenStreetMap (founded in 2004) exemplify this shift by allowing users to actively contribute to mapping data. Users can add points of interest, update road networks, verify geographical features, and share local knowledge. This collaborative approach not only enhances the accuracy and completeness of mapping data but also fosters a sense of community engagement and ownership. UGC has democratized cartography, enabling diverse perspectives and local insights to enrich the global map dataset, thereby broadening the scope and usability of online mapping platforms (Król, 2020; Yan et al., 2020).

Networking and Processing Power

The continual advancements in networking infrastructure and processing power have played a crucial role in advancing online mapping capabilities. Increasing bandwidth and faster internet connections facilitate seamless map loading, real-time updates, and smooth interaction with map features. Enhanced processing capabilities enable mapping applications to perform complex tasks such as routing algorithms, geospatial data analysis, and 3D rendering of landscapes and cityscapes. These technological improvements ensure that online maps can handle large volumes of data efficiently while delivering responsive and interactive user experiences across various devices and platforms.

In short, the integration of GPS technology, the empowerment of User-Generated Content, and the advancements in networking infrastructure and processing power have collectively propelled the evolution of online mapping platforms. These advancements have not only enhanced the accuracy, functionality, and accessibility of digital maps but have also expanded their utility across diverse domains including transportation, urban planning, disaster response, environmental monitoring, and personal navigation. As technology continues to evolve, the future of online mapping holds promises for further innovations that will continue to redefine how we perceive, interact with, and navigate the world around us.

Impact on Traditional Cartography

This section elaborates on the impact of online mapping on traditional cartography.

Democratization of Access

Online mapping has democratized access to spatial information on an unprecedented scale. Unlike traditional paper maps, which often require purchase and can quickly become outdated, online maps offer free and readily available access to detailed geographical data. This accessibility empowers individuals, businesses, and organizations worldwide to access maps instantly from any location with internet connectivity. By eliminating barriers such as cost and geographic distribution, online mapping has democratized the ability to explore, analyze, and utilize spatial information for a wide range of purposes including navigation, planning, research, and education.

Challenge to Established Practices

The rise of online mapping has challenged established practices within the field of cartography. Traditional map-making processes typically relied on controlled data collection, rigorous cartographic standards, and centralized production methods. In contrast, online mapping platforms leverage User-Generated Content (UGC) and real-time updates to prioritize flexibility, inclusivity, and user participation. This shift has broadened the scope of map creation beyond professional cartographers to include contributions from a global community of enthusiasts, experts, and residents. It has also accelerated the pace of map updates, enabling maps to reflect current conditions and evolving landscapes more accurately and swiftly than traditional methods allow.

Shifting Focus

Online mapping has catalyzed a shift in the focus of cartography from static representations to dynamic and interactive experiences. Unlike traditional paper maps that present fixed views of geographical information, online maps offer users the ability to zoom in and out, customize their views, and explore multiple layers of information. This interactive functionality not only enhances usability but also encourages engagement and exploration. Users can overlay various data sets such as satellite imagery, traffic patterns, demographic information, and points of interest, thereby creating personalized and context-rich mapping experiences. This shift towards dynamic and interactive mapping experiences has redefined how individuals perceive and interact with spatial information, fostering a deeper understanding of geographical contexts and facilitating informed decision-making across various sectors.

Hence, online mapping has profoundly impacted traditional cartography by democratizing access to spatial information, challenging established practices with user-driven content and real-time updates, and shifting the focus from static representations to dynamic, interactive experiences. As online mapping technologies continue to evolve and innovate, they are likely to further transform the field of cartography, expanding its capabilities, enhancing its accessibility, and broadening its relevance in our increasingly digital and interconnected world.

COLLABORATION AND KNOWLEDGE CREATION

Online mapping thrives on the collective power of its users. This section delves into the collaborative nature of these communities, exploring how they leverage "collective intelligence" to create a richer and more dynamic picture of the world.

User-Generated Expertise

Adding Points of Interest (POIs)

One of the primary ways users contribute to online mapping platforms is by adding Points of Interest (POIs) (Andrade et al., 2020; Psyllidis et al., 2022). These can include businesses, landmarks, parks, historical sites, restaurants, and other notable locations that may not be readily available on traditional maps. By pinpointing and adding these POIs, users enrich the map's utility by providing valuable information about local attractions and amenities. This not only enhances the map's comprehensiveness but also helps users discover hidden gems and plan their activities more effectively based on their interests and preferences.

Updating Road Networks

Users also play a crucial role in updating road networks on online mapping platforms (Herfort et al., 2021; Minaei, 2020). They can report new road constructions, closures, changes in traffic flow, and road conditions. This real-time information is invaluable for ensuring accurate navigation and route planning, especially in dynamic urban environments were infrastructure changes frequently. By contributing updates to road networks, users help maintain the map's relevance and reliability, enabling others to navigate efficiently and safely.

Detailed Descriptions and Photographs

Beyond basic geographic data, users can enhance online maps by providing detailed descriptions and photographs of locations (Domènech et al., 2020; Gunter & Önder, 2021). This additional information offers insights into the characteristics, ambiance, accessibility, and unique features of specific places. Detailed descriptions can include historical background, cultural significance, operational hours, accessibility information for individuals with disabilities, and other relevant details that enrich users' understanding and experience of the location. Photographs provide visual context, helping users visualize the environment and make informed decisions about visiting or exploring a particular place.

Identifying and Reporting Errors or Outdated Information

Users also serve as vigilant monitors of map accuracy by identifying and reporting errors or outdated information. This proactive role ensures that the map remains reliable and up-to-date, reflecting current conditions and changes in the physical environment. Users can report inaccuracies such as incorrect place names, outdated business information, misplaced markers, or discrepancies in geographic features. By promptly addressing and correcting these issues, users contribute to the overall quality and credibility of the online mapping platform, benefiting all users who rely on accurate spatial information.

In summary, online mapping platforms harness the collective expertise and local knowledge of users to create dynamic, comprehensive, and reliable maps. By actively engaging with these platforms through contributions of POIs, updates to road networks, detailed descriptions and photographs, and error reporting, users not only enhance the utility of maps for themselves but also for the broader community of map users worldwide. This collaborative approach to mapping underscores the transformative impact of user-generated content in shaping the future of digital cartography.

Collective Intelligence

Online mapping platforms leverage the collective intelligence of their user communities by harnessing the diverse local knowledge and expertise contributed by a vast number of users. Unlike traditional methods of map creation that rely on centralized data collection and professional cartographers, online maps benefit from the cumulative insights and contributions of individuals worldwide. This collaborative effort allows online maps to evolve into dynamic repositories of information that surpass the capabilities of any single contributor or traditional mapping approach.

Comprehensive and Nuanced Mapping

Through user-generated content such as Points of Interest (POIs), updates to road networks, detailed descriptions, photographs, and error reports, online maps become more comprehensive and capture nuanced details that traditional methods might overlook. Users contribute their intimate knowledge of local landmarks, businesses, cultural sites, and infrastructure changes, thereby enriching the map with real-time updates and accurate depictions of the physical environment. This collective input ensures that online maps reflect the diverse perspectives and lived experiences of communities around the globe, making them invaluable resources for navigation, exploration, and decision-making.

Enhanced Accuracy and Relevance

The collective intelligence generated through user contributions enhances the accuracy and relevance of online maps. By crowdsourcing data verification and updates, online mapping platforms can quickly identify and correct errors, outdated information, or inaccuracies in geographic representations. This continuous feedback loop between users and the platform ensures that the maps remain current, reliable, and reflective of real-world conditions, thereby improving usability and trustworthiness for all users.

Facilitating Informed Decision-Making

Collective intelligence empowers users to make informed decisions based on a comprehensive understanding of their surroundings. By accessing up-to-date information on road conditions, local amenities, points of interest, and other relevant factors, individuals can plan routes, explore new locations, and navigate unfamiliar environments with confidence. This democratization of spatial knowledge enables users to optimize their daily activities, enhance efficiency, and discover new opportunities for exploration and interaction within their communities.

Hence, the collaborative nature of online mapping platforms exemplifies collective intelligence, where the collective efforts of a diverse user base contribute to the creation of knowledge that transcends individual capabilities. By leveraging the local knowledge, experiences, and contributions of users worldwide, online maps evolve into dynamic, accurate, and invaluable tools that empower individuals and communities to navigate, explore, and engage with the world around them in meaningful and impactful ways.

Benefits of Collaboration

The benefits of collaboration through online mapping communities compared to traditional map-making processes as summarized in Table 2 and elaborated below.

Real-Time Updates

One of the primary advantages of online mapping communities is the ability to provide real-time updates. Unlike traditional map-making processes that rely on periodic updates or surveys, online maps can be continuously updated by users. This real-time capability allows online platforms to swiftly reflect changes on the ground, such as new road constructions, closures, traffic conditions, business openings or closures, and other dynamic developments. Users can contribute updates instantaneously, ensuring that the map remains current and accurate, thereby enhancing its utility for navigation, planning, and decision-making.

Global Coverage

Online mapping platforms benefit from a global user base, which enables them to map even remote and under-documented areas worldwide. Traditional map-making processes may prioritize mapping urban centers and well-traveled regions due to logistical constraints and resource limitations. In contrast, online communities can harness the collective efforts of users spanning diverse geographic locations and cultural backgrounds. This expansive coverage fosters a more comprehensive and inclusive representation of the world, capturing geographic nuances and local insights that might be overlooked by traditional mapping methods. As a result, online maps offer a broader and more detailed depiction of the Earth's landscapes, enhancing accessibility and knowledge dissemination on a global scale.

Niche Expertise

Online mapping communities leverage the specialized knowledge and expertise of local users about their surroundings. These users often possess intimate familiarity with specific areas, including details such as hiking trails, bike paths, scenic viewpoints, historical landmarks, and local businesses. By contributing this niche expertise, users enrich online maps with detailed and accurate information that caters to diverse interests and activities. This localized knowledge enhances the map's utility for recreational purposes, tourism planning, environmental conservation, and community engagement. It also ensures that online maps are tailored to meet the unique needs and preferences of users seeking specific information about particular regions or points of interest.

Table 2. Benefits of collaboration in online mapping

Feature	Description	Advantage
Real-Time Updates	Users can update information on the ground	Faster and more accurate reflection of changes
Global Coverage	User base can contribute to mapping remote areas	More complete picture of the world
Niche Expertise	Local users contribute specialized knowledge	Detailed information specific to an area

In summary, online mapping communities offer distinct advantages over traditional map-making processes by facilitating real-time updates, achieving global coverage through a diverse user base, and incorporating niche expertise from local contributors. These collaborative efforts not only enhance the accuracy, relevance, and usability of online maps but also empower users to engage actively in mapping their environments, contributing to a more dynamic and interconnected global mapping ecosystem.

Examples of Successful Projects

Some examples of successful projects that highlight the power of collaboration in online mapping are shown below.

OpenStreetMap (OSM)

OpenStreetMap (OSM) (https://www.openstreetmap.org/) is a prime example of a successful collaborative mapping project. Launched in 2004, OSM is entirely built by a community of millions of volunteers worldwide who contribute geographic data, update maps, and verify information. The platform offers a free and open alternative to traditional map data providers, allowing users to access and edit maps of nearly every corner of the globe. OSM has been instrumental in disaster response efforts, urban planning initiatives, humanitarian projects, and community mapping exercises. Its comprehensive and constantly evolving dataset showcases the collective effort and expertise of its global community, demonstrating the potential of collaborative mapping to democratize access to spatial information and foster community engagement on a global scale.

Waze

Waze (https://www.waze.com/live-map/) is a community-based traffic and navigation app that relies on user-generated data to provide real-time updates on traffic conditions, accidents, road closures, and other incidents affecting road travel. Users contribute information by reporting incidents, hazards, and speed traps, which are then aggregated and shared with other drivers to improve route planning and navigation. Waze's success lies in its ability to harness the collective intelligence of its user community, turning everyday drivers into active contributors to a dynamic and responsive mapping and navigation ecosystem. By leveraging real-time user reports, Waze enhances the driving experience for millions of users worldwide, optimizing travel times, reducing congestion, and improving overall road safety.

Mapillary

Mapillary (https://www.mapillary.com/) is a collaborative platform that aggregates user-contributed street-level imagery to create a comprehensive 360-degree view of the world's streets and environments. Launched in 2013, Mapillary allows users to capture and upload photos using smartphones or cameras, which are then stitched together using computer vision technology to create navigable street-level views. This crowdsourced imagery provides valuable insights for urban planning, infrastructure management, environmental monitoring, and tourism promotion. By capturing detailed and up-to-date visual data from diverse locations around the globe,

Mapillary complements traditional mapping data with rich contextual information that enhances understanding and decision-making in various domains.

These successful projects exemplify how collaborative mapping initiatives harness the power of community participation and user-generated content to create innovative and impactful solutions for mapping, navigation, and spatial data visualization. By enabling users to actively contribute their knowledge, insights, and experiences, these platforms demonstrate the transformative potential of collective intelligence in shaping the future of digital cartography and enhancing our interaction with the world's geographic information. By harnessing the collective power of users, online mapping communities are revolutionizing the way we understand and interact with the world around us.

CHALLENGES AND CONSIDERATIONS

While online mapping communities offer a wealth of benefits, navigating this digital landscape isn't without its challenges. This section assesses these issues and proposes solutions for responsible online mapping practices.

Data Accuracy and Verification

The nature of user-generated content (UGC) in online mapping presents challenges alongside its many benefits as described below.

The collaborative nature of UGC allows for real-time updates and broad coverage, but it also opens the door to potential misinformation and errors. Accidental mistakes, such as incorrect locations or outdated information, can be introduced by well-meaning users. More concerning is the potential for malicious edits, where individuals deliberately add false information to mislead others. Without robust verification processes, these errors and intentional inaccuracies can proliferate, undermining the reliability of the map data. To address this, many platforms implement moderation systems, peer reviews, and automated detection algorithms to identify and correct inaccuracies swiftly. However, maintaining a balance between open contribution and accurate data remains a continual challenge.

Moreover, UGC can reflect the biases and priorities of its contributors, leading to uneven representation across the map. Areas with a higher concentration of active contributors may be well-documented, while less populated or economically disadvantaged regions might be underrepresented. This bias can result in maps that do not accurately reflect the diversity of experiences and needs across different communities. For instance, affluent neighborhoods might have detailed information about local amenities, while poorer areas might lack even basic mapping coverage.

To mitigate these biases, platforms can promote diversity among contributors, encourage participation from underrepresented regions, and implement algorithms that prioritize coverage in less documented areas. Additionally, collaboration with local organizations and community groups can help ensure a more equitable representation of different areas.

Several strategies can be employed to enhance the accuracy and verification of UGC in online mapping.

- Platforms can use crowdsourced verification methods, where multiple users validate the same piece of information. The consensus from several contributors can help ensure the data's accuracy. For example, a new road or landmark might require confirmation from multiple users before it is permanently added to the map.
- Machine learning and artificial intelligence can be utilized to detect anomalies and inconsistencies in the data. These systems can flag potentially erroneous contributions for further review by human moderators.
- Implementing reputation or trust systems for contributors can help ensure data reliability. Users who consistently provide accurate and helpful information can earn higher trust scores, and their contributions can be given more weight in the verification process.
- Collaborating with local governments, organizations, and community groups can enhance data accuracy. These partnerships can provide authoritative data sources and ensure that maps reflect the needs and realities of local communities.
- Ensuring transparency in the contribution process and holding users accountable for their edits can deter malicious behavior. Clear guidelines, visible edit histories, and the ability to report and dispute inaccuracies can enhance the integrity of the data.

While UGC in online mapping brings significant advantages in terms of real-time updates and comprehensive coverage, it also introduces challenges related to data accuracy and verification. By implementing robust verification processes, fostering diverse participation, and leveraging technology and community partnerships, online mapping platforms can mitigate these challenges and maintain the reliability and usefulness of their maps.

Misuse of Map Data

The availability of highly detailed maps and real-time traffic updates can lead to significant privacy concerns. Users might inadvertently reveal sensitive information about their location, travel patterns, and routines. For instance, location-sharing features can expose a user's real-time whereabouts, potentially making them vulnerable to tracking or unwanted attention. Moreover, data from maps can be aggregated to infer personal habits, frequented places, and other private details. Addressing these concerns requires robust privacy controls, clear user consent mechanisms, and the ability for users to manage their privacy settings. Additionally, anonymizing data and limiting the granularity of publicly available information can help mitigate privacy risks. The detailed and accessible nature of online map data also poses risks of misuse for malicious purposes as listed below.

- Detailed maps and real-time location-sharing features can be exploited by stalkers to track and monitor individuals without their consent. This misuse of map data can lead to severe safety and security concerns for targeted individuals.
- Criminals can use map data to identify and target vulnerable locations, such as isolated homes, businesses with minimal security, or areas with infrequent police patrols. This information can assist in planning and executing criminal activities, thereby increasing the risk to property and personal safety.
- During emergencies, such as natural disasters or public health crises, the misuse of map data can exacerbate the situation. Malicious actors might spread false information about safe zones, evacuation routes, or resource availability, leading to confusion, panic, and potentially dangerous outcomes for affected populations.

Several strategies can be employed to mitigate the risks associated with the misuse of map data as illustrated in the next paragraph.

- Providing users with granular privacy controls allows them to manage who can see their location and travel data. Features such as temporary location sharing, incognito mode, and customizable privacy settings can help protect users' privacy.
- Implementing techniques to anonymize user data and limit the granularity of publicly available information can reduce the risk of misuse. Aggregating data at a higher level (e.g., city or neighborhood) instead of providing exact locations can help protect individual privacy.

- Strengthening security measures on mapping platforms can prevent unauthorized access to sensitive data. This includes implementing encryption, regular security audits, and user authentication protocols.
- Educating users about the potential risks associated with sharing location data and how to use privacy features effectively can empower them to protect their information. Awareness campaigns and clear communication about privacy settings can help users make informed decisions.
- Collaborating with law enforcement and regulatory bodies to monitor and address misuse of map data can enhance safety and security. Establishing channels for reporting and responding to malicious activities can help mitigate the impact of misuse.
- Developing and enforcing ethical guidelines and policies for the use of map data can set standards for responsible behavior. Platforms can establish terms of service that prohibit malicious use and outline consequences for violating these policies.

Hence, while online mapping platforms offer significant benefits, they also present potential risks related to privacy violations and malicious applications. By implementing robust privacy controls, security measures, user education, and ethical guidelines, these platforms can mitigate the risks and ensure that map data is used responsibly and ethically.

Promoting Responsible Online Mapping

User Education

Educating users on responsible editing practices is fundamental. Users should be encouraged to use and cite reliable sources when adding or updating map data. This ensures contributions are based on accurate and credible information. Moreover, be aware of personal biases and strive for objective contributions. Understanding the impact of biased data can help users contribute more balanced information. Additionally, learn the best practices for editing maps, such as avoiding vandalism, respecting local regulations, and following community guidelines.

Community Moderation

Implementing robust moderation techniques helps maintain the integrity of map data: Engage experienced users as volunteer moderators to review contributions and flag suspicious edits. Further, use AI and machine learning algorithms to detect and flag potential errors, malicious edits, or patterns of misuse. Also, provides easy-to-use tools for users to report inaccuracies or malicious content, ensuring quick resolution.

Data Verification Systems

Exploring mechanisms to verify user contributions enhances data reliability. Encourage a system where multiple users review and confirm new data before it becomes part of the map. Require additional details or evidence (such as photos or links to official documents) for significant edits or new entries. Implement processes that require consensus from several contributors for changes to be accepted, particularly in sensitive or highly trafficked areas.

Transparency and User Reputation

Transparency and reputation systems can incentivize responsible contributions by maintaining and displaying a transparent edit history for each map entry, showing who made changes and when. This accountability discourages vandalism and misinformation. Moreover, clearly highlights the source of data and contributions, allowing users to assess the credibility of the information. Further, develop user reputation systems where contributors earn trust scores based on the accuracy and helpfulness of their contributions. Higher scores can grant users more influence and privileges, while repeat offenders can face restrictions.

By fostering responsible online mapping practices through user education, community moderation, data verification, and transparency measures, online mapping platforms can enhance data integrity, reliability, and trust. These strategies collectively ensure that the benefits of collaborative mapping are realized while mitigating the risks associated with user-generated content.

CONCLUSION

The chapter provides the details on the evolution of online mapping platforms from the early 1990s to the present that has revolutionized the way we interact with geographical data, moving from rudimentary digital maps to sophisticated, interactive applications. These developments have democratized access to spatial information, challenged traditional cartographic practices, and shifted the focus from static maps to dynamic, user-interactive experiences. Consequently, online mapping platforms have not only expanded the functionality and accessibility of digital maps but also transformed various domains such as transportation, urban planning, and personal navigation. As technology continues to advance, the future of online mapping holds the promise of further innovations, continually reshaping how we perceive, interact with, and navigate the world around us.

The chapter also underscores the transformative power of user participation in online mapping platforms, highlighting how collective intelligence significantly enhances the quality, comprehensiveness, and utility of digital maps. Users contribute to these platforms by adding Points of Interest (POIs), updating road networks, and providing detailed descriptions and photographs, which collectively enrich the maps with real-time, localized information. This collaborative approach ensures that maps reflect diverse perspectives and up-to-date conditions, thereby improving navigation and decision-making for all users. The chapter also explores the challenges inherent in user-generated content, such as data accuracy, verification, and potential misuse, and proposes strategies to address these issues, including robust moderation, transparency, and user education. Examples of successful collaborative projects like OpenStreetMap, Waze, and Mapillary illustrate the effectiveness of harnessing community input to create dynamic, reliable mapping solutions. Despite the challenges, the chapter concludes that the benefits of collective user contributions far outweigh the drawbacks, emphasizing that responsible practices can mitigate risks and enhance the reliability and impact of online mapping platforms. By leveraging the collective knowledge and experiences of users, these platforms not only democratize access to geographic information but also foster a more interconnected and informed global community.

REFERENCES

Ahmad, M., & Ali, A. (2023). Mapping the future of sustainable development through cloud-based solutions: A case study of openstreetmap. In *Promoting Sustainable Management Through Technological Innovation* (pp. 153–176). IGI Global., DOI: 10.4018/978-1-6684-9979-5.ch011

Andrade, R., Alves, A., & Bento, C. (2020). POI mining for land use classification: A case study. *ISPRS International Journal of Geo-Information*, 9(9), 493. Advance online publication. DOI: 10.3390/ijgi9090493

Borkowska, S., & Pokonieczny, K. (2022). Analysis of OpenStreetMap Data Quality for Selected Counties in Poland in Terms of Sustainable Development. *Sustainability (Basel)*, 14(7), 3728. Advance online publication. DOI: 10.3390/su14073728

Brown, G., Sanders, S., & Reed, P. (2018). Using public participatory mapping to inform general land use planning and zoning. *Landscape and Urban Planning*, 177, 64–74. Advance online publication. DOI: 10.1016/j.landurbplan.2018.04.011

Chen, C., Zhang, D., Wang, Y., & Huang, H. (2021). Enabling Smart Urban Services with GPS Trajectory Data. In *Enabling Smart Urban Services with GPS Trajectory Data*. DOI: 10.1007/978-981-16-0178-1

Chico, H. (2015). *Does MapQuest still exist?' Yes, it does, and it's a profitable business*. Washington Post. https://www.washingtonpost.com/business/economy/does-mapquest-still-exist-as-a-matter-of-fact-it-does/2015/05/22/995d2532-fa5d-11e4-a13c-193b1241d51a_story.html

Domènech, A., Mohino, I., & Moya-Gómez, B. (2020). Using flickr geotagged photos to estimate visitor trajectories in world heritage cities. *ISPRS International Journal of Geo-Information*, 9(11), 646. Advance online publication. DOI: 10.3390/ijgi9110646

Foody, G., Long, G., Schultz, M., & Olteanu-Raimond, A. M. (2024). Assuring the quality of VGI on land use and land cover: Experiences and learnings from the LandSense project. *Geo-Spatial Information Science*, 27(1), 16–37. Advance online publication. DOI: 10.1080/10095020.2022.2100285

Fraisl, D., Campbell, J., See, L., Wehn, U., Wardlaw, J., Gold, M., Moorthy, I., Arias, R., Piera, J., Oliver, J. L., Masó, J., Penker, M., & Fritz, S. (2020). Mapping citizen science contributions to the UN sustainable development goals. *Sustainability Science*, 15(6), 1735–1751. Advance online publication. DOI: 10.1007/s11625-020-00833-7

Gunter, U., & Önder, I. (2021). An Exploratory Analysis of Geotagged Photos From Instagram for Residents of and Visitors to Vienna. *Journal of Hospitality & Tourism Research (Washington, D.C.)*, 45(2), 373–398. Advance online publication. DOI: 10.1177/1096348020963689

Herfort, B., Lautenbach, S., Porto de Albuquerque, J., Anderson, J., & Zipf, A. (2021). The evolution of humanitarian mapping within the OpenStreetMap community. *Scientific Reports*, 11(1), 3037. Advance online publication. DOI: 10.1038/s41598-021-82404-z PMID: 33542423

Hilburn, A., Zawisza, T., Bazan, J., Cruz, R., & Rodriguez, J. (2021). Employing Participatory Risk Mapping (PRM) as a land-use planning method: The case of a derelict former hospital in Laredo, Texas, USA. *Journal of Urban Design*, 26(2), 235–256. Advance online publication. DOI: 10.1080/13574809.2020.1814135

Kantola, S., Fagerholm, N., & Nikula, A. (2023). Utilization and implementation of PPGIS in land use planning and decision-making from the perspective of organizations. *Land Use Policy*, 127, 106528. Advance online publication. DOI: 10.1016/j.landusepol.2022.106528

Khan, Z. T., & Johnson, P. A. (2020). Citizen and government co-production of data: Analyzing the challenges to government adoption of VGI. *The Canadian Geographer. Geographe Canadien*, 64(3), 374–387. Advance online publication. DOI: 10.1111/cag.12619

Król, K. (2020). Evolution of online mapping: From Web 1.0 to Web 6.0. *Geomatics, Landmanagement and Landscape*, 1, 33–51. DOI: 10.15576/GLL/2020.1.33

Lee, J., Lim, J., Pyo, S., & Lee, J. (2023). Aerial online mapping on-board system by real-time object detection for UGV path generation in unstructured outdoor environments. *Journal of Field Robotics*, 40(7), 1754–1765. Advance online publication. DOI: 10.1002/rob.22213

Minaei, M. (2020). Evolution, density and completeness of OpenStreetMap road networks in developing countries: The case of Iran. *Applied Geography (Sevenoaks, England)*, 119, 102246. Advance online publication. DOI: 10.1016/j.apgeog.2020.102246

Murad, A., Faruque, F., Naji, A., Tiwari, A., Qurnfulah, E., Rahman, M., & Dewan, A. (2024). Optimizing health service location in a highly urbanized city: Multi criteria decision making and P-Median problem models for public hospitals in Jeddah City, KSA. *PLoS ONE, 19*(1 January). DOI: 10.1371/journal.pone.0294819

Nagaraj, A. (2021). Information seeding and knowledge production in online communities: Evidence from openstreetmap. *Management Science*, 67(8), 4908–4934. Advance online publication. DOI: 10.1287/mnsc.2020.3764

Petzold, J., Andrews, N., Ford, J. D., Hedemann, C., & Postigo, J. C. (2020). Indigenous knowledge on climate change adaptation: A global evidence map of academic literature. In *Environmental Research Letters* (Vol. 15, Issue 11). DOI: 10.1088/1748-9326/abb330

Psyllidis, A., Gao, S., Hu, Y., Kim, E. K., McKenzie, G., Purves, R., Yuan, M., & Andris, C. (2022). Points of Interest (POI): A commentary on the state of the art, challenges, and prospects for the future. *Computational Urban Science*, 2(1), 20. Advance online publication. DOI: 10.1007/s43762-022-00047-w PMID: 35789810

Santos, D., Santos, C., Santos, J., Filho, A., & Saba, H. (2024). The Importance of the Facility Location Techniques to Assist Companies in Decision-Making for the Installation of Logistics Hub. *Open Journal of Business and Management*, 12(01), 79–89. Advance online publication. DOI: 10.4236/ojbm.2024.121006

Skaalsveen, K., Ingram, J., & Urquhart, J. (2020). The role of farmers' social networks in the implementation of no-till farming practices. *Agricultural Systems*, 181, 102824. Advance online publication. DOI: 10.1016/j.agsy.2020.102824

Taouktsis, X., & Zikopoulos, C. (2024). A decision-making tool for the determination of the distribution center location in a humanitarian logistics network. *Expert Systems with Applications*, 238, 122010. Advance online publication. DOI: 10.1016/j.eswa.2023.122010

Williams, D., O'Brien, D., & Kramers, E. (2003). The Atlas of Canada Web Mapping: The User Counts. *Cartographic Perspectives*, 44(44), 8–28. Advance online publication. DOI: 10.14714/CP44.512

Yan, Y., Feng, C. C., Huang, W., Fan, H., Wang, Y. C., & Zipf, A. (2020). Volunteered geographic information research in the first decade: a narrative review of selected journal articles in GIScience. In *International Journal of Geographical Information Science* (Vol. 34, Issue 9). DOI: 10.1080/13658816.2020.1730848

Zentai, L. (2013). The evolution of cartographic visualization in the Digital Era. *Sharing Knowledge*, 146.

Chapter 10
Empowering Communities:
OpenStreetMap and Social Inclusion

Munir Ahmad
https://orcid.org/0000-0003-4836-6151
Survey of Pakistan, Pakistan

ABSTRACT

This chapter explored how OpenStreetMap (OSM) enhances social inclusion and community participation in mapping. By enabling anyone to contribute, OSM leverages local knowledge for more accurate and detailed maps, addressing the limitations of traditional mapping. Community involvement is fostered through mapping parties, micro-tasking initiatives, and social media integration, promoting ownership and engagement. OSM empowers marginalized groups by documenting their communities, countering misrepresentation, and bridging the digital divide with training and resources. Despite challenges like digital literacy and data quality, solutions such as multilingual resources, robust validation, and offline tools enhance inclusivity. Ultimately, OSM supports sustainable development, disaster preparedness, and equitable resource allocation by integrating diverse perspectives and fostering community-driven mapping efforts.

INTRODUCTION

Globalization has become a central feature of society and the advances in digital technology have changed the appearance and ways of the reality that surrounds us (Autio et al., 2021; Bibri, 2022; Manoharan et al., 2021). Today, due to the avail-

DOI: 10.4018/979-8-3693-3868-1.ch010

ability of digital maps we have got the chance to acquire geographical information at our fingertips. Nevertheless, traditional mapping applications are often inadequate in capturing certain groups, particularly, those in less developed areas. That leads to many discrepancies in terms of available information which can hamper good decisions as well as emergency preparedness and response mechanisms. It is imperative to attain proper coverage and correct representation because, without equal opportunities in access to such elements, the disparities will remain distinct across the geographical areas.

The requirement for inclusive mapping is not just trivial but rather of significant concern as it affects the day-to-day functionality. Without clear maps and comprehensive cartography, poor outcomes can be expected especially when the maps are not detailed enough concerning the areas in question. For example, it can be challenging to identify and access those in need of rescuing such as in the case of humanitarian disasters this translates to a slower response to such situations. Moreover, such cultures often do not have a representation that speaks on behalf of them when it comes to the portrayal of environments. This absence of representation can contribute to continued oppression and limit the environment's ability to help these communities with adequate resources and assistance. This is why inclusive mapping is important not only simply for the purposes of functional and performant logistical and emergency response mapping but also for ensuring that all people's voices can be meaningfully depicted and navigated (Bryant, 2022; Laituri et al., 2023; Mohiuddin & Jabot, 2023; Vogt et al., 2023).

OSM has a range of advantages in dealing with the problems of inadequate and skewed mapping. Due to the possibility of anyone being involved in the production of the maps, OSM provides a favorable platform for the social inclusion of different communities as they are in a better position to map their environments to their best knowledge. This participatory process allows the use of local information, which makes the map data better and more accurate. Due to the openness of OSM, the residents are involved directly thus providing more information that is useful in increasing the level of mapping detail. Thus, OSM not only enhances the reliability of geographical data but also increases motivation and concern among people in the community, making them more persistent (Ahmad & Ali, 2023; Grinberger et al., 2022; Herfort et al., 2021; Muhamad et al., 2023; Schott et al., 2021).

The objective of this chapter is to analyze the relationship between OSM and social inclusion. It will look at how OSM brings together people in communities and provides a platform for participation, development of local content, and support for the underprivileged sections of society. Furthermore, the risks and opportunities involved in this kind of participation will also be highlighted in the chapter with a view of presenting solutions to the likely challenges. Last, the chapter shall conclude by giving a brief of the importance of mapping to the excluded communities and part of positive societal change.

COMMUNITY PARTICIPATION

OSM thrives on the collective effort of its contributors. Unlike traditional, top-down mapping approaches where information flows from a central authority, OSM empowers individuals to add their local knowledge and update existing information. This collaborative spirit fosters a sense of ownership and empowers communities to create maps that truly reflect their needs. Different ways through which communities participate in OSM are summarized in Table 1 and are described below.

Mapping Parties

Mapping parties are organized events that gather individuals with diverse levels of mapping experience to collaborate on creating and improving maps. These events serve as educational opportunities for new mappers, who can learn the basics from seasoned contributors. At the same time, experienced mappers can share their knowledge and work together on larger, more complex projects. These events are not just about collecting valuable geographical data; they also play a crucial role in raising awareness about OpenStreetMap and empowering residents to actively participate in the mapping process. Engaging community members helps to ensure that the maps are accurate and reflective of local realities, fostering a sense of ownership and agency among participants (Brovelli et al., 2018). Hristova et al. (2013) found that social mapping events have a more positive impact on new contributors than experienced contributors.

Mapathons are also the type of mapping parties that focus on gathering data in unmapped areas. User feedback can be used to improve data collection in these types of mapping parties (Gama et al., 2019). Universities integrate mapathons, collaborative events for creating open geospatial data, into their curriculum (Coetzee et al., 2018). Libraries can be a venue for hosting events called mapathons where volunteers contribute to creating maps for disaster relief efforts to help individuals in vulnerable areas by providing them with accurate and up-to-date maps (Quill, 2018).

Micro-tasking Initiatives

Large mapping projects can indeed be overwhelming for beginners. To address this, micro-tasking initiatives break down these projects into smaller, more manageable tasks, enabling anyone with a few minutes to contribute meaningfully. One such initiative is "Missing Maps"(https://www.missingmaps.org/) which focuses on mapping vulnerable communities at risk of epidemics. By dividing the mapping efforts into small, accessible tasks, Missing Maps allows volunteers to contribute to critical humanitarian work without requiring extensive time commitments or expertise (Kriewaldt & Lee, 2021; Mahmud et al., 2022).

Another example is "Wheelmap" (https://wheelmap.org/) which encourages users to identify and map wheelchair-accessible locations worldwide. This initiative empowers users to make significant contributions by simply noting the accessibility of places they visit (Boßmann & Harriehausen-Mühlbauer, 2021; Dzafic et al., 2020). Both initiatives demonstrate how micro-tasking can democratize the mapping process, making it easier for a wide range of participants to get involved and ensure that maps are more comprehensive and inclusive.

Community Challenges and Gamification

Some communities use friendly competition and gamification to boost participation in mapping activities. These challenges often target specific features or areas within a set timeframe, adding a fun and engaging element to the process (Watkinson et al., 2023). For example, the "Mapathon" series organizes online mapping competitions where participants contribute data for a designated region. These events turn mapping into an enjoyable and dynamic activity, fostering a spirit of collaboration and camaraderie among participants. By incorporating elements of competition and game-like rewards, these initiatives can significantly increase engagement and motivate more people to contribute to mapping projects, ultimately enhancing the quality and scope of the maps produced.

Social Media Integration

OpenStreetMap integrates with various social media platforms, enabling users to share their mapping experiences and collaborate online. This integration fosters a sense of community and encourages wider participation. For instance, the #MapMyCity hashtag on X (formally Twitter), Instagram, or LinkedIn allows users to showcase their OSM contributions and inspire others to map their own cities. By sharing their efforts and achievements, mappers can connect with like-minded individuals, exchange tips and advice, and collectively enhance the richness and accuracy of OSM data. This online interaction not only amplifies the reach of OSM but also builds a supportive and engaged community of mappers.

Table 1. Communities' participation in OSM

Participation Method	Description	Example
Mapping Parties	Organized events where community members collaborate to gather and contribute geographic data.	US Mappy Hours are virtual gatherings for the U.S. community to meet new people and discuss OpenStreetMap.
Micro-tasking Initiatives	Breaking down large mapping projects into smaller, more manageable tasks.	Missing Maps focuses on mapping vulnerable communities at risk of epidemics, while Wheelmap tasks users with identifying wheelchair-accessible locations.
Community Challenges & Gamification	Using friendly competition and game elements to increase participation.	Mapathon series organizes online mapping competitions where participants contribute data for a designated region.
Social Media Integration	Sharing mapping experiences and collaborating online through social media platforms.	#MapMyCity hashtag on Twitter allows users to share their OSM contributions and inspire others.

These are just a few examples of how communities actively participate in OSM. By fostering a collaborative environment, leveraging technology, and promoting inclusivity, OSM empowers individuals to become active contributors to the creation of a more comprehensive and representative map of the world.

LOCAL KNOWLEDGE AND INFORMATION GAP

Traditional map data, often based on satellite imagery or government surveys, can overlook the intricate details that define a place. This is where the power of local knowledge comes in. OpenStreetMap empowers communities to contribute their unique understanding of their surroundings, enriching map data in several ways that are depicted in table 2 and elaborated below.

Missing Infrastructure

Official maps often overlook vital elements crucial for effective navigation and service delivery. This gap is where local mappers play a crucial role by adding details like unmapped roads, footpaths, and community landmarks. A compelling example is the mapping of informal settlements by the local residents who actively contributed data on narrow alleyways and hidden pathways that are essential for emergency responders navigating these densely populated areas (Herfort et al., 2021; Raviscioni et al., 2022).

These contributions not only improve the accuracy and completeness of maps but also enhance emergency response capabilities. By mapping previously undocumented routes and landmarks, local mappers empower their communities and facilitate better access to essential services and resources. This grassroots mapping effort demonstrates the transformative impact of community engagement in creating more inclusive and functional maps that meet the specific needs of local populations.

Points of Interest

Commercial maps frequently overlook local businesses, community centers, and cultural sites that hold significant value for residents. OpenStreetMap provides a platform for communities to pinpoint these vital locations, ensuring they are recognized and accessible to others. Integrating indigenous knowledge into OSM, not only enriches the map data but also amplifies the visibility of cultural sites and natural resources that are essential to the community's identity and well-being. This collaborative effort highlights OSM's role in empowering communities to safeguard their heritage and ensure that important locations are accurately represented and accessible to a global audience (Klinkhardt et al., 2021; Minghini et al., 2022).

Hyperlocal Features

Local knowledge also plays a crucial role beyond just filling in missing elements on maps. Communities can actively customize map data to reflect their unique needs, languages, and cultural perspectives. For example, a fishing community might contribute detailed information about tide pools and fish spawning grounds, which are essential for their livelihood but often missing from generic maps. Furthermore, communities with indigenous languages can enrich maps by adding place names and labels in their native tongue. This practice not only enhances the cultural preservation of indigenous heritage but also promotes inclusivity by ensuring that local identities and traditions are accurately represented on the map.

Table 2. Impact of local knowledge on OSM data

Local Knowledge Element	Description	Positive Impact
Missing Infrastructure	Unmapped roads, footpaths, and community landmarks.	Improves navigation and facilitates service delivery (e.g., emergency response).
Points of Interest	Local businesses, community centers, and cultural sites.	Increases visibility and accessibility of these locations.
Hyperlocal Features	Details specific to a community (e.g., tide pools, indigenous languages).	Caters to unique needs and fosters cultural preservation.

Disaster Preparedness

Detailed maps that include information on evacuation routes, shelters, and vulnerable locations are instrumental in empowering communities to prepare for and respond to disasters effectively. For instance, following the devastating Nepal earthquake in 2015, local mappers swiftly updated OpenStreetMap data to reflect the current situation on the ground. They pinpointed damaged infrastructure, blocked roads, and other critical details that were essential for coordinating and prioritizing relief efforts (Bhatta et al., 2016).

In times of crisis, such as natural disasters, having up-to-date and accurate mapping information can make a significant difference in saving lives and minimizing damage. OSM's collaborative and open-source nature allows for rapid updates and contributions from local communities, governmental agencies, and humanitarian organizations. This real-time data sharing and mapping capability enable responders to navigate affected areas more efficiently, identify safe routes for evacuation, and establish temporary shelters where needed (Tzavella et al., 2022).

By leveraging OSM and similar platforms for disaster preparedness and response, communities can proactively enhance their resilience and readiness, ensuring that critical information is readily available and accessible to all stakeholders involved in emergency management.

Resource Allocation

Accurate data on infrastructure, population distribution, and community needs plays a crucial role in enabling governments and non-governmental organizations (NGOs) to allocate resources efficiently. OpenStreetMap data can be utilized to identify remote villages without access to clean water. By mapping out these underserved areas, the project facilitated the targeted delivery of water pumps and sanitation facilities to communities in need.

OSM provided a platform for local mappers to document essential details about infrastructure and community demographics. This data enabled organizations to prioritize and allocate resources effectively, ensuring that aid efforts were directed where they were most urgently required. By leveraging OSM's collaborative mapping capabilities, the project not only improved access to vital resources but also enhanced the resilience of communities by addressing critical infrastructure gaps.

This initiative exemplifies how open-source mapping data can empower stakeholders to make informed decisions and take targeted actions that have a tangible impact on improving the quality of life for underserved populations. By continuing to expand and update mapping efforts, governments and NGOs can better address community needs and achieve more equitable resource allocation.

Community Development

Inclusive maps have a profound impact on community development by empowering residents to advocate for their needs and showcase their unique attributes. When local businesses are listed on OpenStreetMap, they gain visibility and can attract a broader customer base, thereby stimulating economic growth and local entrepreneurship. Similarly, cultural landmarks documented by community members not only preserve heritage but also enhance tourism potential, attracting visitors interested in experiencing the authentic character of an area (Ahmad, 2023; Balducci, 2021).

Accurate and comprehensive maps play a pivotal role in promoting sustainable development within communities. By accurately reflecting the landscape and resources available, these maps assist in urban planning, infrastructure development, and disaster preparedness. Moreover, they provide a platform for residents to participate in decision-making processes and advocate for improvements in services and amenities.

Overall, inclusive mapping on platforms like OSM fosters community engagement, economic vitality, and cultural preservation. It enables communities to harness their strengths and address their challenges effectively, contributing to a more sustainable and prosperous future for all residents. By incorporating the invaluable insights of local communities, OpenStreetMap transcends the realm of navigation, becoming a powerful tool for empowerment, disaster preparedness, and sustainable development.

EMPOWERING MARGINALIZED GROUPS

Social inclusion lies at the heart of OpenStreetMap. The platform empowers marginalized groups to reclaim their narratives and represent themselves accurately on the map. This section explores how OSM fosters a platform for marginalized groups.

Mapping Vulnerable Communities

Mapping vulnerable communities using OpenStreetMap is a transformative practice that addresses the invisibility often faced by marginalized groups residing in informal settlements, indigenous lands, or unrecognized areas. Traditional maps frequently overlook these communities, limiting their access to essential services and resources. OSM empowers residents to take charge of mapping their own neighborhoods, and documenting key locations such as homes, schools, healthcare facilities, and community infrastructure. By actively participating in mapping initiatives, residents not only enhance navigation within their communities but also assert their existence and needs. This grassroots approach challenges negative stereotypes and misconceptions associated with informal settlements, fostering a more accurate and inclusive representation of these areas.

By leveraging OSM, vulnerable communities can amplify their voices, promote social equity, and pave the way for targeted interventions that address their specific needs. This collaborative mapping effort not only enhances local empowerment but also contributes to broader initiatives aimed at achieving sustainable development and social justice.

Bridging the Digital Divide

Addressing the digital divide is crucial to ensuring that marginalized communities can actively participate in initiatives like OpenStreetMap. Lack of access to technology and mapping skills often presents barriers that prevent these communities from contributing to and benefiting from OSM data. To bridge this gap, several initiatives are in practice

- Organizations like Missing Maps (https://www.missingmaps.org/) conduct training workshops in underserved areas. These workshops equip residents with essential mapping skills, teaching them how to contribute valuable data to OSM. By empowering local communities to map their own neighborhoods, Missing Maps not only improves the accuracy of map data but also enhances community resilience and preparedness for emergencies.
- Projects like TeachOSM (https://teachosm.org/) aim to assist students in mapping concepts. This is a project launched in 2016 by OpenStreetMap US, that empowers educators of all levels to integrate open-source mapping and OpenStreetMap tools into their curriculum. They provide resources like lesson plans and training opportunities, and also maintain a platform for educators to collaborate on projects.

By providing training and educational opportunities, these initiatives empower marginalized communities to overcome technological barriers and participate meaningfully in OSM. Bridging the digital divide not only promotes inclusivity in mapping efforts but also enhances community empowerment and resilience in the face of social, economic, and environmental challenges.

Countering Misrepresentation

OpenStreetMap serves as a powerful tool for countering misrepresentation and empowering marginalized communities to reclaim their narratives. Traditional maps frequently perpetuate negative stereotypes or overlook the existence and contributions of indigenous and marginalized groups. OSM allows these communities to actively participate in mapping their ancestral lands, documenting traditional knowledge routes, and asserting their cultural heritage and rights.

A notable example is seen in indigenous communities in the Philippines, who have utilized OSM to map and document their ancestral lands comprehensively. By recording their traditional knowledge routes, sacred sites, and historical landmarks on OSM, these communities challenge historical misrepresentations and assert their rightful place on the map. This grassroots mapping effort not only preserves indigenous cultures but also serves as a tool for advocating for land rights and cultural preservation.

Through OSM, marginalized communities gain visibility and recognition on a global platform, ensuring that their perspectives and contributions are accurately represented. By participating in mapping initiatives, these communities reclaim their narratives, promote cultural diversity, and advocate for social justice and equality. OSM thus plays a pivotal role in fostering inclusivity, empowering communities, and challenging existing biases within mapping and geographical representation. OSM can be employed by marginalized groups in various ways that are elaborated below.

- Accurate maps that showcase the presence and needs of marginalized communities serve as powerful advocacy tools. By documenting their communities on OSM, these groups can demonstrate their existence and highlight areas requiring improved living conditions, access to land rights, and basic services. This data empowers communities to advocate for their rights and demand equitable treatment from authorities and policymakers.
- OSM enables detailed mapping of infrastructure, population distribution, and community needs within marginalized areas. This information helps governments, NGOs, and humanitarian organizations allocate resources more effectively. By pinpointing specific locations and identifying areas lacking essential services, OSM data ensures that interventions and service delivery efforts are targeted where they are most urgently needed, thus improving the overall quality of life for marginalized populations.
- Traditional maps often perpetuate negative stereotypes or overlook the realities of marginalized communities. By documenting their own realities on OSM, marginalized groups can counter these misrepresentations. They can accurately depict their cultural heritage, traditional knowledge, and contributions to society, thereby promoting a more inclusive and accurate representation of their communities on a global scale.

OSM serves as a vital platform for marginalized groups to assert their rights, improve service delivery, and challenge inaccurate portrayals. By actively participating in mapping initiatives, these communities not only enhance their visibility and representation but also advocate for social justice, equity, and respect for their unique cultural identities and contributions. OSM empowers marginalized groups to become active participants in shaping the way they are seen and represented on the map. This fosters a sense of agency, promotes social inclusion, and paves the way for a more just and equitable world.

CHALLENGES AND SOLUTIONS

While the participatory nature of OSM fosters inclusivity, it also presents challenges that need to be addressed to ensure equitable participation for all.

Challenges

There are several challenges associated with OSM and similar collaborative mapping platforms are listed below.

- Not everyone has access to technology or the necessary digital literacy skills to contribute effectively to OSM. This digital divide can disproportionately affect individuals from low-income communities or geographically isolated areas, limiting their ability to participate in mapping projects and benefit from the information shared through OSM.
- The predominance of English in the OSM user interface and documentation poses a significant barrier for non-English speakers. This linguistic limitation can hinder their full participation in mapping activities, understanding project guidelines, and contributing their local knowledge accurately. Overcoming language barriers is crucial for fostering inclusivity and ensuring that diverse perspectives are represented in global mapping efforts.
- The open and decentralized nature of OSM allows anyone to contribute data, which can lead to concerns about data quality and potential biases. Contributors' perspectives, cultural backgrounds, and access to information may influence how data is recorded and mapped, potentially leading to unintentional inaccuracies or misrepresentations. Ensuring data accuracy and minimizing biases requires ongoing efforts in community engagement, validation processes, and maintaining transparency in data sources and methodologies.

Solutions

Some solutions to address challenges in OpenStreetMap and enhance inclusivity are as follows.

- Initiatives like "Missing Maps" organize training workshops in underserved communities. These programs aim to equip residents with essential mapping skills, bridging the digital literacy gap and empowering them to contribute effectively to OSM. By providing hands-on training and resources, these workshops enable community members to document their local knowledge and improve the accuracy of map data.
- OSM is actively working on developing multilingual resources to cater to a diverse global audience. This includes translating the user interface, documentation, and support materials into various languages. By offering information in local languages, OSM enhances accessibility and encourages broader participation from non-English speakers. Multilingual resources also include creating tutorials and guides that are culturally relevant and accessible to users worldwide.
- Robust moderation and validation processes are essential to maintain data quality and accuracy in OSM. Experienced mappers within the community can review new contributions, identify inconsistencies, and verify the accuracy of information. Community-driven validation helps ensure that mapped data reflects ground truth and minimizes potential biases. Additionally, automated validation tools can be employed to check for errors, improve data consistency, and enhance the reliability of mapped information.
- Recognizing the challenges posed by limited internet connectivity in some areas, OSM has developed offline mapping tools. These tools allow individuals to collect mapping data without requiring a continuous internet connection. Users can gather information offline using mobile devices or GPS units and upload their data to OSM when internet access becomes available. Offline mapping tools facilitate participation from remote or isolated communities, ensuring that their contributions are included in the global mapping dataset.

By implementing these solutions, OSM can enhance inclusivity, improve data quality, and empower communities worldwide to participate actively in mapping their environments and advocating for their needs effectively. These initiatives contribute to a more comprehensive and accurate representation of diverse communities and landscapes on the global map. By acknowledging these challenges and implementing effective solutions, the OSM community can strive toward a more inclusive mapping experience. This ensures that everyone, regardless of background or location, has the opportunity to contribute their unique perspective and shape the map of our world.

CONCLUSION

OpenStreetMap addresses the challenges of inadequate and biased mapping by providing a participatory platform that includes diverse communities, enabling them to map their environments accurately. This participatory approach leverages local knowledge, resulting in more detailed and reliable maps, while fostering community engagement and social inclusion. The chapter examines the relationship between OSM and social inclusion, highlighting how OSM facilitates community participation, content development, and support for underprivileged groups, while addressing potential risks and proposing solutions. Community participation in OSM is fostered through organized events like mapping parties and mapathons, micro-tasking initiatives like Missing Maps and Wheelmap, and gamification to boost engagement. Integration with social media further amplifies community involvement. The use of local knowledge in OSM addresses gaps in traditional maps, capturing missing infrastructure, points of interest, and hyperlocal features that are crucial for effective navigation and service delivery. This is especially important in disaster preparedness, where detailed maps can enhance emergency response. Accurate data from OSM also aids in resource allocation and community development, empowering residents to advocate for their needs and preserve their cultural heritage. OSM's inclusivity extends to marginalized groups, allowing them to document their communities, challenge misrepresentation, and bridge the digital divide through initiatives like Missing Maps and TeachOSM. Despite challenges such as digital literacy, language barriers, and data quality concerns, solutions like training workshops, multilingual resources, robust validation processes, and offline mapping tools enhance OSM's inclusivity and reliability. By addressing these challenges, OSM ensures that diverse perspectives are represented, empowering communities to actively participate in mapping and fostering positive societal change.

REFERENCES

Ahmad, M. (2023). Exploring the Role of OpenStreetMap in Mapping Religious Tourism in Pakistan for Sustainable Development. In J. P. D. M. Vítor, A. G. da R. N. João, L. de J. P. Maria, & A. de M. C. Liliana (Eds.), *Experiences, Advantages, and Economic Dimensions of Pilgrimage Routes* (pp. 23–40). IGI Global. DOI: 10.4018/978-1-6684-9923-8.ch002

Ahmad, M., & Ali, A. (2023). Mapping the future of sustainable development through cloud-based solutions: A case study of openstreetmap. In *Promoting Sustainable Management Through Technological Innovation* (pp. 153–176). IGI Global., DOI: 10.4018/978-1-6684-9979-5.ch011

Autio, E., Mudambi, R., & Yoo, Y. (2021). Digitalization and globalization in a turbulent world: Centrifugal and centripetal forces. *Global Strategy Journal*, 11(1), 3–16. Advance online publication. DOI: 10.1002/gsj.1396

Balducci, F. (2021). Is OpenStreetMap a good source of information for cultural statistics? The case of Italian museums. *Environment and Planning. B, Urban Analytics and City Science*, 48(3), 503–520. Advance online publication. DOI: 10.1177/2399808319876949

Bhatta, G. P., Dangol, S., & Sapkota, R. K. (2016). Role of Land Professionals and Spatial Data Infrastructure in Disaster Risk Reduction: In the Context of Post 2015 Nepal Earthquake: General Review. *Nepalese Journal on Geoinformatics*, 15, 59–65. DOI: 10.3126/njg.v15i1.51187

Bibri, S. E. (2022). The Social Shaping of the Metaverse as an Alternative to the Imaginaries of Data-Driven Smart Cities: A Study in Science, Technology, and Society. *Smart Cities*, 5(3), 832–874. Advance online publication. DOI: 10.3390/smartcities5030043

Boßmann, C., & Harriehausen-Mühlbauer, B. (2021). Customizable Navigation on Mobile Devices for Physically Impaired People. *International Conference on Information and Communication Technologies for Ageing Well and E-Health, ICT4AWE - Proceedings, 2021-April.* DOI: 10.5220/0010527002440255

Brovelli, M. A., Mooney, P., Biagi, L., Brambilla, M., Celino, I., Ciceri, E., Dorigatti, N., Huang, H., Minghini, M., & Venkatachalam, V. (2018). *Mapping Parties at FOSS4G Europe: Fun.* Outcomes and Lessons Learned., DOI: 10.1007/978-3-319-70878-2_1

Bryant, J. (2022). *Digital mapping and inclusion in humanitarian response*. ODI.

Coetzee, S., Minghini, M., Solis, P., Rautenbach, V., & Green, C. (2018). Towards understanding the impact of Mapathons - Reflecting on youthmappers experiences. *International Archives of the Photogrammetry, Remote Sensing and Spatial Information Sciences - ISPRS Archives, 42*(4W8). DOI: 10.5194/isprs-archives-XLII-4-W8-35-2018

Dzafic, D., Candiotti, J. L., & Cooper, R. A. (2020). Improving wheelchair route planning through instrumentation and navigation systems. *Proceedings of the Annual International Conference of the IEEE Engineering in Medicine and Biology Society, EMBS, 2020-July*. DOI: 10.1109/EMBC44109.2020.9176481

Gama, K., Gonçalves, B. A., Rautenbach, V., Coetzee, S., Sastry, N., Green, C., & Fourie, N. (2019). Mapathons and hackathons to crowdsource the generation and usage of geographic data. *ACM International Conference Proceeding Series*. DOI: 10.1145/3316287.3316293

Grinberger, A. Y., Minghini, M., Yeboah, G., Juhász, L., & Mooney, P. (2022). Bridges and Barriers: An Exploration of Engagements of the Research Community with the OpenStreetMap Community. *ISPRS International Journal of Geo-Information*, 11(1), 54. Advance online publication. DOI: 10.3390/ijgi11010054

Herfort, B., Lautenbach, S., Porto de Albuquerque, J., Anderson, J., & Zipf, A. (2021). The evolution of humanitarian mapping within the OpenStreetMap community. *Scientific Reports*, 11(1), 3037. Advance online publication. DOI: 10.1038/s41598-021-82404-z PMID: 33542423

Hristova, D., Quattrone, G., Mashhadi, A., & Capra, L. (2013). The life of the party: Impact of social mapping in OpenStreetMap. *Proceedings of the 7th International Conference on Weblogs and Social Media, ICWSM 2013*. DOI: 10.1609/icwsm.v7i1.14416

Klinkhardt, C., Woerle, T., Briem, L., Heilig, M., Kagerbauer, M., & Vortisch, P. (2021). Using openstreetmap as a data source for attractiveness in travel demand models. In *Transportation Research Record* (Vol. 2675, Issue 8). DOI: 10.1177/0361198121997415

Kriewaldt, J., & Lee, S. J. (2021). Digital volunteerism: Missing maps: Crowd sourcing to support humanitarian responses for a better future. *Geography Bulletin*, •••, 19–21.

Laituri, M., Luizza, M. W., Hoover, J. D., & Allegretti, A. M. (2023). Questioning the practice of participation: Critical reflections on participatory mapping as a research tool. *Applied Geography (Sevenoaks, England)*, 152, 102900. Advance online publication. DOI: 10.1016/j.apgeog.2023.102900

Mahmud, Z., Chauhan, A., Sarkar, D., & Soden, R. (2022). Revisiting Engagement in Humanitarian Mapping: An Updated Analysis of Contributor Retention in OpenStreetMap. *Conference on Human Factors in Computing Systems - Proceedings*. DOI: 10.1145/3491101.3519728

Manoharan, A. P., Ingrams, A., Kang, D., & Zhao, H. (2021). Globalization and Worldwide Best Practices in E-Government. *International Journal of Public Administration*, 44(6), 465–476. Advance online publication. DOI: 10.1080/01900692.2020.1729182

Minghini, M., Sarretta, A., & Napolitano, M. (2022). OpenStreetMap Contribution to Local Data Ecosystems in COVID-19 Times: Experiences and Reflections from the Italian Case. *Data*, 7(4), 39. Advance online publication. DOI: 10.3390/data7040039

Mohiuddin, M. B., & Jabot, M. (2023). Activating Education for Sustainable Development Goals Through YouthMappers. In *Sustainable Development Goals Series: Vol. Part F2734*. DOI: 10.1007/978-3-031-05182-1_8

Muhamad, N., Muhamad Hakimi, F. H., & Mahadzir, M. D. A. (2023). Community Activation for Disaster Risk Reduction Through OpenStreetMap: A Scoping Review. *Journal of Advanced Geospatial Science & Technology*, 3(2), 25–50. Advance online publication. DOI: 10.11113/jagst.v3n2.68

Quill, T. M. (2018). Humanitarian Mapping as Library Outreach: A Case for Community-Oriented Mapathons. *Journal of Web Librarianship*, 12(3), 160–168. Advance online publication. DOI: 10.1080/19322909.2018.1463585

Raviscioni, S., Rojas Bolanos, M. A., Gaspari, F., Ponti, C., Biraghi, C. A., & Tadi, M. (2022). COLLABORATIVE MAPPING STRATEGY IN SUPPORT OF SLUM UPGRADING: THE CASE OF BOGOTÁ. *International Archives of the Photogrammetry, Remote Sensing and Spatial Information Sciences - ISPRS Archives, 43*(B4-2022). DOI: 10.5194/isprs-archives-XLIII-B4-2022-273-2022

Schott, M., Grinberger, A. Y., Lautenbach, S., & Zipf, A. (2021). The impact of community happenings in openstreetmap-establishing a framework for online community member activity analyses. *ISPRS International Journal of Geo-Information*, 10(3), 164. Advance online publication. DOI: 10.3390/ijgi10030164

Tzavella, K., Skopeliti, A., & Fekete, A. (2022). Volunteered geographic information use in crisis, emergency and disaster management: A scoping review and a web atlas. *Geo-Spatial Information Science*. Advance online publication. DOI: 10.1080/10095020.2022.2139642

Vogt, A., Flacke, J., Pfeffer, K., Hoefsloot, F. I., Strugar Kolesnik, J., & Schnell, J. (2023). Development of an inclusive Mapping Application in a Co-Design Process. *AGILE: GIScience Series*, 4, 1–8. Advance online publication. DOI: 10.5194/agile-giss-4-48-2023

Watkinson, K., Huck, J. J., & Harris, A. (2023). Using gamification to increase map data production during humanitarian volunteered geographic information (VGI) campaigns. *Cartography and Geographic Information Science*, 50(1), 79–95. Advance online publication. DOI: 10.1080/15230406.2022.2156389

Chapter 11
Fostering Engagement and Trust in E-Learning Communities Through Social Media Platforms

Sreethi Rebeka R.
Christ University, India

Rejoice Thomas
https://orcid.org/0000-0002-8701-6720
Christ University, India

ABSTRACT

This chapter explores the integration of social media platforms in e-learning environments, focusing on their roles in fostering engagement, promoting collaboration, and building trust within virtual educational communities. It analyzes how social media enhances learner interaction, discussing best practices for using platform features to encourage active participation and facilitate collaborative learning experiences. Strategies for fostering trust and community through transparent communication and inclusive practices are also examined. Drawing on theoretical frameworks of social presence and community of inquiry, this study highlights the potential of social media to create dynamic and interactive learning environments. By addressing privacy concerns and ethical considerations, the chapter offers insights into leveraging social media effectively to enhance engagement and learning outcomes in online education.

DOI: 10.4018/979-8-3693-3868-1.ch011

INTRODUCTION

In today's interconnected world, e-learning communities increasingly leverage social media platforms to create interactive and dynamic learning environments. This chapter explores the symbiotic relationship between e-learning and social media, examining how these platforms can empower educators and learners while addressing challenges related to safety and trust. By embracing the potential of social media, we can harness its power to foster meaningful educational interactions and cultivate a sense of community among participants.

E-learning has revolutionized education, breaking down geographical barriers and providing access to resources and expertise from around the globe. However, the effectiveness of these online learning environments hinges on the ability to engage participants and build a trusted community. With their inherent interactive and participatory nature, social media platforms offer a unique opportunity to enhance the e-learning experience. They provide spaces for learners to collaborate, share ideas, and support one another, creating a vibrant and engaging educational atmosphere (Perez et al., 2023).

This chapter delves into how social media can be integrated into e-learning communities to enhance engagement and build trust. It examines the strategies educators can employ to create safe and supportive environments, the role of social media in fostering peer-to-peer interactions, and how these platforms can be used to personalize learning experiences. Additionally, it addresses the challenges and risks associated with using social media in educational settings, including issues related to privacy, security, and the digital divide.

Through a comprehensive analysis of these topics, this chapter aims to provide educators, administrators, and policymakers with insights and practical strategies for leveraging social media to build robust, safe, and trustworthy e-learning communities. By understanding and addressing the complexities of this relationship, we can create more effective and inclusive online learning environments that truly harness the potential of social media to enrich education.

BACKGROUND:

Integrating social media platforms into e-learning environments has transformed educational practices, offering new avenues for engagement, collaboration, and personalized learning experiences. Traditional educational models increasingly incorporate social media to enhance student interaction, encourage active participation, and foster community among learners. However, this integration also challenges privacy, security, and ethical considerations that must be addressed to ensure effective and safe learning environments (Alalwan, 2022).

This chapter explores strategies for fostering engagement and trust within e-learning communities through the effective use of social media platforms. It examines how educators can leverage social media to enhance student engagement, promote collaborative learning, and cultivate a sense of trust and community among participants.

The objectives of this chapter are multifaceted, exploring integrating social media platforms within e-learning environments. Firstly, the chapter aims to critically analyze how social media platforms facilitate engagement and interaction among learners in virtual educational settings, examining their role in enhancing communication channels and fostering collaborative learning experiences. Secondly, it seeks to delve into best practices for utilizing social media features effectively to promote active participation and create dynamic, interactive learning environments. Lastly, the chapter investigates strategies to cultivate trust and nurture a sense of community within e-learning communities through transparent communication methods and inclusive practices. By addressing these objectives, the chapter aims to provide insights into harnessing the potential of social media to optimize engagement, collaboration, and community-building in online educational contexts.

This chapter focuses on various social media platforms commonly used in educational settings, such as Facebook groups, Twitter chats, and LinkedIn communities. It will explore case studies and examples of successful implementations of social media integration in e-learning to illustrate effective engagement and trust-building strategies. The scope includes discussions on privacy concerns, security measures, and ethical considerations associated with using social media in educational contexts.

The conceptual framework for this chapter draws on theories of social presence, community of inquiry, and social constructivism. It explores how these theoretical perspectives can inform the understanding of how social media platforms facilitate communication, collaboration, and knowledge construction within virtual learning communities.

The theoretical framework further builds upon concepts from educational psychology, digital communication theories, and social network analysis. It provides a theoretical lens through which to analyze the impact of social media on learner engagement, trust development, and community building in e-learning environments. By addressing these components, the chapter aims to comprehensively explore strategies and frameworks for effectively leveraging social media platforms to foster engagement and trust in e-learning communities.

THE CONVERGENCE OF E-LEARNING AND SOCIAL MEDIA

The education landscape has undergone a significant transformation with the advent of digital technology. Traditional classroom-based learning has been complemented and, in some cases, replaced by e-learning platforms that provide flexibility, accessibility, and a wealth of resources to learners worldwide. E-learning has evolved from simple online courses to comprehensive virtual learning environments that offer interactive content, real-time feedback, and personalized learning paths. This evolution has been driven by technological advances, increasing internet penetration, and the growing demand for continuous, lifelong learning (Alenezi, 2023).

The digital age has seen the rise of Massive Open Online Courses (MOOCs), Learning Management Systems (LMS), and other online educational tools that facilitate the dissemination of knowledge. These platforms enable learners to access various educational materials, participate in discussions, and collaborate on projects, regardless of physical location. The ability to learn at one's own pace and the convenience of accessing resources anytime and anywhere have made e-learning an attractive option for students and professionals alike (Perez et al., 2023).

Social media platforms have become integral to our daily lives, influencing how we communicate, share information, and engage with content. Social media offers unique opportunities to enhance the learning experience in educational settings. Platforms such as Facebook, Twitter, LinkedIn, Instagram, and YouTube provide educators and learners with tools to create, share, and discuss educational content innovatively (Bik & Goldstein, 2013; Perez et al., 2023).

Social media facilitates peer-to-peer interaction, allowing learners to connect, share insights, and collaborate on projects. It also enables educators to reach a wider audience, share resources, and engage with students outside traditional classroom settings. Using social media in education can promote active learning, foster community, and provide real-time feedback and support (Misra, 2023).

Integrating social media into e-learning environments offers numerous advantages. Social media platforms are inherently engaging, encouraging active participation and interaction among learners through multimedia content such as videos, infographics, and live streams, making learning more effective and enjoyable. Additionally, social media fosters community building, creating a sense of collaboration, support, and belonging among learners, which is especially beneficial in e-learning settings where physical interaction is limited. These platforms also provide access to many resources, including articles, videos, and expert opinions, enriching the learning experience with diverse perspectives and up-to-date information. Furthermore, social media enables real-time communication and feedback, allowing educators to promptly address questions and concerns, improving the overall learning experience and providing immediate support to learners (Salloum et al., 2019).

Integrating social media into e-learning environments presents several challenges. Privacy and security concerns are paramount, as educators and institutions must ensure that personal information is protected and that the platforms comply with relevant data protection regulations. Additionally, social media can be a significant source of distraction for learners, making it crucial to balance its educational benefits with its potential to divert attention. The digital divide is another critical issue, as not all learners have equal access to social media and digital technologies, necessitating efforts to address accessibility and ensure inclusivity. Quality control is also a concern, given the vast amount of information available on social media, making it difficult to verify the accuracy and quality of educational content. Educators must diligently curate and verify resources to maintain high standards (Misra, 2023; Salloum et al., 2019). Educators can effectively integrate social media into e-learning environments by understanding and addressing these challenges, creating powerful, engaging, and trustworthy educational experiences.

ENSURING SAFETY AND TRUST IN VIRTUAL LEARNING SPACES

In virtual learning spaces, safety risks are a significant concern that educators and administrators must address to ensure a secure environment for learners. These risks include cyberbullying, where individuals may face harassment or intimidation from peers; data breaches, where personal information can be exposed or stolen; and the spread of misinformation, which can undermine the credibility of educational content. Additionally, the anonymity of online interactions can sometimes lead to inappropriate behaviour and a lack of accountability. Understanding these risks is the first step in creating a safe online learning community, as it allows educators to anticipate potential issues and develop proactive measures to address them (Kassem et al., 2017).

To mitigate the safety risks associated with social media in e-learning, it is essential to implement comprehensive strategies that promote safe online practices. Educators and institutions should use secure, reputable platforms with robust privacy and security features. Educating participants about online safety, including recognizing and reporting cyberbullying, protecting personal information, and evaluating the credibility of online content, is crucial. Establishing and enforcing clear policies on acceptable behaviour, privacy settings, and the use of personal data can help maintain a safe online environment. Regular monitoring of online interactions and prompt response to any issues that arise are also necessary to prevent and address harmful behaviour effectively (Jo, 2023).

Transparent communication is a cornerstone of building trust in virtual learning spaces. Educators and administrators should maintain open lines of communication with learners, clearly outlining the policies, expectations, and procedures related to online safety and conduct. It includes providing clear information on how data is collected, used, and protected and the steps taken to ensure a secure learning environment. Regular updates and open discussion forums can help address learners' concerns, fostering a sense of trust and community (Bik & Goldstein, 2013; Perez et al., 2023). By being transparent and responsive, educators can build trust that enhances the learning experience and encourages active participation and engagement in virtual learning spaces.

ENGAGEMENT STRATEGIES FOR EFFECTIVE LEARNING

Social media platforms offer many features that can be leveraged to enhance learner engagement in e-learning environments. Utilizing multimedia content, such as videos, infographics, and live streams, can make learning more dynamic and visually appealing. Interactive features like polls, quizzes, and discussion threads enable learners to actively participate and contribute to the learning process. Social media's shareability allows for disseminating educational content beyond the confines of a single course, encouraging broader discussions and collaborative learning. Additionally, personalized notifications and targeted content recommendations can keep learners engaged and motivated by catering to their interests and learning progress (Li & Wong, 2020).

Gamification involves integrating game design elements into the learning experience to boost motivation and engagement. Techniques such as point scoring, leaderboards, badges, and challenges can create a sense of competition and achievement among learners. Interactive learning methods, including simulations, virtual labs, and role-playing exercises, allow learners to apply theoretical knowledge in practical, hands-on scenarios. These approaches make learning more enjoyable and enhance knowledge retention and developing critical thinking skills (Saleem et al., 2021). By transforming traditional learning activities into engaging and interactive experiences, educators can foster a deeper connection to the material and sustain learner interest over time.

Building a sense of community and fostering peer interaction is essential for effective learning in virtual environments. Social media platforms can facilitate these connections by providing spaces for learners to collaborate, share ideas, and support each other. Group projects, study circles, and peer review activities encourage learners to collaborate, exchange feedback, and build a supportive network. Online forums and social media groups dedicated to specific courses or topics can be hubs for ongoing discussions and resource sharing (Alalwan, 2022; Lowenthal et al., 2023). By nurturing a collaborative and inclusive community, educators can create a learning environment where learners feel connected, valued, and motivated to participate actively.

SOCIAL MEDIA TOOLS AND TECHNOLOGIES FOR E-LEARNING

Effectively utilizing social media platforms in e-learning involves adopting best practices that maximize engagement and learning outcomes. First, select platforms that align with the educational goals and audience preferences, ensuring they are user-friendly and widely accessible. Establish clear guidelines and expectations for online behaviour to maintain a respectful and productive learning environment. Encourage active participation by regularly posting engaging content, initiating discussions, and responding promptly to learners' queries and comments. Additionally, create dedicated groups or pages for specific courses or topics to organize content and facilitate focused interactions. Regularly updating and curating content ensures it remains relevant and valuable to learners (Li & Wong, 2020; Stewart, 2015).

Integrating multimedia and visual content into e-learning can significantly enhance the learning experience by catering to diverse learning styles and making complex information more accessible. Use videos to demonstrate concepts, provide tutorials, and share expert insights, as they can be more engaging than text alone. Infographics and diagrams can simplify and clarify complex ideas, making them easier to understand and remember. Live streaming sessions, such as webinars or Q&A sessions, offer real-time interaction and can foster a sense of connection between educators and learners. Incorporating these various forms of multimedia content can make learning more interactive, visually appealing, and effective (Clark, 2021).

Social media platforms offer robust analytics tools that can be harnessed to personalize the learning experience. Educators can gain valuable insights into their behaviour and learning needs by analyzing data on learners' interactions, engagement levels, and content preferences. This information can be used to tailor content and activities to individual learners, providing personalized recommendations and feedback. Tracking metrics such as completion rates, time spent on different activities, and participation in discussions can help identify areas where learners may need additional support or resources(Khor & Mutthulakshmi, 2024). Leveraging analytics allows for a more targeted and responsive approach to e-learning, enhancing its effectiveness and addressing each learner's unique needs.

PROMOTING INCLUSIVITY AND DIVERSITY

Creating inclusive digital learning environments ensures that all learners feel valued and supported. It involves designing courses and content catering to diverse learning styles, backgrounds, and abilities. Use inclusive language and imagery that reflect various cultures, identities, and experiences. Encourage diverse perspectives by inviting contributions from all participants and fostering an environment where everyone feels comfortable sharing their thoughts and ideas. Providing multiple engagement means, such as discussion forums, video lectures, and interactive activities, can accommodate different learning preferences and enhance inclusivity (Mintz et al., 2024).

Addressing accessibility in e-learning communities is critical to ensuring all learners have equal opportunities to participate and succeed. It involves designing digital content that meets accessibility standards, such as the Web Content Accessibility Guidelines (WCAG). Ensure that all multimedia content, including videos and images, is accompanied by captions, transcripts, and descriptive text. Use accessible design principles, such as high-contrast colours, readable fonts, and keyboard navigation, to make content usable for learners with disabilities. Providing alternative formats and resources, as well as offering technical support, can help overcome barriers and create a more inclusive learning environment (Ingavélez-Guerra et al., 2021).

Cultivating cultural sensitivity and respect in e-learning communities is vital for promoting diversity and inclusivity. Educators should be aware of cultural differences and strive to create respectful content and representative of various cultures. Incorporate diverse perspectives and examples in course materials to reflect the global nature of the learning community. Encourage open discussions about cultural issues and provide opportunities for learners to share their cultural experiences and viewpoints. Address any instances of cultural insensitivity or bias promptly and constructively (Livingston et al., 2022; Mintz et al., 2024). Educators can create a more inclusive and supportive e-learning community by fostering an environment of mutual respect and understanding.

CASE STUDIES AND SUCCESS STORIES

Several e-learning communities have successfully leveraged social media platforms to create dynamic and engaging educational experiences. For instance, Khan Academy utilizes platforms like YouTube and Facebook to share instructional videos and interact with learners globally, fostering a supportive community around its educational content. Another example is Coursera, which utilizes LinkedIn and Twitter to connect learners with instructors, facilitate discussions, and share course updates. These platforms enable learners to access resources, collaborate with peers, and receive real-time feedback, enhancing their learning journey.

Initiatives aimed at ensuring trust and safety in e-learning communities have proven impactful in maintaining a positive learning environment. Platforms like edX and Udacity implement strict privacy policies and offer secure communication channels to protect learner data and prevent unauthorized access. They also provide clear guidelines on acceptable behaviour and actively monitor content to address misconduct or inappropriate conduct promptly. These efforts help build trust among participants and contribute to a safe and respectful online learning environment.

Effective engagement strategies in e-learning have yielded valuable lessons for educators and administrators. Platforms like LinkedIn Learning and Skillshare use personalized learning paths and recommendations based on user preferences and behaviour analytics to keep learners engaged and motivated. Incorporating interactive elements like quizzes, forums, and live webinars encourages active participation and enhances knowledge retention. Furthermore, leveraging multimedia content such as videos and infographics makes learning more accessible and appealing to diverse audiences. These strategies highlight the importance of adapting content delivery methods to meet the needs and preferences of learners, thereby maximizing engagement and learning outcomes in e-learning environments.

RECOMMENDATIONS AND SOLUTIONS

To effectively integrate social media into e-learning environments while addressing associated challenges, educators should prioritize implementing stringent privacy policies and security measures to safeguard student data, ensuring compliance with regulations like GDPR or CCPA. Clear usage guidelines must be established, delineating acceptable behaviours and content-sharing policies to minimize distractions and maintain a focused learning environment. Ongoing education and training initiatives for educators and students are crucial, focusing on responsible social media use, privacy settings, and digital citizenship. Careful platform selection should prioritize those that align with educational objectives, offer robust privacy features, and facilitate engagement and collaboration through multimedia content and real-time communication tools. Monitoring mechanisms should be implemented to track student interactions and content, supplemented by responsive technical support to address issues promptly and ensure a positive user experience. Collaboration among stakeholders—educators, administrators, parents, and students—is essential for fostering understanding and effectively navigating the benefits and challenges of social media in education. Regular evaluation and adaptation based on feedback and analytics will further refine practices, optimizing social media integration to enhance engagement, collaboration, and personalized learning in e-learning environments while upholding student privacy and responsible digital engagement.

FUTURE DIRECTIONS AND EMERGING TRENDS

Looking ahead, the future of virtual education and e-learning will be profoundly influenced by emerging technologies and the evolution of social media. Artificial intelligence (AI) advances are poised to revolutionize learning experiences through personalized tutoring systems, adaptive assessments, and intelligent content recommendations. Virtual and augmented reality (VR/AR) technologies will likely create immersive learning environments that simulate real-world scenarios, enhancing student engagement and understanding. Additionally, the integration of blockchain technology holds promise for secure credentialing and decentralized learning platforms, ensuring trust and transparency in certification processes.

Predictions for the future of virtual education include a shift towards more flexible and accessible learning modalities catering to diverse learner needs and preferences. Lifelong learning will become increasingly emphasized, with continuous upskilling and reskilling becoming essential in a rapidly evolving job market. Moreover, the global reach of virtual education will democratize access to high-quality learning resources, bridging geographical and socioeconomic divides.

Ethical considerations and policy implications will play a crucial role in shaping the future of virtual education. Issues such as data privacy, digital literacy, equity in access to technology, and the ethical use of AI will need careful consideration and regulation. Policymakers must ensure that educational technologies are used responsibly and inclusively, safeguarding learner rights and promoting equitable educational opportunities.

In embracing these emerging trends and addressing associated ethical challenges, educators, policymakers, and stakeholders can collaboratively pave the way for a future where virtual education is innovative and practical, but also ethical, accessible, and equitable for learners worldwide.

DISCUSSION

Integrating social media into e-learning environments represents a significant evolution in educational practices, offering both opportunities and challenges. With their interactive and participatory nature, social media platforms have fundamentally altered how educators engage with students and facilitate learning experiences. By leveraging these platforms, educators can enhance student engagement through multimedia content, real-time communication, and collaborative learning activities.

One of the key advantages of integrating social media in e-learning is its ability to foster community building and peer interaction. Platforms like Facebook groups, Twitter chats, and LinkedIn communities enable learners to connect with peers, share ideas, and collaborate on projects, transcending geographical boundaries and enhancing the sense of belonging within virtual classrooms. This community-centric approach supports collaborative learning and encourages students' participation and knowledge sharing.

Moreover, social media facilitates personalized learning experiences by allowing educators to tailor content and resources to individual learner preferences and needs. Through analytics and data-driven insights, educators can track student progress, identify learning gaps, and deliver targeted interventions, optimizing each student's learning journey.

However, the integration of social media in e-learning has its challenges. Privacy and security concerns remain prominent, requiring educators and institutions to implement robust data protection measures and educate students about online safety practices. The potential for distraction and misuse of social media also necessitates careful management and clear guidelines on acceptable use within educational contexts.

The future of e-learning and social media integration will likely be shaped by technological advancements such as AI, VR/AR, and blockchain. These technologies enhance personalized learning experiences, create immersive educational simulations, and ensure secure credentialing and certification processes.

While integrating social media in e-learning offers numerous benefits in engagement, collaboration, and personalized learning, it also requires careful consideration of privacy, security, and ethical implications. By navigating these challenges thoughtfully and embracing emerging technologies responsibly, educators can harness the full potential of social media to create enriching and effective learning environments for students worldwide.

CONCLUSION

Integrating social media and emerging technologies into e-learning has transformed educational landscapes, offering new avenues for engagement, collaboration, and personalized learning. Ensuring safety, inclusivity, and ethical practices will be paramount to fostering a positive and effective learning environment as we navigate these advancements. The future of virtual education holds promise for continued innovation, with AI, VR/AR, and blockchain poised to enhance learning experiences further and expand access to education globally. However, addressing challenges such as data privacy, digital equity, and ethical considerations will require thoughtful policies and proactive measures. By embracing these opportunities and challenges, educators and policymakers can shape a future where virtual education not only meets the diverse needs of learners but also empowers individuals and communities worldwide.

REFERENCES

Alalwan, N. (2022). Actual use of social media for engagement to enhance students' learning. *Education and Information Technologies*, 27(7), 9767–9789. DOI: 10.1007/s10639-022-11014-7 PMID: 35399784

Alenezi, M. (2023). Digital learning and digital institution in higher education. *Education Sciences*, 13(1), 88. DOI: 10.3390/educsci13010088

Bik, H. M., & Goldstein, M. C. (2013). An introduction to social media for scientists. *PLoS Biology*, 11(4), e1001535. DOI: 10.1371/journal.pbio.1001535 PMID: 23630451

Clark, R. C. (2021). Multimedia learning in e-Courses. In *Cambridge University Press eBooks* (pp. 537–551). DOI: 10.1017/9781108894333.054

Ingavélez-Guerra, P., Otón-Tortosa, S., Hilera-González, J., & Sánchez-Gordón, M. (2021). The use of accessibility metadata in e-learning environments: A systematic literature review. *Universal Access in the Information Society*, 22(2), 445–461. DOI: 10.1007/s10209-021-00851-x

Jo, H. (2023). From Classroom to Screen: Analyzing the Mechanisms Shaping E-Learning Benefits amidst COVID-19. *Journal of the Knowledge Economy*. Advance online publication. DOI: 10.1007/s13132-023-01614-0

Kassem, M., Benomran, L., & Teizer, J. (2017). Virtual environments for safety learning in construction and engineering: Seeking evidence and identifying gaps for future research. *Visualization in Engineering*, 5(1), 16. Advance online publication. DOI: 10.1186/s40327-017-0054-1

Khor, E. T., & Mutthulakshmi, K. (2024). A systematic review of the role of learning analytics in supporting personalized learning. *Education Sciences*, 14(1), 51. DOI: 10.3390/educsci14010051

Li, K. C., & Wong, B. T. (2020). Social media in Higher Education: A Review of Their uses, benefits and Limitations. *Communications in Computer and Information Science*, 1302, 248–257. DOI: 10.1007/978-981-33-4594-2_21

Livingston, E., Houston, E., Carradine, J., Fallon, B., Akmeemana, C., Nizam, M., & McNab, A. (2022). Global student perspectives on digital inclusion in education during COVID-19. *Global Studies of Childhood*, 13(4), 341–357. DOI. 10.1177/20436106221102617

Lowenthal, P. R., Horan, A., DeArmond, M. C., Lomellini, A., Egan, D., Johnson, M., Moeller, K. N., Keldgord, F., Kuohn, J., Jensen, S., Stamm, A., & Pounds, D. (2023). Classroom community and online learning: A synthesis of Alfred Rovai's research. *TechTrends*, 67(6), 931–944. DOI: 10.1007/s11528-023-00904-3

Mintz, J., Connolly, C., O'Brien, E., Daniela, L., & Ceallaigh, T. Ó. (2024). Inclusive Digital Education: Contexts, Practices and Perspectives. *Computers in the Schools*, 41(2), 115–119. DOI: 10.1080/07380569.2024.2340873

Misra, D. P. (2023). Social media for education and research: Practical considerations. *Journal of the Royal College of Physicians of Edinburgh/˜the Royal College of Physicians ofEdinburgh, 53*(1), 4–6. https://doi.org/DOI: 10.1177/14782715231158008

Perez, E., Manca, S., Fernández-Pascual, R., & Guckin, C. M. (2023). A systematic review of social media as a teaching and learning tool in higher education: A theoretical grounding perspective. *Education and Information Technologies*, 28(9), 11921–11950. DOI: 10.1007/s10639-023-11647-2

Saleem, A. N., Noori, N. M., & Ozdamli, F. (2021). Gamification Applications in e-learning: A Literature review. *Technology. Knowledge and Learning*, 27(1), 139–159. DOI: 10.1007/s10758-020-09487-x

Salloum, S. A., Al-Emran, M., Habes, M., Alghizzawi, M., Ghani, M. A., & Shaalan, K. (2019). It is important to understand the impact of social media practices on the acceptance of E-Learning Systems. In *Advances in intelligent systems and computing* (pp. 360–369). DOI: 10.1007/978-3-030-31129-2_33

Stewart, O. G. (2015). A critical review of the literature on social media's affordances in the classroom. *E-Learning and Digital Media*, 12(5–6), 481–501. DOI: 10.1177/2042753016672895

ADDITIONAL READING

Darwish, D. (2024). Chatbot Concepts and Basics. In *Advances in Computational Intelligence and Robotics book series* (pp. 1–25). DOI: 10.4018/979-8-3693-1830-0.ch001

Darwish, D. (2024). Chatbots vs. AI Chatbots vs. Virtual Assistants. In *Advances in Computational Intelligence and Robotics book series* (pp. 26–50). DOI: 10.4018/979-8-3693-1830-0.ch002

Darwish, D. (2024). Web 3. In *Advances in Web Technologies and Engineering book series* (pp. 1–28). DOI: 10.4018/979-8-3693-1532-3.ch001

Dragomir, M., Rúas-Araújo, J., & Horowitz, M. (2024). Beyond online disinformation: Assessing national information resilience in four European countries. *Humanities & Social Sciences Communications*, 11(1), 101. Advance online publication. DOI: 10.1057/s41599-024-02605-5

Gomez-Vasquez, L. (2021). Social media academic communities for learning, networking and career support. In *Proceedings of the 8th European Conference on Social Media, ECSM 2021* (pp. 75-81). Virtual, Online. https://doi.org/DOI: 10.34190/ESM.21.025

Pareek, S., & Goncalves, J. (2024). Peer–supplied credibility labels were used as an online misinformation intervention. *International Journal of Human-computer Studies, p. 188*, 103276. DOI: 10.1016/j.ijhcs.2024.103276

Singha, R., & Singha, S. (2023). Faith and Culture in Education: Fostering Inclusive Environments. In DeHart, J. (Ed.), *The Role of Faith and Religious Diversity in Educational Practices* (pp. 149–172). IGI Global., DOI: 10.4018/978-1-6684-9184-3.ch007

Singha, R., & Singha, S. (2024). Application of Experiential, Inquiry-Based, Problem-Based, and Project-Based Learning in Sustainable Education. In Goi, C. L. (Ed.), *Teaching and Learning for a Sustainable Future: Innovative Strategies and Best Practices* (Vol. 1, pp. 109–128). IGI Global., DOI: 10.4018/978-1-6684-9859-0.ch006

Singha, R., Singha, S., Ruben, V. M., Natal, M. S., Longkumer, A., & Haokip, A. D. (2024). The Ethics of Collaborating With Social Media Influencers: Influencers and Psychological Well-Being. In Bi, N., & Zhang, R. (Eds.), *Global Perspectives on Social Media Influencers and Strategic Business Communication* (pp. 326–342). IGI Global., DOI: 10.4018/979-8-3693-0912-4.ch016

Singha, S. (2023). Culturally Relevant Teaching in Humanities: E-Book Creation, Blogging, and Bookmaking. In Frazier, D. M. (Ed.), *Teaching Humanities With Cultural Responsiveness at HBCUs and HSIs* (pp. 121–146). IGI Global., DOI: 10.4018/978-1-6684-9782-1.ch006

Singha, S. (2024). Exploring Motivations of Social Media Influencers in Content Production. In Bi, N., & Zhang, R. (Eds.), *Global Perspectives on Social Media Influencers and Strategic Business Communication* (pp. 26–40). IGI Global., DOI: 10.4018/979-8-3693-0912-4.ch002

Singha, S. (2024). Social Media's Influence on Consumer Decision-Making: A Roadmap for Success. In Sahin, F., & Soylemez, C. (Eds.), *Globalized Consumer Insights in the Digital Era* (pp. 85–109). IGI Global., DOI: 10.4018/979-8-3693-3811-7.ch004

Singha, S., & Singh, R. (2024). Cross-Disciplinary Collaborations and Partnerships for Sustainability Education: Including Community-Based Learning, Industry Partnerships, and International Collaborations. In Goi, C. L. (Ed.), *Teaching and Learning for a Sustainable Future: Innovative Strategies and Best Practices* (Vol. 1, pp. 17–37). IGI., DOI: 10.4018/978-1-6684-9859-0.ch002

Singha, S., & Singha, R. (2023). Protecting Data and Privacy: Cloud-based solutions for intelligent transportation applications. *Scalable Computing: Practice and Experience*, 24(3), 257–276. DOI: 10.12694/scpe.v24i3.2381

Trivedi, S. K., Singh, A., Yadav, M., Kumar, A., & Srivastava, P. R. (2024). Intention to use social media in online and blended learning: Potential predictors and mediation of collectivism. *IEEE Transactions on Engineering Management*, 71, 1–14. DOI: 10.1109/TEM.2023.3257422

KEY TERMS AND DEFINITIONS

Community Moderation: Oversight and management of online interactions within e-learning communities to maintain a respectful, inclusive, and productive environment.

Digital Inclusivity: Ensuring equal access and opportunities for all learners, regardless of their digital literacy level, socioeconomic background, or geographic location, in online educational settings.

E-Learning Communities: Online groups of learners and educators who interact and collaborate virtually to achieve educational goals through digital platforms.

Engagement Strategies: Methods and approaches used to encourage active participation, interaction, and involvement of learners in educational activities and discussions.

Online Education: Educational activities and programs delivered over the Internet, enabling remote access to learning resources and interactions.

Social Media Integration: Incorporating social media platforms like Facebook, Twitter, and LinkedIn into e-learning environments to enhance communication, collaboration, and engagement.

Trust-Building: Processes and strategies aimed at fostering confidence, reliability, and mutual respect among participants in virtual learning communities.

Chapter 12
Evaluating the Influence of YouTube Vlogs on Hotel Booking Decisions:
An Information Adoption Model Approach

Suman Lata
Amity University, Noida, India

Krishma Rana
Central University of Jammu, India

ABSTRACT

With the popularity of social media, YouTube Vlogs are playing a crucial role for travelers' hotel booking. YouTube Vloggers create videos of their travelling experiences and upload which help the novice travelers to make an informed choice about their decision on hotel booking. The current study examines what determines travelers to adopt information from YouTube Vlogs for online hotel bookings and how it influences their intentions. A research model was prepared and further, analyzed by sampling 256 Indian travelers who used YouTube Vlogs prior to their hotel booking. The hypotheses of this paper were analyzed by applying structural equation modeling (SEM) using partial least squares (PLS). The findings of this study identified that information quality, source credibility, and trust emerged as crucial factors influencing the adoption of YouTube Vlogs for hotel booking among travelers. This study expanded the information adoption model by introducing a new element, specifically the inclusion of the construct of trust.

DOI: 10.4018/979-8-3693-3868-1.ch012

1. INTRODUCTION

The advancement of internet technologies has led to the emergence of novel platforms, including social media, blogs, video content, reviews, and testimonials, impacting how information is exchanged between consumers and marketers (Mohamed, & Shoufan, 2024). The high demand for the internet has resulted in the expansion of online communities, enabling users to share their opinions, commonly referred to as electronic word of mouth (eWOM). (Ray, Bala & Dwivedi, 2020). Researchers and marketers alike acknowledge the significant role of eWom in providing advantages to firms (Chu & Kim, 2018). Social media is a crucial tool for consumers seeking information from peers and friends to ensure satisfaction before making a purchase (Cherif et al., 2024). Video blogs, among various social media platforms, are considered more convincing and appealing than traditional blogs due to their visual representation (Adu-Marfo et., 2024). Since its establishment in 2005, YouTube has rapidly become a globally recognized video-sharing platform all across the world (Bond, & Miller, 2024). Furthermore, YouTube is identified as the second-largest search engine globally after Google. Content published on YouTube Vlogs is highly relevant and reaches millions of users worldwide (Rufino, 2024). YouTube serves a prominent role in diverse industries, including education, film, and music (Nugroho, & Wang, 2024). It is considered more advantageous for users in meeting their needs compared to other social media platforms (Selem et al., 2024).

YouTube has emerged as a prominent medium for consumers, particularly in the service industry where the quality is challenging to predict before experiencing (Park et al., 2024). Its multimedia-rich visual content makes it a preferred medium for prospective customers compared to text-based reviews and ratings. Both marketers and vloggers utilize videos to influence their customers in purchasing decisions (Ho-Mai et al., 2024). Various investigations have delved into hotel booking intentions within different contexts, encompassing eWOM (Motahar, 2024; Fatiha, 2024; Lee & Lee, 2024), social media (Bilinski, 2024; Sivathanu, & Pillai., 2023; Le & Ryu, 2023; Ray, 2020; Andreu, Beckman & Miller, 2020; El-Said, 2020), website quality (Kim et al., 2022; Chan, Wu & Vipulakom, 2020; Ongsakul, Ali, Wu, Duan, Cabanoglu & Ryu, 2020; Silaban et al., 2022), and hotel rating schemes (Usman, 2021; Wang, Sun & Wen 2019; Xia, Vu, Lan, Law & Li, 2019). Owing to its visual appeal, YouTube is widely embraced by consumers globally (Lee, 2018). Consumers show a preference for Instagram over other social media platforms due to its visual elements (Djafarova and Rushworth, 2019). Despite the recent surge in the popularity of vlogs, which are extensively used for product marketing, their impact on customer decision-making has not been explored to the same extent as other social media platforms (Bond & Miller, 2024). Visual eWOM (Vlogs) has received relatively less attention from researchers (Rufino, 2024). Therefore, this study fills the existing gap by exploring the following research query: In what way do tourists embrace information via YouTube vlogs, and how does it impact their intentions to make hotel bookings? To delve into this matter, we employ the information adoption model, incorporating trust into the foundational model. This research contributes to the sparse literature on YouTube adoption within the hospitality industry, offering empirical evidence by investigating the role of trust alongside the information adoption model in the acceptance of vlogs for hotel booking intentions.

2. LITERATURE REVIEW

In the literature review, the search for relevant papers was conducted on Google Scholar using diverse keywords such as eWom impact on hotel bookings, YouTube Vlogs, User-generated content, information adoption model, and online hotel bookings. The search yielded over 200 results, from which 87 papers pertinent to the study's focus were selected. A comprehensive exploration of prior studies on the information adoption model within the context of eWom was extensively addressed by various researchers. The information adoption model posits that consumers embrace information through two routes: Central Routes, also known as Information Quality, and Peripheral Routes, termed Source Credibility (Saputri, 2024). Consumers exhibit a preference for obtaining information through central routes rather than peripheral routes (Zhang et al., 2024). Additionally, research by Salem et al. (2024) suggested that information quality and source credibility positively influence consumers' perceived eWom credibility. Horrich et al., (2024) argued that active users utilize both routes when seeking information from online reviews about hotel bookings. Meanwhile, Tseng and Wang (2016) found that perceived risk influences dual-route information adoption processes on travel websites, effectively persuading consumers to adopt information via perceived usefulness (Khan et al., 2024).

Beyond the information adoption model, the technology acceptance model (TAM) has been employed in various studies, including eWom intention, mobile apps, and online reviews. Despite its widespread use, TAM is associated with several limitations, such as low explanatory power, neglect of hindrances in technology adoption, and a focus solely on perceived usefulness, disregarding information development and social context considerations. Given these limitations, the present study opts for the information adoption theory to find the impact of YouTube Vlogs on consumers' hotel booking intentions. Trust influences consumers' willingness to rely on others and plays a dominant role in their online purchase decision. Recognizing its importance, this study integrates the trust construct with the information adoption theory, emphasizing its crucial role in helping consumers adopt information from computer-mediated sources. Previous literature has identified key dimensions of hotel trust, including integrity, competence, and reliability (Ahmed et al., 2024; Rafdinal et al., 2024; Nazari Ardabili et al., 2024. Positive reviews on consumer opinion platforms are identified as crucial in building trust, as consumers often turn to reviews to mitigate risks associated with buying situations, enhancing their trust and the perceived usefulness of reviews (Mathavan et al., 2024; Shahzad et al., 2024).

3. CONCEPTUAL MODEL AND HYPOTHESES DEVELOPMENT

3.1Information quality

Information quality is described as "the audience's subjective perception of the arguments in the persuasive message as strong and cogent on the one hand versus weak and spacious on the other (Usman, 2021)." Past literature has explored information quality in various contexts, including food online-to-offline commerce (Bitzenbauer et al., 2024; Mohamed, & Shoufan, 2024; Kang & Namkung, 2020), social media (Efe et al., 2024), electronic word of mouth in hospitality (Martinez, Harrero & Salmones, 2020), and purchase intentions (Masele, & Mwita, 2024; Lin et al., 2024; Demirtas, & Alici, 2024). Therefore, we hypothesize that the information quality provided by YouTube vloggers about hotels positively influences tourists' information usefulness for hotel booking intentions. Thus, our hypothesis is:

H1: Information quality positively influences tourist's information usefulness for hotel booking intentions through YouTube vloggers.

3.2 Source credibility

Source credibility describes as "the extent to which the receiver perceives the source to be expert and competent from which he is acquiring information" (Petty & Caciopo, 2012). Various studies have delved into source credibility (Zahrah, 2024; Arora & Lata, 2020; Kong, & Fang, 2024; Hong & Pittman, 2020; Keni et al., 2024; Lata & Rana, 2021; Kim, Melton, Min & Kim, 2020; Martinez, Herrero & Salmones, 2020). Notably, vloggers' content is deemed more relevant when videos are uploaded by experienced travelers. Therefore, we predict that the source credibility of YouTube vlogs about hotel booking can be one of the determinants of consumers' online hotel booking intentions. Thus, our hypothesis is:

H2: Source credibility positively influences tourist's information usefulness for hotel booking intentions through YouTube vloggers.

3.3 Trust

Trust is described as 'a readiness of a person to rely on a substitute partner in whom one has confidence' (Habbal et al., 2024). Users trust the information and content shared by other users on social media when the provided information is reliable and consistent (Nugroho, & Wang, 2024). Consumers may not be familiar with the service delivery and facilities, but they expect the hotels to fulfill their promises. Trust has been studied in various contexts, including online travel purchases (Darmayasa, & Hardika, 2024; Khare, Dixit & Sarkar, 2020), consumer trust in Airbnb (Wang, Asaad & Filieri, 2020), social media (Yu et al, 2024), and hotel apps (Akhtar, & Siddiqi, 2024). If users trust vlogs within an online community, the likelihood of the usefulness of YouTube vlogs will be higher. Therefore, we hypothesize:

H3: Trust positively influences tourist's information usefulness for hotel booking intentions through YouTube vloggers.

3.4 Information usefulness

Information usefulness is characterized by customers' perception of online reviews as significant and beneficial in guiding their purchasing decisions (Salem et al., 2024). Past literature has shown that information usefulness is a prominent factor influencing consumers when deciding to purchase a product or service (Fatiha, 2024). Studies have explored information usefulness in various contexts, including purchase intentions (Hussain et al., 2024; Park, & Lee, 2024; Sigala, 2024; Ventre & Kolbe, 2020) and social media (Kapri, & Sharma, 2024). Therefore, we hypothesize:

H4: Information usefulness positively influences tourist's hotel booking intentions through YouTube vloggers.

4. RESEARCH METHODOLOGY

4.1 Questionnaire Preparation

The questionnaire of this study was prepared by using past literature to measure the construct. The items of questionnaire have covered five constructs; the questionnaire items of information quality, source credibility and information usefulness were taken from (Nguyen, 2024); the questionnaire items of trust were taken from (Akhtar, & Siddiqi, 2024); and the questionnaire items of hotel booking intention were adapted from (Ho-Mai et al., 2024). The items of the questionnaire of this study were measured on five points Likert scale, ranging from 1 ("strongly disagree") to 5 ("strongly agree").

4.2 Sample and Data collection

To collect data from the respondents, a quantitative survey approach was used to analyze the impact of YouTube vlogs on travelers' hotel bookings intentions. Data from respondents was collected through a self-administered survey questionnaire employing closed-ended questions. The data was gathered from various hotels which are resided in Delhi. Prior to final data collection, a meeting was scheduled with the general manager and permission was taken for the participation of guests. The guests were invited to the hotel lobby and asked to participate. Before the distribution of questionnaire to respondents, few screening questions were asked to ensure that the respondents are representative of universe i.e. Do you use YouTube Vlogs, Do you use YouTube Vlogs while hotel booking. It was ensured the target population must have used YouTube Vlogs at least once or twice in the past six months. After questionnaires were provided to selected guests, initially they seemed shy and confused but as they read questionnaire thoroughly, they got open and provided responses. The convenience sampling method was applied while collecting the response from the guests how YouTube Vlogs influence their decisions while online hotel booking. A total number of 370 questionnaires were distributed among the respondents. The filled 290 were received back from respondents which were keenly screened by the researchers, and it was found that 34 questionnaires contain some missing values, hence these questionnaires were discarded. Finally, 256 valid responses were selected for data analysis, a response rate of 69.1%. The data were collected from Delhi in the month of October 2023. Table 1 indicates the respondents' profile.

Table 1. Demographic profile of the respondents

	Characteristics	Frequency	Percentage
Gender	Male	159	62.1%
	Female	97	37.9%
Age	Below 20	47	18.3%
	21-35	90	35.1%
	36-50	52	20.3%
	51-65	37	14.5%
	Above 65	30	11.8%
Employment Status	Employed	125	48.8%
	Self-Employed	40	15.6%
	Student	70	27.3%
	Others	21	8.3%

5. DATA ANALYSES AND RESULTS

In survey-based research, PLS-Structural Equation Modeling (SEM) is recognized as a crucial tool, particularly in the field of tourism and travel, where it is widely and frequently employed (Jeon, Ali & Lee, 2018). Additionally, PLS is advantageous as it necessitates a small sample size and can calculate path estimates even in the presence of non-normality, as highlighted by studies such as Cheah et al. (2024) and Beldiq (2024). Since PLS doesn't provide significance tests and path estimates directly (Jacqueline et al., 2024), so bootstrapping technique is employed to achieve it. The PLS algorithm offers flexibility to each indicator, and indicators that demonstrate a weak relationship with their latent construct and with other indicators receive lower weightings, as explained by Santoso et al., (2023).

5.1 The measurement model

The evaluation of the PLS measurement model included the scrutiny of convergent and discriminant validity, as well as the reliability of all constructs. Convergent validity in the measurement model was appraised by analyzing composite reliability, Cronbach's alpha, and average variance extracted, following the guidelines of Fornell and Larcker (1981). Cronbach's alpha provided alpha values for all indicators, treating them with equal reliability and showing consistent outer loadings for the constructs. All values surpassed the specified threshold values, as indicated in Table 2.

Table 2. Items loadings, composite reliability, AVE, Cronbach Alpha coefficients

Construct	Scale Item	Loadings	Composite Reliability	AVE	Cronbach Alpha
	AQ1	0.903			
	AQ2	0.680			
Argument Quality (AQ)	AQ3	0.857	0.858	0.671	0.755
	SC1	0.915			
	SC2	0.838			
Source Credibility (SC)	SC3	0.817	0.893	0.736	0.825
	TR1	0.897			
	TR2	0.741			
Trust (TR)	TR3	0.886	0.881	0.713	0.799
	IU1	0.726			
	IU2	0.863			
Information Usefulness (IU)	IU3	0.863	0.859	0.671	0.755
	HB1	0.912			
Hotel Booking Intention	HB2	0.839			
(HBI)	HB3	0.618	0.838	0.639	0.749

Discriminant Validity refers to an "extent in which the reflection of one variable doesn't show the reflection of some other variable" (Afthanorhan, 2021). It is confirmed when the square root of the Average Variance Extracted exceeds the correlation between the constructs, as indicated in Table 3 (Hilkenmeier et al., 2020).

Table 3. Discriminant validity of constructs

	AQ	**SC**	**TR**	**TR**	**HBI**
AQ	**0.819**				
SC	0.150	**0.858**			
TR	-0.013	0.336	**0.844**		
IU	0.249	0.466	0.423	**0.819**	
HBI	0.531	0.421	0.355	0.672	**0.799**

5.2 Structural Model

In the structured model, two values which have highest explanatory power are squared multiple correlations (R^2) and path coefficient (β) values. The R^2 of endogenous variable depicts the percentage of variance whereas the (β) values show the strength of relationship between the constructs (Chin, 1998). R-Square of endogenous is considered as substantial=0.670, moderate=0.333, and weak=0.190 (Ramayah et ql., 2018). The R square value obtained in this study for Information

Usefulness is 0.338 and R square value of Hotel Booking Intention is 0.452 that exhibits the model has the moderate power of explaining the influence of all constructs on Information Usefulness and Hotel Booking Intentions. To analyze the path coefficients, bootstrapping procedure with 5000 iterations were applied. The results of path coefficients are described in Figure 1 and Table 4. The construct with highest β value shows that the construct has the most significant effect and lower β value indicates that the construct has the less effect on the endogenous latent variables. From Figure 1, it shows that source credibility has the highest impact on information usefulness with the path coefficient (β = 0.330) and information quality has the lowest impact with the path coefficient (β = 0.203). Further the mediation of information usefulness plays the most significant impact on the hotel booking intentions with path coefficient (β = 0.672).

Figure 1. Result of structured model

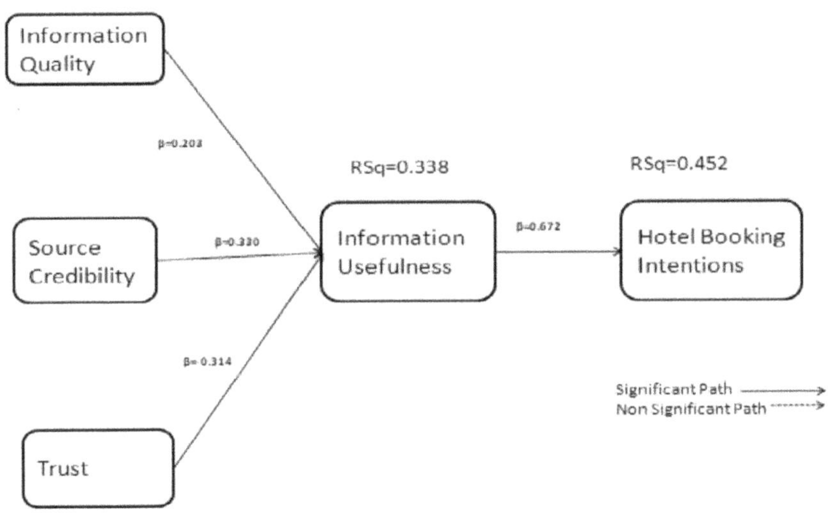

Figure 2. t-statistics

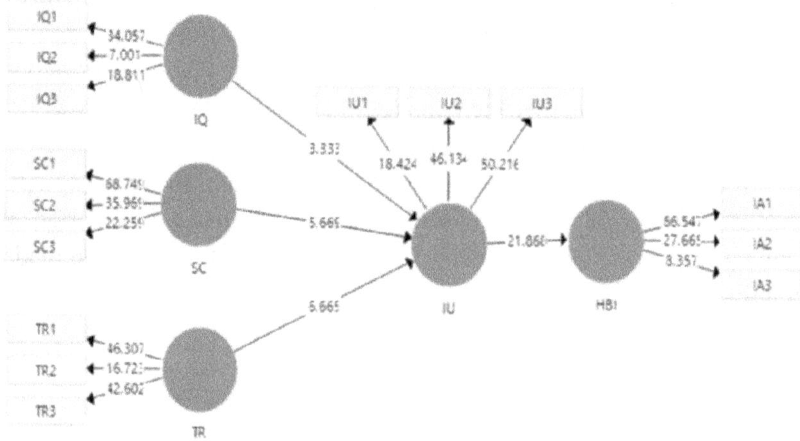

Table 4. Summary of test results for the structured model

Hypotheses	Path	Standardized Coefficient	P value	Supported	Constructs	R-Squared
H1	IQ-IU	0.203	0.001	Yes	Information Usefulness	0.338
H2	SC-IU	0.330	0.000	Yes		
H3	TR-IU	0.314	0.000	Yes		
H4	IU-HBI	0.672	0.000	Yes	Hotel Booking Intentions	0.452

6. DISCUSSIONS

This research focuses on understanding key influences of information adoption constructs on hotel booking intentions. The finding of this study shows that the dual-route process occurs on YouTube vlogs adoption while booking a hotel. The results of this study confirmed the Sussman & Siegal (2003) information adoption model. The high-quality information substantially improves the travel planning of tourists (Mohamed, & Shoufan, 2024). Consumers trust the information when the provided content meets their satisfaction (Bond, & Miller, 2023). Information provided with rich quality is relevant, appropriate, and up to date, it fulfills the tourist's need (Nugroho, & Wang, 2024). The relationship between information quality and information usefulness (H1) is found significant (β=0.203, p<0.05). The findings of this study was found to be consistent with the (Kang & Namkung, 2019) which was conducted on consumer's decision making for purchasing food product through O2Ocommerce. previous studies which were done in different context of eWom (Selem et al., 2024; Bilinski, 2024). The result indicates that hotel patrons' booking intention is affected by YouTube vloggers because they consider it reliable and true.

Further, H2 examined the relationship between source credibility and information usefulness. This study found that consumers perceive YouTube Vlogs as a credible source as well as they perceive that Vloggers are highly expert and provide reliable information on the basis of their experiences. The study indicates the significant positive relationship between source credibility and information usefulness (β=0.330, p<0.05) which indicates that user perceives the high credibility of YouTube vloggers who share their videos regarding their hotel experiences. Sivathanu, & Pillai, (2023), the higher the consumer perceives source expertise the more persuasive the message is. Source's higher credibility leads consumer for the information usefulness. le et al., (2023) pointed out that source credibility is a fundamental element that not only influences an individual's overall attitude but also his/her buying intentions. The findings of this study are found consistent with the previous research (Mathavan et al., 2024; Ahmed et al., 2024; Kang & Namkung, 2019).

The subsequent Hypothesis (H3) of the study also found a significant relationship between trust and information usefulness (β=0.314, p<0.05). As expected, trust positively influences the information usefulness for hotel booking. Nazari Ardabili et al., (2024) pointed in their study that transaction trusts positively impact the intentions for mutual transaction between travel wholesalers and retailers. Further, Rafdinal et al., (2024) also pointed out in their study that consumers trust positively moderates the relationship among online service quality, value, and satisfaction. Recently, Wang et al. (2015) found that e-trust plays prominent role of mediator between hotel website quality and online hotel booking intentions. Chu and Kim (2011) stated that trust is considered as a prominent factor for consumers to know the information value in social networking. This study has also identified the direct role of trust on YouTube vloggers for hotel booking, whereas previous studies have taken trust as mediator only (Keni et al., 2024; Darmayasa, & Hardika, 2024). The meta-analysis conducted by Ismagilova et al., (2019) also stated that trust is a strong antecedent which led a consumer to purchase.

This study also found information usefulness as most significant factor between influence variables and hotel booking intentions (β=0.672, p<0.05), which indicates internet users perceive YouTube vlogger useful for their hotel booking intentions. In our best knowledge, this study is the first in the hospitality sector, which has taken an attempt to understand the role of YouTube vlogs on online hotel booking intentions.

6.1Theoretical Contributions

The findings of this study contribute to the YouTube vloggers adoption literature in emerging market context. Various studies have researched in context of online reviews, eWOM, social media etc. but specific study on the YouTube vloggers adoption for hotel booking is still at the nascent stage. Our research adds in the scant literature concerned with the YouTube vlogs impact on hotel booking intentions. The proposed conceptual model has been constructed from literature and supported with empirical evidence. This model has been taken from Sussman and Siegal (2003) and added a new dimension trust in this study. The present research has conducted in Indian context and to the best of researchers' knowledge, this is the first study that has analyzed the influence of YouTube vlogs on online hotel booking intentions in India. Finally, this study added in the scarce literature of YouTube vloggers adoption of travelers in context of hotel bookings.

6.2 Implications for practice

This study has withdrawn some managerial implications for YouTube vloggers, hotel practitioners and researchers. Due to perceived benefits received, travelers are willing to adopt social media while planning their trip. Travelers rely more on the content published by users rather than the official site. However, the important finding of this study states that travelers trust the content published by YouTube vloggers regarding hotel bookings. So, the content of YouTube vlogs is considered to be designed carefully to provide the required information to travelers for their hotel bookings. The level of accuracy and relevance should be high in the content. Second, the information provided by the YouTube vloggers also triggers the travelers for hotel booking. The hotel should provide some benefits to the customers (free breakfast, special discounts) which make these customers produce positive response through their vlogs. In addition, it may generate content through customers by intrinsic incentives. Though, hotels managers must give great intention towards the recommendations provided by customers and pacify them to believe that their requests are addressed. For instance, hotels should accept online advice from customers and should enact highly given suggestions. The acceptance of online suggestion system has been already adopted by various brands such as Starbucks and its platform My Starbucks Idea (http://mystarbucksidea.force.com/apex/ideaHome), and through this, it found amazing results and consumers are pleased and committed as they know that their suggestions have been addressed. Furthermore, it is crucial for hotel managers to consistently deliver the best and promised amenities to customers, as this encourages positive feedback. Interestingly, hotels receiving only positive reviews may be viewed with skepticism. Instead of merely deleting negative reviews from websites, hotel managers should address weaknesses, enhance service quality, and continually monitor reviews and videos. Developing strategies to counter negative content is essential. Since hotel responses are visible to all readers, adept handling of negative reviews is noticeable and commendable. Effectively managing negative feedback not only satisfies and appeases dissatisfied guests but also motivates them to share positive content about genuine service recovery (Yu et al., 2024; Zhang, & Tang, 2024). Uploaded content should avoid vagueness and steer clear of fake reviews to protect the hotels' reputation.

7. CONCLUSION

With the prevalence of social media and web 2.0, the immense growth of online two-way communication and diversity in content has taken place. Consumers remain highly engaged in online content, especially on YouTube due to its visual representation for decision making. YouTube vlogs are considered more trustworthy as compared to official website by consumers for hotel bookings. It successfully fetches the attention of marketers, who actively use eWom as a new marketing tool. This study has provided important insights to hoteliers. By understanding how much experienced users content play important role for novice travelers and influence their intentions and will aid hotel managers in the betterment of their services and so it increases hotel sales. This research advances present understanding of the travelers' information adoption behavior from YouTube vlogs and leads to the richer understanding of its influence on travelers' hotel booking intentions.

Limitation of the study

The study's limitations can serve as a guide for future directions. The model presented in this paper has only accounted for less than half of the variance in hotel booking intention, indicating that there may be crucial indicators not considered in this investigation. So, studies done in future should focus on other variables of hotel booking intentions. The other variables are valence, visual cues, dispersion, positive and negative eWOM. Further, the study can also analyze the various factors that resist the travelers for the YouTube vloggers adoption for hotel booking. Lastly, the respondents taken in this study are from India; therefore, the finding of this study cannot be applied in another country. Users from different regions and country might perceive a different outlook towards the YouTube vloggers adoption for hotel bookings. Lastly, this study will provide help to the researchers and hotel practitioners to understand the role of YouTube vloggers on tourist's hotel booking intentions.

REFERENCES

Adu-Marfo, A. O., Kwapong, O. A. T. F., Oheneba-Sakyi, Y., & Miller-Young, J. (2024). Understanding teachers' usage of YouTube as a pedagogical tool: A qualitative case study of basic school teachers in Ghana. *E-Learning and Digital Media*, •••, 20427530241239393. DOI: 10.1177/20427530241239393

Afthanorhan, A., Ghazali, P. L., & Rashid, N. (2021, May). Discriminant validity: A comparison of CBSEM and consistent PLS using Fornell & Larcker and HTMT approaches. [). IOP Publishing.]. *Journal of Physics: Conference Series*, 1874(1), 012085. DOI: 10.1088/1742-6596/1874/1/012085

Ahmed, Y. A., Shehzad, H. M. F., Khurshid, M. M., Abbas Hassan, O. H., Abdalla, S. A., & Alrefai, N. (2024). Examining the effect of interoperability factors on building information modelling (BIM) adoption in Malaysia. *Construction Innovation*, 24(2), 606–642. DOI: 10.1108/CI-12-2021-0245

Akhtar, N., & Siddiqi, U. I. (2024). Effects of service providers' self-disclosure on booking platforms on consumers' trust, hesitation, and booking intentions: Moderating role of social media influencers. *Journal of Hospitality Marketing & Management*, 33(4), 470–498. DOI: 10.1080/19368623.2023.2281445

Akhtar, N., & Siddiqi, U. I. (2024). Effects of service providers' self-disclosure on booking platforms on consumers' trust, hesitation, and booking intentions: Moderating role of social media influencers. *Journal of Hospitality Marketing & Management*, 33(4), 470–498. DOI: 10.1080/19368623.2023.2281445

Arora, N., & Lata, S. (2020). YouTube channels influence on destination visit intentions: An empirical analysis on the base of information adoption model. *Journal of Indian Business Research*, 12(1), 23–42. DOI: 10.1108/JIBR-09-2019-0269

Beldiq, E. A., Callula, B., Yusuf, N. A., & Zahra, A. R. A. (2024). Unlocking organizational potential: Assessing the impact of technology through smartpls in advancing management excellence. *APTISI Transactions on Management*, 8(1), 40–48.

Bilinski, P. (2024). The content of tweets and the usefulness of YouTube and Instagram in corporate communication. *European Accounting Review*, 33(1), 279–311. DOI: 10.1080/09638180.2022.2084759

Bitzenbauer, P., Höfler, S., Veith, J. M., Winkler, B., Zenger, T., & Kulgemeyer, C. (2024). Exploring the relationship between surface features and explaining quality of YouTube explanatory videos. *International Journal of Science and Mathematics Education*, 22(1), 25–48. DOI: 10.1007/s10763-022-10351-w

Bond, B. J., & Miller, B. (2024). YouTube as my space: The relationships between YouTube, social connectedness, and (collective) self-esteem among LGBTQ individuals. *New Media & Society*, 26(1), 513–533. DOI: 10.1177/14614448211061830

Chan, S. H. J., Wu, S., & Vipulakom, K. (2020). Young consumers' behavioural intention based on hotel websites. *Anatolia*, 31(1), 1–18. DOI: 10.1080/13032917.2019.1684959

Chang, Y. C., Ku, C. H., & Chen, C. H. (2019). Social media analytics: Extracting and visualizing Hilton hotel ratings and reviews from TripAdvisor. *International Journal of Information Management*, 48, 263–279. DOI: 10.1016/j.ijinfomgt.2017.11.001

Cheah, J. H., Magno, F., & Cassia, F. (2024). Reviewing the SmartPLS 4 software: the latest features and enhancements.

Cherif, K. M., Azzouz, L., & Bendania, A. (2024). *Algerian secondary school students' preferences for the use of YouTube in their informal learning*. Educational Technology Quarterly.

Chu, S. C., & Kim, J. (2018). The current state of knowledge on electronic word-of-mouth in advertising research. *International Journal of Advertising*, 37(1), 1–13. DOI: 10.1080/02650487.2017.1407061

Darmayasa, I. N., & Hardika, N. S. (2024). Core tax administration system: The power and trust dimensions of slippery slope framework Tax Compliance model. *Cogent Business & Management*, 11(1), 2337358. DOI: 10.1080/23311975.2024.2337358

Demirtas, M. S., & Alici, N. (2024). The reliability and quality of YouTube videos as a source of breath holding spell. *Italian Journal of Pediatrics*, 50(1), 8. DOI: 10.1186/s13052-023-01570-0 PMID: 38238792

Djafarova, E., & Rushworth, C. (2017). Exploring the credibility of online celebrities' Instagram profiles in influencing the purchase decisions of young female users. *Computers in Human Behavior*, 68, 1–7. DOI: 10.1016/j.chb.2016.11.009

Efe, I. E., Tesch, C., & Subedi, P. (2024). YouTube as a source of patient information on awake craniotomy: Analysis of content quality and user engagement. *World Neurosurgery: X*, 21, 100249. DOI: 10.1016/j.wnsx.2023.100249 PMID: 38090193

Fatiha, M. (2024). The effectiveness of electronic promotion channels for booking platforms: comparative study between Namlatic Hotel Booking and Booking. com. *Journal of Contemporary Business and Economic Studies Vol, 7*(01).

Fatiha, M. (2024). The effectiveness of electronic promotion channels for booking platforms: comparative study between Namlatic Hotel Booking and Booking. com. *Journal of Contemporary Business and Economic Studies Vol, 7*(01).

Fornell, C., & Larcker, D. F. (1981). Structural equation models with unobservable variables and measurement error: Algebra and statistics. *JMR, Journal of Marketing Research*, 18(3), 382–388. DOI: 10.1177/002224378101800313

Habbal, A., Ali, M. K., & Abuzaraida, M. A. (2024). Artificial Intelligence Trust, Risk and Security Management (AI TRiSM): Frameworks, applications, challenges and future research directions. *Expert Systems with Applications*, 240, 122442. DOI: 10.1016/j.eswa.2023.122442

Hilkenmeier, F., Bohndick, C., Bohndick, T., & Hilkenmeier, J. (2020). Assessing distinctiveness in multidimensional instruments without access to raw data–a manifest Fornell-Larcker criterion. *Frontiers in Psychology*, 11, 223. DOI: 10.3389/fpsyg.2020.00223 PMID: 32210863

Ho-Mai, N. T., Tran, V. T., Nguyen, V. K., Do, U. T. T., Truong, T. B., & Tran, P. T. K. (2024). The pathways of increasing online celebrity brand equity and followers' hotel booking intention: A serial multiple mediation model. *Journal of Research in Interactive Marketing*. Advance online publication. DOI: 10.1108/JRIM-08-2023-0265

Ho-Mai, N. T., Tran, V. T., Nguyen, V. K., Do, U. T. T., Truong, T. B., & Tran, P. T. K. (2024). The pathways of increasing online celebrity brand equity and followers' hotel booking intention: A serial multiple mediation model. *Journal of Research in Interactive Marketing*. Advance online publication. DOI: 10.1108/JRIM-08-2023-0265

Horrich, A., Ertz, M., & Bekir, I. (2024). The effect of information adoption via social media on sustainable consumption intentions: The moderating influence of gender. *Current Psychology (New Brunswick, N.J.)*, 43(18), 1–14. DOI: 10.1007/s12144-023-05526-9

Hulland, J. (1999). Use of partial least squares (PLS) in strategic management research: A review of four recent studies. *Strategic Management Journal*, 20(2), 195–204. DOI: 10.1002/(SICI)1097-0266(199902)20:2<195::AID-SMJ13>3.0.CO;2-7

Hussain, K., Nusair, K., Junaid, M., & Aman, W. (2024). A two-actor model for understanding user engagement with content creators: Applying social capital theory. *Computers in Human Behavior*, 156, 108237. DOI: 10.1016/j.chb.2024.108237

Ismagilova, E., Slade, E., Rana, N. P., & Dwivedi, Y. K. (2020). The effect of characteristics of source credibility on consumer behaviour: A meta-analysis. *Journal of Retailing and Consumer Services*, 53, 101736. Advance online publication. DOI: 10.1016/j.jretconser.2019.01.005

Jacqueline, G., Senjaya, Y. P. A., Firli, M. Z., & Yadila, A. B. (2024). Application of SmartPLS in Analyzing Critical Success Factors for Implementing Knowledge Management in the Education Sector. *APTISI Transactions on Management*, 8(1), 49–57. DOI: 10.33050/atm.v8i1.2201

Kang, J. W., & Namkung, Y. (2019). The role of personalization on continuance intention in food service mobile apps. *International Journal of Contemporary Hospitality Management*. Advance online publication.

Kang, J. W., & Namkung, Y. (2019). The role of personalization on continuance intention in food service mobile apps. *International Journal of Contemporary Hospitality Management*. Advance online publication.

Kapri, S. S., & Sharma, A. (2024). Digital marketing impact on rural Homestay booking and role of destination image. *Anatolia*, •••, 1–13. DOI: 10.1080/13032917.2024.2319075

Keni, K., Wilson, N., & Teoh, A. P. (2024). Antecedents of viewers' watch behavior toward YouTube videos: Evidence from the most populous Muslim-majority country. *Journal of Islamic Marketing*, 15(2), 446–469. DOI: 10.1108/JIMA-01-2023-0008

Khan, A. M., Soroya, S. H., & Mahmood, K. (2024). Impact of information credibility on social media information adoption behavior: A systematic literature review. *Library Hi Tech*, 42(1), 261–283. DOI: 10.1108/LHT-03-2022-0165

Kim, J., Melton, R., Min, J. E., & Kim, B. Y. (2020). Who says what?: Exploring the impacts of content type and blog type on brand credibility, brand similarity and eWOM intention. *Journal of Fashion Marketing and Management*. Advance online publication.

Kim, T., Jo, H., Yhee, Y., & Koo, C. (2022). Robots, artificial intelligence, and service automation (RAISA) in hospitality: Sentiment analysis of YouTube streaming data. *Electronic Markets*, 32(1), 259–275. DOI: 10.1007/s12525-021-00514-y

Kong, H., & Fang, H. (2024). Research on the Effectiveness of Virtual Endorsers: A Study Based on the Match-Up Hypothesis and Source Credibility Model. *Sustainability (Basel)*, 16(5), 1761. DOI: 10.3390/su16051761

Lata, S., & Rana, K. (2021). WHAT ARE THE DETERMINANTS OF CONSUMERS'ONLINE REVIEWS ADOPTION FOR HOTEL BOOKINGS: A STRUCTURAL EQUATION MODELLING APPROACH. *Enlightening Tourism. A Pathmaking Journal, 11*(1), 171-193.

Le, H. T. P. M., & Ryu, S. (2023). The eWOM adoption model in the hospitality industry: The moderating effect of the vlogger's review. *Journal of Hospitality and Tourism Technology*, 14(2), 225–244. DOI: 10.1108/JHTT-08-2021-0233

Lee, J., & Lee, H. K. (2024). Exploring direct and indirect cultural experiences: A study of global consumers' Hanbok experience and engagement mediated via YouTube. *Fashion and Textiles*, 11(1), 19. DOI: 10.1186/s40691-024-00385-9

Lin, M. E., Ayo-Ajibola, O., Castellanos, C. X., West, J., Luu, N., Kim, I., & Kokot, N. C. (2024). Assessing Laryngectomy Patient Education on YouTube: Investigating Quality and Reliability. *OTO Open*, 8(1), e113. DOI: 10.1002/oto2.113 PMID: 38299048

Martínez, P., Herrero, Á., & García-de los Salmones, M. D. M. (2020). Determinants of eWOM on hospitality CSR issues. In Facebook we trust? *Journal of Sustainable Tourism*, 1-19.

Masele, J. J., & Mwita, D. (2024). Online Television Subscription in Tanzania: Examination of the Influence of Information Quality, Video quality and technology ease of use. *ORSEA JOURNAL, 13*(2).

Mathavan, B., Vafaei-Zadeh, A., Hanifah, H., Ramayah, T., & Kurnia, S. (2024). Understanding the purchase intention of fitness wearables: Using value-based adoption model. *Asia-Pacific Journal of Business Administration*, 16(1), 101–126. DOI: 10.1108/APJBA-04-2022-0166

Mathavan, B., Vafaei-Zadeh, A., Hanifah, H., Ramayah, T., & Kurnia, S. (2024). Understanding the purchase intention of fitness wearables: Using value-based adoption model. *Asia-Pacific Journal of Business Administration*, 16(1), 101–126. DOI: 10.1108/APJBA-04-2022-0166

Mohamed, F., & Shoufan, A. (2024). Users' experience with health-related content on YouTube: An exploratory study. *BMC Public Health*, 24(1), 86. DOI: 10.1186/s12889-023-17585-5 PMID: 38172765

Mohamed, F., & Shoufan, A. (2024). Users' experience with health-related content on YouTube: An exploratory study. *BMC Public Health*, 24(1), 86. DOI: 10.1186/s12889-023-17585-5 PMID: 38172765

Motahar, P. S., Tavakoli, R., & Mura, P. (2024). Social media influencers' visual framing of Iran on YouTube. *Tourism Recreation Research*, 49(2), 270–282. DOI: 10.1080/02508281.2021.2014252

Nazari Ardabili, D., Amin, F., & Fayyazi, B. M. (2024). Designing an Adoption Model for Electronic Human Resource Management in Service-Oriented Organizations: A Case Study of Tehran Municipality. *Journal of Information Technology Management*, 16(2), 91–111.

Nguyen, D. T. B., & Nguyen, V. T. K. (2024). The Impact of Electronic Word-of-Mouth on the Purchase Intention of Tourists on Online Hotel Booking Applications. [IJABIM]. *International Journal of Asian Business and Information Management*, 15(1), 1–19. DOI: 10.4018/IJABIM.342086

Nugroho, A., & Wang, W. T. (2024). Credibility of Youtube product reviews and customers' product return intention: A product fit uncertainty perspective. *Information Technology & People*, 37(4), 1560–1586. DOI: 10.1108/ITP-11-2021-0838

Ongsakul, V., Ali, F., Wu, C., Duan, Y., Cobanoglu, C., & Ryu, K. (2020). Hotel website quality, performance, telepresence and behavioral intentions. *Tourism Review*. Advance online publication.

Park, J. Y., & Lee, H. E. (2024). How Consumer Photo Reviews and Online Platform Types Influence Luxury Hotel Booking Intentions Through Envy. *Journal of Travel Research*, •••, 00472875241247317. DOI: 10.1177/00472875241247317

Park, J. Y., & Lee, H. E. (2024). How Consumer Photo Reviews and Online Platform Types Influence Luxury Hotel Booking Intentions Through Envy. *Journal of Travel Research*, •••, 00472875241247317. DOI: 10.1177/00472875241247317

Petty, R. E., & Cacioppo, J. T. (2012). *Communication and persuasion: Central and peripheral routes to attitude change*. Springer Science & Business Media.

Rafdinal, W., Wibisono, N., & Setiawati, L. (2024). Customer-centric virtual reality applications adoption in the hospitality industry: quality-value-based adoption model. *Journal of Hospitality and Tourism Insights*.

Ramayah, T. J. F. H., Cheah, J., Chuah, F., Ting, H., & Memon, M. A. (2018). Partial least squares structural equation modeling (PLS-SEM) using smartPLS 3.0. *An updated guide and practical guide to statistical analysis*, 978-967.

Ray, A., Bala, P. K., & Dwivedi, Y. K. (2020). Exploring values affecting e-Learning adoption from the user-generated-content: A consumption-value-theory perspective. *Journal of Strategic Marketing*, •••, 1–23.

Roy, S. K., Fatema, M. R., Islam, M. J., & Huda, M. N. (2020). Reviewing YouTube as a compelling tool for the promotion of tourism. *International Journal of Managing Account*, 2(5), 96–104.

Rufino, G. G.Rufino, Gilliane G. (2024). Methods Used in YouTube for Teaching and Learning English Language: A Systematic Literature Review. *International Journal of English Language Studies*, 6(1), 82–97. DOI: 10.32996/ijels.2024.6.1.9

Santoso, N. P. L., Sunarjo, R. A., & Fadli, I. S. (2023). Analyzing the Factors Influencing the Success of Business Incubation Programs: A SmartPLS Approach. *ADI Journal on Recent Innovation*, 5(1), 60–71. DOI: 10.34306/ajri.v5i1.985

Saputri, M. E. (2024). Faktor-Faktor Information Adoption Model terhadap Purchase Intention: Studi pada Media Sosial Tiktok Azarine Cosmetic. *Al-Kharaj: Jurnal Ekonomi. Keuangan & Bisnis Syariah*, 6(5), 3778–3790.

Selem, K. M., Shoukat, M. H., Khalid, R., & Raza, M. (2024). Guest interaction with hotel booking website information: Scale development and validation of antecedents and consequences. *Journal of Hospitality Marketing & Management*, 33(5), 626–648. DOI: 10.1080/19368623.2023.2279174

Shahzad, K., Zhang, Q., & Khan, M. K. (2024). Blockchain technology adoption in supply chain management: An investigation from UTAUT and information system success model. *International Journal of Shipping and Transport Logistics*, 18(2), 165–190. DOI: 10.1504/IJSTL.2024.137893

Sigala, M. (2024). Social Media and Crisis Communication: Managing or Creating a Crisis? Lessons Learnt from Hotel Amarilis. In *Case Based Research in Tourism, Travel, and Hospitality* (pp. 61–82). Springer. DOI: 10.1007/978-981-97-1891-7_4

Silaban, P. H., Chen, W. K., Nababan, T. S., Eunike, I. J., & Silalahi, A. D. K. (2022). How travel vlogs on YouTube influence consumer behavior: A use and gratification perspective and customer engagement. *Human Behavior and Emerging Technologies*, 2022, 1–16. DOI: 10.1155/2022/4432977

Sivathanu, B., & Pillai, R. (2023). The effect of deepfake video advertisements on the hotel booking intention of tourists. *Journal of Hospitality and Tourism Insights*, 6(5), 1669–1687. DOI: 10.1108/JHTI-03-2022-0094

Tseng, S. Y., & Wang, C. N. (2016). Perceived risk influence on dual-route information adoption processes on travel websites. *Journal of Business Research*, 69(6), 2289–2296. DOI: 10.1016/j.jbusres.2015.12.044

Usman, J. (2021). The Discourse of Propaganda in Traveloka's YouTube Advertising Videos. *Indonesian Journal of EFL and Linguistics*, 5(1), 175–194.

Ventre, I., & Kolbe, D. (2020). The Impact of Perceived Usefulness of Online Reviews, Trust and Perceived Risk on Online Purchase Intention in Emerging Markets: A Mexican Perspective. *Journal of International Consumer Marketing*, 32(4), 1–13. DOI: 10.1080/08961530.2020.1712293

Wang, X., Sun, J., & Wen, H. (2019). Tourism seasonality, online user rating and hotel price: A quantitative approach based on the hedonic price model. *International Journal of Hospitality Management*, 79, 140–147. DOI: 10.1016/j.ijhm.2019.01.007

Wang, Y., Asaad, Y., & Filieri, R. (2020). What makes hosts trust Airbnb? Antecedents of hosts' trust toward Airbnb and its impact on continuance intention. *Journal of Travel Research*, 59(4), 686–703. DOI: 10.1177/0047287519855135

Yoo, M., Singh, A. K., & Loewy, N. (2024). Predicting hotel booking cancelation with machine learning techniques. *Journal of Hospitality and Tourism Technology*, 15(1), 54–69. DOI: 10.1108/JHTT-07-2022-0227

Yu, H., Ryoo, Y., & Han, E. (2024). Mind over matter: How biased perceptions of political knowledge influence selection and evaluation of political YouTube channels. *Internet Research*, 34(2), 474–494. DOI: 10.1108/INTR-09-2021-0677

Zahrah, I. N. (2024). Vlogger and Brand Credibility Perception: A Systematic Literature Review of Endorsement Effectiveness in Youtube Vlogs. *Jurnal Indonesia Sosial Teknologi*, 5(2), 445–459. DOI: 10.59141/jist.v5i2.905

Zhang, D., Ma, J., & He, Z. (2024). The effect of emotional changes in composite reviews on consumers' information adoption from a dual perspective. *Industrial Management & Data Systems*, 124(6), 2205–2229. DOI: 10.1108/IMDS-06-2023-0396

Zhang, R. Y., & Tang, C. H. H. (2024). The impact of partitioned pricing on hotel booking and the moderating effect of temporal distance. *International Journal of Hospitality Management*, 116, 103621. DOI: 10.1016/j.ijhm.2023.103621

KEY TERMS AND DEFINITIONS

Hotel Booking Intention: Traveler's buy intent or the purpose or reason behind a statement or action as part of a customer's journey toward a purchase.

Information Adoption Model: This model explains how individuals adopt information and thus change their intentions and behaviors within the computer-mediated communication platforms.

Information Usefulness: Information usefulness as "the perception of an individual that he holds on to the provided information and how he can use new information to boost performance.

Online Reviews: Online reviews are voluntary evaluations of products, services, or businesses by internet users who have used, purchased, or experienced them

Online Videos: Online video is defined as a digital video that is distributed over the internet

Travelers' Behavior: Travel behavior refers to the allocation of resources, such as time and money, to activities and movements from one place to another

YouTube Vlogs: A video that documents a person's life and is usually posted online for an audience.

Chapter 13
Virtual Communities: Current Status and Challenges

M. R. Ramesh
https://orcid.org/0000-0002-1648-9387
Indira Gandhi Centre for Atomic Research, Kalpakkam, India

ABSTRACT

Virtual communities have transformed the landscape of social interaction, creating dynamic and multifaceted spaces for individuals to connect, share, and collaborate across geographical boundaries. This chapter delves into the current status of virtual communities, examining their evolution from early internet forums to sophisticated social networks and online platforms. We will explore the diverse forms these communities take, including interest-based groups, professional networks, and support communities, highlighting their role in fostering social capital and collective intelligence.

The chapter will address the significant challenges that virtual communities face today. Key issues include managing digital identities, ensuring privacy and security, combating misinformation, and maintaining engagement and participation. We will discuss the implications of algorithmic curation and echo chambers on community dynamics and the potential for online harassment and toxicity. Additionally, the chapter will consider the ethical and regulatory landscape governing virtual communities, emphasizing the need for balanced approaches that protect users while promoting open discourse.

Through a comprehensive review of current research and case studies, this chapter aims to provide a nuanced understanding of the benefits and pitfalls of virtual communities. It will offer insights into the strategies and best practices for fostering healthy, vibrant, and resilient online communities. By examining both the technological advancements and socio-cultural impacts, this chapter seeks to

DOI: 10.4018/979-8-3693-3868-1.ch013

contribute to the ongoing discourse on the future of virtual communities in our increasingly digital world.

1. INTRODUCTION TO VIRTUAL COMMUNITIES

1.1 Definition and Scope

A virtual community is a social network of individuals who interact through specific social media platforms, internet forums, or other online spaces, forming a collective with shared interests, goals, or activities, (Rheingold, 2000). Unlike traditional communities bound by geography, virtual communities transcend physical limitations, connecting people across the globe. These communities are diverse in their structure and function, ranging from professional networks like LinkedIn to hobbyist groups on Reddit, immersive virtual worlds such as Second Life, and social media giants like Facebook and Twitter.

The scope of this chapter encompasses the evolution, status, and challenges of virtual communities. It will delve into the origins and historical development of these communities, their various forms, and functions today, and the multifaceted challenges they face, including issues of privacy, security, and the digital divide.

1.2 Historical Context

The concept of virtual communities' dates back to the early days of the internet. The genesis can be traced to the late 1970s and early 1980s with the advent of Bulletin Board Systems (BBS). These were computer servers running software that allowed users to connect and share messages, files, and other information. BBSs were local, often hosted by enthusiasts who provided a space for users to discuss topics ranging from technology to hobbies, (Kozinets, 2010).

Parallel to BBS, Usenet emerged in 1980, developed by Tom Truscott and Jim Ellis. Usenet allowed users to post messages in newsgroups, which were organized hierarchically by subject. This platform laid the groundwork for many aspects of online communication, including threaded discussions and moderated groups. Usenet's decentralized nature foreshadowed the peer-to-peer networks and open-source communities that would follow.

As internet accessibility increased in the 1990s, virtual communities expanded beyond niche tech circles. America Online (AOL) played a pivotal role, providing millions of users with easy internet access and fostering vibrant communities through chat rooms and forums. Simultaneously, the World Wide Web's rise brought web-based communities, epitomized by GeoCities, which allowed users to create personal web pages and link them in thematic neighborhoods, (Ellison & Boyd, 2008).

The late 1990s and early 2000s saw the emergence of more sophisticated virtual communities. Platforms like LiveJournal and Blogger enable personal expression and community formation around blogs. Meanwhile, massively multiplayer online role-playing games (MMORPGs) such as Ultima Online and EverQuest created immersive virtual worlds where players could interact in complex social and economic systems, (Haythornthwaite & Wellman, 2002).

The explosion of social media in the mid-2000s fundamentally transformed virtual communities. Sites like MySpace and Facebook redefined social networking, emphasizing real-world connections and identity verification. Twitter introduced microblogging, fostering real-time communication and community building around trending topics. Simultaneously, professional networks like LinkedIn established spaces for career-oriented interactions, (Kollock & Smith, 1999).

The evolution continued with the advent of mobile technology and ubiquitous internet access. Platforms like Instagram and Snapchat catered to a visually-oriented, always-connected generation, while Reddit became a hub for diverse communities, each centered around specific interests, known as subreddits. Virtual worlds evolved with Second Life, which allowed users to create and inhabit a detailed virtual existence, blending social, economic, and creative dimensions, (Boyd & Ellison, 1997).

1.3 Current Status and Challenges

Today, virtual communities are integral to the social fabric of the internet. They play critical roles in various domains, including social interaction, professional networking, gaming, education, and activism. The COVID-19 pandemic underscored their importance as people turned to online communities for socialization, work, and support amid physical distancing measuresm, (Jones, 1997) (Preece, 2000).

However, the proliferation of virtual communities brings several challenges:

- Privacy and Security: With vast amounts of personal data shared online, virtual communities face significant privacy and security concerns. High-profile data breaches and the misuse of personal information by companies like Facebook have heightened awareness and regulatory scrutiny.
- Moderation and Governance: The balance between free speech and harmful content is a persistent challenge. Platforms must navigate the complexities of moderating content to prevent abuse, misinformation, and harassment while respecting users' rights to expression.
- Digital Divide: Access to virtual communities is not universal. Socioeconomic disparities, technological infrastructure, and digital literacy affect participa-

tion, perpetuating inequalities in who can benefit from these spaces, (Turkle, 1997).

- Psychological Impact: The impact of virtual communities on mental health is a growing area of concern. Issues like social media addiction, cyberbullying, and the pressure to maintain a certain online persona can have profound psychological effects.Economic Exploitation: The commercialization of virtual communities raises questions about the exploitation of user-generated content and labor. Platforms monetize user activity through targeted advertising and data mining, often without adequate compensation to the users who generate the content, (Wellman & Gulia, 1999).

2. TECHNOLOGICAL FOUNDATIONS

2.1 Infrastructure

The bedrock of virtual communities is their technological infrastructure, which encompasses internet connectivity, servers, and cloud computing. High-speed internet connectivity is the linchpin that supports seamless interaction within virtual communities. It enables real-time communication, streaming, and the sharing of large files, fostering a sense of immediacy and presence among users. Reliable and fast internet access is crucial, particularly in rural or underdeveloped regions, where connectivity gaps can create digital divides and limit participation in global virtual communities.

Servers are another critical component, providing the backbone for data storage, processing, and retrieval. They host websites, forums, and applications, ensuring that content is accessible 24/7. With the growth of virtual communities, the demand for robust server infrastructure has increased, requiring scalable solutions that can handle massive user loads without compromising performance. This need has driven advancements in server technologies, including the use of powerful processors, efficient cooling systems, and enhanced security measures to protect against cyber threats.

Cloud computing has revolutionized the way virtual communities operate by offering scalable and flexible resources on-demand. It allows for the storage and processing of vast amounts of data, supporting the dynamic and expansive nature of online interactions. Cloud services provide the infrastructure necessary for hosting platforms and tools used by virtual communities, enabling users to access content and applications from anywhere in the world. This flexibility has been instrumental in supporting the growth of remote work, online education, and social networking.

2.2 Platforms and Tools

The platforms and tools that underpin virtual communities are diverse and continually evolving. Social media networks like Facebook, Twitter, and Instagram play a pivotal role in connecting individuals and groups, providing spaces for sharing content, engaging in discussions, and forming relationships. These platforms leverage algorithms to curate content, enhancing user engagement by delivering personalized experiences. However, the reliance on algorithms also raises concerns about echo chambers and the spread of misinformation, presenting challenges for maintaining healthy virtual communities.

Online forums, such as Reddit and specialized discussion boards, offer a more focused environment for community building around specific interests or topics. These forums enable users to exchange knowledge, seek advice, and collaborate on projects. The structure of these platforms, often organized into threads and subforums, facilitates in-depth discussions and the development of niche communities. Moderation tools are essential in these settings to ensure respectful interactions and to manage the spread of harmful content.

Collaborative software, including tools like Slack, Microsoft Teams, and Discord, has become integral to virtual communities, especially in professional and educational contexts. These platforms support real-time communication, file sharing, and project management, fostering collaboration and productivity. Features such as video conferencing, screen sharing, and integration with other applications enhance the user experience, making it easier for teams to work together remotely. The rise of these tools has been accelerated by the COVID-19 pandemic, which necessitated a shift to virtual collaboration.

2.3 Emerging Technologies

Emerging technologies are poised to further transform virtual communities, offering new possibilities and addressing existing challenges. Virtual reality (VR) and augmented reality (AR) are at the forefront of this evolution, providing immersive experiences that can enhance social interactions and educational opportunities. VR creates entirely digital environments where users can interact as if they were physically present, fostering a deeper sense of connection. AR, on the other hand, overlays digital information onto the real world, enriching experiences without fully immersing users in a virtual space. These technologies hold promise for applications in gaming, training, remote work, and social networking, though their widespread adoption is contingent on advancements in hardware and content development.

Blockchain technology also has significant implications for virtual communities, particularly in terms of security and trust. Blockchain offers a decentralized approach to data management, ensuring transparency and reducing the risk of data breaches. In virtual communities, it can be used to verify identities, manage digital assets, and create tamper-proof records of interactions. This can enhance trust among users, particularly in peer-to-peer marketplaces and collaborative projects, where verifying authenticity and maintaining accountability are crucial.

Artificial intelligence (AI) is another transformative force, with applications ranging from content moderation to personalized user experiences. AI algorithms can analyze vast amounts of data to detect and remove inappropriate content, helping to maintain safe and respectful virtual environments. Additionally, AI can enhance user engagement by providing personalized recommendations, automating routine tasks, and enabling more natural interactions through chatbots and virtual assistants. As AI technology continues to advance, its role in virtual communities is likely to expand, offering new ways to enhance connectivity, security, and user satisfaction.

In conclusion, the technological foundations of virtual communities are multifaceted, encompassing essential infrastructure, diverse platforms and tools, and emerging technologies. These elements collectively support the vibrant and dynamic nature of virtual interactions, enabling people to connect, collaborate, and share in ways that transcend physical boundaries. As technology continues to evolve, it will undoubtedly shape the future of virtual communities, presenting both opportunities and challenges that will need to be navigated with care.

3. SOCIAL DYNAMICS WITHIN VIRTUAL COMMUNITIES

3.1 Community Building

The foundation of any virtual community lies in the intricate processes of community building and maintenance. These processes encompass the dynamics of membership, the roles members assume, and the leadership structures that guide interactions. Community building in virtual spaces is significantly influenced by the platform's design, the purpose of the community, and the norms established by its members. Membership dynamics involve the ways individuals join, participate in, and sometimes leave communities. These dynamics are often marked by the initial attraction to the community's core values or interests, sustained engagement through active participation, and occasionally, disengagement due to conflicts or shifts in personal interests.

Roles within virtual communities are diverse, ranging from passive observers to active contributors and leaders. Members often naturally gravitate towards roles that fit their skills and interests, such as content creators, moderators, or support providers. Leadership within virtual communities can be formal, with designated roles like administrators or moderators, or informal, emerging through recognized contributions and influence. Effective leadership is crucial for fostering a sense of belonging and ensuring the community's growth and resilience. Leaders often set the tone for interactions, resolve conflicts, and guide the community towards its objectives.

3.2 Identity and Interaction

The formation and expression of identity in virtual communities are complex processes that differ from those in physical spaces. Online, individuals have the opportunity to construct and reconstruct their identities through selective self-presentation and interaction. This fluidity allows for experimentation with different aspects of identity, which can be empowering but also challenging. The anonymity or pseudonymity afforded by many platforms enables users to explore parts of their identity that they might suppress in offline interactions.

Interactions within virtual communities range from casual conversations to deep, meaningful exchanges. The nature of these interactions is shaped by the community's focus, the communication tools available, and the norms established by its members. Online interactions can foster strong social bonds, creating a sense of camaraderie and mutual support. However, they can also lead to misunderstandings and conflicts due to the lack of non-verbal cues and the potential for misinterpretation of written text.

The role of identity in these interactions is pivotal. Members often seek validation and recognition from their peers, which can reinforce their sense of belonging and self-worth. The virtual space thus becomes a platform for social validation, where likes, comments, and other forms of engagement serve as indicators of acceptance and appreciation. These dynamics underscore the importance of thoughtful communication and empathy within virtual communities to maintain healthy interactions.

3.3 Governance and Moderation

Governance and moderation are critical components in managing virtual communities. Effective governance models ensure that the community remains aligned with its goals, values, and norms. These models can vary widely, from hierarchical structures with clear roles and responsibilities to more decentralized, participatory approaches where decisions are made collectively. The choice of governance model often reflects the community's size, purpose, and the level of formality desired by its members.

Moderation practices are essential for maintaining a productive and respectful environment. Moderators play a key role in enforcing community guidelines, addressing disruptive behavior, and resolving conflicts. They must balance the need for control with the desire to allow free expression and foster open dialogue. The challenges of moderation are numerous, including dealing with harassment, managing spam, and navigating the fine line between censorship and the protection of community standards.

One of the significant challenges in governance and moderation is ensuring inclusivity and fairness. This involves creating an environment where diverse perspectives are welcomed and valued, and where all members feel safe and respected. Effective moderation practices require clear guidelines, transparency in decision-making, and mechanisms for accountability. The use of technology, such as automated moderation tools, can aid in managing large communities, but human judgment remains indispensable in handling nuanced situations.

In conclusion, the social dynamics within virtual communities are complex and multifaceted. Building and maintaining a community requires understanding the intricacies of membership dynamics, roles, and leadership. The formation and expression of identity online are fluid processes that influence interactions within these communities. Effective governance and moderation are essential to foster a healthy and productive environment. As virtual communities continue to evolve, understanding these dynamics will be crucial in addressing the challenges they face and enhancing the experiences of their members.

4. ECONOMIC IMPACT OF VIRTUAL COMMUNITIES

Virtual communities have evolved into significant economic entities, driving a diverse range of monetization models, fostering intricate virtual economies, and presenting both lucrative opportunities and inherent risks. This chapter delves into the economic dimensions of virtual communities, examining the mechanisms through which they generate revenue, the structure and functioning of their virtual economies, and the potential benefits and challenges they pose to participants and businesses.

4.1 Monetization Models

Virtual communities employ various monetization strategies to generate revenue, primarily through subscriptions, advertising, and in-app purchases. Each model offers distinct advantages and challenges, influencing the financial sustainability and user experience within these communities.

Subscriptions form the backbone of many virtual communities, providing a steady revenue stream in exchange for access to premium content or features. Platforms like LinkedIn and Patreon thrive on subscription models, offering exclusive content, networking opportunities, and enhanced functionalities to paying members. This model ensures a predictable income and fosters a committed user base. However, it necessitates continuous delivery of high-value content to justify the recurring costs, posing a challenge in maintaining subscriber engagement over time.

Advertising is another prevalent revenue model, with platforms such as Facebook and YouTube leveraging vast user data to offer targeted advertising opportunities. By analyzing user behavior, preferences, and demographics, these platforms create highly personalized ad experiences, enhancing the effectiveness and profitability of their advertising efforts. While this model can be highly lucrative, it raises concerns about user privacy and data security, necessitating stringent regulatory compliance and ethical considerations.

In-app purchases represent a significant revenue source, particularly within gaming communities and social media platforms. Users spend real money to acquire virtual goods, enhance their avatars, or unlock special features, as seen in games like Fortnite and mobile applications like TikTok. This model capitalizes on the psychological appeal of customization and status within the virtual community, driving significant profit margins. However, it also attracts scrutiny regarding the ethical implications of microtransactions and the potential for fostering addictive behaviors.

4.2 Virtual Economies

Virtual economies are sophisticated ecosystems where virtual goods, services, and currencies circulate, mirroring real-world economic principles yet existing entirely within digital realms. These economies are essential for the functionality and sustainability of virtual communities, creating value and enabling transactions among participants.

Virtual goods encompass a wide array of items, from digital clothing and accessories for avatars to virtual real estate and collectibles. These goods often hold significant value, driven by their rarity, aesthetic appeal, or functional benefits within the virtual environment. For instance, platforms like Second Life and Roblox have thriving marketplaces where users buy and sell virtual assets, sometimes at prices comparable to real-world items.

Virtual services extend beyond goods, offering various forms of labor and expertise within the virtual community. This includes virtual event planning, digital art creation, and virtual consultancy. The gig economy within virtual communities mirrors its real-world counterpart, with platforms such as Fiverr and Upwork facilitating the exchange of virtual services for real money.

Virtual currencies are the lifeblood of these economies, enabling transactions and trade. These currencies can be platform-specific, like Linden Dollars in Second Life, or more universal, such as cryptocurrencies like Bitcoin and Ethereum. Virtual currencies facilitate seamless transactions, though they also introduce complexities related to currency exchange, inflation, and regulatory oversight.

4.3 Opportunities and Risks

The economic opportunities within virtual communities are vast, offering individuals and businesses new avenues for income generation, innovation, and market expansion. However, these opportunities are accompanied by significant risks that must be navigated to ensure sustainable growth and participation.

Opportunities for individuals include earning income through content creation, virtual services, and entrepreneurial ventures within virtual marketplaces. Platforms like YouTube, Twitch, and Etsy empower creators to monetize their skills and reach global audiences. For businesses, virtual communities offer a unique marketing channel, customer engagement opportunities, and avenues for product innovation. Brands can leverage virtual communities to conduct market research, launch virtual products, and build brand loyalty through immersive experiences.

Risks are inherent in the dynamic and often volatile nature of virtual economies. Regulatory challenges loom large, as governments struggle to keep pace with the rapid evolution of virtual commerce. Issues such as intellectual property rights, taxation, and consumer protection require robust legal frameworks to ensure fair play and security. Additionally, the potential for economic disparity and exploitation within virtual communities cannot be overlooked. The reliance on microtransactions and the emergence of virtual monopolies can exacerbate inequality, creating a digital divide that mirrors real-world socio-economic disparities.

Security risks are also paramount, with virtual communities being prime targets for cyber-attacks, fraud, and data breaches. Ensuring the security and privacy of users is crucial for maintaining trust and fostering a thriving virtual economy. This necessitates advanced cybersecurity measures, transparent data handling practices, and continuous vigilance against emerging threats.

In conclusion, the economic impact of virtual communities is profound, shaping new monetization models, intricate virtual economies, and presenting both opportunities and risks. As these digital ecosystems continue to evolve, stakeholders must navigate the complexities with foresight and adaptability, ensuring that virtual communities remain vibrant, inclusive, and economically viable.

5. CHALLENGES AND FUTURE DIRECTIONS

Virtual communities have become an integral part of the digital landscape, offering spaces for social interaction, knowledge sharing, and collaboration. However, the rapid expansion and increasing influence of these communities have brought forth significant challenges. This chapter delves into four critical areas: privacy and security, misinformation and content moderation, the digital divide, and governance and regulation. Addressing these challenges is essential for fostering healthy and inclusive virtual environments.

5.1 Privacy and Security

One of the foremost challenges in virtual communities is protecting user privacy and ensuring security. With the vast amounts of personal data shared online, users are increasingly vulnerable to privacy breaches and cyber-attacks. Virtual communities often collect detailed personal information, which can be exploited by malicious actors if not adequately protected.

Ensuring privacy involves implementing robust encryption methods, secure authentication processes, and transparent data handling practices. It is also crucial to educate users about the importance of privacy settings and safe online behavior. However, balancing user privacy with the need for community moderation and engagement can be tricky. For example, anonymity can protect user identity but may also enable harmful behavior, such as trolling or cyberbullying. Striking a balance between these competing interests remains a significant challenge.

5.2 Misinformation and Content Moderation

The proliferation of misinformation and fake news is another pressing issue within virtual communities. The speed and reach of information dissemination online mean that false information can quickly spread, causing real-world consequences. This is particularly concerning in areas such as public health, politics, and social justice, where misinformation can lead to public harm and undermine trust in institutions.

Content moderation is a critical tool in combating misinformation. It involves identifying and removing harmful content, promoting accurate information, and sometimes, sanctioning users who violate community guidelines. However, effective content moderation is fraught with difficulties. Automated systems can be too rigid or inaccurate, while human moderators can be overwhelmed by the volume of content. Moreover, content moderation raises concerns about censorship and freedom of expression, as decisions about what constitutes harmful content can be subjective and context-dependent.

5.3 Digital Divide

The digital divide represents the gap between those who have access to digital technologies and those who do not. This divide can be based on various factors, including geography, socioeconomic status, education, and age. It presents a significant barrier to equitable participation in virtual communities.

Efforts to bridge the digital divide must address both access and literacy. Providing affordable internet access and devices is a foundational step, but it is equally important to ensure that individuals have the skills and knowledge to use these technologies effectively. Community-based programs, public policies, and international cooperation can play crucial roles in these efforts. However, the pace of technological advancement means that the goalposts are continually moving, necessitating ongoing attention and adaptation.

5.4 Governance and Regulation

Effective governance and regulation are essential for managing the complexities of virtual communities. As these communities often operate across national boundaries, they pose unique challenges for traditional regulatory frameworks. Issues such as data privacy, intellectual property, and online harassment require coordinated responses that balance local laws with the global nature of the internet.

Governance involves setting and enforcing rules that guide behavior within virtual communities. This can be done by platform owners, community managers, or through self-regulation by users. However, developing fair and effective governance structures is challenging. It requires transparency, accountability, and participation from diverse stakeholders. Regulations, on the other hand, need to be adaptable to technological changes and enforceable across different jurisdictions. International cooperation is vital to address cross-border issues effectively.

5.5 Future Directions

Looking ahead, addressing these challenges requires a multifaceted approach that combines technological innovation, policy development, and community engagement. Advances in artificial intelligence and machine learning can improve privacy protections and content moderation, while international agreements can harmonize regulations and standards.

Furthermore, fostering digital literacy and inclusivity is essential for narrowing the digital divide. This involves not only providing access to technology but also ensuring that individuals have the skills and support needed to participate fully in virtual communities.

In conclusion, while virtual communities offer immense potential for connection and collaboration, they also pose significant challenges that must be addressed to ensure they remain safe, inclusive, and beneficial for all users. By tackling issues of privacy, misinformation, access, and governance head-on, we can help shape a future where virtual communities enhance rather than undermine our digital and social landscapes.

6. CONCLUSION

Virtual communities have become an integral part of modern society, revolutionizing the way individuals interact, share information, and form relationships. This chapter has explored the multifaceted nature of virtual communities, their current status, and the numerous challenges they face. As we reflect on these discussions, several key points emerge that highlight the evolving landscape of virtual communities and offer insights into their future trajectories.

6.1 Current Status of Virtual Communities

The contemporary virtual community is characterized by its diversity and ubiquity. These communities span various platforms, from social media networks like Facebook and Twitter to specialized forums and interest-based groups on Reddit and Discord. The proliferation of virtual communities is driven by advancements in technology, particularly the widespread availability of high-speed internet and the increasing penetration of smartphones. This technological foundation has enabled seamless connectivity, allowing individuals from across the globe to engage in real-time interactions.

Virtual communities today serve a myriad of purposes. They provide spaces for social interaction, professional networking, collaborative projects, and support groups for various causes. Social media platforms have become central hubs for personal communication, political discourse, and cultural exchange. Meanwhile, professional networks like LinkedIn facilitate career development and business connections. Additionally, niche communities cater to specific interests, hobbies, and support needs, fostering a sense of belonging among members with shared passions or experiences.

6.2 Challenges Facing Virtual Communities

Despite their many benefits, virtual communities face significant challenges that threaten their sustainability and effectiveness. One of the primary issues is the question of privacy and data security. With the increasing amount of personal information shared online, the risk of data breaches and misuse of information has become a critical concern. Users are often unaware of how their data is collected, stored, and used, leading to potential vulnerabilities and a lack of trust in virtual platforms.

Another challenge is the prevalence of misinformation and disinformation. The ease with which false information can spread in virtual communities has profound implications for public discourse and societal cohesion. This issue is exacerbated by algorithm-driven echo chambers that reinforce pre-existing biases and limit exposure to diverse perspectives. Consequently, combating misinformation requires robust content moderation policies and the promotion of media literacy among users.

The issue of online harassment and toxicity also poses a significant challenge. Virtual communities can sometimes foster negative behavior, including bullying, hate speech, and other forms of harassment. Such toxic environments can deter participation and harm individuals' mental well-being. Effective community management and the implementation of clear guidelines and enforcement mechanisms are essential to creating safe and inclusive spaces.

Additionally, the digital divide remains a barrier to equitable participation in virtual communities. Access to technology and internet connectivity is unevenly distributed, with marginalized groups often facing greater obstacles. Bridging this gap is crucial to ensuring that the benefits of virtual communities are accessible to all, regardless of socioeconomic status or geographic location.

6.3 Future Developments and Evolving Roles

Looking ahead, the future of virtual communities will likely be shaped by ongoing technological advancements and societal shifts. One potential development is the integration of virtual and augmented reality (VR/AR) technologies, which could offer more immersive and interactive experiences. These technologies have the potential to transform virtual communities into spaces that more closely mimic physical interactions, enhancing the sense of presence and connection among members.

Artificial intelligence (AI) will also play a pivotal role in the evolution of virtual communities. AI-driven tools can improve content moderation, personalize user experiences, and facilitate more meaningful interactions. However, the use of AI also raises ethical considerations, including issues of bias, transparency, and accountability.

The role of virtual communities in society is likely to expand as they become increasingly embedded in various aspects of daily life. In education, virtual learning communities can provide flexible and accessible opportunities for lifelong learning. In the workplace, remote collaboration tools will continue to evolve, supporting hybrid work models and global teams. Moreover, virtual communities will remain vital for social activism and community organizing, providing platforms for collective action and advocacy.

To navigate the future effectively, it is essential to address the challenges facing virtual communities. This requires a collaborative effort among technology developers, policymakers, community managers, and users. By prioritizing privacy, combating misinformation, fostering inclusivity, and bridging the digital divide, we can ensure that virtual communities continue to thrive and contribute positively to society.

In conclusion, virtual communities have transformed the way we connect and interact, offering numerous opportunities while also presenting significant challenges. As we move forward, the ongoing evolution of these communities will be shaped by technological innovations and our collective efforts to create safe, inclusive, and equitable digital spaces. The future of virtual communities holds great promise, and by addressing current challenges, we can harness their full potential to enhance our social, professional, and cultural lives.

REFERENCES

Boyd, D., & Ellison, N. (2007). Social Network Sites: Definition, History, and Scholarship. *Journal of Computer-Mediated Communication*, 13(1), 210–230. DOI: 10.1111/j.1083-6101.2007.00393.x

Ellison, N., & Boyd, D. M. (2013). Sociality through social network sites.

Haythornthwaite, C., & Wellman, B. (2002). *The Internet in Everyday Life: An Introduction*. Blackwell. DOI: 10.1002/9780470774298.ch

Jones, S. G. (1997). *Virtual Culture: Identity and Communication in Cybersociety*. Sage Publications.

Kollock, P., & Smith, M. (Eds.). (1999). *Communities in Cyberspace*. Routledge.

Kozinets, R. V. (2010). *Netnography: Doing Ethnographic Research Online*. Sage Publications.

Preece, J. (2000). *Online Communities: Designing Usability, Supporting Sociability*. John Wiley & Sons.

Rheingold, H. (2000). *The Virtual Community: Homesteading on the Electronic Frontier*. Addison-Wesley Professional. DOI: 10.7551/mitpress/7105.001.0001

Turkle, S. (1997). *Life on the Screen: Identity in the Age of the Internet*. Simon & Schuster.

Wellman, B., & Gulia, M. (1999). Virtual Communities as Communities: Net Surfers Don't Ride Alone. In Kollock, P., & Smith, M. (Eds.), *Communities in Cyberspace*.

Chapter 14
Ethics and Conduct: Navigating the Moral Landscape of Virtual

Muhammad Usman Tariq
https://orcid.org/0000-0002-7605-3040
University College Cork, Ireland

ABSTRACT

The chapter dives into the complicated interaction between moral contemplations and online behavior inside virtual communities. It investigates the advancing moral challenges confronted by clients, stage suppliers, and mediators in keeping up moral guidelines and cultivating positive intelligent in advanced spaces. Through a comprehensive examination of key moral standards, such as security assurance, substance balance, algorithmic inclination, and computerized consideration, the chapter highlights the complex ethical problems inborn in overseeing virtual communities. Drawing upon real-world cases and insightful inquiries, it illustrates the multifaceted nature of moral decision-making in online situations. It underscores the significance of maintaining moral values amid mechanical headways and societal shifts. Moreover, the chapter emphasizes the need for proactive measures and moral carefulness to address issues such as online badgering, deception, and computerized imbalance.

INTRODUCTION

Morals in virtual communities may be a multifaceted space that intertwines conventional moral standards with the special characteristics of online intuition. With the expansion of the web and the rise of social media stages, gatherings, and other advanced communities, the need to obtain it and apply moral benchmarks in

DOI: 10.4018/979-8-3693-3868-1.ch014

these situations has become progressively foremost. Morals in virtual communities include standards of genuineness, regard, protection, and obligation that oversee how people associate, share data, and construct connections online. These standards point to cultivating a secure, conscious, and reliable computerized environment. A basic aspect of online morals is the administration of namelessness. Whereas anonymity can allow clients to specify conclusions without fear of revenge, it can also lead to reckless behavior such as trolling, cyberbullying, and spreading deception. For occurrence, stages such as Reddit, which regularly permits mysterious posting, have had to create comprehensive control approaches to moderate hurtful behaviors and maintain moral guidelines (Massanari, 2017).

Protection is another foundation of online morals. In virtual communities, clients regularly share individual data, which makes the security of this information vital. Breaches of security can lead to noteworthy results, such as character robbery, enthusiastic trouble, and monetary misfortune. The Cambridge Analytica scandal, where the individual information of millions of Facebook clients was collected without assent, underscores the basic requirement for rigid security and moral information while taking care of hones (Isaak & Hanna, 2018; Tariq, 2024).

BACKGROUND

The Effect of Virtual Community Flow on Moral Behavior

The flow inside virtual communities essentially impact moral behavior, forming how clients see and follow moral guidelines. These elements incorporate bunch standards, the nearness of mediators, the platform's plan, and the community's overarching culture. Gather standards are unwritten rules that administer behavior within a community. They are created naturally and can unequivocally impact members' activities. For example, in professional online communities such as LinkedIn, standards energize polished skills and useful talk. In contrast, in more casual settings, such as gaming gatherings, the standards may endure or energize more forcefully and competitively (Kollock & Smith, 1996). When gathering standards adjusted to moral standards, they can advance positive behavior, but when they do not, they can lead to moral breaches.

Control plays a significant role in maintaining moral benchmarks in virtual communities. Mediators are regularly dependent on upholding rules, tending to offence, and directing dialogue to stay beneficial and aware. Successful moderation can prevent untrustworthy behaviors, such as abhor discourse, badgering, and deception. Wikipedia depends intensely on a community of volunteer arbitrators to preserve its substance's precision and unwavering quality, exhibiting the significance of control in maintaining moral benchmarks (Specialty and Bruckman, 2008).

A stage's plan can also affect moral behavior. Highlights, such as announcement instruments, substance channels, and client confirmation forms can advance or prevent moral intuition. Stages prioritizing client security and moral behavior regularly execute strong announcement frameworks, clear community rules, and instructive assets for advanced citizenship. Twitter's advancing arrangements of hate speech and badgering represent how stage plans and approach upgrades can impact client behavior and moral measures (Gillespie, 2018; Tariq, 2024).

Another basic element is the culture of a virtual community formed by individuals and their intelligences. A community with a culture of regard, inclusivity, and responsibility is likely to foster ethical behavior among individuals. However, a poisonous culture can sustain untrustworthy behavior. The contrast in societies can be seen in comparing communities such as Stack Flood, which emphasizes regard and bolster for those looking for information, with less directed gatherings that will tolerate or energize negative behaviors (Mamykina et al., 2011).

Case Example

A related case of ethics in virtual communities' concerns taking care of deception amid the spread of COVID-19. Social media sites such as Facebook, Twitter, and YouTube have confronted noteworthy challenges in combating the spread of incorrect data about infection, medications, and antibodies. The quick spread of deception posed moral situations and almost flexibility in discourse versus open security. These platforms had to adjust the have to give clients precise data regarding their rights to specific assorted perspectives. Activities like Facebook's with fact-checking organisations and Twitter's arrangement of labelling deluding tweets almost COVID-19 highlight these stages' moral obligations in guaranteeing the spread of dependable data (Cinelli et al., 2020; Tariq, 2024).

Another case is moral contemplations that encompass online gaming communities. In games such as the World of Warcraft" and "Fortnite," players frequently shape tight-knit bunches or societies in which cooperation and communication are fundamental. These communities must explore the issues of consideration, badgering, and reasonable play. Diversion designers and community directors execute codes of conduct and announcement frameworks to preserve a positive and moral environment. The case of "Alliance of Legends" illustrates this well, where the developer, Riot Recreations, presented the Tribunal framework, permitting players to take an interest in investigating reports of untrustworthy behavior, in this manner advancing a community-driven approach to ethics (Kou & Nardi, 2013).

Morals in virtual communities may be a complex and advancing field, required by the particular nature of online intuition and the challenges that they present. Understanding and executing moral standards in these situations is significant for cultivating client trust, respect, and security. The effect of virtual community flow, including group standards, control, stage plans, and community culture, is critical in forming moral behavior. By examining real-world cases and case thinks, it becomes apparent that maintaining moral measures in virtual communities requires progressive exertion, collaboration, and development from both stage suppliers and clients. As computerized spaces develop and advance, so must the moral systems that oversee them, guaranteeing that virtual communities remain places of positive, conscious, and significant interaction.

Analysis of Challenges to Ethical Conduct in Online Spaces

The rapid expansion of online spaces has revolutionized communication, learning, and social interaction; however, it also presents several moral challenges. The Internet's worldwide nature interfaces people from different social foundations, making situations where moral conduct can be troublesome to explore and implement. Two noteworthy challenges to moral conduct in online spaces are the impact of secrecy on individual responsibility and the contrasts in social and social standards among assorted community individuals (Tariq, 2024). Secrecy in online spaces may be a double-edged sword. It offers clients the flexibility to specify themselves without fear of prompt individual repercussions, but also reduces individual responsibility, driving them to moral challenges. When people feel untraceable, they may lock in behaviors they would something else maintain a strategic distance from face-to-face intuition, such as trolling, cyberbullying, and the spread of untrue data (Suler, 2004).

For example, in stages like 4chan, clients can post names, frequently contributing to the spread of destructive substances and badgering. In such stages, the need for individual responsibility can encourage clients to lock in extraordinary behaviors, knowing that they are unlikely to confront coordinated results. This environment can cultivate a culture where untrustworthy conduct is normalized, making the development and implementation of moral measures troublesome (Bernstein et al., 2011; Tariq, 2024). In addition, namelessness can complicate efforts to combat deception. Amid the widespread COVID-19 outbreak, mysterious accounts on social media platforms are critical sources of inaccurate data about the infection and antibodies. The secrecy of these accounts makes it challenging for stage directors to track and check the spread of deception, posturing noteworthy dangers of open well-being (Cinelli et al., 2020).

In any case, it is important to recognize that secrecy serves basic positive functions. It permits clients to look back on delicate issues such as mental well-being or compulsion, without fear of disgrace. Stages such as Reddit have bolstered communities in which secrecy makes a difference. People feel secure enough to share their encounters and seek assistance (Andalibi et al., 2016). Subsequently, the challenge lies in adjusting the defensive perspective of namelessness with the responsibility to preserve moral conduct.

Contrasts in Social and Social Standards Among Assorted Community Individuals

The worldwide nature of online spaces brings together people from assorted social foundations, each with its own standards and values. These differing qualities can enhance online intelligence, but also lead to noteworthy moral challenges. Contrasts in social and social standards can cause errors and clashes, as activities considered satisfactory in one culture may be regarded as improper or hostile in another (Herring, 1996).

Humour and parody change broadly across societies. A joke considered funny in one social setting may be viewed as hostile or ill-bred in another. This social disparity can lead to clashes and moral predicaments, almost constituting satisfactory behavior in a worldwide online community. Twitter, a platform with a worldwide client base, regularly sees such clashes, where tweets expected to be jokes by one client can incite backfire from clients with distinctive social foundations (Reagle, 2015).

Dialect boundaries advance and complicate this intuition. Miscommunication due to dialect contrasts can lead to errors and inadvertent offences. Indeed, territorial slang and informal expressions inside English-speaking communities can cause confusion and potential moral clashes. Stages such as Facebook and YouTube, which have clients from around the world, frequently confront challenges in moderating substances that are socially touch or relevantly complex (Tandoc et al., 2018).

The challenge of socially differing qualities is also apparent in online gaming communities, where players from different parts of the world are associated in real-time. Diversions such as the "Alliance of Legends" and "Overwatch" bring together players with diverse social foundations and social standards. Engineers and community supervisors must explore these contrasts to create comprehensive situations that consider differing viewpoints while maintaining ethical measures. Revolt Diversions, the "Alliance of Legends' designer, has executed worldwide codes of conduct and territorial balance groups to address these social and moral challenges (Kou & Nardi, 2013).

Moreover, moral challenges emerge when online platforms implement policies and guidelines that are not aligned with the social values of all clients. For example, substance control arrangements that are also unbending can be seen as censorship in a few societies, while being seen as essential for maintaining goodness in others. Adjusting between respecting social differences and upholding steady moral measures may be a ceaseless challenge for stages worldwide, such as Facebook and Instagram (Gillespie, 2018).

A striking illustration of the moral challenges posed by secrecy and social diversity is the contention encompassing the subreddit r/Donald. This community, which upheld the previous U.S. President Donald Trump frequently locked in behaviors such as badgering, doxing (distributing private data), and spreading scheme hypotheses. The secrecy of Reddit clients makes it difficult to hold people responsible for their activities. Moreover, the community's standards clashed with the broader Reddit community guidelines, creating moral predicaments around free speech versus hurtful conduct. Inevitably, Reddit prohibited subreddits, highlighting the platform's battle to balance secrecy, social contrasts, and moral behavior (Marwick & Lewis, 2017).

Another illustration is the moral suggestions for social differences in substance control in TikTok. This stage, prevalent among a worldwide group of onlookers, confronted feedback for supposedly smothering content from users in marginalized communities and those examining delicate political issues. The differences in social standards across its client base made it challenging for TikTok to create and uphold substance-balance approaches that were seen as reasonable and moral by all clients. This circumstance underscores the difficulty of maintaining ethical conduct in a socially assorted online space (Milhorance, 2020).

The challenges to moral conduct in online spaces are significant and multifaceted, driven by the effects of secrecy on individual responsibility and contrasts in social and social standards among different community individuals. Anonymity can secure clients and empower unscrupulous behavior, requiring a sensitive adjustment to guarantee responsibility for security. Social differences improve online intelligence, but lead to mistaken assumptions and clashes, requiring touchy and comprehensive approaches to substance control and community administration. Real-world illustrations such as the contentions of Reddit and TikTok outline the complexities of these challenges. As online spaces advance, there must be methodologies to address these moral problems, ensuring that advanced communities remain conscious, comprehensive, and responsible.

DEVELOPING ETHICAL GUIDELINES FOR VIRTUAL COMMUNITIES

As the advanced scene advances, the requirement for vigorous moral rules in virtual communities has become increasingly critical. These rules ensure that online intuition is aware, comprehensive, and useful. Creating viable moral rules includes understanding the key standards of moral behavior and recognizing the basic parts played by community directors and mediators in maintaining these benchmarks.

Key Standards for Moral Behavior in Online Communities

A few key standards establish moral behavior in online communities. These standards were outlined to advance positive intelligence and protect clients from harm.

Regard and Civility

The rule of regard is at the center of any moral rule. Individuals in virtual communities should treat each other with affability and thought, dodging-damaging dialects, individual assault, and badgering. For instance, LinkedIn energizes proficient and conscious talk, emphasizing the importance of maintaining a gracious tone in differences (Suler, 2004).

Trustworthiness and Astuteness

Genuineness is significant for maintaining trust in a community. Clients should be empowered to share data honestly and maintain strategic distance from deceiving others. This rule is especially imperative in communities centered on data sharing, such as Wikipedia, where the exactness and unwavering quality of substance are foremost (Specialty & Bruckman, 2008).

Protection and Secrecy

Ensuring user protection can be a principal moral concern. Rules should diagram how individual data are handled and guarantee that users' information is not shared without assent. Even though sometimes criticized, Facebook's security arrangements point to granting clients control over their data and how it is utilized (Isaak & Hanna, 2018).

Inclusivity and Non-Discrimination

Moral rules ought to advance inclusivity and disallow separation based on race, sexual orientation, sexual introduction, religion, or any other characteristics. These guidelines make a difference in creating an inviting environment for all clients. Stages such as Reddit have presented anti-harassment approaches to cultivate inclusivity and avoid biased behavior (Massanari, 2017).

Responsibility and Obligation

Clients should be held responsible for their activities within the community. This incorporates taking responsibility for the substance they share and understanding the effect of their behavior on others. Twitter, for example, has actualized approaches to holding clients responsible for abusive discourse and badgering by implementing suspensions and bans for violators (Gillespie, 2018). Empowering sympathy and advertising to bolster individual communities can fortify a community's moral texture. Online bolster bunches and gatherings, such as those on Reddit for mental health, exemplify how compassion and back can be indispensable to community intelligence (Andalibi et al., 2016).

THE ROLE OF COMMUNITY DIRECTORS AND MEDIATORS IN MAINTAINING MORAL MEASURES

Community supervisors and arbitrators are important in maintaining moral measures in virtual communities. Their duties include upholding rules, settling clashes, and cultivating a positive community culture. Community supervisors and arbitrators guarantee that built-up moral rules follow. They screen talks, address infringements, and execute punishments when necessary. For example, mediators on sites such as Reddit and Facebook effectively expel posts that abuse community benchmarks and issue notices or bans to irritate clients (Marwick & Lewis, 2017).

Clashes are unavoidable in any community and fall to arbitrators to intervene in debates and guarantee that they are settled reasonably and usefully. Compelling strife determination requires arbitrators to be unbiased, compassionate, and talented. The control group on Wikipedia is known for its organized approach to strife determination, utilizing dialogue and consensus building to address debate (Strong et al., 2008).

Past the run-the-show requirement, community supervisors and moderators also played a pivotal role in forming the community's culture. Empowering positive behavior and highlighting illustrations of constructive interactions can impact the general tone of the community. This proactive approach can be seen in stages such as the Stack Flood, where arbitrators and experienced clients show conscious and accommodating behavior to preserve a collaborative environment (Mamykina et al., 2011).

Instructive Activities

Community supervisors and arbitrators can create instructive activities to advise clients about the community's moral rules and the importance of moral behavior. This may include onboarding sessions for modern individuals, customary overhauls on community measures, and assets on advanced citizenship. Twitter's visit overhauls and client notices around approach changes outline how instructive endeavors can offer assistance in maintaining moral measures (Gillespie, 2018).

Straightforwardness and Communication

Successful control requires straightforward and clear communication with the community. Clients ought to understand why certain activities are undertaken and how choices are made. This transparency builds beliefs and makes clients feel that they have contributed more to the community's moral benchmarks. Reddit and Facebook regularly distribute straightforward reports, specifying their balanced endeavors and decision-making forms (Newton, 2020).

Adjusting to Alter

Virtual communities are energetic, and moral rules must be advanced in reaction to modern challenges and changing client behaviors. Community managers and arbitrators must be versatile, persistently evaluate, and upgrade rules to address developing issues. The reaction of different social media platforms to the spread of deception amid widespread COVID-19 highlights the need for spry and responsive control hones (Cinelli et al., 2020).

Case of Moral Rule

One illustrative case of moral rule advancement and enforcement is Reddit's dealing with r/Donald subreddit. First, the subreddit was used by supporters of Donald Trump to discuss political issues. Be that as it may, it became infamous for abusing Reddit's substance approaches by locking badgering, spreading deception, and prompting savagery. Reddit's arbitrators endeavored to implement moral rules through notices and brief bans, but eventually the stage chosen was to boycott the subreddit to maintain community measures (Marwick & Lewis, 2017).

Another case is Wikipedia's approach to maintaining moral conduct among editors. Wikipedia's rules emphasize a lack of bias, unquestionable status, and civility. This stage depends on an expansive volunteer base of editors and chairpersons to uphold these rules. Debates are settled through talks and agreements, and rehash violators can be prohibited from altering. This collaborative and straightforward approach is viable for maintaining Wikipedia's validity and ethical standards (Specialty and Bruckman, 2008).

Creating moral rules for virtual communities may be a complex, but basic error. Key standards, such as regard, genuineness, protection, inclusivity, responsibility, and compassion shape the establishment of these rules. Community supervisors and mediators are fundamental in implementing these benchmarks, settling clashes, advancing a positive culture, teaching clients, guaranteeing straightforwardness, and adjusting to change. Real-world illustrations from stages such as Reddit, Twitter, and Wikipedia illustrate the challenges and challenges in maintaining moral conduct in different online situations. As virtual communities proceed to develop and advance, progressive endeavors to refine and implement moral rules will be pivotal to keeping up secure, conscious, and beneficial advanced spaces.

CASE STUDIES: ETHICAL DILEMMAS AND RESOLUTIONS

Virtual communities offer exceptional opportunities for social interactions, data sharing, and collaboration. However, these spaces also display special moral situations that require cautious thoughts and determination. Analysing real-life scenarios in which moral clashes have emerged inside virtual communities can provide important insights into the techniques utilized to address and resolve these issues.

Case Study 1: Reddit's r/The Donald Subreddit

Moral Predicament

The r/The Donald subreddit, committed to supporters of the previous U.S. President Donald Trump became the central point of moral contention because of its substance. As often as possible, individuals in this community posted incendiary and derisive discourse, scheme hypotheses, and affectations to savagery. These activities damaged Reddit's approach to badgering, despising discourse, and deception, creating a critical moral struggle between free discourse and community security.

Determination Methodology

Reddit's chairpersons first took a graduated approach to the issues in r/The Donald. They issued notices, forced transitory bans, and required the subreddit arbitrators to uphold stricter controls on substance. Despite these endeavors, the subreddit proceeded to cultivate hurtful behavior. In June 2020, after numerous episodes of rough substance and falling flat to comply with Reddit's community rules, the stage was chosen for a time boycott, r/Donald (Marwick & Lewis, 2017). This determination highlights the significance of implementing moral benchmarks when confronting backfire from a vocal client base. By prioritizing community security and the following arrangements, Reddit illustrated a commitment to maintaining a healthy and conscious online environment (Tariq, 2024).

Case Study 2: Wikipedia's Publication Debate

Moral Predicament

The free online Wikipedia reference book depends on many volunteer editors to preserve and upgrade its substance. This collaborative show can lead to moral situations, especially when editors oppose the idea of non-partisanship and integrity of data. One striking struggle included the Wikipedia page for Gamergate, a disputable development related to sexism and badgering in the video amusement industry. Editors were profoundly isolated on how to show the development, with a few contending for a center on its moral concerns and others on related badgering (Specialty & Bruckman, 2008).

Determination Procedure

Wikipedia's approach to resolving such debates emphasizes discourse, agreement, and straightforwardness. In the case of the Gamergate page, editors locked in broad dialogues on the article's conversation page to reach an agreement that adjusted the viewpoints. Wikipedia's arrangements on unquestionable status and nonpartisanship guided these talks, guaranteeing that the ultimate substance was well sourced and adjusted. When agreement could not be effectively accomplished, the debate was heightened to Wikipedia's Intervention Committee, which gave an official determination based on the community's rules.

This case outlines the adequacy of an organized, straightforward, and community-driven approach for settling moral clashes. Wikipedia effectively explored a disagreeable issue by cultivating an open discourse and following clear publication standards.

Case Study 3: Facebook's Cambridge Analytica Embarrassment

Moral Problem

Cambridge Analytica outrage uncovered noteworthy moral issues concerning client protection and information misuse. In 2018, it was discovered that Cambridge Analytica gathered individual information from millions of Facebook clients without their consent, utilizing this data to focus on political publicization. This breach raised moral questions about information protection, an educated assent, and the obligations of social media stages to secure client data (Isaak & Hanna, 2018).

Determination Procedure

In reaction to this outrage, Facebook took a few measures to address moral breaches and reestablish client beliefs. These include improving information protection settings, giving clients more noteworthy control over their data, and expanding the straightforwardness of information collection hones. Facebook also limits third-party access to client information and presents stricter arrangements for app engineers. Moreover, the company propelled an open relations campaign to communicate these changes and emphasize its commitment to client protection.

Cambridge Analytica's embarrassment's determination underscores the need for strong information security approaches and straightforward communication with clients. Facebook's activities aim to amend moral violations and anticipate future breaches, highlighting the significance of responsibility and proactive measures for maintaining moral measures.

Case Study 4: Twitter's Reaction to Deception

Moral Problem

Twitter, a major social media platform, has confronted noteworthy challenges in combating misinformation, especially amid the widespread COVID-19 pandemic and 2020 U.S. presidential decisions. The rapid spread of untrue data on these themes posed genuine moral predicaments because it debilitated open well-being and undermined equitable forms. Twitter must adjust the standards of free speech to avoid the hurt caused by deception (Gillespie, 2018).

Determination Technique

Twitter has adopted a multifaceted approach to address the deception issue. The stage presented arrangements to name and, in a few cases, expel deceiving tweets about COVID-19 and race. It also partnered with fact-checking organisations to confirm data and give clients precise information. In addition, Twitter actualized changes to its calculation to decrease the permeability of incorrect data and advance solid sources. The company communicated these changes directly to its clients, clarifying the reasoning behind their activities. This highlights the significance of flexibility and straightforwardness in relation to moral situations in virtual communities. Twitter's endeavors to moderate deception illustrate how stages can take dynamic steps to maintain moral measures while adjusting competing values.

Case Study 5: Twitch's Dealing with Badgering and Mishandle

Moral Situation

Jerk, a live spilling platform primarily utilized by gamers, has battled with issues of badgering and mishandling, especially for female streamers. Reports of sexist comments, stalking, and facilitated badgering campaigns have raised significant moral concerns regarding client security and stage obligation. Jerk's challenge was to create a secure and inclusive environment while permitting free expression and community building (Chess & Shaw, 2015).

Determination Technique

Jerk reacted by reinforcing its badgering approaches and executing more vigorous authorization instruments. The stage presented instruments for streamers to better oversee their communities, such as upgraded balance capabilities, robotized sifting of hostile dialects, and stricter punishments for approach infringement. Jerk moreover propelled instructive activities to raise mindfulness around badgering and advance positive behavior among its clients. Customary straightforward reports have been upgraded on the platform's endeavors to combat manhandling and to move forward with community guidelines.

Twitch's approach underscores the need for comprehensive methodologies to address moral issues in virtual communities. By combining approach authorization, client strengthening, and instruction, Jerk pointed to the formation of a more secure and more aware environment for all clients.

This case outlines the moral problems that can emerge in virtual communities and the techniques used to resolve them. To avoid discourse and deception to ensure client security and combat harassment, platforms must navigate complex moral scenes to preserve beliefs and integrity. Effective solutions include clear rules, active enforcement, community engagement, and straightforward communication. As spaces advance, the capacity to adjust and maintain moral benchmarks will remain vital for cultivating sound and aware online communities.

PROMOTING A CULTURE OF TRUST AND SAFETY

In this rapidly advancing age, advancing the culture of belief and security in virtual communities is fundamental. Belief cultivates client engagement and collaboration, whereas security guarantees that all members can associate without fear of badgering or hurting. Viable procedures for building beliefs and guaranteeing security are important for the supportability and victory of online communities.

Procedures for Building Believe Among Community Individuals

Straightforwardness and Open Communication

Straightforwardness in arrangements, decision-making forms, and activities taken by community pioneers is foundational to building beliefs. Clients who understand the rules and their reasons are more likely to believe in the stage and its administration. For example, Wikipedia's straightforward publication and struggle determination forms, which are open to public viewing, offer assistance in constructing beliefs among its supporters and clients (Specialty & Bruckman, 2008).

Reliable Authorization of Rules

Applying community rules guarantees that all individuals are treated decently, which is significant for beliefs. Conflicting requirements can lead to the discernment of predisposition and favoritism, undermining beliefs. Despite this backfire, Reddit's approach to prohibiting subreddits like r/The Donald for rehashed arrangement infringement underscores the significance of steady run-the-show authorization in keeping up beliefs (Marwick & Lewis, 2017).

Community Association and Strengthening

Including community members in decision-making enables them to cultivate a sense of proprietorship. Stages such as Stack Flood empower clients' interests in balance through a notoriety framework that permits experienced clients to audit and hail substances. This participatory approach makes a difference in the construction of a collaborative and reliable community (Mamykina et al., 2011).

Clear and Available Rules

Providing clear, effective open rules helps clients understand the desire for behavior inside the community. Stages such as Facebook and Twitter frequently upgrade their community benchmarks and provide nitty-gritty clarifications on their approaches to clients. This clarity helps anticipate errors and build beliefs within the platform's administration (Gillespie, 2018).

Input Components

Setting up channels for client criticism and illustrating responsiveness to concerns can improve beliefs. Twitter's search for client input on approach changes and giving standard upgrades on how input tends to embody how criticism components can cultivate belief (Gillespie, 2018).

Measures to Guarantee the Security and Well-being of Members in Virtual Situations

Vigorous Balance Frameworks

A viable balance is essential for maintaining a secure environment. This incorporates mechanized systems to identify destructive substances and human mediators that can survey settings and subtlety. The utilization of AI to distinguish and expel harmful substances, combined with a large group of human arbitrators, outlines a comprehensive approach to maintaining security (Newton, 2020).

Anti-Harassment Approaches

Clear anti-harassment approaches are essential to secure clients. Stages must characterize badgering broadly and provide cases to assist clients in understanding what constitutes unsatisfactory behavior. Jerk, a live-streaming stage, has implemented strict anti-harassment arrangements and apparatuses for streamers to oversee their communities, helping secure clients from mishandling (Chess & Shaw, 2015).

Back Frameworks for Casualties

Providing support for badgering and managing victims is crucial to their well-being. This could incorporate access to mental well-being resources, detailed instruments, and devoted support groups. Reddit's execution of back devices for users encountering badgering is significant for providing resources to assist casualties (Massanari, 2017).

Security Assurances

Guaranteeing client protection is essential to creating a secure online environment. It incorporates strong information assurance measures and clear protection arrangements. The European Union's Common Information Security Control (GDPR) has set high benchmarks for information assurance, and numerous platforms have embraced all-inclusive offerings for client protection and security (Isaak & Hanna, 2018).

Instruction and Mindfulness

Teaching clients about online security, protection, and conscious behavior can prevent numerous issues soon after they emerge. Stages like Instagram have propelled instructive campaigns to raise awareness of cyberbullying and how to report it, making a difference in creating a more informed and secure community (Andalibi et al., 2016).

Secure Spaces for Powerless Bunches

Making and maintaining secure spaces for helpless bunches is fundamental to inclusivity and security. Facebook has executed apparatuses and approaches to back LGBTQ+ clients, counting highlights to protect against badgering and to provide assets for mental well-being support (Isaak & Hanna, 2018).

Cases and Examples

Wikipedia's Approach to Believe and Security

Wikipedia's worldwide global victory can be credited to its straightforward administration and strong security measures. The platform's open-altering demonstration is backed by clear rules, straightforward debate determination preparation, and a solid community of volunteer editors who screen substances. This demonstration made a significant difference. Wikipedia maintains high belief and security despite being a large, decentralized community (Strong et al., 2008).

Facebook's Information Security Activities

Following the Cambridge Analytica embarrassment, Facebook attempted noteworthy measures to modify its beliefs and guarantee client security. The stage upgraded security settings, restricted third-party access to information, and expanded transparency regarding information hones. These steps were pivotal in tending toward moral breaches and reestablishing client trust (Isaak & Hanna, 2018).

Reddit's Community-Based Moderation

Reddit's approach to balance includes engaging community mediators in implementing rules inside their subreddits. This decentralized show permits custom-fitted control that reflects the standards of each community while maintaining large stages. The platform's reaction to the r/The_Donald discussion illustrates the significance of consistent requirements and community associations in maintaining beliefs and safety (Marwick & Lewis, 2017).

Twitter's Dealing with Deception

Amid the COVID-19 outbreak, Twitter confronted the challenge of combating deception while maintaining free discourse. The platform introduced arrangements to name and evaluate untrue data, joined forces with fact-checking organisations, and balanced its calculations to advance sound sources. This multifaceted approach is fundamental to moral situations related to deception and ensuring open well-being (Gillespie, 2018).

Twitch's Anti-Harassment Measures

Twitch implemented comprehensive measures to combat badgering and to guarantee client security. These include improved control instruments, strict arrangements against hate discourse and badgering, and bolster frameworks for casualties. Twitch's endeavors highlight the significance of a proactive and multilayered approach to maintaining a secure and comprehensive community (Chess & Shaw, 2015).

Promoting a culture of belief and security in virtual communities is crucial to maintainability and victory. Building beliefs requires straightforward, steady-state authorization, community inclusion, clear communication, and responsive input components. Guaranteeing security includes strong control, anti-harassment arrangements, back frameworks for casualties, security securities, instructive activities, and securing space for vulnerable groups. Case ponders from stages such as Wikipedia, Facebook, Reddit, Twitter, and Jerk outline compelling techniques for cultivating beliefs and security. As online communities advance, these standards and measures will remain vital in tending toward moral challenges and promoting positive intuition.

THE ROLE OF POLICIES AND REGULATIONS

The rise of virtual communities has required the advancement of approaches and directions to administer behavior, guarantee security, and advance moral conduct. These systems are basic for creating situations where clients can connect, share data, and collaborate without fear of badgering or hurt. Analysing existing approaches and the effect of direction provides an understanding of how virtual spaces can be overseen in cultivating moral behavior.

Examination of Existing Approaches that Oversee Behavior in Virtual Spaces

Community Rules and Terms of Benefit

Most virtual communities build a set of community rules and terms of benefit (TOS) to characterize satisfactory behavior and lay out the infringement results. For instance, Reddit's community rules emphasize regard, protection, and denial of badgering and abhor discourse. These rules are supplemented by the TOS's understanding that clients must acknowledge upon joining the stage. Clear and available rules assist clients in achieving their desires and defining the boundaries of worthy behavior (Massanari, 2017).

Substance Control Arrangements

Substance control approaches are essential to maintain a secure and conscious environment. These approaches regularly use computerized frameworks and human mediators to survey and oversee user-generated substances. Facebook's balance approach incorporates the expulsion of substances that damage community measures, such as hate discourse, realistic viciousness, and deception. The platform's use of manufactured insights (AI) to distinguish and hail harmful substances and, recently, human surveys have been a case of how innovation can be utilized to uphold arrangements successfully (Gillespie, 2018).

Anti-Harassment and Anti-Bullying Approaches

Particular arrangements focusing on badgering and bullying are essential to ensure defenseless clients. Jerk, a live-gushing stage, has executed comprehensive anti-harassment approaches that incorporate the utilization of computerized apparatuses to channel hostile dialects and strengthen streamers to oversee their communities through control highlights. These arrangements are planned to avoid badgering and guarantee secure space for all clients, especially those from marginalized bunches (Chess & Shaw, 2015).

Security Approaches

Protection arrangements oversee how client information is collected, utilized, and ensured. The European Union's Common Information Security Direction (GDPR) could be a point of interest system that orders exacting information assurance measures and requires stages to get unequivocal assent from clients, sometimes recently collecting individual data. Stages such as Facebook and Google have overhauled their security arrangements to comply with GDPR, highlighting the significance of administrative systems in securing client security (Isaak & Hanna, 2018).

Client Assertion and Announcing Instruments

Client understanding regularly incorporates components to announce the infringement of arrangements. For example, Twitter's client assertion traces strategies for announcing injurious behavior and provides apparatuses for clients to piece or quiet accounts that lock in badgering. Announcing components are vital for engaging clients to require activity against untrustworthy behavior and for stages to respond successfully to infringement (Gillespie, 2018).

The Effect of Directions on Cultivating Moral Conduct inside Communities

Advancing Responsibility

Directions and approaches advance responsibility by establishing clear rules and consequences for infringement. When clients know that their activities are being observed and that there are repercussions for unscrupulous behavior, they are more likely to follow community guidelines. The steady requirement of these approaches is fundamental for maintaining beliefs and order within virtual communities (Strong et al., 2008).

Upgrading Client Security

Directions on client security, such as anti-harassment and anti-bullying approaches, are essential for creating comprehensive and secure situations. By effectively tending to destructive behavior and providing bolsters for casualties, stages can cultivate a sense of security and well-being among clients. Twitch's endeavors to combat badgering through comprehensive approaches and back frameworks outline the positive effects of such directions on client security (Chess & Shaw, 2015).

Believing is essential to the victory of any virtual community. Arrangements and directions that are straightforward, reliably implemented, and adjusted according to users' desires offer assistance in constructing and maintaining belief. For example, Wikipedia's straightforward administrative demonstration, which includes clear publication approaches and open struggle determination forms, has been instrumental in building belief among its supporters and clients (Specialty & Bruckman, 2008).

Guaranteeing Reasonableness and Balance

Controls play a pivotal role in advancing reasonableness and correspondence within virtual communities. Anti-discrimination policies, such as those forbidding despise discourse and guaranteeing breaks, even with treatment for all clients, are fundamental for cultivating comprehensive situations. Reddit's choice to boycott subreddits that advance abhor discourse and segregation reflects a commitment to decency and uniformity (Marwick and Lewis, 2017).

Empowering Mindful Behavior

Directions can energize mindful behavior by teaching clients the effects of their activities and advancing positive intuition. Instructive activities, such as Instagram campaigns to raise mindfulness around cyberbullying and mental well-being well-being, offer assistance in helping clients understand the significance of awareness and moral behavior online (Andalibi et al., 2016).

Legitimate Compliance and Corporate Duty

Administrative systems, such as the GDPR, compel states to comply with lawful information and client security guidelines. Compliance with such directions illustrates corporate obligations and commitment to moral obligations. Facebook's endeavors to upgrade information protection and transparency following the Cambridge Analytica outrage highlight regulatory compliance's significance in revamping beliefs and guaranteeing moral conduct (Isaak and Hanna, 2018).

Case Examples

Facebook's Compliance with GDPR

The implementation of the GDPR in 2018 had a noteworthy effect on how the stages handle client information. Facebook's compliance with the GDPR involved changing its security arrangements, obtaining unequivocal assent from clients for information collection, and making it more straightforward. Most information can be handled in a straightforward manner. These changes guaranteed lawful compliance and upgraded client beliefs and information assurance (Isaak and Hanna, 2018).

Reddit's Community Rules Authorization

Reddit's approach to upholding community rules through client strengthening and a reliable balance has been successful in maintaining moral measures. The platform's choice to boycott subreddits such as r/The Donald for rehashed approach infringement illustrated a commitment to maintaining community benchmarks and guaranteeing an awareness of the environment (Marwick & Lewis, 2017).

Twitter's Deception Arrangements

Amid the widespread COVID-19 outbreak, Twitter executed arrangements to combat deception by labelling and expelling incorrect data. These measures were planned to ensure open well-being and access precise data. Twitter's proactive approach to deception highlights the role of controlling moral behavior and protecting clients (Gillespie, 2018).

Wikipedia's Straightforward Administration

Wikipedia's straightforward publication arrangements and open-struggle determination forms have been essential for building beliefs and guaranteeing moral conduct. The platform's decentralized administration, which includes community interest in decision-making, advances responsibility, and decency, illustrates the effectiveness of straightforward controls in cultivating moral behavior (Specialty & Bruckman, 2008).

Arrangements and controls are fundamental for administering behavior in virtual communities and cultivating moral conduct. Community rules, substance control approaches, anti-harassment measures, security protection, and reporting instruments are basic components of these systems. The effect of directions is obvious in advancing responsibility, improving client security, building beliefs, guaranteeing reasonableness, empowering dependable behavior, and guaranteeing legitimate compliance. Case ponders from Facebook, Reddit, Twitter, and Wikipedia outline the positive impacts of well-designed arrangements and directions in keeping up moral benchmarks and making secure, comprehensive virtual situations. As virtual communities advance, the continuous improvement and requirement for successful approaches and controls will remain significant in advancing moral conduct and ensuring clients.

ETHICAL CONSIDERATIONS FOR COMMUNITY DESIGN

Within the computerized age, where virtual stages serve as central points for social interaction and collaboration, moral contemplations are vital in forming community plans. The plan and highlights of virtual stages can impact client behavior and intelligence, making it basic to prioritize moral standards for their improvement. This exposition investigates how virtual stage plans and highlights can advance moral intuition and the significance of comprehensive and available community plans for differing needs.

How the Plan and Highlights of Virtual Stages Can Advance Moral Intelligent

User-Friendly Interface

A user-friendly interface is essential for advancing the moral intelligence of virtual communities. Stages ought to be natural and simple to explore, permitting clients to consistently engage with substances and to associate with others. Clear labelling, steady plan components, and natural routes contribute to positive client involvement and energize moral behavior. For example, social media sites, such as Facebook and Twitter, prioritize straightforwardness and ease of use, encouraging moral intuition among clients (Gillespie, 2018).

Protection Controls

Protection controls are fundamental for securing user data and cultivating beliefs in virtual communities. Stages should provide strong protection that permits clients to control who can access their content and how their information is shared. Facebook's security settings, which empower clients to customize their group of viewers for each post and oversee their information-sharing inclinations, engage clients in forming educated choices about their security (Isaak & Hanna, 2018).

Substance Control Devices

Substance balance instruments help to maintain a secure and conscious environment by permitting stages to screen and expel substances. Robotized channels, detailing components, and human mediators are crucial for implementing community rules and avoiding hurtful behaviors. Jerk, a live-spilling stage, gives substance makers apparatuses to directly chat, channel hostile dialects, and boycott clients who abuse community benchmarks, advancing moral intelligence among clients (Chess & Shaw, 2015).

Algorithmic Straightforwardness

Straightforwardness in algorithmic decision making is vital for advancing moral intelligence and moderating the spread of deception and inclination. Stages ought to provide clients with an understanding of how calculations work and how they impact substance dissemination and proposals. Twitter's choice to present straightforward measures, such as clarifying why certain tweets are prescribed or why certain accounts appear in users' timelines, improves client beliefs and advances moral behavior (Gillespie, 2018).

Accessibility Highlights

Availability guarantees that virtual stages are comprehensive and available to clients with assorted needs. Planning stages with highlights, such as screen peruser compatibility, console route, and movable content estimation, accommodate users with inabilities and advances that are of interest. Social media sites, such as Instagram, have executed availability highlights, such as alt-content portrayals for pictures, to guarantee that all clients can lock in with substance and take an interest in discussions (Andalibi et al., 2016).

The Significance of Comprehensive and Available Community Plan to Bolster Different Needs

Guaranteeing Rise to Get to

A comprehensive and available community plan guarantees the rise of virtual stages for clients with assorted needs. Planning stages with availability highlight the expulsion boundaries for cooperation and advance inclusivity. In this case, Facebook's commitment to availability incorporates highlights, such as alt content depictions for pictures, screen peruser compatibility, and console alternate routes, empowering clients with the inability to lock in completely with the stage (Isaak & Hanna, 2018).

Cultivating Differing Qualities and Representation

A comprehensive community plan advances differences and representations by pleasing clients with diverse foundations, societies, and personalities. Stages ought to consider their client base's differing needs and inclinations when designing highlights and interfaces. Instagram's endeavors to advance differences and representation incorporate highlights, such as gender-neutral pronouns and customizable profile choices, making a more comprehensive environment for clients (Andalibi et al., 2016).

Addressing Predisposition and Separation

A comprehensive plan can help address predisposition and segregation inside virtual communities by guaranteeing that the stages are open and inviting all clients. The planning stages highlight that advanced differences, values, and incorporation can moderate the impacts of inclination and separation and cultivate a culture of regard and acknowledgement. Twitter's commitment to predisposition and segregation incorporates activities to advance different representations in substance balance and algorithmic decision-making, making a difference in forming a more comprehensive and impartial stage (Gillespie, 2018).

Engaging Marginalized Communities

A comprehensive community plan enables marginalized communities by giving them a voice and stage for expression. Stages ought to prioritize highlights and approaches that open the voices of marginalized bunches and guarantee their security and well-being. Twitches' activities to back LGBTQ+ makers and combat badgering through anti-harassment arrangements and balance devices illustrate a commitment to enable marginalized communities and cultivate a culture of inclusivity (Chess & Shaw, 2015).

Case Studies and Illustrations

Facebook's Openness Activities

Facebook has actualized different openness highlights to guarantee that its stage is comprehensive and available to clients with different needs. These highlights incorporate alt content depictions for images, screen peruser compatibility, console alternate routes, and empower clients with the inability to lock in completely with the stage. Facebook's commitment to availability reflects its commitment to advancing inclusivity and rising to get to all clients (Isaak and Hanna, 2018).

Instagram's Differing Qualities and Consideration Endeavors

Instagram has presented a few highlights to advance its differences and incorporation into its community. These highlights incorporate gender-neutral pronouns and customizable profile alternatives, permitting clients to precisely identify their personalities. Instagram's endeavors to cultivate differences and representations contribute to a more comprehensive and inviting environment for clients from assorted foundations (Andalibi et al., 2016).

Twitter's Inclination Relief Methodologies

Twitter has executed methodologies to address predisposition and segregation during its stage. These techniques incorporate advancing differing representations in substance control and algorithmic decision making to guarantee decency and value. Twitter's commitment to inclination and separation reflects its acknowledgement of the significance of creating a comprehensive and evenhanded environment for all clients (Gillespie, 2018).

Moral contemplations are instrumental in forming plans, highlighting virtual stages, and advancing positive intelligence in online communities. User-friendly interfacing, protection controls, substance balance instruments, algorithmic straightforwardness, and accessibility highlights are basic components of a moral community plan. A comprehensive and available community plan is essential for supporting differing needs, cultivating different qualities and representations, tending to predisposition and segregation, and enabling marginalized communities. Case ponders from Facebook, Instagram, and Twitter outline the significance of prioritizing moral standards in community plans and the positive effect of comprehensive and available highlights on client engagement and well-being. As virtual communities evolve, continuous commitment to a moral community plan will be essential for creating secure, comprehensive, and evenhanded online situations.

FUTURE DIRECTIONS IN VIRTUAL COMMUNITY ETHICS

As virtual communities advance and extend, modern moral challenges emerge, requiring inventive arrangements and a forward-thinking approach. The rapid pace of mechanical progression presents complexities that require cautious thought to guarantee the moral keenness of online intelligence. This study investigates rising moral challenges in quickly advancing virtual spaces and the potential for modern advances, such as AI control, to shape the moral scene.

Developing Moral Challenges in Quickly Advancing Virtual Spaces

Algorithmic Predisposition and Segregation

The expanding dependence on calculations to minister substances and personalize client encounters raises concerns regarding inclination and separation. Calculations can sustain the existing inclinations displayed when preparing information, leading to unfair results. Tending to algorithmic predisposition requires straightforward, responsible, and continuous assessment of algorithmic frameworks to relieve the chance of hurt to marginalized communities (Gillespie, 2018).

Security and Information Assurance

Collecting and utilizing individual information via virtual stages raises moral concerns regarding security and information assurance. As stages accumulate endless sums of client information focused on promoting algorithmic decision-making, there is a need for vigorous information assurance directions and instruments to guarantee client security and assent. Adjusting personalized encounters and client security remains a significant moral challenge (Isaak and Hanna, 2018).

Substance Balance and Free Discourse

Substance control approaches confront the examination of their effects on free discourse and censorship. Adjusting the ought to evacuate destructive substances, such as abhor speech and misinformation, with the conservation of free expression could be a complex moral predicament. Stages must explore securing clients from hurt and maintaining the standards of free discourse, considering social, lawful, and social settings (Gillespie, 2018).

Computerized Disparity

Computerized separate compound incongruities in virtual communities propagate disparities based on financial status, topography, and socioeconomic factors. Guaranteeing impartial access to virtual spaces requires obstructing web networks, computerized education, and innovation. Disappointment in addressing computerized imbalance can encourage marginalized groups, which are now impeded, driving social prohibition and unjust support in online communities (Warschauer, 2003).

Online Badgering and Cyberbullying

The namelessness and disinhibition afforded by virtual spaces contributes to the predominance of online badgering and cyberbullying. Ensuring clients from badgering while protecting their flexibility of expression poses moral challenges for stage control. Unused approaches to combating online badgering, such as algorithmic location and client strengthening, are required to create more secure and comprehensive virtual situations (Massanari, 2017).

The Potential for Unused Innovations to Shape the Moral Scene

AI Control and Content Sifting

The advent of manufactured insights (AI) presents opportunities and challenges for substance control in virtual communities. AI calculations can be used to robotize the location and expulsion of destructive substances, moving forward with proficiency and versatility. Be that as it may, AI control raises concerns about precision, predisposition, and unintended results. Moral AI plan standards, such as decency, straightforwardness, and responsibility, ensure that AI control improves rather than undermining moral measures (Gillespie, 2018).

Blockchain and Decentralization

Blockchain innovation offers the potential to decentralize virtual communities by engaging clients with more prominent control over their information and intuition. The decentralized stages built on blockchain conventions prioritize protection, straightforwardness, and client independence. Blockchain-based communities face challenges in administration, adaptability, and administrative compliance. Moral contemplations in blockchain plans guarantee inclusivity, responsibility, and maintainability (Böhme et al., 2015).

Virtual Reality and Immersive Encounters

Virtual reality (VR) innovation empowers immersive encounters that obscure boundaries between virtual and physical situations. Moral contemplations in VR plans guarantee client security, assent, and privacy in immersive spaces. The VR stages must address virtual badgering, personality control, and mental well-being. Planning VR encounters that prioritize client offices, sympathy, and moral engagement is essential for cultivating positive intelligence in virtual communities (Lugrin et al., 2019).

Moral AI Assistants and Chatbots

AI-powered virtual collaborators and chatbots offer personalized feedback and help in virtual communities. Moral contemplations in the AI partner plan incorporate straightforwardness, responsibility, and client assents. AI associates must consider client security, dodge-propagating inclinations, and maintain moral benchmarks in decision-making. Guaranteeing that AI associates prioritize client well-being, independence, and educated assent is essential for building beliefs and cultivating moral intelligence (Coeckelbergh, 2020).

Social Effect of Rising Innovations

The social effect of developing innovations in virtual communities has expanded past specialized contemplations of moral, social, and political measurements. Mechanical progress shapes social standards, control elements, and moral systems inside virtual spaces. Moral premonition and proactive engagement with partners are fundamental for expecting and tending toward the social consequences of rising innovations. Stages must facilitate exchanges with clients, specialists, and policymakers to guarantee that innovation advancement adjusts to moral values and societal needs (van Est et al., 2017).

As virtual communities advance, the exploration of moral scenes becomes increasingly complex. Developing innovations offers unused openings and challenges in forming ethical measurements of online intuition. Developing moral challenges requires a multidisciplinary approach that combines mechanical innovation with ethical reflection and social duties. Stages must prioritize straightforwardness, responsibility, client strengthening, and inclusivity in their plan and administration forms to cultivate moral intuition and create secure, comprehensive, and evenhanded virtual communities.

CONCLUSION

In conclusion, the moral scene of virtual communities is multifaceted, continually advancing, and requires cautious thought to maintain the standards of reasonableness, inclusivity, protection, and responsibility. A few key moral contemplations have been developed through this talk, enveloping challenges and openings for cultivating positive intuition and forming long-term online spaces.

Securing client protection and guaranteeing information security are the foremost issues in virtual communities. Stages must execute vigorous protection arrangements, obtain educated assent for information collection, and give clients control over their data. Adjusting ought to evacuate hurtful substances while preserving free expression presents a noteworthy moral challenge. Stages must create straightforward substance balance arrangements that maintain community measures regarding users' rights from precise perspectives. Calculations are central to forming client encounters and substance dispersion in virtual communities. Tending to algorithmic predisposition requires straightforward, responsible, and continuous assessment to relieve the chance of unfair results. Bridging advanced isolation and guaranteeing evenhanded access to virtual spaces are fundamental for advancing inclusivity and social cohesion. Stages must address boundaries in web networks, computer proficiency, and innovation to anticipate the marginalization of distraught bunches. Combating online badgering and cyberbullying requires proactive measures including client strengthening, algorithmic discovery, and community control. Stages must create secure and strong situations that protect clients from harm while protecting their opportunities for expression. The significance of moral watchfulness cannot be exaggerated as virtual communities advance and grow. While innovative progressions offer opportunities for modern association and collaboration, they also display moral challenges that require conscious thought and proactive engagement.

Moral vigilance in online spaces is essential for safeguarding client rights, promoting differences and incorporation, and maintaining faith and acuity in virtual communities. Stages must prioritize moral standards in their planning, administration, and decision-making forms, cultivating a culture of straightforwardness, responsibility, and social obligation. Eventually, the continuous significance of moral carefulness lies in its capacity to shape the long-run of virtual communities for the superior. By maintaining moral measures and cultivating moral behavior, online spaces can end up in dynamic, comprehensive, and engaging situations in which clients can flourish and emphatically contribute to society. In conclusion, moral carefulness is not simply an obligation, but a shared commitment to creating online spaces that reflect our values, regard our rights, and improve our lives. As we explore the complexities of virtual communities, let us stay careful in maintaining moral standards and forming a future in which everybody can take an interest, contribute, and have a place.

REFERENCES

Ahmed, S. I., Radhakrishnan, S., Nair, B. B., & Thiruvengadathan, R. (2021). Efficient hyperparameter-tuned machine learning approach for estimation of supercapacitor performance attributes. *Journal of Physics Communications*, 5(11), 115011. DOI: 10.1088/2399-6528/ac3574

Andalibi, N., Ozturk, P., & Forte, A. (2016). Sensitive self-disclosures, responses, and social support on Instagram: The case of #depression. In *Proceedings of the 2017 ACM Conference on Computer Supported Cooperative Work and Social Computing (CSCW 2017)* (pp. 1485–1500).

Böhme, R., Christin, N., Edelman, B., & Moore, T. (2015). Bitcoin: Economics, technology, and governance. *The Journal of Economic Perspectives*, 29(2), 213–238. DOI: 10.1257/jep.29.2.213

Chess, S., & Shaw, A. (2015). A conspiracy of fishes, or, how we learned to stop worrying about #GamerGate and embrace hegemonic masculinity. *Journal of Broadcasting & Electronic Media*, 59(1), 208–220. DOI: 10.1080/08838151.2014.999917

Coeckelbergh, M. (2020). *AI ethics: Social and ethical implications of algorithms, data, and artificial intelligence*. Cambridge University Press. DOI: 10.7551/mitpress/12549.001.0001

Forte, A., & Bruckman, A. (2008). Scaling consensus: Increasing decentralization in Wikipedia governance. In *Proceedings of the 41st Annual Hawaii International Conference on System Sciences (HICSS)* (p. 157). DOI: 10.1109/HICSS.2008.383

Gillespie, T. (2018). *Custodians of the internet: Platforms, content moderation, and the hidden decisions that shape social media*. Yale University Press.

Isaak, J., & Hanna, M. J. (2018). User data privacy: Facebook, Cambridge Analytica, and privacy protection. *Computer*, 51(8), 56–59. DOI: 10.1109/MC.2018.3191268

Lugrin, J. L., Longpré, S., & El Saddik, A. (2019). Towards ethical guidelines for virtual reality. *IEEE Transactions on Technology and Society*, 1(1), 48–58.

Marwick, A. E., & Lewis, R. (2017). *Media manipulation and disinformation online*. Data & Society Research Institute.

Massanari, A. L. (2017). Gamergate and the Fappening: How Reddit's algorithm, governance, and culture support toxic technocultures. *New Media & Society*, 19(3), 329–346. DOI: 10.1177/1461444815608807

Tariq, M. U. (2024). Harnessing Persuasive Technologies for Enhanced Learner Engagement and Motivation. In M. Sanmugam, D. Lim, N. Mohd Barkhaya, W. Wan Yahaya, & Z. Khlaif (Eds.), *Power of Persuasive Educational Technologies in Enhancing Learning* (pp. 30-62). IGI Global. https://doi.org/DOI: 10.4018/979-8-3693-6397-3.ch002

Tariq, M. U. (2024). Smart Transportation Systems: Paving the Way for Sustainable Urban Mobility. In Munuhwa, S. (Ed.), *Contemporary Solutions for Sustainable Transportation Practices* (pp. 254–283). IGI Global., DOI: 10.4018/979-8-3693-3755-4.ch010

Tariq, M. U. (2024). Integration of IoMT for Enhanced Healthcare: Sleep Monitoring, Body Movement Detection, and Rehabilitation Evaluation. In Liu, H., Tripathy, R., & Bhattacharya, P. (Eds.), *Clinical Practice and Unmet Challenges in AI-Enhanced Healthcare Systems* (pp. 70–95). IGI Global., DOI: 10.4018/979-8-3693-2703-6.ch004

Tariq, M. U. (2024). Cybersecurity Risk Assessment Models and Theories in the Travel and Tourism Industry. In Thealla, P., Nadda, V., Dadwal, S., Oztosun, L., & Cantafio, G. (Eds.), *Corporate Cybersecurity in the Aviation, Tourism, and Hospitality Sector* (pp. 1–17). IGI Global., DOI: 10.4018/979-8-3693-2715-9.ch001

Tariq, M. U. (2024). Data Breach Incidents and Prevention in the Hospitality Industry. In Thealla, P., Nadda, V., Dadwal, S., Oztosun, L., & Cantafio, G. (Eds.), *Corporate Cybersecurity in the Aviation, Tourism, and Hospitality Sector* (pp. 181–199). IGI Global., DOI: 10.4018/979-8-3693-2715-9.ch010

Tariq, M. U. (2024). Navigating the Personalization Pathway: Implementing Adaptive Learning Technologies in Higher Education. In Minh Tung, T. (Ed.), *Adaptive Learning Technologies for Higher Education* (pp. 265–291). IGI Global., DOI: 10.4018/979-8-3693-3641-0.ch012

Tariq, M. U. (2024). Enhancing Students and Learning Achievement as 21st-Century Skills Through Transdisciplinary Approaches. In Kumar, R., Ong, E., Anggoro, S., & Toh, T. (Eds.), *Transdisciplinary Approaches to Learning Outcomes in Higher Education* (pp. 220–257). IGI Global., DOI: 10.4018/979-8-3693-3699-1.ch007

Tariq, M. U. (2024). Multi-Agent Models in Healthcare System Design. In Dall'Acqua, L. (Ed.), *Bioethics of Cognitive Ergonomics and Digital Transition* (pp. 143–170). IGI Global., DOI: 10.4018/979-8-3693-2667-1.ch008

Tariq, M. U. (2024). Social Innovations for Improving Healthcare. In Chandan, H. (Ed.), *Social Innovations in Education, Environment, and Healthcare* (pp. 302–317). IGI Global., DOI: 10.4018/979-8-3693-2569-8.ch015

Tariq, M. U. (2024). Leveraging AI for Entrepreneurial Innovation in Healthcare. In Özsungur, F. (Ed.), *Generating Entrepreneurial Ideas With AI* (pp. 192–216). IGI Global., DOI: 10.4018/979-8-3693-3498-0.ch009

Tariq, M. U. (2024). Leading Smart Technologies and Innovations for E-Business 5.0: Applications and Management Frameworks. In Popkova, E. (Ed.), *Smart Technologies and Innovations in E-Business* (pp. 25–46). IGI Global., DOI: 10.4018/978-1-6684-7840-0.ch002

Tariq, M. U. (2024). Crafting Authentic Narratives for Sustainable Branding. In Rodrigues, P. (Eds.), *Compelling Storytelling Narratives for Sustainable Branding* (pp. 194–229). IGI Global., DOI: 10.4018/979-8-3693-3326-6.ch011

Tariq, M. U. (2024). The role of AI in skilling, upskilling, and reskilling the workforce. In Doshi, R., Dadhich, M., Poddar, S., & Hiran, K. (Eds.), *Integrating generative AI in education to achieve sustainable development goals* (pp. 421–433). IGI Global., DOI: 10.4018/979-8-3693-2440-0.ch023

Tariq, M. U. (2024). AI-powered language translation for multilingual classrooms. In Doshi, R., Dadhich, M., Poddar, S., & Hiran, K. (Eds.), *Integrating generative AI in education to achieve sustainable development goals* (pp. 29–46). IGI Global., DOI: 10.4018/979-8-3693-2440-0.ch002

Tariq, M. U. (2024). AI and the future of talent management: Transforming recruitment and retention with machine learning. In Christiansen, B., Aziz, M., & O'Keeffe, E. (Eds.), *Global practices on effective talent acquisition and retention* (pp. 1–16). IGI Global., DOI: 10.4018/979-8-3693-1938-3.ch001

Tariq, M. U. (2024). Application of blockchain and Internet of Things (IoT) in modern business. In Sinha, M., Bhandari, A., Priya, S., & Kabiraj, S. (Eds.), *Future of customer engagement through marketing intelligence* (pp. 66–94). IGI Global., DOI: 10.4018/979-8-3693-2367-0.ch004

Tariq, M. U. (2024). The role of AI ethics in cost and complexity reduction. In Tennin, K., Ray, S., & Sorg, J. (Eds.), *Cases on AI ethics in business* (pp. 59–78). IGI Global., DOI: 10.4018/979-8-3693-2643-5.ch004

Tariq, M. U. (2024). Challenges of a metaverse shaping the future of entrepreneurship. In Inder, S., Dawra, S., Tennin, K., & Sharma, S. (Eds.), *New business frontiers in the metaverse* (pp. 155–173). IGI Global., DOI: 10.4018/979-8-3693-2422-6.ch011

Tariq, M. U. (2024). Neurodiversity inclusion and belonging strategies in the workplace. In J. Vázquez de Príncipe (Ed.), *Resilience of multicultural and multigenerational leadership and workplace experience* (pp. 182-201). IGI Global. https://doi.org/DOI: 10.4018/979-8-3693-1802-7.ch009

Tariq, M. U. (2024). AI and IoT in flood forecasting and mitigation: A comprehensive approach. In Ouaissa, M., Ouaissa, M., Boulouard, Z., Iwendi, C., & Krichen, M. (Eds.), *AI and IoT for proactive disaster management* (pp. 26–60). IGI Global., DOI: 10.4018/979-8-3693-3896-4.ch003

Tariq, M. U. (2024). Empowering student entrepreneurs: From idea to execution. In Cantafio, G., & Munna, A. (Eds.), *Empowering students and elevating universities with innovation centers* (pp. 83–111). IGI Global., DOI: 10.4018/979-8-3693-1467-8.ch005

Tariq, M. U. (2024). The transformation of healthcare through AI-driven diagnostics. In Sharma, A., Chanderwal, N., Tyagi, S., Upadhyay, P., & Tyagi, A. (Eds.), *Enhancing medical imaging with emerging technologies* (pp. 250–264). IGI Global., DOI: 10.4018/979-8-3693-5261-8.ch015

Tariq, M. U. (2024). The role of emerging technologies in shaping the global digital government landscape. In Guo, Y. (Ed.), *Emerging developments and technologies in digital government* (pp. 160–180). IGI Global., DOI: 10.4018/979-8-3693-2363-2.ch009

Tariq, M. U. (2024). Equity and inclusion in learning ecosystems. In Al Husseiny, F., & Munna, A. (Eds.), *Preparing students for the future educational paradigm* (pp. 155–176). IGI Global., DOI: 10.4018/979-8-3693-1536-1.ch007

Tariq, M. U. (2024). Empowering educators in the learning ecosystem. In Al Husseiny, F., & Munna, A. (Eds.), *Preparing students for the future educational paradigm* (pp. 232–255). IGI Global., DOI: 10.4018/979-8-3693-1536-1.ch010

Tariq, M. U. (2024). Revolutionizing health data management with blockchain technology: Enhancing security and efficiency in a digital era. In Garcia, M., & de Almeida, R. (Eds.), *Emerging technologies for health literacy and medical practice* (pp. 153–175). IGI Global., DOI: 10.4018/979-8-3693-1214-8.ch008

Tariq, M. U. (2024). Emerging trends and innovations in blockchain-digital twin integration for green investments: A case study perspective. In Jafar, S., Rodriguez, R., Kannan, H., Akhtar, S., & Plugmann, P. (Eds.), *Harnessing blockchain-digital twin fusion for sustainable investments* (pp. 148–175). IGI Global., DOI: 10.4018/979-8-3693-1878-2.ch007

Tariq, M. U. (2024). Emotional intelligence in understanding and influencing consumer behavior. In Musiolik, T., Rodriguez, R., & Kannan, H. (Eds.), *AI impacts in digital consumer behavior* (pp. 56–81). IGI Global., DOI: 10.4018/979-8-3693-1918-5.ch003

Tariq, M. U. (2024). Fintech startups and cryptocurrency in business: Revolutionizing entrepreneurship. In Kankaew, K., Nakpathom, P., Chnitphattana, A., Pitchayadejanant, K., & Kunnapapdeelert, S. (Eds.), *Applying business intelligence and innovation to entrepreneurship* (pp. 106–124). IGI Global., DOI: 10.4018/979-8-3693-1846-1.ch006

Tariq, M. U. (2024). Multidisciplinary service learning in higher education: Concepts, implementation, and impact. In S. Watson (Ed.), *Applications of service learning in higher education* (pp. 1-19). IGI Global. https://doi.org/DOI: 10.4018/979-8-3693-2133-1.ch001

Tariq, M. U. (2024). Enhancing cybersecurity protocols in modern healthcare systems: Strategies and best practices. In Garcia, M., & de Almeida, R. (Eds.), *Transformative approaches to patient literacy and healthcare innovation* (pp. 223–241). IGI Global., DOI: 10.4018/979-8-3693-3661-8.ch011

Tariq, M. U. (2024). Advanced wearable medical devices and their role in transformative remote health monitoring. In Garcia, M., & de Almeida, R. (Eds.), *Transformative approaches to patient literacy and healthcare innovation* (pp. 308–326). IGI Global., DOI: 10.4018/979-8-3693-3661-8.ch015

Tariq, M. U. (2024). Leveraging artificial intelligence for a sustainable and climate-neutral economy in Asia. In Ordóñez de Pablos, P., Almunawar, M., & Anshari, M. (Eds.), *Strengthening sustainable digitalization of Asian economy and society* (pp. 1–21). IGI Global., DOI: 10.4018/979-8-3693-1942-0.ch001

Tariq, M. U. (2024). Metaverse in business and commerce. In Kumar, J., Arora, M., & Erkol Bayram, G. (Eds.), *Exploring the use of metaverse in business and education* (pp. 47–72). IGI Global., DOI: 10.4018/979-8-3693-5868-9.ch004

Van Est, R., Van den Hoven, J., & Lokhorst, G.-J. (2017). Social and ethical implications of creating artificial moral agents for healthcare. *Science and Engineering Ethics*, 23(2), 431–448. PMID: 27380187

Warschauer, M. (2003). *Technology and social inclusion: Rethinking the digital divide*. MIT Press. DOI: 10.7551/mitpress/6699.001.0001

KEY TERMS AND DEFINITIONS

Algorithmic Bias: The tendency of automated systems, such as algorithms used in virtual communities.

Anonymity: The state of anonymity online allows freedom of expression without fear of reprisal.

Content Moderation: The Process of Overseeing and Managing User-generated Content in Virtual Communities.

Cyberbullying: The use of digital platforms to harass, threaten, and humiliate individuals is a significant ethical issue in virtual communities.

Digital Divide: The gap between individuals or communities with varying levels of access to digital technologies.

Privacy: The right of individuals in virtual communities to control their personal information and protect it from unauthorised access or misuse.

Virtual Communities: Online platforms where individuals interact, share information, and build relationships.

Chapter 15
Exploring Tomorrow:
Evolution of Virtual Communities and Social Media

Sreethi Rebeka R.
Christ University, India

Rejoice Thomas
https://orcid.org/0000-0002-8701-6720
Christ University, India

ABSTRACT

This chapter explores the future of virtual communities and social media platforms, probing into emerging trends, technological innovations, and societal shifts. It examines the evolution of AR and VR experiences, the role of AI in personalization and content curation, and the emergence of decentralized and blockchain-based social networks. It envisions a future where virtual communities foster inclusivity, trust, and empowerment by addressing cross-cultural communication, language barriers, and global collaboration. By navigating ethical considerations and embracing diversity, these digital landscapes offer transformative connectivity, innovation, and cultural exchange opportunities.

INTRODUCTION

The landscape of virtual communities and social media is constantly evolving, driven by technological innovations and changing societal norms. Today, these platforms play a central role in connecting, communicating, and collaborating online. They have transcended mere tools for social interaction to become integral components of our daily lives, influencing everything from personal relationships to

DOI: 10.4018/979-8-3693-3868-1.ch015

professional networking, education, and political activism (Joshi et al., 2023). Virtual communities, defined as groups of individuals interacting primarily through digital means, have proliferated across various platforms, offering a sense of belonging and shared purpose to millions worldwide. Social media platforms like Facebook, X, and Instagram, as well as emerging ones such as TikTok and Clubhouse, have revolutionized not only how we share information but also how we perceive and construct our identities. These platforms provide the infrastructure for virtual communities to thrive, fostering connections as strong and impactful as those formed in physical spaces (Li et al., 2020). As we look towards the future, the trajectory of virtual communities promises to be transformative, reshaping how individuals interact and engage in digital spaces. Several key factors are driving this transformation. Emerging technologies such as artificial intelligence (AI), virtual reality (VR), augmented reality (AR), and blockchain are set to redefine the boundaries of virtual interaction. These technologies will enhance the immersive experience, create more secure and transparent systems for trust-building, and enable new forms of digital economies and governance (Wu & Mariano, 2023).

Changes in societal attitudes towards digital interaction, privacy, and citizenship influence how virtual communities are structured and managed. As digital natives grow up and become the majority, their expectations for digital interactions will push platforms to innovate and adapt continuously. The global economy and environmental concerns are also crucial in shaping virtual communities. Remote work, driven by economic needs and environmental sustainability goals, is increasing reliance on virtual communities for professional collaboration and support. As virtual communities become more diverse, they are also becoming more inclusive, reflecting a broader range of cultural expressions and practices. This cultural integration is vital for fostering global connectivity and understanding in an increasingly interconnected world (Lin et al., 2024).

Governments and regulatory bodies are beginning to recognize the significant impact of virtual communities. They are enacting laws and guidelines to ensure these digital spaces are safe, equitable, and respectful of user rights. This chapter will explore these factors in detail, examining the emerging trends and technologies shaping the future of virtual communities and social media platforms. By envisioning future scenarios, we aim to understand how these digital landscapes will evolve and adapt, fostering new forms of connectivity, trust, and empowerment. This exploration will provide valuable insights into the opportunities and challenges, helping stakeholders proactively navigate and shape virtual communities' future. The evolution of virtual communities and social media is not just a technological journey but a human one, reflecting our deepest desires for connection, collaboration, and community in an ever-changing world.

BACKGROUND

Virtual communities and social media platforms have become integral to modern society, reshaping how people communicate, collaborate, and interact online. Originating from early internet forums and chat rooms, virtual communities have evolved into sophisticated digital ecosystems facilitating connections between individuals across geographical boundaries. The rise of social media platforms such as Facebook, Twitter, Instagram, and TikTok has accelerated the growth of virtual communities, offering users many ways to share content, engage with others, and form online relationships. These platforms have become hubs for social interaction, information sharing, entertainment, and commerce, attracting billions of users worldwide.

Technological advancements, including the proliferation of smartphones, high-speed internet access, and AI and blockchain technologies, have further transformed virtual communities, enabling new connectivity, personalization, and decentralization. Augmented reality (AR) and virtual reality (VR) experiences enhance the immersive nature of online interactions, while AI-powered algorithms shape content discovery and recommendation. Amidst these developments, challenges such as privacy concerns, misinformation, algorithmic bias, and online harassment have emerged, raising questions about virtual communities' ethical and societal implications. Additionally, cultural and language barriers can hinder effective communication and collaboration in these digital spaces, highlighting the need for inclusive design and cross-cultural understanding.

Despite these challenges, virtual communities hold immense potential for fostering global collaboration, cultural exchange, and social change. By addressing these challenges and leveraging the opportunities afforded by emerging technologies, virtual communities can continue to evolve as vibrant, inclusive, and empowering spaces for individuals and communities worldwide.

This study examines the evolution and impact of virtual communities and social media platforms in the digital age. It seeks to explore the dynamics of online interactions, the role of emerging technologies, and the societal implications of virtual communities on a global scale.

This study aims to analyze various aspects of virtual communities and social media platforms, exploring their evolution from early internet forums to modern social media networks. It will examine how technological advancements such as AR, VR, AI, and blockchain have influenced the development and dynamics of these communities. The research will address virtual communities' challenges and opportunities regarding privacy, security, and ethical considerations. Additionally, it will investigate the role of virtual communities in fostering cross-cultural communication, collaboration, and social change. Furthermore, the study will consider the implications of influencer culture, content moderation, and community governance on the functioning and sustainability of virtual communities.

This study aims to investigate the evolution and trends of virtual communities and social media platforms, exploring how they have transformed over time. It seeks to delve into the impact of emerging technologies, such as AR, VR, AI, and blockchain, on the dynamics of these communities. The study will examine the challenges and opportunities that virtual communities face in the digital age, particularly regarding privacy, security, and ethical considerations. Additionally, it will analyze the role of virtual communities in promoting cross-cultural communication and collaboration. Furthermore, the research will assess the implications of influencer culture, content moderation, and community governance on the functioning and sustainability of virtual communities.

This study's conceptual framework is built upon several vital concepts pivotal to understanding the dynamics and significance of virtual communities in today's digital landscape. Virtual Communities are online platforms or spaces where individuals converge to interact, share information, and establish social connections. They serve as digital hubs fostering communication and collaboration across geographical boundaries.

Social Media Platforms enable users to create, share, and engage with content within a social framework. Social media platforms play a crucial role in facilitating the formation and sustenance of virtual communities by providing tools for communication, content dissemination, and community building. Emerging Technologies like Augmented Reality (AR), Virtual Reality (VR), Artificial Intelligence (AI), and blockchain are revolutionizing the landscape of virtual communities. These innovations offer new avenues for immersive experiences, personalized interactions, and secure transactions within online social spaces.

Cross-cultural communication is an arena for communication and interaction among individuals from diverse cultural backgrounds. Cross-cultural communication within these digital realms highlights the complexities of navigating cultural differences and fostering understanding in a globalized world. Influencer Culture refers to individuals who wield significant influence on social media platforms due to their large following and content creation. Influencers play a crucial role in shaping virtual communities' trends, opinions, and behaviours, often as focal points of attention and engagement.

Community Governance, such as virtual communities, establish rules, norms, and mechanisms to govern member behaviour and interactions. Community governance structures regulate content moderation, dispute resolution, and community management, shaping the culture and dynamics of virtual social spaces. By elucidating these key concepts, our study provides a comprehensive framework for analyzing the complexities and implications of virtual communities in contemporary society.

Through an interdisciplinary lens, we aim to explore the interactions, trends, and transformative potentials inherent in these digital ecosystems, offering insights into their role in shaping social relations, cultural dynamics, and technological innovation.

This study will adopt a multidisciplinary approach, integrating theories from sociology, communication studies, and technology to offer a robust understanding of virtual communities in contemporary society. Here is a breakdown of the theoretical frameworks that will guide our investigation. The Social Capital Theory lens will allow us to explore how virtual communities serve as platforms for developing and exchanging social capital among members. We will explore how connections forged within these digital realms contribute to trust, reciprocity, and individual cooperation.

From the perspective of media ecology theory, we will examine the intricate interplay between digital technologies and the structure of virtual communities. Our analysis will focus on how these technologies shape communication patterns, information flows, and the overall ecology of virtual social spaces. Diffusion of Innovations Theory will provide insights into the processes through which emerging technologies are adopted and diffused within virtual communities. We will investigate factors influencing the spread of innovations, such as communication dynamics, social networks, and the perceived benefits of new technologies.

We will explore the sociocultural and historical contexts that shape online interactions and community dynamics by applying the Cultural-Historical Activity Theory framework. Our inquiry will examine how cultural norms, historical legacies, and socio-political factors influence virtual communities' formation, evolution, and practices. By integrating these theoretical perspectives, our study aims to offer a comprehensive understanding of virtual communities, shedding light on their functions, dynamics, and significance in contemporary society. By unravelling the complexities of these digital social spaces, we seek to contribute to both theoretical advancements and practical insights for individuals, communities, and policymakers navigating the ever-evolving landscape of online interactions.

THE RISE OF AUGMENTED REALITY (AR) AND VIRTUAL REALITY (VR) EXPERIENCES

As we move further into the digital age, augmented reality (AR) and virtual reality (VR) are poised to significantly reshape the landscape of virtual communities and social media. These immersive technologies promise to enhance how we interact, providing new dimensions of engagement and connection. Augmented reality (AR) overlays digital information in the real world, creating a blended experience that enhances our perception of reality. This technology can potentially revolutionize social interactions in several ways: AR can make digital communication more interactive and engaging. For instance, AR filters and effects in apps like Snapchat and Instagram allow users to modify their appearances or environments in real-time, adding a layer of creativity to personal interactions (Han & Bailenson, 2024; Miller et al., 2019).

AR enables users to share contextual information seamlessly. For example, during a virtual meeting, participants can overlay charts, documents, and other visual aids into their physical space, making discussions more dynamic and informative. AR can facilitate location-based social interactions. Platforms like Pokémon have demonstrated how AR can encourage users to explore their surroundings and interact with others in shared physical and digital spaces. AR can enhance educational and collaborative experiences by providing interactive, hands-on learning opportunities. It is particularly valuable in professional and academic settings, where complex concepts can be visualized and manipulated in real-time (Ta, 2024; Wen, 2020).

Virtual reality (VR) offers fully immersive digital environments, creating new social interaction and community-building realms. The impact of VR on virtual communities includes. VR platforms like VRChat and AltspaceVR create immersive social spaces where users can meet, interact, and form communities in ways that feel physically present. These environments can mimic real-world settings or create fantastical worlds limited only by imagination.VR has the unique ability to foster empathy and a sense of presence. By experiencing situations from another's perspective, users can develop a deeper understanding and connection with others. It can be particularly impactful in social causes, therapeutic settings, and conflict resolution (Hadjipanayi et al., 2024).

VR enables hosting virtual events, such as concerts, conferences, and social gatherings, providing a sense of togetherness despite physical distances. These events can offer rich, interactive experiences beyond what traditional online platforms can provide.VR allows for highly customizable environments, enabling communities to create spaces that reflect their values and interests. It can lead to more inclusive and accessible virtual communities where everyone can find a place that feels like home. As AR and VR technologies become more prevalent, addressing the ethical considerations associated with their use in virtual communities is crucial. Immersive technologies often require significant personal data to function effectively. Ensuring the privacy and security of this data is paramount, as breaches could lead to severe consequences for users' personal and professional lives. The immersive nature of AR and VR can lead to digital addiction and impact mental health. Developing guidelines and strategies to promote healthy usage and supporting those who may struggle with excessive use is essential. Ensuring that AR and VR experiences are accessible to people with disabilities is necessary. It includes designing interfaces everyone uses and providing alternative ways to experience content for those who cannot use traditional VR or AR devices (Carlson, 2023).

Immersive environments can be prone to harassment and inappropriate behaviour. Establishing robust content moderation and safety protocols is critical to creating respectful and welcoming virtual spaces. Developers and designers must adhere to ethical practices when creating AR and VR experiences. It includes considering the long-term impacts of their designs on users and society and striving to develop technologies that enhance human well-being. The rise of AR and VR is set to transform the future of virtual communities and social media, offering exciting new possibilities for interaction and engagement. However, it is essential to navigate these advancements with careful consideration of their ethical implications to ensure they contribute positively to our digital lives.

AI-POWERED PERSONALIZATION AND CONTENT CURATION

Artificial Intelligence (AI) is increasingly shaping how we interact with social media and virtual communities. By leveraging sophisticated algorithms, AI can enhance user experiences through personalized content curation, improved engagement, and the creation of tailored digital environments. However, these advancements also bring challenges, particularly concerning privacy and the authenticity of AI-generated content. AI's role in social media is multifaceted, encompassing several key areas algorithms analyze user behaviour to curate personalized content feeds. By understanding preferences and predicting interests, AI ensures that users are presented with the most relevant and engaging content, keeping them hooked to the platform. AI powers recommendation systems that suggest friends, groups, events, and products based on users' past interactions and interests. These systems enhance user experience by connecting individuals with content and communities they will likely find meaningful.

AI-driven chatbots and virtual assistants facilitate real-time interaction and support within social media platforms. These tools can respond instantly to user queries, recommend actions, and even moderate discussions to maintain a positive environment, helping identify and mitigate security threats such as cyberbullying, harassment, and misinformation. By analyzing patterns and flagging harmful content, AI creates safer digital spaces for users. The personalization algorithms that drive AI-powered content curation present a double-edged sword. While they significantly enhance user experience by tailoring content to individual preferences, they also raise critical concerns about privacy and data security.

Personalization requires extensive data collection, including user behaviour, preferences, and interactions. It raises concerns about how this data is collected, stored, and used. Ensuring transparency and user consent is crucial to maintaining trust. The extensive data collection necessary for personalization can lead to privacy invasions if not appropriately managed. Users may be uncomfortable with the extent of data being gathered about their online activities, leading to calls for stricter data protection regulations. Personalization algorithms can reinforce existing biases by continually presenting content that aligns with users' past behaviour, creating echo chambers. Addressing this bias requires the development of algorithms that promote diverse and balanced content exposure. Empowering users with control over their personalization settings can help balance customization and privacy. Providing options to manage data sharing, content preferences, and advertisement settings allows users to tailor their experiences without compromising privacy (Csisjournalism, 2022).

AI-generated content is poised to become a significant component of virtual communities, offering opportunities and challenges. AI can generate a wide range of content, from text and images to videos and interactive experiences. It can help meet the growing demand for content and enable creators to produce high-quality materials more efficiently. AI-generated content can be tailored to individual users, enhancing engagement and making interactions feel more personal. For instance, AI can create customized messages, recommendations, and even virtual avatars that reflect users' preferences. AI tools can assist in creative processes, offering suggestions, automating repetitive tasks, and enabling new forms of artistic expression. This collaboration can expand the creative potential of individuals and communities.

The rise of AI-generated content raises questions about authenticity and trust. Users may find distinguishing between human-created and AI-generated content challenging, leading to potential issues with misinformation and manipulation. Ensuring that AI-generated content is used ethically involves addressing issues like intellectual property rights, content authenticity, and the potential for misuse. Establishing guidelines and regulatory frameworks will be essential in navigating these challenges. AI-powered personalization and content curation are transforming the landscape of social media and virtual communities, offering enhanced experiences and new possibilities for interaction. However, balancing these advancements with ethical considerations, privacy concerns, and the need for authenticity will be crucial in shaping a positive and sustainable digital future.

DECENTRALIZED AND BLOCKCHAIN-BASED SOCIAL NETWORKS

The advent of blockchain technology is opening new frontiers in developing decentralized social networks, fundamentally altering how trust, control, and community dynamics are managed in the digital realm. These platforms promise to empower users, enhance security, and provide a more transparent and equitable social media experience. Blockchain technology offers a transparent and immutable ledger that can revolutionize trust dynamics in social media. Blockchain's transparent nature ensures that all transactions and interactions are recorded on a public ledger. This transparency can build trust among users, as activities and data cannot be easily manipulated or hidden (Mlika et al., 2024).

Blockchain's immutability ensures that once data is recorded, it cannot be altered or deleted without consensus. This feature guarantees the integrity of user-generated content and interactions, reducing the risk of fraud and misinformation (Hisseine et al., 2022). Blockchain can provide decentralized identity verification systems, enhancing privacy and security. Users can control their personal information and prove their identity without relying on centralized authorities, reducing the risk of data breaches. Smart contracts, self-executing contracts with terms directly written into code, can be used to automate governance and moderation processes in social networks. These contracts can enforce community rules and handle disputes transparently and fairly. Decentralized social networks, built on blockchain technology, shift power from centralized entities to individual users, fostering greater autonomy and control. In decentralized networks, users retain ownership of their data. They can decide how their information is used, shared, and monetized, reversing the traditional model where platform owners control user data (Mlika et al., 2024).

Decentralized platforms are less susceptible to censorship, as no central authority can unilaterally remove content or ban users. It empowers individuals to express themselves freely, although it also necessitates robust community governance to manage harmful content. Blockchain-based social networks often incorporate cryptocurrency tokens to incentivize participation and contribution. Users can earn tokens for creating content, engaging with posts, contributing to platform governance, and fostering an active and engaged community. Users can participate in the management of decentralized networks through token-based voting systems. This democratic approach ensures platform decisions reflect the community's collective will rather than a few stakeholders' interests.

While blockchain-powered social networks offer numerous advantages, they also present unique challenges and opportunities. Blockchain networks often need help with scalability issues, as they need help to handle many transactions quickly and efficiently. Developing scalable solutions is crucial for the widespread adoption of decentralized social networks. The complexity of blockchain technology can be a barrier for mainstream users. Improving user interfaces and educating users about blockchain concepts are essential to making these platforms more accessible. While blockchain provides robust security features, it is not immune to attacks. Ensuring the security of blockchain networks against threats like hacking and fraud is critical for maintaining user trust.

The decentralized nature of blockchain-based networks can pose challenges for regulatory compliance. Navigating legal frameworks and ensuring adherence to regulations across different jurisdictions is necessary to avoid potential legal issues. Blockchain, particularly proof-of-work-based systems, can be resource-intensive and have a significant environmental footprint. Exploring more sustainable alternatives, like proof-of-stake, is essential for the long-term viability of these platforms. Decentralized governance models require active participation from users to be effective. Encouraging engagement and ensuring fair representation in decision-making processes can be challenging but is essential for a healthy community. Blockchain technology is set to transform social media by providing decentralized, transparent, and secure platforms. While there are challenges to overcome, user empowerment and community-building opportunities are immense, promising a future where digital interactions are more equitable and user-centric.

COMMUNITY GOVERNANCE AND DIGITAL CITIZENSHIP

As virtual communities and social media platforms continue to evolve, so too do the models for governance and the expectations of digital citizenship. This section explores how community norms and governance models are being redefined, the role of digital citizenship in these virtual spaces, and the potential regulatory frameworks that will shape the future of social media. The governance of virtual communities involves establishing rules, norms, and mechanisms to manage behaviour, ensure security, and foster a positive environment. As these communities grow more complex, innovative governance models are emerging. Leveraging blockchain and other decentralized technologies, some platforms are adopting decentralized governance models. It involves distributing decision-making power among users, often through mechanisms like token-based voting. Such models can enhance transparency and accountability, giving users a direct say in managing communities. AI and machine learning algorithms are significant in moderating content and enforcing community standards. These technologies can quickly identify and address harmful behaviour, although they must be carefully designed to avoid biases and ensure fairness.

Encouraging active participation from community members in governance processes can lead to more democratic and inclusive decision-making. Tools like community forums, surveys, and town hall meetings can facilitate this engagement, allowing users to contribute to developing and enforcing norms and policies. Many platforms adopt hybrid governance models combining centralized, decentralized, and participatory governance elements. This approach can balance efficiency with user empowerment, ensuring robust management while incorporating diverse perspectives. Digital citizenship encompasses the responsible and ethical behaviour of individuals in online spaces. In the context of virtual communities, it involves several key aspects.

Ensuring users have the skills and knowledge to navigate digital spaces safely and effectively. It includes understanding privacy settings, recognizing misinformation, and engaging respectfully with others. Digital citizens should adhere to ethical standards, including respect for others, honesty, and integrity. Promoting positive behaviour and discouraging harmful actions like cyberbullying, harassment, and spreading false information are vital for healthy communities. Digital citizenship also involves active participation in community governance and public discourse. It can include voting in community decisions, contributing to discussions, and helping to shape the platform's future (Clements, 2023).

Protecting one's privacy and respecting the privacy of others are fundamental aspects of digital citizenship. Users should be aware of data protection practices and take steps to secure their personal information. Embracing and promoting diversity and inclusion within virtual communities is essential. It involves recognizing and valuing different perspectives, experiences, and identities and working to ensure that all members feel welcome and respected. As social media continues to influence society, regulatory frameworks are evolving to address the challenges and opportunities these platforms present (Bromell, 2022).

Regulations like the General Data Protection Regulation (GDPR) in Europe set stringent data protection and user privacy standards. Future frameworks will likely build on these principles, ensuring that users have control over their data and that platforms handle information responsibly. Governments and regulatory bodies increasingly focus on content moderation, requiring platforms to remove harmful content and ensure safe environments. Balancing freedom of expression with the need to prevent harm is a critical challenge in developing these policies. Regulations may mandate greater transparency from social media companies regarding their algorithms, data practices, and decision-making processes. It can help build trust and ensure platforms are accountable to their users and the public (Lepri et al., 2017; Quinn, 2021).

Ensuring a competitive landscape in the social media industry is another regulatory focus. Preventing monopolistic practices and promoting competition can foster innovation and give users more choices. The internet's borderless nature means that international cooperation is essential for effective regulation. Harmonizing regulations across jurisdictions and collaborating on enforcement can help address global challenges like misinformation and cybercrime. Beyond legal requirements, developing ethical standards and best practices can guide social media companies in creating responsible and user-centric platforms. Industry associations and independent watchdogs can play a role in establishing and promoting these standards. Community governance and digital citizenship are critical components of the future of virtual communities and social media. By redefining governance models, fostering responsible digital behaviour, and developing robust regulatory frameworks, we can create more equitable, secure, and empowering digital environments for all users.

THE EVOLUTION OF INFLUENCER CULTURE

Influencer culture has become a defining aspect of social media and virtual communities, significantly impacting marketing strategies and consumer behaviour. As this culture evolves, it brings new opportunities and challenges in influencer marketing, ethics, and the dynamics between micro and macro influencers. Influencer marketing is set to undergo significant transformations driven by technological advancements and changing consumer expectations. Advances in AR and VR will enable influencers to create more personalized and immersive experiences for their followers. Brands can collaborate with influencers to offer virtual try-ons, interactive tutorials, and virtual reality experiences that deepen consumer engagement (Du et al., 2022).

AI and big data analytics will be crucial in shaping influencer marketing strategies. By analyzing vast amounts of data, brands can identify the most effective influencers for their campaigns, optimize content delivery, and measure ROI more accurately. Influencers will increasingly adopt direct-to-consumer models, leveraging their platforms to launch their product lines and brands. This trend will blur the lines between influencer and entrepreneur, offering new avenues for revenue generation. Social media platforms are integrating e-commerce functionalities, allowing influencers to sell products directly through their posts and live streams. This seamless integration will streamline the purchase process and enhance the effectiveness of influencer marketing (Beichert et al., 2024).

Brands will focus more on niche markets and micro-communities, leveraging influencers with more minor, highly engaged followers. This approach allows for more targeted and authentic brand engagement. As the influencer industry matures, issues of ethics and authenticity become increasingly important. Regulatory bodies are enforcing stricter guidelines on transparency and disclosure in influencer marketing. Influencers must disclose sponsored content to maintain trust and comply with advertising standards. Authenticity remains a critical factor in influencer success. Followers value genuine recommendations and personal stories over overtly commercial content. Influencers who maintain authenticity are likelier to build lasting trust and loyalty (Lee & Eastin, 2021).

Influencers are increasingly expected to use their platforms responsibly, promoting positive values and contributing to social causes. Ethical behaviour, including honesty, inclusivity, and environmental consciousness, is becoming a benchmark for influencer credibility. With their broad reach, influencers are responsible for combating misinformation and promoting accurate information. It involves fact-checking content, collaborating with credible sources, and being transparent about their expertise and limitations (Zniva et al., 2023). Influencers who actively engage with their communities, respond to comments, and foster meaningful interactions are likelier to maintain their influence. Building a sense of community around shared values and interests enhances loyalty and trust.

MICRO VS MACRO INFLUENCERS: TRENDS AND IMPLICATIONS

The distinction between micro and macro influencers shapes the dynamics of influencer marketing, each offering unique advantages and challenges. Micro-influencers, typically with 1,000 to 100,000 followers, often have higher engagement rates than macro influencers—their more minor, more dedicated following results in more personal and interactive relationships. Micro-influencers usually cater to specific niches, allowing brands to reach targeted audiences with tailored messages. It can lead to more effective and meaningful brand interactions. Collaborating with micro-influencers is generally more cost-effective than partnering with macro-influencers. Brands can work with multiple micro-influencers to diversify their reach and impact.

Micro-influencers are perceived as more relatable and authentic, often seen as regular individuals sharing their passions. This authenticity can enhance brand credibility. Macro influencers, with over 100,000 followers, offer brands the advantage of broad reach and visibility. They are ideal for large-scale campaigns aiming to increase brand awareness. Macro influencers are often more experienced in creating high-quality content and managing brand partnerships. This professionalism can lead to more polished and impactful campaigns. Macro influencers hold significant sway in their respective fields and can influence trends and consumer behaviour on a large scale. Their endorsements can carry substantial weight. Collaborating with macro influencers can be costly and competitive, as they often have relationships with multiple brands. Additionally, their large following can sometimes lead to lower engagement rates due to a more generalized audience (Chen et al., 2024).

The evolution of influencer culture is reshaping how brands engage with consumers, emphasizing the importance of authenticity, ethical behaviour, and strategic targeting. As technology advances and consumer expectations evolve, influencers will play a pivotal role in virtual communities, driving trends and fostering connections between brands and audiences. Balancing the strengths of micro and macro influencers, maintaining ethical standards, and leveraging new technologies will be essential to successful influencer marketing in the future.

GLOBALIZATION AND CULTURAL EXCHANGE IN VIRTUAL SPACES

The globalization of virtual communities and social media platforms has created unprecedented opportunities for cross-cultural communication and collaboration. Virtual communities unite individuals from diverse cultural backgrounds, fostering cross-cultural communication and understanding. Social media platforms and virtual communities often reflect a mosaic of cultural identities. This diversity enriches discussions, broadens perspectives, and promotes a deeper understanding of global issues (Yuna et al., 2022). The international nature of virtual spaces allows for sharing of stories and experiences from different parts of the world. This exchange of narratives can challenge stereotypes, highlight commonalities, and celebrate cultural uniqueness. Virtual communities provide a platform for intercultural dialogue, where individuals can discuss cultural practices, values, and traditions. These conversations can build bridges between cultural groups and promote mutual respect (Qie & Kang, 2023).

Effective cross-cultural communication requires cultural sensitivity and awareness. Users must navigate cultural differences in communication styles, social norms, and values to interact respectfully and meaningfully. Despite the potential for cultural exchange, language and cultural barriers can hinder effective communication in virtual communities. The variety of languages spoken by users can create communication challenges. Language barriers can lead to misunderstandings, misinterpretations, and exclusion of non-native speakers from discussions. Advances in AI-powered translation tools are helping to bridge language gaps. Real-time translation features in social media platforms enable users to communicate across language barriers, though these tools are only sometimes perfect and can sometimes miss nuances (Steigerwald et al., 2022).

Language is deeply intertwined with cultural context. Idioms, humour, and cultural references may translate poorly, leading to potential miscommunications. Providing cultural context and explanations can help mitigate these issues. Platforms can promote inclusivity by supporting multiple languages and providing resources for learning about different cultures. User interfaces should be designed to accommodate diverse linguistic and cultural backgrounds, making virtual spaces accessible to a broader audience. Moderation policies should be culturally informed to address issues like hate speech, discrimination, and cultural insensitivity. Training moderators in cultural competence can enhance their ability to manage diverse virtual communities effectively. Virtual communities can potentially drive global collaboration, enabling individuals and organizations to collaborate across geographical boundaries. Virtual communities facilitate the exchange of knowledge and expertise on a worldwide scale. Collaborative platforms allow professionals, researchers, and enthusiasts to share insights, resources, and best practices across borders. Social media has been instrumental in organizing global movements and campaigns. Climate change, human rights, and social justice have garnered international support through virtual communities, amplifying their impact (Liu et al., 2012).

Virtual spaces enable collaborative projects that involve participants from different countries. Online tools and platforms support teamwork, allowing individuals to co-create content, conduct research, and develop innovations regardless of their physical location. Virtual communities can host cultural exchange programs where participants share their cultural heritage, traditions, and perspectives. These programs promote understanding and appreciation of cultural diversity (Dooly & Vinagre, 2021). Online educational platforms and virtual classrooms can bring together students and educators worldwide. These initiatives foster global learning experiences and encourage the exchange of academic resources and methodologies. Virtual communities allow global entrepreneurs to connect, share ideas, and collaborate on business ventures. These networks can lead to international partnerships and innovative business solutions that address global markets (Messinger et al., 2021). Globalization and cultural exchange in virtual spaces transform how individuals and communities interact, collaborate, and learn from one another. By facilitating cross-cultural communication, addressing language and cultural barriers, and acting as catalysts for global collaboration, virtual communities are paving the way for a more interconnected and culturally aware world. These developments promise greater understanding, innovation, and cooperation across borders, enriching individual experiences and collective progress.

SOLUTIONS AND RECOMMENDATIONS

Develop and integrate more advanced translation technologies and cultural context features into social media platforms to overcome language and cultural barriers. These tools should provide accurate translations while preserving nuances and cultural sensitivities. To promote respectful and inclusive interactions, offer cultural sensitivity training to platform moderators, influencers, and users. This training should focus on understanding diverse cultural norms, values, and communication styles to foster empathy and reduce misunderstandings. Implement inclusive design practices in developing social media platforms to accommodate diverse linguistic and cultural backgrounds. It includes supporting multiple languages, providing accessibility features, and incorporating cultural representation in design elements.

Establish clear community moderation guidelines that reflect cultural diversity and sensitivity. Encourage community members to report cultural insensitivity or discrimination and enforce consequences for violations to maintain a respectful and safe environment. Facilitate intercultural dialogue and exchange within virtual communities by organizing cultural events, discussion forums, and educational initiatives. Encourage users to share their cultural experiences, traditions, and perspectives to foster understanding and appreciation. Collaborate with cultural organizations, NGOs, and academic institutions to promote cross-cultural awareness and knowledge on social media platforms. It can involve hosting joint campaigns, sharing educational resources, and supporting cultural events and initiatives.

Empower cultural influences from diverse backgrounds to amplify their voices and perspectives on social media platforms. Provide support and resources to help them reach broader audiences and promote cross-cultural understanding through their content. Educate users about the importance of cultural sensitivity and inclusivity in virtual communities. Provide resources, guidelines, and best practices for respectful cross-cultural communication and encourage active participation in promoting cultural diversity and understanding. By implementing these solutions and recommendations, social media platforms can create more inclusive, respectful, and culturally diverse virtual spaces where users from all backgrounds feel valued, respected, and empowered to engage in meaningful cross-cultural interactions.

FUTURE RESEARCH DIRECTIONS

Investigate the impact of emerging technologies such as augmented reality (AR), virtual reality (VR), and artificial intelligence (AI) on the dynamics of virtual communities. Explore how these technologies shape user interactions, community structures, and engagement levels. Examine the ethical implications of AI-powered personalization and content curation in virtual communities. Investigate algorithmic bias, privacy concerns, and manipulating user behaviour, and propose frameworks for responsible AI deployment. Research decentralized governance models in blockchain-based social networks and their effectiveness in promoting transparency, fairness, and user empowerment. Explore the challenges and opportunities of decentralized decision-making processes in virtual communities.

Develop and evaluate cross-cultural communication strategies and interventions for virtual communities. Investigate how cultural differences impact communication dynamics online and identify practical approaches for promoting intercultural understanding and collaboration. Assess the long-term effects of influencer culture on consumer behaviour, brand engagement, and social norms. Explore how influencer marketing strategies evolve and their implications for advertising ethics and consumer trust. Explore the design and implementation of global collaboration platforms for cross-border initiatives, educational projects, and social movements. Investigate the factors contributing to successful global collaboration and the challenges of online coordinating diverse teams.

Examine the cultural adaptation of social media platforms to diverse cultural contexts and user preferences. Investigate how platforms can customize their features, content, and user experience to better accommodate different cultural norms and values. Study the role of virtual communities in building resilience and facilitating crisis response during global events such as pandemics, natural disasters, and social upheavals. Explore how online networks mobilize resources, disseminate information, and provide support during crises. Develop and evaluate digital citizenship education programs for promoting responsible online behaviour, critical thinking skills, and media literacy. Investigate effective strategies for teaching digital citizenship in schools, workplaces, and community settings.

Assess the environmental impact of virtual communities and social media platforms, particularly regarding energy consumption, carbon emissions, and electronic waste. Explore sustainable design practices and technologies to reduce the environmental footprint of digital platforms. By focusing on these future research directions, scholars can deepen our understanding of virtual communities, address emerging challenges, and harness the potential of digital technologies for fostering global connectivity, cultural exchange, and social progress.

DISCUSSION

Virtual communities have undergone a remarkable evolution since their inception. From the early days of Internet forums and bulletin boards, where individuals with common interests gathered to share information and discuss topics, they have transformed into sophisticated social media platforms connecting billions of users worldwide. The advent of emerging technologies such as augmented reality (AR), virtual reality (VR), artificial intelligence (AI), and blockchain has significantly influenced the dynamics of virtual communities. AR and VR technologies have introduced immersive experiences, allowing users to interact with digital content in novel ways. AI algorithms power content recommendation systems, personalizing user experiences and shaping online interactions. Blockchain technology revolutionizes community governance and trust mechanisms, enabling decentralized social networks and secure transactions.

Virtual communities have profound societal implications, both positive and negative. On the one hand, they facilitate global communication, collaboration, and cultural exchange, breaking down geographical barriers and fostering connections between people from diverse backgrounds. They provide platforms for social activism, enabling grassroots movements and amplifying marginalized voices. On the other hand, virtual communities raise concerns about privacy, security, and ethical conduct. Misformation, cyberbullying, and algorithmic bias pose challenges that require careful consideration and mitigation strategies. One of the key benefits of virtual communities is their ability to facilitate cross-cultural communication. They provide opportunities for individuals from different cultural backgrounds to engage in dialogue, share perspectives, and learn from one another. However, cultural and language barriers can sometimes hinder effective communication and collaboration. Strategies such as multilingual support, cultural sensitivity training, and inclusive design are essential for promoting cross-cultural understanding and inclusivity in virtual communities.

Influencer culture has emerged as a dominant force in virtual communities, with individuals gaining significant influence and authority through their online presence. Influencers shape consumer trends, promote products and services, and drive engagement on social media platforms. However, the rise of influencer culture also raises questions about authenticity, transparency, and the ethical responsibilities of influencers. Striking a balance between commercial interests and maintaining trust with their audience constantly challenges influencers. Effective governance is crucial for the sustainability and well-being of virtual communities. Community governance mechanisms define the rules, norms, and decision-making processes that govern behaviour and interactions within these communities. Decentralized governance models, enabled by blockchain technology, offer promising avenues for democratizing decision-making and increasing user autonomy. However, implementing effective governance structures requires careful consideration of scalability, accountability, and inclusivity factors.

Virtual communities and social media platforms have become integral to contemporary society, shaping how we communicate, collaborate, and interact online. While they offer immense opportunities for connectivity, cultural exchange, and social change, they also present challenges that require thoughtful solutions. By leveraging emerging technologies, fostering cross-cultural understanding, promoting ethical conduct, and implementing effective governance mechanisms, we can harness the full potential of virtual communities for the benefit of individuals and society as a whole.

CONCLUSION

The future of virtual communities and social media is poised for transformative change, driven by technological advancements and evolving societal norms. As we explore these digital landscapes, it becomes clear that several key trends will shape how we connect, communicate, and collaborate online. Integrating augmented reality (AR) and virtual reality (VR) will create more immersive and interactive social experiences, enhancing how we engage with digital content and each other. AI-powered personalization and content curation will revolutionize social media, offering tailored experiences while balancing customization with privacy concerns. The rise of decentralized and blockchain-based social networks promises to redefine trust and empower users through greater control over their data and interactions.

Community governance and digital citizenship will be critical in managing these evolving spaces, with new models of governance emerging to ensure fairness, inclusivity, and security. The ethical considerations of influencer culture and the dynamic between micro and macro influencers will continue to influence marketing strategies and brand engagement. Globalization and cultural exchange in virtual spaces foster cross-cultural communication and collaboration, breaking down language and cultural barriers. Virtual communities will be pivotal in facilitating global movements, collaborative projects, and educational initiatives, enriching our collective understanding and cooperation.

As we navigate this future, embracing these advancements' opportunities while addressing their challenges is essential. By fostering trust, ensuring ethical behaviour, and promoting inclusivity, we can build virtual communities that connect and empower us to create a more interconnected and equitable digital world.

REFERENCES

Beichert, M., Bayerl, A., Goldenberg, J., & Lanz, A. (2024). Revenue generation through influencer marketing. *Journal of Marketing*, 88(4), 40–63. Advance online publication. DOI: 10.1177/00222429231217471

Bromell, D. (2022). Challenges in regulating online content. In *Springer eBooks* (pp. 29–53). DOI: 10.1007/978-3-030-95550-2_2

Carlson, C. G. (2023). Virtual and augmented simulations in mental health. *Current Psychiatry Reports. Current Psychiatry Reports*, 25(9), 365–371. DOI: 10.1007/s11920-023-01438-4 PMID: 37624512

Chen, J., Zhang, Y., Cai, H., Liu, L., Liao, M., & Fang, J. (2024). A comprehensive overview of micro-influencer marketing: Decoding the current landscape, impacts, and trends. *Behavioral Sciences (Basel, Switzerland)*, 14(3), 243. DOI: 10.3390/bs14030243 PMID: 38540546

Csisjournalism. (2022). *Thinking Outside the Bubble: Addressing Polarization and Disinformation on Social Media*. CSIS Journalism Bootcamp. https://journalism.csis.org/thinking-outside-the-bubble-addressing-polarization-and-disinformation-on-social-media/

Dooly, M., & Vinagre, M. (2021). Research into practice: Virtual exchange in language teaching and learning. *Language Teaching*, 55(3), 392–406. DOI: 10.1017/S0261444821000069

Du, Z., Liu, J., & Wang, T. (2022). Augmented reality marketing: A systematic literature review and an agenda for future inquiry. *Frontiers in Psychology*, 13, 925963. Advance online publication. DOI: 10.3389/fpsyg.2022.925963 PMID: 35783783

Hadjipanayi, C., Christofi, M., Banakou, D., & Michael-Grigoriou, D. (2024). Cultivating empathy through narratives in virtual reality: A review. *Personal and Ubiquitous Computing*, 28(3-4), 507–519. Advance online publication. DOI: 10.1007/s00779-024-01812-w

Han, E., & Bailenson, J. N. (2024). *Social interaction in VR*. Oxford Research Encyclopedia of Communication., DOI: 10.1093/acrefore/9780190228613.013.1489

Hisseine, M. A., Chen, D., & Yang, X. (2022). The application of blockchain in social media: A systematic literature review. *Applied Sciences (Basel, Switzerland)*, 12(13), 6567. DOI: 10.3390/app12136567

Joshi, Y., Lim, W. M., Jagani, K., & Kumar, S. (2023). Social media influencer marketing: Foundations, trends, and ways forward. *Electronic Commerce Research.* Advance online publication. DOI: 10.1007/s10660-023-09719-z

Lee, J. A., & Eastin, M. S. (2021). Perceived authenticity of social media influencers: Scale development and validation. *Journal of Research in Interactive Marketing*, 15(4), 822–841. DOI: 10.1108/JRIM-12-2020-0253

Lepri, B., Oliver, N., Letouzé, E., Pentland, A., & Vinck, P. (2017). Fair, transparent, and accountable algorithmic decision-making processes. *Philosophy & Technology*, 31(4), 611–627. DOI: 10.1007/s13347-017-0279-x

Li, F., Larimo, J., & Leonidou, L. C. (2020). Social media marketing strategy: Definition, conceptualization, taxonomy, validation, and future agenda. *Journal of the Academy of Marketing Science*, 49(1), 51–70. DOI: 10.1007/s11747-020-00733-3

Lin, Z., Gukasyan, G., & Nasyrova, L. (2024). Virtual reality in cultural education: Cultural integration and academic performance of migrant students in the context of cultural capital. *Education and Information Technologies.* Advance online publication. DOI: 10.1007/s10639-024-12450-3

Liu, X., Wang, G. A., Johri, A., Zhou, M., & Fan, W. (2012). Harnessing global expertise: A comparative study of expertise profiling methods for online communities. *Information Systems Frontiers*, 16(4), 715–727. DOI: 10.1007/s10796-012-9385-6

Messinger, P. R., Smirnov, K., & Ge, X. (2021). Virtual communities. In *Springer eBooks* (pp. 1–17). DOI: 10.1007/978-3-319-98390-5_161-1

Miller, M. R., Jun, H., Herrera, F., Villa, J. Y., Welch, G., & Bailenson, J. N. (2019). Social interaction in augmented reality. *PLoS One*, 14(5), e0216290. DOI: 10.1371/journal.pone.0216290 PMID: 31086381

Mlika, F., Karoui, W., & Romdhane, L. B. (2024). Trustworthy decentralization based on blockchain tools for social network architectures. *Social Network Analysis and Mining*, 14(1), 95. Advance online publication. DOI: 10.1007/s13278-024-01252-7

Qie, N., & Kang, X. (2023). Capabilities influencing cross-cultural communication in digital contexts: Exploration with a Chinese sample. In *Lecture notes in computer science* (pp. 126–141). DOI: 10.1007/978-3-031-35939-2_10

Quinn, P. (2021). Research under the GDPR – a level playing field for public and private sector research? *Life Sciences, Society and Policy*, 17(1), 4. Advance online publication. DOI: 10.1186/s40504-021-00111-z PMID: 33648586

Steigerwald, E., Ramírez-Castañeda, V., Brandt, D. Y. C., Báldi, A., Shapiro, J. T., Bowker, L., & Tarvin, R. D. (2022). Overcoming language barriers in academia: Machine translation tools and a vision for a multilingual future. *BioScience/Bioscience, 72*(10), 988–998. DOI: 10.1093/biosci/biac062

Ta, T. (2024, May 28). *Breaking the Monotony: How AR VR could Revolutionize Virtual meetings*. Travancore Analytics. https://www.travancoreanalytics.com/ar-vr-in-virtual-meetings/

Wen, Y. (2020). Augmented reality enhanced cognitive engagement: Designing classroom-based collaborative learning activities for young language learners. *Educational Technology Research and Development*, 69(2), 843–860. DOI: 10.1007/s11423-020-09893-z

Wu, S., & Mariano, B. (2023). Emerging technologies and global health: A systematic review generating bibliometric evidence for innovation management. *BMJ Innovations*, 9(3), 165–176. DOI: 10.1136/bmjinnov-2022-001064

Yuna, D., Xiaokun, L., Jianing, L., & Lu, H. (2022). Cross-cultural communication on social media: Review from the cultural psychology and neuroscience perspective. *Frontiers in Psychology*, 13. Advance online publication. DOI: 10.3389/fpsyg.2022.858900 PMID: 35356358

Zniva, R., Weitzl, W. J., & Lindmoser, C. (2023). Be constantly different! How to manage influencer authenticity. *Electronic Commerce Research*, 23(3), 1485–1514. DOI: 10.1007/s10660-022-09653-6

ADDITIONAL READING

Cusick, J. A., George, E. A., Greenway, E., Watve, M., Graham, K., & Raby, C. L. (2024). Is it time to get over the X? Assessing social media conferences' global impact and future in animal behaviour. *Animal Behaviour*, pp. *213*, 33–50. DOI: 10.1016/j.anbehav.2024.04.001

Darwish, D. (2024). The Driving Forces Behind Web 3 Growth. In Darwish, D. (Ed.), *Decentralizing the Online Experience With Web3 Technologies* (pp. 29–56). IGI Global., DOI: 10.4018/979-8-3693-1532-3.ch002

Darwish, D. (2024). Chatbot Concepts and Basics. In Darwish, D. (Ed.), *Design and Development of Emerging Chatbot Technology* (pp. 1–25). IGI Global., DOI: 10.4018/979-8-3693-1830-0.ch001

Darwish, D. (Ed.). (2024). *Emerging Trends in Cloud Computing Analytics, Scalability, and Service Models*. IGI Global., DOI: 10.4018/979-8-3693-0900-1

Darwish, D. (Ed.). (2024). *Decentralizing the Online Experience With Web3 Technologies*. IGI Global., DOI: 10.4018/979-8-3693-1532-3

Darwish, D. (2024). Chatbots vs. AI Chatbots vs. Virtual Assistants. In Darwish, D. (Ed.), *Design and Development of Emerging Chatbot Technology* (pp. 26–50). IGI Global., DOI: 10.4018/979-8-3693-1830-0.ch002

Darwish, D. (2024). The Technology Impacts and AI Solutions for the Tourism Industry. In Kumar, S., Talukder, M., & Pego, A. (Eds.), *Utilizing Smart Technology and AI in Hybrid Tourism and Hospitality* (pp. 23–50). IGI Global., DOI: 10.4018/979-8-3693-1978-9.ch002

Gunnes, M., Løe, I., & Kalseth, J. (2024). Exploring the impact of information and communication technologies on loneliness and social isolation in community-dwelling older adults: A scoping review of reviews. *BMC Geriatrics*, 24(1), 215. Advance online publication. DOI: 10.1186/s12877-024-04837-1 PMID: 38431561

Li, X., Johnston, K. A., & Feng, J. (2024). Virtual community engagement: Engaging virtual communities for nation branding through sports. *Public Relations Review*, 50(3), 102440. DOI: 10.1016/j.pubrev.2024.102440

Rofik, N. (2024). Ungkapan Kesat dalam Penggunaan Implikatur di Media Sosial pada Musim Pilihan Raya. *Pertanika Journal of Social Science & Humanities*, 32(S1), 139–160. DOI: 10.47836/pjssh.32.S1.06

Schukow, C. P., Punjabi, L. S., & Abdul-Karim, F. W. (2023). #PathX: # PathTwitter's transformation and a discussion on different social media platforms used by pathologists in 2024. *Advances in Anatomic Pathology*. Advance online publication. DOI: 10.1097/PAP.0000000000000424 PMID: 38047394

Singha, R., & Singha, S. (2023). Economic sustainability, mindfulness, and diversity in the age of artificial intelligence and machine learning. In Raj, P., Soundarabai, P. B., & Augustine, P. (Eds.), *Machine Intelligence: Computer Vision and Natural Language Processing* (pp. 273–285). Taylor & Francis Group., DOI: 10.1201/9781003424550-15

Singha, R., & Singha, S. (2024). Enhancing Wellbeing: Exploring the Impact of Augmented Reality and Virtual Reality. In Hiran, K., Doshi, R., & Patel, M. (Eds.), *Applications of Virtual and Augmented Reality for Health and Wellbeing* (pp. 55–74). IGI Global., DOI: 10.4018/979-8-3693-1123-3.ch004

Singha, R., & Singha, S. (2024). Transitioning to Digital Merchandise: Integrating Metaverse Into Retail Offerings. In Rezaei, S., & Ansary, A. (Eds.), *Artificial Intelligence of Things (AIoT) for Productivity and Organizational Transition* (Vol. 1, pp. 26–51). IGI Global., DOI: 10.4018/979-8-3693-0993-3.ch002

Singha, R., Singha, S., Ruben, V. M., Natal, M. S., Longkumer, A., & Haokip, A. D. (2024). The Ethics of Collaborating With Social Media Influencers: Influencers and Psychological Wellbeing. In Bi, N., & Zhang, R. (Eds.), *Global Perspectives on Social Media Influencers and Strategic Business Communication* (pp. 326–342). IGI Global., DOI: 10.4018/979-8-3693-0912-4.ch016

Singha, S. (2024). Unveiling Gender Dynamics in Digital Capitalism: Navigating the Path to Social Gender Equality (Vol. 1). In i. Topçu (Ed.), *Digital Capitalism in the New Media Era* (Vol. 1, pp. 161–186). IGI Global. DOI: 10.4018/979-8-3693-1182-0.ch009

Singha, S. (2024). Exploring Motivations of Social Media Influencers in Content Production. In Bi, N., & Zhang, R. (Eds.), *Global Perspectives on Social Media Influencers and Strategic Business Communication* (pp. 26–40). IGI Global., DOI: 10.4018/979-8-3693-0912-4.ch002

Singha, S. (2024). Social Media's Influence on Consumer Decision-Making: A Roadmap for Success. In Sahin, F., & Soylemez, C. (Eds.), *Globalized Consumer Insights in the Digital Era* (pp. 85–109). IGI Global., DOI: 10.4018/979-8-3693-3811-7.ch004

Singha, S., & Singha, R. (2023). Protecting Data and Privacy: Cloud-based solutions for intelligent transportation applications. *Scalable Computing: Practice and Experience*, 24(3), 257–276. DOI: 10.12694/scpe.v24i3.2381

Singha, S., Singha, R., Rebeka, S. P., & Ruben, V. M. (2023). Sustainable marketing in e-commerce: Strategies for environmental impact reduction. In Masengu, R., Bigirimana, S., Chiwaridzo, O. T., Benson, R., & Blossom, C. (Eds.), *Sustainable Marketing, Branding, and Reputation Management: Strategies for a Greener Future* (pp. 444–464). IGI Global., DOI: 10.4018/979-8-3693-0019-0.ch023

Zozaya-Durazo, L. D., Sádaba-Chalezquer, C., & Feijoo-Fernández, B. (2023). "Fake or not, I am sharing it": Teen perception about disinformation in social networks. *Young Consumers*. Advance online publication. DOI: 10.1108/YC-06-2022-1552

KEY TERMS AND DEFINITIONS

Community Empowerment: The process of enabling virtual community members to take control, make decisions, and drive change within their digital environments.

Digital Connectivity: The state of being connected to others via digital networks, enabling instant communication and information exchange across global distances.

Future Trends: Emerging patterns, technologies, and behaviours are expected to shape the development and usage of virtual communities and social media in the coming years.

Social Media: Online platforms that enable users to create, share, and engage with content, fostering communication, networking, and social interaction.

Technological Evolution: The continuous development and advancement of technology lead to new tools, platforms, and capabilities that transform how virtual communities and social media function.

Trust Dynamics: The relationships and factors that influence trust between members of virtual communities, including privacy, security, transparency, and reliability.

Virtual Communities: Online groups where individuals with shared interests, goals, or values interact, communicate, and build relationships, often facilitated by digital platforms.

Compilation of References

Abarca, V. M. G., Palos-Sanchez, P. R., & Rus-Arias, E. (2020). Working in Virtual Teams: A Systematic Literature Review and a Bibliometric Analysis. *IEEE Access : Practical Innovations, Open Solutions*, 8, 168923–168940. DOI: 10.1109/ACCESS.2020.3023546

Abbas, N., Whitfield, J., Atwell, E., Bowman, H., Pickard, T., & Walker, A. (2022). Online chat and chatbots to enhance mature student engagement in higher education. International Journal of Lifelong Education, 41(3), 308-326. https://doi.org/tandfonline.comDOI: 10.1080/02601370.2022.2066213

Abbas, A. F., Jusoh, A., Mas'od, A., Alsharif, A. H., & Ali, J. (2022). Bibliometrix analysis of information sharing in social media. *Cogent Business and Management*, 9(1), 2016556. Advance online publication. DOI: 10.1080/23311975.2021.2016556

Abbas, S., Alnoor, A., Yin, T. S., Sadaa, A. M., Muhsen, Y. R., Khaw, K. W., & Ganesan, Y. (2023). Antecedents of trustworthiness of social commerce platforms: A case of rural communities using multi-group SEM & MCDM methods. [HTML]. *Electronic Commerce Research and Applications*, 62, 101322. DOI: 10.1016/j.elerap.2023.101322

Abeza, G. (2021). Sport Communication. *Sport Management Digest (1),* 1, 1-8. https://digestsm.com/digest/sport-communication/

Abeza, G., O'Reilly, N., Sanderson, J., & Frederick, E. (2021). *Social media in sport: Theory and practice*. World Scientific Publishing Co. Pte. Ltd., https://books.google.pt/books?id=loM8EAAAQBAJ&pg=PR4&dq=Abeza,+Gashaw,+O'Reilly,+Norman,+Sanderson,+Jimmy+%26+Frederick,+Evan.+(2021).+Social+media+in+sport:+Theory+and+practice.+London:+World+Scientific+Publishing+Co.+Pte.+Ltd.&hl=pt-PT&sa=X&ved=2ahUKEwij3bX_3er8AhXaTaQEHSqFDB0Q6AF6BAgHEAI#v=onepage&q=Abeza%2C%20Gashaw%2C%20O'Reilly%2C%20Norman%2C%20Sanderson%2C%20Jimmy%20%26%20Frederick%2C%20Evan.%20(2021).%20Social%20media%20in%20sport%3A%20Theory%20and%20practice.%20London%3A%20World%20Scientific%20Publishing%20Co.%20Pte.%20Ltd.&f=false DOI: 10.1142/12299

Abood, O. G., Elsadd, M. A., & Guirguis, S. K. (2017). Investigation of cryptography algorithms used for security and privacy protection in smart grid. In *2017 Nineteenth International Middle East Power Systems Conference (MEPCON)* (pp. 644–649). https://doi.org/DOI: 10.1109/MEPCON.2017.8301249

Abosag, I., Roper, S., & Hind, D. (2010). Examining the relationship between brand emotion and brand extension among supporters of professional football clubs. *European Journal of Marketing*, (46), 9, 1233–1251. https://www.emerald.com/insight/content/doi/10.1108/03090561211247810/full/html

Adamic, L. A., & Glance, N. (2005). The political blogosphere and the 2004 US election: divided they blog. *Proceedings of the 3rd International Workshop on Link Discovery*, 36–43. DOI: 10.1145/1134271.1134277

Adu-Marfo, A. O., Kwapong, O. A. T. F., Oheneba-Sakyi, Y., & Miller-Young, J. (2024). Understanding teachers' usage of YouTube as a pedagogical tool: A qualitative case study of basic school teachers in Ghana. *E-Learning and Digital Media*, •••, 20427530241239393. DOI: 10.1177/20427530241239393

Afthanorhan, A., Ghazali, P. L., & Rashid, N. (2021, May). Discriminant validity: A comparison of CBSEM and consistent PLS using Fornell & Larcker and HTMT approaches. []. IOP Publishing.]. *Journal of Physics: Conference Series*, 1874(1), 012085. DOI: 10.1088/1742-6596/1874/1/012085

Ahmad, M. (2023). Exploring the Role of OpenStreetMap in Mapping Religious Tourism in Pakistan for Sustainable Development. In J. P. D. M. Vítor, A. G. da R. N. João, L. de J. P. Maria, & A. de M. C. Liliana (Eds.), *Experiences, Advantages, and Economic Dimensions of Pilgrimage Routes* (pp. 23–40). IGI Global. DOI: 10.4018/978-1-6684-9923-8.ch002

Ahmad, M., & Ali, A. (2023). Mapping the future of sustainable development through cloud-based solutions: A case study of openstreetmap. In *Promoting Sustainable Management Through Technological Innovation* (pp. 153–176). IGI Global., DOI: 10.4018/978-1-6684-9979-5.ch011

Ahmed, S. I., Radhakrishnan, S., Nair, B. B., & Thiruvengadathan, R. (2021). Efficient hyperparameter-tuned machine learning approach for estimation of supercapacitor performance attributes. *Journal of Physics Communications*, 5(11), 115011. DOI: 10.1088/2399-6528/ac3574

Ahmed, Y. A., Shehzad, H. M. F., Khurshid, M. M., Abbas Hassan, O. H., Abdalla, S. A., & Alrefai, N. (2024). Examining the effect of interoperability factors on building information modelling (BIM) adoption in Malaysia. *Construction Innovation*, 24(2), 606–642. DOI: 10.1108/CI-12-2021-0245

Aichner, T., Grünfelder, M., Maurer, O., & Jegeni, D. (2021). Twenty-five years of social media: a review of social media applications and definitions from 1994 to 2019. Cyberpsychology, behavior, and social networking, 24(4), 215-222. https://doi.org/ liebertpub.comDOI: 10.1089/cyber.2020.0134

Akhtar, N., & Siddiqi, U. I. (2024). Effects of service providers' self-disclosure on booking platforms on consumers' trust, hesitation, and booking intentions: Moderating role of social media influencers. *Journal of Hospitality Marketing & Management*, 33(4), 470–498. DOI: 10.1080/19368623.2023.2281445

Akpuokwe, C. U., Chikwe, C. F., & Eneh, N. E. (2024). Innovating business practices: The impact of social media on fostering gender equality and empowering women entrepreneurs. Magna Scientia Advanced Research and Reviews, 10(2), 032-043. https://doi.org/ magnascientiapub.comDOI: 10.30574/msarr.2024.10.2.0042

Al Shehab, N. A. (2022). the dark side of social media: Spreading misleading information during covid-19 crisis. Advances in Data Science and Intelligent Data Communication Technologies for COVID-19 [HTML]. *Innovative Solutions Against COVID*, 19, 277–306. DOI: 10.1007/978-3-030-77302-1_15

Alalwan, N. (2022). Actual use of social media for engagement to enhance students' learning. *Education and Information Technologies*, 27(7), 9767–9789. DOI: 10.1007/s10639-022-11014-7 PMID: 35399784

Albert, N., Merunka, D., & Valette-Florence, P. (2009). The feeling of love toward a brand: Concept and measurement. *Advances in Consumer Research. Association for Consumer Research (U. S.)*, 36, 300–307. https://www.researchgate.net/publication/49136328_The_Feeling_of_Love_Toward_a_Brand_Concept_and_Measurement

Albert, R., & Barabási, A.-L. (2002). Statistical mechanics of complex networks. *Reviews of Modern Physics*, 74(1), 47–97. DOI: 10.1103/RevModPhys.74.47

Alenezi, A. M., & Shahi, K. K. (2015). Interactive e-learning through second life with blackboard technology. *Procedia: Social and Behavioral Sciences*, 176, 891–897. https://www.sciencedirect.com/science/article/pii/S1877042815005923. DOI: 10.1016/j.sbspro.2015.01.555

Alenezi, M. (2023). Digital learning and digital institution in higher education. *Education Sciences*, 13(1), 88. DOI: 10.3390/educsci13010088

Alexander, R., Ravi, A., Barclay, H., Sawhney, I., Chester, V., Malcolm, V., ... & Langdon, P. E. (2020). Guidance for the treatment and management of COVID-19 among people with intellectual disabilities. Journal of Policy and Practice in Intellectual Disabilities, 17(3), 256-269. https://doi.org/ wiley.comDOI: 10.1111/jppi.12352

Ali, W., Din, I. U., Almogren, A., & Kim, B.-S. (2022). A novel privacy preserving scheme for smart-grid-based home area networks. *Sensors (Basel)*, 22(2269), 2269. Advance online publication. DOI: 10.3390/s22062269 PMID: 35336439

Alonso-Dos-Santos, M., Rejón Guardia, F., Pérez Campos, C., Calabuig-Moreno, F., & Ko, Y. J. (2018). Engagement in sports virtual brand communities. *Journal of Business Research*, 89, 273–279. DOI: 10.1016/j.jbusres.2017.12.053

Anagnostopoulos, C., Parganas, P., Chadwick, S., & Fenton, A. (2018). Branding in pictures: Using Instagram as a brand management tool in professional team sport organisations. *European Sport Management Quarterly*, 18(4), 4, 413–438. DOI: 10.1080/16184742.2017.1410202

Anaya, K. L., & Pollitt, M. G. (2021). How to procure flexibility services within the electricity distribution system: Lessons from an international review of innovation projects. *Energies*, 14(4475), 4475. Advance online publication. DOI: 10.3390/en14154475

Andalibi, N., Ozturk, P., & Forte, A. (2016). Sensitive self-disclosures, responses, and social support on Instagram: The case of #depression. In *Proceedings of the 2017 ACM Conference on Computer Supported Cooperative Work and Social Computing (CSCW 2017)* (pp. 1485–1500).

Anderson, B. (1983). *Imagined Communities: Reflections on the Origin and Spread of Nationalism*. Verso.

Andrade, R., Alves, A., & Bento, C. (2020). POI mining for land use classification: A case study. *ISPRS International Journal of Geo-Information*, 9(9), 493. Advance online publication. DOI: 10.3390/ijgi9090493

Antonelli, M., Penfold, R. S., Merino, J., Sudre, C. H., Molteni, E., Berry, S., ... & Steves, C. J. (2022). Risk factors and disease profile of post-vaccination SARS-CoV-2 infection in UK users of the COVID Symptom Study app: a prospective, community-based, nested, case-control study. The Lancet Infectious Diseases, 22(1), 43-55. https://doi.org/ thelancet.comDOI: 10.1016/S1473-3099(21)00460-6

Arafat, S. Y., Kar, S. K., Menon, V., Alradie-Mohamed, A., Mukherjee, S., Kaliamoorthy, C., & Kabir, R. (2020). Responsible factors of panic buying: an observation from online media reports. Frontiers in Public Health, 8, 603894. https://doi.org/frontiersin.orgDOI: 10.3389/fpubh.2020.603894

Aragão, F., Farias, F., Mota, M., & Freitas, A. (2016). Curtiu, comentou, comprou. A mídia social digital Instagram e o consumo. *Revista Ciências Administrativas (22),* 1, 130-161. https://www.redalyc.org/articulo.oa?id=475655250006

Archambault, L., Leary, H., & Rice, K. (2022). Pillars of online pedagogy: A framework for teaching in online learning environments. [HTML]. *Educational Psychologist*, 57(3), 178–191. Advance online publication. DOI: 10.1080/00461520.2022.2051513

Arora, N., & Lata, S. (2020). YouTube channels influence on destination visit intentions: An empirical analysis on the base of information adoption model. *Journal of Indian Business Research*, 12(1), 23–42. DOI: 10.1108/JIBR-09-2019-0269

Asad, M. M., Naz, A., Churi, P., & Tahanzadeh, M. M. (2021). Virtual reality as pedagogical tool to enhance experiential learning: a systematic literature review. Education Research International, 2021, 1-17. https://doi.org/hindawi.comDOI: 10.1155/2021/7061623

Autio, E., Mudambi, R., & Yoo, Y. (2021). Digitalization and globalization in a turbulent world: Centrifugal and centripetal forces. *Global Strategy Journal*, 11(1), 3–16. Advance online publication. DOI: 10.1002/gsj.1396

Backlinko. (2024). Roblox User and Growth Stats You Need to Know in 2024. Retrieved from https://backlinko.com/roblox-users

Bagrow, J. P. (2008). Evaluating local community methods in networks. *Journal of Statistical Mechanics*, 2008(05), P05001. Advance online publication. DOI: 10.1088/1742-5468/2008/05/P05001

Baiden, B. K., & Chen, X. (2017). Security and privacy in smart grid: A review. *Renewable & Sustainable Energy Reviews*, 72, 698–706. DOI: 10.1016/j.rser.2017.01.069

Bakshy, E., Messing, S., & Adamic, L. A. (2015). Exposure to ideologically diverse news and opinion on Facebook. *Science*, 348(6239), 1130–1132. DOI: 10.1126/science.aaa1160 PMID: 25953820

Balducci, F. (2021). Is OpenStreetMap a good source of information for cultural statistics? The case of Italian museums. *Environment and Planning. B, Urban Analytics and City Science*, 48(3), 503–520. Advance online publication. DOI: 10.1177/2399808319876949

Balliauw, M., Onghena, E., & Mulkens, S. (2020). Identifying factors affecting the value of advertisements on football clubs' and players' social media: A discrete choice analysis. *International Journal of Sports Marketing & Sponsorship*, •••, 1–25. DOI: 10.1108/IJSMS-12-2019-0138

Barabási, A.-L., & Albert, R. (1999). Emergence of scaling in random networks. *Science*, 286(5439), 509–512. DOI: 10.1126/science.286.5439.509 PMID: 10521342

Bardzell, S., & Shankar, K. (2007, July). Video game technologies and virtual design: a study of virtual design teams in a metaverse. *In International Conference on Virtual Reality* (pp. 607-616). Springer, Berlin, Heidelberg. Retrieved from https://link.springer.com/chapter/10.1007/978-3-540-73335-5_65

Barnes, S. J., Mattsson, J., & Hartley, N. (2015). Assessing the value of real-life brands in Virtual Worlds. *Technological Forecasting and Social Change*, 92, 12–24. https://www.sciencedirect.com/science/article/abs/pii/S0040162514003035. DOI: 10.1016/j.techfore.2014.10.017

Basinger, E. D., Delaney, A. L., & Williams, C. (2023). Uncertainty management in online sexual health forums. [HTML]. *Health Communication*, 38(5), 875–884. Advance online publication. DOI: 10.1080/10410236.2021.1980253 PMID: 34605355

Beichert, M., Bayerl, A., Goldenberg, J., & Lanz, A. (2024). Revenue generation through influencer marketing. *Journal of Marketing*, 88(4), 40–63. Advance online publication. DOI: 10.1177/00222429231217471

Beldiq, E. A., Callula, B., Yusuf, N. A., & Zahra, A. R. A. (2024). Unlocking organizational potential: Assessing the impact of technology through smartpls in advancing management excellence. *APTISI Transactions on Management*, 8(1), 40–48.

Bellhäuser, H., Liborius, P., & Schmitz, B. (2022). Fostering self-regulated learning in online environments: positive effects of a web-based training with peer feedback on learning behavior. Frontiers in psychology. https://doi.org/frontiersin.orgDOI: 10.3389/fpsyg.2022.813381

Beniger, J. R. (1987). The Personalization of Mass Media and the Growth of PseudoCommunity. *Communication Research*, 14(3), 352–371. DOI: 10.1177/009365087014003005

Berdejo-Espinola, V., Suárez-Castro, A. F., Amano, T., Fielding, K. S., Oh, R. R. Y., & Fuller, R. A. (2021). Urban green space use during a time of stress: A case study during the COVID-19 pandemic in Brisbane, Australia. People and Nature, 3(3), 597-609. https://doi.org/ wiley.comDOI: 10.1002/pan3.10218

Betley, E. C., Sigouin, A., Pascua, P. A., Cheng, S. H., MacDonald, K. I., Arengo, F., ... & Sterling, E. J. (2023). Assessing human well-being constructs with environmental and equity aspects: A review of the landscape. People and Nature, 5(6), 1756-1773. https://doi.org/wiley.comDOI: 10.1002/pan3.10293

Bhatta, G. P., Dangol, S., & Sapkota, R. K. (2016). Role of Land Professionals and Spatial Data Infrastructure in Disaster Risk Reduction: In the Context of Post 2015 Nepal Earthquake: General Review. *Nepalese Journal on Geoinformatics*, 15, 59–65. DOI: 10.3126/njg.v15i1.51187

Bibri, S. E., Allam, Z., & Krogstie, J. (2022). The Metaverse as a virtual form of data-driven smart urbanism: platformization and its underlying processes, institutional dimensions, and disruptive impacts. Computational Urban Science. https://doi.org/springer.comDOI: 10.1007/s43762-022-00051-0

Bibri, S. E. (2022). The Social Shaping of the Metaverse as an Alternative to the Imaginaries of Data-Driven Smart Cities: A Study in Science, Technology, and Society. *Smart Cities*, 5(3), 832–874. Advance online publication. DOI: 10.3390/smartcities5030043

Bik, H. M., & Goldstein, M. C. (2013). An introduction to social media for scientists. *PLoS Biology*, 11(4), e1001535. DOI: 10.1371/journal.pbio.1001535 PMID: 23630451

Bilinski, P. (2024). The content of tweets and the usefulness of YouTube and Instagram in corporate communication. *European Accounting Review*, 33(1), 279–311. DOI: 10.1080/09638180.2022.2084759

Billiet, A., Dufays, F., Friedel, S., & Staessens, M. (2021). The resilience of the cooperative model: How do cooperatives deal with the COVID-19 crisis?. Strategic Change. https://doi.org/ nih.govDOI: 10.1002%2Fjsc.2393

Bitzenbauer, P., Höfler, S., Veith, J. M., Winkler, B., Zenger, T., & Kulgemeyer, C. (2024). Exploring the relationship between surface features and explaining quality of YouTube explanatory videos. *International Journal of Science and Mathematics Education*, 22(1), 25–48. DOI: 10.1007/s10763-022-10351-w

Blondel, V. D., Guillaume, J.-L., Lambiotte, R., & Lefebvre, E. (2008). Fast unfolding of communities in large networks. *Journal of Statistical Mechanics*, 2008(10), P10008. Advance online publication. DOI: 10.1088/1742-5468/2008/10/P10008

Böhme, R., Christin, N., Edelman, B., & Moore, T. (2015). Bitcoin: Economics, technology, and governance. *The Journal of Economic Perspectives*, 29(2), 213–238. DOI: 10.1257/jep.29.2.213

Bojic, L. (2022). Metaverse through the prism of power and addiction: what will happen when the virtual world becomes more attractive than reality?. European Journal of Futures Research. https://doi.org/ springer.comDOI: 10.1186/s40309-022-00208-4

Bolger, R. K. (2021). Finding Wholes in the Metaverse: Posthuman Mystics as Agents of Evolutionary Contextualization. *Religions*, 12(9), 768. https://www.mdpi.com/2077-1444/12/9/768. DOI: 10.3390/rel12090768

Bond, B. J., & Miller, B. (2024). YouTube as my space: The relationships between YouTube, social connectedness, and (collective) self-esteem among LGBTQ individuals. *New Media & Society*, 26(1), 513–533. DOI: 10.1177/14614448211061830

Borges, F. (2019). Soccer Clubs as Media Organizations: A Case Study of Benfica TV and PSG TV. *International Journal of Sport Communication*, 12(12), 275–294. DOI: 10.1123/ijsc.2019-0001

Borkowska, S., & Pokonieczny, K. (2022). Analysis of OpenStreetMap Data Quality for Selected Counties in Poland in Terms of Sustainable Development. *Sustainability (Basel)*, 14(7), 3728. Advance online publication. DOI: 10.3390/su14073728

Boßmann, C., & Harriehausen-Mühlbauer, B. (2021). Customizable Navigation on Mobile Devices for Physically Impaired People. *International Conference on Information and Communication Technologies for Ageing Well and E-Health, ICT4AWE - Proceedings, 2021-April.* DOI: 10.5220/0010527002440255

Boulianne, S. (2020). Social media use and participation: A meta-analysis of current research. *Information Communication and Society*, 23(2), 248–266.

Bowe, M., Gray, D., Stevenson, C., McNamara, N., Wakefield, J. R., Kellezi, B., ... & Costa, S. (2020). A social cure in the community: A mixed-method exploration of the role of social identity in the experiences and well-being of community volunteers. European Journal of Social Psychology, 50(7), 1523-1539. https://doi.org/ wiley.comDOI: 10.1016/j.futures.2023.103258

Boyd, D. M., & Ellison, N. B. (2007). Social network sites: Definition, history, and scholarship. *Journal of Computer-Mediated Communication*, 13(1), 210–230. DOI: 10.1111/j.1083-6101.2007.00393.x

Brogan, C. & Smith, J. (2020). Trust agents: Using the web to build influence, improve reputation, and earn trust. amazonaws.com

Bromell, D. (2022). Challenges in regulating online content. In *Springer eBooks* (pp. 29–53). DOI: 10.1007/978-3-030-95550-2_2

Brooks, S., & Hogan, B. (2021). Professional networking on LinkedIn: The role of social capital. *Journal of Social Media in Society*, 10(1), 45–63.

Brovelli, M. A., Mooney, P., Biagi, L., Brambilla, M., Celino, I., Ciceri, E., Dorigatti, N., Huang, H., Minghini, M., & Venkatachalam, V. (2018). *Mapping Parties at FOSS4G Europe: Fun*. Outcomes and Lessons Learned., DOI: 10.1007/978-3-319-70878-2_1

Brown, G., Sanders, S., & Reed, P. (2018). Using public participatory mapping to inform general land use planning and zoning. *Landscape and Urban Planning*, 177, 64–74. Advance online publication. DOI: 10.1016/j.landurbplan.2018.04.011

Bryant, J. (2022). *Digital mapping and inclusion in humanitarian response*. ODI.

Bui, T. (2023). How Roblox can attract more adult players: a case study of a Finnish start-up.https://www.theseus.fi/handle/10024/851390

Butterworth, M. (2021). *Communication and Sport* (Volume 28). Germany: Walter de Gruyter GmbH & Co KG. https://books.google.pt/books?id=nls8EAAAQBAJ&pg=PT112&dq=Communication+and+sport&hl=pt-PT&sa=X&ved=2ahUKEwiIyJev4ur8AhWMr6QKHbxrAxEQ6AF6BAgIEAI#v=onepage&q=Communication%20and%20sport&f=false

Cadwalladr, C., & Graham-Harrison, E. (2018). The Cambridge Analytica files. The Guardian. Retrieved from https://www.theguardian.com/news/series/cambridge-analytica-files

Callaghan, V. (2011). *Immersive Education: Taking K-12 Distance Learning to the Next Level*. Springer Science & Business Media. Retrieved from https://books.google.be/books?hl=en&lr=&id=Idgbf828DdsC&oi=fnd&pg=PA83&dq=Adidas+and+universities+in+Second+Life&ots=fpNsMqWcND&sig=LzSPQSHuO2B710i_cysmmECwzgg&redir_esc=y#v=onepage&q=Adidas%20and%20universities%20in%20Second%20Life&f=false

Cao, H., Liu, S., Guan, Z., & Zhang, X. (2017). Achieving differential privacy of data disclosure from non-intrusive load monitoring in smart grid. In *Cyberspace Safety and Security* (pp. 32–42). https://doi.org/DOI: 10.1007/978-3-319-69471-9_3

Cao, Y., & Smith, P. (2021). LinkedIn as a platform for professional networking and career development. *Journal of Career Development*, 48(2), 150–165.

Carlson, C. G. (2023). Virtual and augmented simulations in mental health. *Current Psychiatry Reports. Current Psychiatry Reports*, 25(9), 365–371. DOI: 10.1007/s11920-023-01438-4 PMID: 37624512

Carpenter, J., Tani, T., Morrison, S., & Keane, J. (2022). Exploring the landscape of educator professional activity on Twitter: An analysis of 16 education-related Twitter hashtags. [HTML]. *Professional Development in Education*, 48(5), 784–805. DOI: 10.1080/19415257.2020.1752287

Castro-Cosío, A. (2023). 'Informal' Financial Practices in the South Bronx: Family, Compadres, and Acquaintances. [HTML]. *Journal of Family and Economic Issues*. Advance online publication. DOI: 10.1007/s10834-023-09912-0

Celliers, M., & Hattingh, M. (2020). A systematic review on fake news themes reported in literature. In Responsible Design, Implementation and Use of Information and Communication Technology: 19th IFIP WG 6.11 Conference on e-Business, e-Services, and e-Society, I3E 2020, Skukuza, South Africa, April 6–8, 2020 [Springer International Publishing. nih.gov]. *Proceedings*, 19(Part II), 223–234.

Chakraborty, T., Srinivasan, S., Ganguly, N., Bhowmick, S., & Mukherjee, A. (2013). Constant Communities in Complex Networks. *Scientific Reports*, 3(1), 1825. DOI: 10.1038/srep01825 PMID: 23661107

Chang, Y. C., Ku, C. H., & Chen, C. H. (2019). Social media analytics: Extracting and visualizing Hilton hotel ratings and reviews from TripAdvisor. *International Journal of Information Management*, 48, 263–279. DOI: 10.1016/j.ijinfomgt.2017.11.001

Chan, S. H. J., Wu, S., & Vipulakom, K. (2020). Young consumers' behavioural intention based on hotel websites. *Anatolia*, 31(1), 1–18. DOI: 10.1080/13032917.2019.1684959

Cheah, J. H., Magno, F., & Cassia, F. (2024). Reviewing the SmartPLS 4 software: the latest features and enhancements.

Chen, C., Zhang, D., Wang, Y., & Huang, H. (2021). Enabling Smart Urban Services with GPS Trajectory Data. In *Enabling Smart Urban Services with GPS Trajectory Data*. DOI: 10.1007/978-981-16-0178-1

Chen, J., Fay, S., & Wang, Q. (2021). The impact of influencer marketing on consumer behavior. *JMR, Journal of Marketing Research*, 58(1), 90–110.

Chen, J., Zhang, Y., Cai, H., Liu, L., Liao, M., & Fang, J. (2024). A comprehensive overview of micro-influencer marketing: Decoding the current landscape, impacts, and trends. *Behavioral Sciences (Basel, Switzerland)*, 14(3), 243. DOI: 10.3390/bs14030243 PMID: 38540546

Chen, L., Baird, A., & Straub, D. (2020). A linguistic signaling model of social support exchange in online health communities. [HTML]. *Decision Support Systems*, 130, 113233. Advance online publication. DOI: 10.1016/j.dss.2019.113233

Cherif, K. M., Azzouz, L., & Bendania, A. (2024). *Algerian secondary school students' preferences for the use of YouTube in their informal learning*. Educational Technology Quarterly.

Chess, S., & Shaw, A. (2015). A conspiracy of fishes, or, how we learned to stop worrying about #GamerGate and embrace hegemonic masculinity. *Journal of Broadcasting & Electronic Media*, 59(1), 208–220. DOI: 10.1080/08838151.2014.999917

Chico, H. (2015). *Does MapQuest still exist?' Yes, it does, and it's a profitable business*. Washington Post. https://www.washingtonpost.com/business/economy/does-mapquest-still-exist-as-a-matter-of-fact-it-does/2015/05/22/995d2532-fa5d-11e4-a13c-193b1241d51a_story.html

Chudyk, A. M., Stoddard, R., McCleary, N., Duhamel, T. A., Shimmin, C., Hickes, S., & Schultz, A. S. (2023). Exploring patient and caregiver perceptions of the meaning of the patient partner role: a qualitative study. Research Involvement and Engagement, 9(1), 106. https://doi.org/springer.comDOI: 10.1186/s40900-023-00511-9

Chu, S. C., & Kim, J. (2018). The current state of knowledge on electronic word-of-mouth in advertising research. *International Journal of Advertising*, 37(1), 1–13. DOI: 10.1080/02650487.2017.1407061

Clark, R. C. (2021). Multimedia learning in e-Courses. In *Cambridge University Press eBooks* (pp. 537–551). DOI: 10.1017/9781108894333.054

Clauset, A., Newman, M. E. J., & Moore, C. (2004). Finding community structure in very large networks. *Physical Review. E*, 70(6), 066111. DOI: 10.1103/PhysRevE.70.066111 PMID: 15697438

Clavio, G. (2013). Emerging social media and applications in sport. In Pedersen, P. (Ed.), *Handbook of sport communication* (pp. 259–268). Routledge., DOI: 10.4324/9780203123485.ch26

Coeckelbergh, M. (2020). *AI ethics: Social and ethical implications of algorithms, data, and artificial intelligence*. Cambridge University Press. DOI: 10.7551/mit-press/12549.001.0001

Coetzee, S., Minghini, M., Solis, P., Rautenbach, V., & Green, C. (2018). Towards understanding the impact of Mapathons - Reflecting on youthmappers experiences. *International Archives of the Photogrammetry, Remote Sensing and Spatial Information Sciences - ISPRS Archives, 42*(4W8). DOI: 10.5194/isprs-archives-XLII-4-W8-35-2018

Coghlan, S., Miller, T., & Paterson, J. (2021). Good proctor or "big brother"? Ethics of online exam supervision technologies. Philosophy & Technology. https://doi.org/ springer.comDOI: 10.1007/s13347-021-00476-1

Cohen, A. P. (1985). *The Symbolic Construction of Community*. Routledge & Kegan Paul. DOI: 10.4324/9780203323373

Cornelissen, J. P., Akemu, O., Jonkman, J. G., & Werner, M. D. (2021). Building character: The formation of a hybrid organizational identity in a social enterprise. Journal of Management Studies, 58(5), 1294-1330. https://doi.org/ wiley.comDOI: 10.1111/joms.12640

Creswell, J. (2009). *Research Design: Qualitative, quantitative and mixed methods approaches*. California: Sage Publications, 3, 1-173. https://www.ucg.ac.me/skladiste/blog_609332/objava_105202/fajlovi/Creswell.pdf

Cruz, J. M., Schregel, J. P., & Zülch, H. (2021). Measuring robustness: Sustainable success factors affecting professional football clubs. *Sport, Business and Management*, 3(12), 1–19. DOI: 10.1108/SBM-03-2021-0041

Csisjournalism. (2022). *Thinking Outside the Bubble: Addressing Polarization and Disinformation on Social Media*. CSIS Journalism Bootcamp. https://journalism.csis.org/thinking-outside-the-bubble-addressing-polarization-and-disinformation-on-social-media/

Dadaczynski, K., Okan, O., Messer, M., Leung, A. Y., Rosário, R., Darlington, E., & Rathmann, K. (2021). Digital health literacy and web-based information-seeking behaviors of university students in Germany during the COVID-19 pandemic: cross-sectional survey study. Journal of medical Internet research, 23(1), e24097. https:// doi.org/ jmir.orgDOI: 10.2196/24097

Danon, L., Díaz-Guilera, A., & Arenas, A. (2006). The effect of size heterogeneity on community identification in complex networks. *Journal of Statistical Mechanics*, 2006(11), 11010–P11010. DOI: 10.1088/1742-5468/2006/11/P11010

Darmayasa, I. N., & Hardika, N. S. (2024). Core tax administration system: The power and trust dimensions of slippery slope framework Tax Compliance model. *Cogent Business & Management*, 11(1), 2337358. DOI: 10.1080/23311975.2024.2337358

Das, K. V., Jones-Harrell, C., Fan, Y., Ramaswami, A., Orlove, B., & Botchwey, N. (2020). Understanding subjective well-being: perspectives from psychology and public health. Public Health Reviews, 41, 1-32. https://doi.org/springer.comDOI: 10.1186/s40985-020-00142-5

Davis, A., Murphy, J. D., Owens, D., Khazanchi, D., & Zigurs, I. (2009). Avatars, people, and virtual worlds: Foundations for research in metaverses. *Journal of the Association for Information Systems*, 10(2), 90–117. https://digitalcommons.unomaha.edu/cgi/viewcontent.cgi?referer=https://scholar.google.com.tw/scholar?hl=nl&as_sdt=0%2C5&q=study+on+working+relations+in+metaverse&oq=working+&httpsredir=1&article=1021&context=isqafacpub. DOI: 10.17705/1jais.00183

De Haas, H. (2021). A theory of migration: the aspirations-capabilities framework. Comparative migration studies. https://doi.org/springer.comDOI: 10.1186/s40878-020-00210-4

Deloitte. (2021). *Deloitte Football Money League 2021*. Deloitte. Consultado em: 15 de novembro de 2021. https://www2.deloitte.com/uk/en/pages/sports-business - group/articles/deloitte-football-money-league.html

Demand Sage. (2024). Roblox Statistics For 2024. Retrieved from https://www.demandsage.com/how-many-people-play-roblox/

Demirtas, M. S., & Alici, N. (2024). The reliability and quality of YouTube videos as a source of breath holding spell. *Italian Journal of Pediatrics*, 50(1), 8. DOI: 10.1186/s13052-023-01570-0 PMID: 38238792

Dey, B. L., Yen, D., & Samuel, L. (2020). Digital consumer culture and digital acculturation. *International Journal of Information Management*, 51, 102057. brunel.ac.uk. DOI: 10.1016/j.ijinfomgt.2019.102057

Diário de Notícias. (20 de março de 2017). *Paixão pelo futebol é "uma forma de amor tribal", conclui estudo.* Diário de Notícias. Consultado em: 26 de novembro de 2021. https://www.dn.pt/sociedade/paixao-pelo-futebol-e-uma-forma-de-amor-tribal-conclui-estudo-5735943.html

Diestelmeier, L. (2019). Unlocking flexibility with law: Developing a legal framework for smart electricity systems.

Diestelmeier, L. (2021). A legal framework for smart grids. In Energy Law, Climate Change and the Environment (pp. 645–655). University of Groningen. https://doi.org/DOI: 10.4337/9781788119689.IX.54

Dille, K. B. & Røkenes, F. M. (2021). Teachers' professional development in formal online communities: A scoping review. Teaching and Teacher Education. https://doi.org/ sciencedirect.comDOI: 10.1016/j.tate.2021.103431

Dionísio, P., Leal, C., & Moutinho, L. (2008). Fandom affiliation and tribal behaviour: A sports marketing application. *Qualitative Market Research*, 11(1), 17–39. DOI: 10.1108/13522750810845531

Djafarova, E., & Rushworth, C. (2017). Exploring the credibility of online celebrities' Instagram profiles in influencing the purchase decisions of young female users. *Computers in Human Behavior*, 68, 1–7. DOI: 10.1016/j.chb.2016.11.009

Dolata, M. & Schwabe, G. (2023). What is the Metaverse and who seeks to define it? Mapping the site of social construction. Journal of Information Technology. https://doi.org/sagepub.comDOI: 10.1177/02683962231159927

Domènech, A., Mohino, I., & Moya-Gómez, B. (2020). Using flickr geotagged photos to estimate visitor trajectories in world heritage cities. *ISPRS International Journal of Geo-Information*, 9(11), 646. Advance online publication. DOI: 10.3390/ijgi9110646

Dooly, M., & Vinagre, M. (2021). Research into practice: Virtual exchange in language teaching and learning. *Language Teaching*, 55(3), 392–406. DOI: 10.1017/S0261444821000069

Dowd, A. (2022). Vanishing acts: The crisis of our loss of kinship with the more-than-human world. [HTML]. *The Journal of Analytical Psychology*, 67(5), 1270–1295. Advance online publication. DOI: 10.1111/1468-5922.12863 PMID: 36440726

Duarte, A. (2023). The relationship between Brands and Consumers. In *Social Brand Management in a Post Covid-19 Era* (pp. 3–16). Routledge., DOI: 10.4324/9781003382331-2

Duhne, P. G. S., Delgadillo, J., & Lutz, W. (2022). Predicting early dropout in online versus face-to-face guided self-help: A machine learning approach. Behaviour Research and Therapy. https://doi.org/sciencedirect.comDOI: 10.1016/j.brat.2022.104200

Duka, M., Sikora, M., & Strzelecki, A. (2023). From Web Catalogs to Google: A Retrospective Study of Web Search Engines Sustainable Development. Sustainability. https://doi.org/mdpi.comDOI: 10.3390/su15086768

Duvall, S. S. (2020). Too famous to protest: Far-right online community bonding over collective desecration of Colin Kaepernick, fame, and celebrity activism. [HTML]. *The Journal of Communication Inquiry*, 44(3), 256–278. Advance online publication. DOI: 10.1177/0196859920911650

Du, Z., Liu, J., & Wang, T. (2022). Augmented reality marketing: A systematic literature review and an agenda for future inquiry. *Frontiers in Psychology*, 13, 925963. Advance online publication. DOI: 10.3389/fpsyg.2022.925963 PMID: 35783783

Dzafic, D., Candiotti, J. L., & Cooper, R. A. (2020). Improving wheelchair route planning through instrumentation and navigation systems. *Proceedings of the Annual International Conference of the IEEE Engineering in Medicine and Biology Society, EMBS, 2020-July*. DOI: 10.1109/EMBC44109.2020.9176481

Efe, I. E., Tesch, C., & Subedi, P. (2024). YouTube as a source of patient information on awake craniotomy: Analysis of content quality and user engagement. *World Neurosurgery: X*, 21, 100249. DOI: 10.1016/j.wnsx.2023.100249 PMID: 38090193

El Morr, C., Maule, C., Ashfaq, I., Ritvo, P., & Ahmad, F. (2020). Design of a Mindfulness Virtual Community: A focus-group analysis. Health informatics journal, 26(3), 1560-1576. https://doi.org/sagepub.comDOI: 10.1177/1460458219884840

Ellis, C. A., Gibbs, S. J., & Rein, G. L. (1991). Groupware - Some Issues and Experiences. *Communications of the ACM*, 34(1), 38–58. DOI: 10.1145/99977.99987

Ellison, N., & Boyd, D. M. (2013). Sociality through social network sites.

Ellison, N. B., Steinfield, C., & Lampe, C. (2007). The benefits of Facebook "friends": Social capital and college students' use of online social network sites. *Journal of Computer-Mediated Communication*, 12(4), 1143–1168. DOI: 10.1111/j.1083-6101.2007.00367.x

Ellison, N. B., Vitak, J., Gray, R., & Lampe, C. (2022). Cultivating social resources on social network sites: Facebook relationship maintenance behaviors and their implications for social capital. *New Media & Society*, 24(1), 15–37.

ERDdS, P., & R&wi, A. (1959). On random graphs I. *Publ. Math. Debrecen, 6*(290–297), 18.

Erdos, P., & Rényi, A. (1960). On the evolution of random graphs. *Publ. Math. Inst. Hung. Acad. Sci*, 5(1), 17–60.

Eyal, P., David, R., Andrew, G., Zak, E., & Ekaterina, D. (2021). Data quality of platforms and panels for online behavioral research. Behavior research methods, 1-20. https://doi.org/springer.comDOI: 10.3758/s13428-021-01694-3

Faisal, M., Cardenas, A. A., & Mashima, D. (2015). How the quantity and quality of training data impacts re-identification of smart meter users? In *2015 IEEE International Conference on Smart Grid Communications (SmartGridComm)*. https://doi.org/DOI: 10.1109/SmartGridComm.2015.7436272

Farhangi, H. (2010). The path of the smart grid. *IEEE Power & Energy Magazine*, 8(1), 18–28. DOI: 10.1109/MPE.2009.934876

Fatiha, M. (2024). The effectiveness of electronic promotion channels for booking platforms: comparative study between Namlatic Hotel Booking and Booking. com. *Journal of Contemporary Business and Economic Studies Vol, 7*(01).

Fayez, O., Ismail, H., & Aboelnagah, H. (2023). Emerging virtual communities of practice during crises: A sustainable model validating the levels of peer motivation and support. *Sustainability*, 15(7), 5691.

Fazlali, M., Moradi, E., & Tabatabaee Malazi, H. (n.d.). *Adaptive Parallel Louvain Community Detection on a Multicore Platform*.

Federação Portuguesa de Futebol. (2021). Sobre a FPF. Consultado em: 20 de novembro de 2021. https://www.fpf.pt/Institucional/Sobre-a-FPF/História-FPF

Fenton, A., Keegan, B.J. & Parry, K.D. (2021). Understanding Sporting Social Media Brand Communities, Place and Social Capital: A Netnography of Football Fans. *Sage Journals,* 1-21. https://doi.org/DOI: 10.1177/216747952098614

Fiedler, M. (1975). A property of eigenvectors of nonnegative symmetric matrices and its application to graph theory. *Czechoslovak Mathematical Journal*, 25(4), 619–633. DOI: 10.21136/CMJ.1975.101357

Finlay, J. M., Kler, J. S., O'Shea, B. Q., Eastman, M. R., Vinson, Y. R., & Kobayashi, L. C. (2021). Coping during the COVID-19 pandemic: a qualitative study of older adults across the United States. Frontiers in public health, 9, 643807. https://doi.org/ frontiersin.orgDOI: 10.3389/fpubh.2021.643807

Flavian, C., Guinaliu, M., & Torres, E. (2005). The Influence of Corporate Image on Customer Trust, a Comparative Analysis in Traditional versus Internet Banking. *Internet Research*, 15, 447–470. DOI: 10.1108/10662240510615191

Foody, G., Long, G., Schultz, M., & Olteanu-Raimond, A. M. (2024). Assuring the quality of VGI on land use and land cover: Experiences and learnings from the LandSense project. *Geo-Spatial Information Science*, 27(1), 16–37. Advance online publication. DOI: 10.1080/10095020.2022.2100285

Fornell, C., & Larcker, D. F. (1981). Structural equation models with unobservable variables and measurement error: Algebra and statistics. *JMR, Journal of Marketing Research*, 18(3), 382–388. DOI: 10.1177/002224378101800313

Forster, R. (2016). Louvain community detection with parallel heuristics on GPUs. *2016 IEEE 20th Jubilee International Conference on Intelligent Engineering Systems (INES)*, 227–232. DOI: 10.1109/INES.2016.7555126

Forster, R. (2018). *Parallel Louvain Community Detection Optimized for GPUs.* http://arxiv.org/abs/1805.10904

Forte, A., & Bruckman, A. (2008). Scaling consensus: Increasing decentralization in Wikipedia governance. In *Proceedings of the 41st Annual Hawaii International Conference on System Sciences (HICSS)* (p. 157). DOI: 10.1109/HICSS.2008.383

Fraisl, D., Campbell, J., See, L., Wehn, U., Wardlaw, J., Gold, M., Moorthy, I., Arias, R., Piera, J., Oliver, J. L., Masó, J., Penker, M., & Fritz, S. (2020). Mapping citizen science contributions to the UN sustainable development goals. *Sustainability Science*, 15(6), 1735–1751. Advance online publication. DOI: 10.1007/s11625-020-00833-7

Frandsen, K. (2016). Sports organizations in a new wave of mediatization. *Communication & Sport*, 4(4), 385–400. DOI: 10.1177/2167479515588185

Freelon, D., McIlwain, C. D., & Clark, M. D. (2018). Beyond the hashtags: #Ferguson, #Blacklivesmatter, and the online struggle for offline justice. *New Media & Society*, 20(4), 1025–1045.

Fuks, H., Raposo, A., Gerosa, M. A., Pimentel, M., Filippo, D., & Lucena, C. (2008). Inter- and Intra-Relationships between Communication Coordination and Cooperation in the Scope of the 3C Collaboration Model. Computer Supported Cooperative Work in Design, *12th International Conference*, 148-153.

Gach, O., & Hao, J.-K. (2014). *Improving the Louvain Algorithm for Community Detection with Modularity Maximization.*, DOI: 10.1007/978-3-319-11683-9_12

Gacs, A., Goertler, S., & Spasova, S. (2020). Planned online language education versus crisis-prompted online language teaching: Lessons for the future. [HTML]. *Foreign Language Annals*, 53(2), 380–392. Advance online publication. DOI: 10.1111/flan.12460

Gallego, M. D., Bueno, S., & Noyes, J. (2016). Second Life adoption in education: A motivational model based on Uses and Gratifications theory. *Computers & Education*, 100, 81–93. https://www.sciencedirect.com/science/article/abs/pii/S0360131516301105. DOI: 10.1016/j.compedu.2016.05.001

Gama, K., Gonçalves, B. A., Rautenbach, V., Coetzee, S., Sastry, N., Green, C., & Fourie, N. (2019). Mapathons and hackathons to crowdsource the generation and usage of geographic data. *ACM International Conference Proceeding Series*. DOI: 10.1145/3316287.3316293

Gantz, W. (2013). Reflections on communication and sport: On fanship and social relationships. *Communication & Sport*, 1(1), 176–187. DOI: 10.1177/2167479512467446

Gartenberg, C. & Zenger, T. (2023). The firm as a subsociety: Purpose, justice, and the theory of the firm. Organization Science. https://doi.org/ informs.orgDOI: 10.1287/orsc.2022.1650

Ghamrawi, N. (2022). Teachers' virtual communities of practice: A strong response in times of crisis or just another Fad?. Education and information technologies. https://doi.org/ springer.comDOI: 10.1007/s10639-021-10857-w

Ghosh, S., Halappanavar, M., Tumeo, A., Kalyanaraman, A., Lu, H., Chavarria-Miranda, D., Khan, A., & Gebremedhin, A. (2018). Distributed louvain algorithm for graph community detection. *Proceedings - 2018 IEEE 32nd International Parallel and Distributed Processing Symposium, IPDPS 2018*, 885–895. DOI: 10.1109/IPDPS.2018.00098

Gilbert, R., Thadani, V., Handy, C., Andrews, H., Sguigna, T., Sasso, A., & Payne, S. (2014). The psychological functions of avatars and alt (s): A qualitative study. *Computers in Human Behavior*, 32, 1–8. https://www.sciencedirect.com/science/article/abs/pii/S0747563213004287. DOI: 10.1016/j.chb.2013.11.007

Gillespie, T. (2018). *Custodians of the internet: Platforms, content moderation, and the hidden decisions that shape social media*. Yale University Press.

Gillespie, T. (2018). *Custodians of the Internet: Platforms, content moderation, and the hidden decisions that shape social media*. Yale University Press.

Girvan, M., & Newman, M. E. J. (2002a). Community structure in social and biological networks. *Proceedings of the National Academy of Sciences of the United States of America*, 99(12), 7821–7826. DOI: 10.1073/pnas.122653799 PMID: 12060727

Giulianotti, R. (2002). Supporters, Followers, Fans, and Flaneurs: A Taxonomy of Spectator Identities in Football. *Journal of Sport and Social Issues*, 26(1), 25–46. DOI: 10.1177/0193723502261003

Giulianotti, R., & Robertson, R. (2012). Mapping the global football field: A sociological model of transnational forces within the world game. *The British Journal of Sociology*, 63(2), 216–240. DOI: 10.1111/j.1468-4446.2012.01407.x PMID: 22670645

Goh, Z., Eva, N., Kiazad, K., Jack, G. A., De Cieri, H., & Spreitzer, G. M. (2022). An integrative multilevel review of thriving at work: Assessing progress and promise. Journal of Organizational Behavior, 43(2), 197-213. https://doi.org/ umich.eduDOI: 10.1002/job.2571

Gong, X., Li, J., Liang, H., Yu, R., & Wu, Y. (2021). Privacy preservation in big data analytics for smart grids: A survey. *IEEE Transactions on Industrial Informatics*, 17(8), 5736–5746. DOI: 10.1109/TII.2021.3055049

González-Anta, B., Pérez de la Fuente, I., Zornoza, A., & Orengo, V. (2023). Building Sustainable Virtual Communities of Practice: A Study of the Antecedents of Intention to Continue Participating. *Sustainability (Basel)*, 15(21), 15657. DOI: 10.3390/su152115657

Gorini, A., Gaggioli, A., & Riva, G. (2008). A second life for eHealth: Prospects for the use of 3-D virtual worlds in clinical psychology. *Journal of Medical Internet Research*, 10(3), e1029. https://www.jmir.org/2008/3/e21. DOI: 10.2196/jmir.1029 PMID: 18678557

Gramates, L. S., Agapite, J., Attrill, H., Calvi, B. R., Crosby, M. A., Dos Santos, G., ... & Strelets, V. B. (2022). FlyBase: a guided tour of highlighted features. Genetics, 220(4), iyac035. https://doi.org/oup.comDOI: 10.1093/genetics/iyac035

Granovetter, M. S. (1973). The strength of weak ties. *American Journal of Sociology*, 78(6), 1360–1380. DOI: 10.1086/225469

Greenhow, C., Graham, C. R., & Koehler, M. J. (2022). Foundations of online learning: Challenges and opportunities. [HTML]. *Educational Psychologist*, 57(3), 131–147. Advance online publication. DOI: 10.1080/00461520.2022.2090364

Grenfell, J. (2013). Immersive interfaces for art education teaching and learning in virtual and real world learning environments. *Procedia: Social and Behavioral Sciences*, 93, 1198–1211. https://www.sciencedirect.com/science/article/pii/S1877042813034617. DOI: 10.1016/j.sbspro.2013.10.016

Grinberger, A. Y., Minghini, M., Yeboah, G., Juhász, L., & Mooney, P. (2022). Bridges and Barriers: An Exploration of Engagements of the Research Community with the OpenStreetMap Community. *ISPRS International Journal of Geo-Information*, 11(1), 54. Advance online publication. DOI: 10.3390/ijgi11010054

Grover, P., Kar, A. K., & Dwivedi, Y. (2022). The evolution of social media influence - A literature review and research agenda. *International Journal of Information Management Data Insights*, 2(2), 100116. DOI: 10.1016/j.jjimei.2022.100116

Grutzpalk, J., & Jarolimek, S. (2024). The importance of police public relations in assembly situations. In *Public Order Policing: A Professional's Guide to International Theories, Case Studies, and Best Practices* (pp. 399–411). Springer International Publishing. [HTML], DOI: 10.1007/978-3-031-43856-1_18

Gunter, U., & Önder, I. (2021). An Exploratory Analysis of Geotagged Photos From Instagram for Residents of and Visitors to Vienna. *Journal of Hospitality & Tourism Research (Washington, D.C.)*, 45(2), 373–398. Advance online publication. DOI: 10.1177/1096348020963689

Gu, Y., & Zhu, J. (2023). The effect of online review and interaction on value co-creation in tourism virtual community. *Cogent Social Sciences*, 9(2), 2261234. DOI: 10.1080/23311886.2023.2261234

Habbal, A., Ali, M. K., & Abuzaraida, M. A. (2024). Artificial Intelligence Trust, Risk and Security Management (AI TRiSM): Frameworks, applications, challenges and future research directions. *Expert Systems with Applications*, 240, 122442. DOI: 10.1016/j.eswa.2023.122442

Hacker, J., Vom Brocke, J., Handali, J., Otto, M., & Schneider, J. (2020). Virtually in this together–how web-conferencing systems enabled a new virtual togetherness during the COVID-19 crisis. European Journal of Information Systems, 29(5), 563-584. https://doi.org/ tandfonline.comDOI: 10.1080/0960085X.2020.1814680

Hadjipanayi, C., Christofi, M., Banakou, D., & Michael-Grigoriou, D. (2024). Cultivating empathy through narratives in virtual reality: A review. *Personal and Ubiquitous Computing*, 28(3-4), 507–519. Advance online publication. DOI: 10.1007/s00779-024-01812-w

Haimson, O. L., Dame-Griff, A., Capello, E., & Richter, Z. (2021). Tumblr was a trans technology: the meaning, importance, history, and future of trans technologies. Feminist media studies, 21(3), 345-361. https://doi.org/ tandfonline.comDOI: 10.1080/14680777.2019.1678505

Haleem, A., Javaid, M., Qadri, M. A., & Suman, R. (2022). Understanding the role of digital technologies in education: A review. Sustainable Operations and Computers, 3, 275-285. https://doi.org/sciencedirect.comDOI: 10.1016/j.susoc.2022.05.004

Haleem, A., Javaid, M., Qadri, M. A., Singh, R. P., & Suman, R. (2022). Artificial intelligence (AI) applications for marketing: A literature-based study. International Journal of Intelligent Networks, 3, 119-132. https://doi.org/ sciencedirect.comDOI: 10.1016/j.ijin.2022.08.005

Han, E., & Bailenson, J. N. (2024). *Social interaction in VR*. Oxford Research Encyclopedia of Communication., DOI: 10.1093/acrefore/9780190228613.013.1489

Harkin, L. J., Beaver, K., Dey, P., & Choong, K. A. (2020). Secret groups and open forums: defining online support communities from the perspective of people affected by cancer. Digital Health. http://dx.doi.org/sagepub.comDOI: 10.1177/2055207619898993

Hartman, R., & Simova, T. (2021). How changing API terms changed Instagram's domain? A bibliometric analysis. *7th International Conference on Computer Technology Applications, ICCTA 2021*, 73–79. https://doi.org/DOI: 10.1145/3477911.3477923

Hassouneh, D., & Brengman, M. (2014). A motivation-based typology of social virtual world users. *Computers in Human Behavior*, 33, 330–338. https://www.sciencedirect.com/science/article/abs/pii/S0747563213003117. DOI: 10.1016/j.chb.2013.08.012

Haythornthwaite, C., & Wellman, B. (2002). *The Internet in Everyday Life: An Introduction*. Blackwell. DOI: 10.1002/9780470774298.ch

Hemphill, R., Forsythe, L. P., Heckert, A. L., Amolegbe, A., Maurer, M., Carman, K. L., ... & Esmail, L. (2020). What motivates patients and caregivers to engage in health research and how engagement affects their lives: qualitative survey findings. Health Expectations, 23(2), 328-336. https://doi.org/wiley.comDOI: 10.1080/1369118X.2020.1764606

Herden, C. J., Alliu, E., Cakici, A., Cormier, T., Deguelle, C., Gambhir, S., . . . Edinger-Schons, L. M. (2021, March). "Corporate Digital Responsibility" New corporate responsibilities in the digital age. In Sustainability Management Forum| NachhaltigkeitsManagementForum (Vol. 29, No. 1, pp. 13-29). Berlin/Heidelberg: Springer Berlin Heidelberg. https://doi.org/ springer.comDOI: 10.1007/s00550-020-00509-x

Herencia, C. A. B. (2021). La narrativa digital del fútbol. Desintermediación de la agenda a través de las redes sociales de los clubes [The digital narrative of soccer. Disintermediation of the agenda through the social networks of the clubs]. *Revista Académica sobre Documentación Digital y Comunicación Interactiva, (22),* 85-96. https://orcid.org/0000-0002 8990-7949

Herfort, B., Lautenbach, S., Porto de Albuquerque, J., Anderson, J., & Zipf, A. (2021). The evolution of humanitarian mapping within the OpenStreetMap community. *Scientific Reports*, 11(1), 3037. Advance online publication. DOI: 10.1038/s41598-021-82404-z PMID: 33542423

Herold, R., & Hertzog, C. (2015). The smart grid and privacy. In *Data Privacy for the Smart Grid* (pp. 1–10). https://doi.org/DOI: 10.1201/b18005-1

He, X., Pun, M.-O., & Kuo, C.-C. J. (2012). *Secure and efficient cryptosystem for smart grid using homomorphic encryption. In 2012 IEEE PES Innovative Smart Grid Technologies.* ISGT., DOI: 10.1109/ISGT.2012.6175676

He, X., Zhang, Y., Liu, X., Huang, D., & Liu, Y. (2022). A comprehensive survey on privacy-preserving techniques in smart grid communications. *IEEE Transactions on Industrial Informatics*, 18(6), 4467–4483. DOI: 10.1109/TII.2021.3053940

He, Y., Luo, F., Sun, M., & Ranzi, G. (2023). Privacy-preserving and hierarchically federated framework for short-term residential load forecasting. *IEEE Transactions on Smart Grid*, 14(6), 1–1. DOI: 10.1109/TSG.2023.3268633

Hilburn, A., Zawisza, T., Bazan, J., Cruz, R., & Rodriguez, J. (2021). Employing Participatory Risk Mapping (PRM) as a land-use planning method: The case of a derelict former hospital in Laredo, Texas, USA. *Journal of Urban Design*, 26(2), 235–256. Advance online publication. DOI: 10.1080/13574809.2020.1814135

Hilkenmeier, F., Bohndick, C., Bohndick, T., & Hilkenmeier, J. (2020). Assessing distinctiveness in multidimensional instruments without access to raw data–a manifest Fornell-Larcker criterion. *Frontiers in Psychology*, 11, 223. DOI: 10.3389/fpsyg.2020.00223 PMID: 32210863

Hillery, G. A.Jr. (1955). Definitions of Community: Areas of Agreement. *Rural Sociology*, 20, 779–791.

Hisseine, M. A., Chen, D., & Yang, X. (2022). The application of blockchain in social media: A systematic literature review. *Applied Sciences (Basel, Switzerland)*, 12(13), 6567. DOI: 10.3390/app12136567

Hjorteset, M. A., & Böcker, L. (2020). Car sharing in Norwegian urban areas: examining interest, intention and the decision to enrol. Transportation research part D: transport and environment, 84, 102322. https://doi.org/sciencedirect.comDOI: 10.1016/j.trd.2020.102322

Hoeller, D., Rudin, N., Sako, D., & Hutter, M. (2024). Anymal parkour: Learning agile navigation for quadrupedal robots. [HTML]. *Science Robotics*, 9(88), eadi7566. Advance online publication. DOI: 10.1126/scirobotics.adi7566 PMID: 38478592

Hoffner, C. A., & Bond, B. J. (2022). Parasocial relationships, social media, & well-being. [HTML]. *Current Opinion in Psychology*, 45, 101306. Advance online publication. DOI: 10.1016/j.copsyc.2022.101306 PMID: 35219157

Hoicka, C. E., Lowitzsch, J., Brisbois, M. C., Kumar, A., & Camargo, L. R. (2021). Implementing a just renewable energy transition: Policy advice for transposing the new European rules for renewable energy communities. Energy Policy, 156, 112435. https://doi.org/ sciencedirect.comDOI: 10.1016/j.enpol.2021.112435

Holmes, W., Porayska-Pomsta, K., Holstein, K., Sutherland, E., Baker, T., Shum, S. B., ... & Koedinger, K. R. (2022). Ethics of AI in education: Towards a community-wide framework. International Journal of Artificial Intelligence in Education, 1-23. https://doi.org/ springer.comDOI: 10.1007/s40593-021-00239-1

Ho-Mai, N. T., Tran, V. T., Nguyen, V. K., Do, U. T. T., Truong, T. B., & Tran, P. T. K. (2024). The pathways of increasing online celebrity brand equity and followers' hotel booking intention: A serial multiple mediation model. *Journal of Research in Interactive Marketing*. Advance online publication. DOI: 10.1108/JRIM-08-2023-0265

Hootsuite. (2021). *Digital 2021: Global Overview Report*. Data Reportal. Consultado em: 3 de janeiro de 2022. https://datareportal.com/reports/digital-2021-global -overview-report

Horrich, A., Ertz, M., & Bekir, I. (2024). The effect of information adoption via social media on sustainable consumption intentions: The moderating influence of gender. *Current Psychology (New Brunswick, N.J.)*, 43(18), 1–14. DOI: 10.1007/s12144-023-05526-9

Howard, P. N., & Hussain, M. M. (2011). The role of digital media. *Journal of Democracy*, 22(3), 35–48. DOI: 10.1353/jod.2011.0041

Hristova, D., Quattrone, G., Mashhadi, A., & Capra, L. (2013). The life of the party: Impact of social mapping in OpenStreetMap. *Proceedings of the 7th International Conference on Weblogs and Social Media, ICWSM 2013*. DOI: 10.1609/icwsm.v7i1.14416

Huang, C. (2022). Time spent on social network sites and psychological well-being: A meta-analysis. *Cyberpsychology, Behavior, and Social Networking*, 25(1), 13–19. PMID: 28622031

Huangfu, Z., Ruan, Y., Zhao, J., Wang, Q., & Zhou, L. (2022). Accessing the influence of community experience on brand loyalty toward virtual Brand Community: developing country perspective. Frontiers in Psychology, 13, 865646. https://doi .org/frontiersin.orgDOI: 10.3389/fpsyg.2022.865646

Hu, B., Li, W., Huo, X., Liang, Y., Gao, M., & Pei, P. (2016). Improving Louvain Algorithm for Community Detection. *Proceedings of the 2016 International Conference on Artificial Intelligence and Engineering Applications*. DOI: 10.2991/aiea-16.2016.20

Hulland, J. (1999). Use of partial least squares (PLS) in strategic management research: A review of four recent studies. *Strategic Management Journal*, 20(2), 195–204. DOI: 10.1002/(SICI)1097-0266(199902)20:2<195::AID-SMJ13>3.0.CO;2-7

Hunt, K. A., Bristol, T., & Bashaw, R. E. (1999). A conceptual approach to classifying sports fans. *Journal of Services Marketing*, 13(6), 6, 439–452. DOI: 10.1108/08876049910298720

Hussain, G., Naz, T., Shahzad, N., & Bajwa, M. J. (2021). Social Media Marketing in Sports and using social media platforms for sports fan engagement. *Journal of Contemporary Issues in Business and Government*, (27), 6, 1460–1474. DOI: 10.47750/cibg.2021.27.05.145

Hussain, K., Nusair, K., Junaid, M., & Aman, W. (2024). A two-actor model for understanding user engagement with content creators: Applying social capital theory. *Computers in Human Behavior*, 156, 108237. DOI: 10.1016/j.chb.2024.108237

Huvila, I., Holmberg, K., Ek, S., & Widén-Wulff, G. (2010). Social capital in second life. *Online Information Review*, 34(2), 295–316. https://www.emerald.com/insight/content/doi/10.1108/14684521011037007/full/html. DOI: 10.1108/14684521011037007

Hysa, B., Karasek, A., & Zdonek, I. (2021). Social media usage by different generations as a tool for sustainable tourism marketing in society 5.0 idea. Sustainability. https://doi.org/ mdpi.comDOI: 10.3390/su13031018

Information Commissioner's Office (ICO). (2009). Privacy impact assessment handbook, Version 2.0. https://www.huntonprivacyblog.com/wp-content/uploads/sites/28/2013/09/PIAhandbookV2.pdf

Ingavélez-Guerra, P., Otón-Tortosa, S., Hilera-González, J., & Sánchez-Gordón, M. (2021). The use of accessibility metadata in e-learning environments: A systematic literature review. *Universal Access in the Information Society*, 22(2), 445–461. DOI: 10.1007/s10209-021-00851-x

Inman, C., Wright, V. H., & Hartman, J. A. (2010). Use of Second Life in K-12 and higher education: A review of research. *Journal of Interactive Online Learning*, 9(1). https://www.ncolr.org/jiol/issues/pdf/9.1.3.pdf

Isaak, J., & Hanna, M. J. (2018). User data privacy: Facebook, Cambridge Analytica, and privacy protection. *Computer*, 51(8), 56–59. DOI: 10.1109/MC.2018.3191268

Islam, S., Zografopoulos, I., Hossain, M. T., Badsha, S., & Konstantinou, C. (2023). *A resource allocation scheme for energy demand management in 6G-enabled smart grid. In 2023 IEEE Power & Energy Society Innovative Smart Grid Technologies Conference (ISGT)*. IEEE., DOI: 10.1109/ISGT51731.2023.10066396

Ismagilova, E., Rana, N. P., Slade, E. L., & Dwivedi, Y. K. (2021). A meta-analysis of the factors affecting eWOM providing behaviour. *European Journal of Marketing*, 55(4), 1067–1102. http://dx.doi.org/https://doi.org/10.1108/EJM-07-2018-0472. DOI: 10.1108/EJM-07-2018-0472

Ismagilova, E., Slade, E., Rana, N. P., & Dwivedi, Y. K. (2020). The effect of characteristics of source credibility on consumer behaviour: A meta-analysis. *Journal of Retailing and Consumer Services*, 53, 101736. Advance online publication. DOI: 10.1016/j.jretconser.2019.01.005

Jacobson, J. (2021). The essential guide to the business & law of esports & professional video gaming. https://doi.org/[HTML]DOI: 10.1201/9781003143963

Jacqueline, G., Senjaya, Y. P. A., Firli, M. Z., & Yadila, A. B. (2024). Application of SmartPLS in Analyzing Critical Success Factors for Implementing Knowledge Management in the Education Sector. *APTISI Transactions on Management*, 8(1), 49–57. DOI: 10.33050/atm.v8i1.2201

Jamil, K., Dunnan, L., Gul, R. F., Shehzad, M. U., Gillani, S. H. M., & Awan, F. H. (2022). Role of social media marketing activities in influencing customer intentions: a perspective of a new emerging era. Frontiers in psychology, 12, 808525. https://doi.org/frontiersin.orgDOI: 10.3389/fpsyg.2021.808525

Javid, E. T., Nazari, M., & Ghaeli, M. R. (2019). Social media and e-commerce: A scientometrics analysis. *International Journal of Data and Network Science*, 3(3), 269–290. DOI: 10.5267/j.ijdns.2019.2.001

Jenkins, H. (2006). *Confronting the challenges of participatory culture: Media education for the 21st century. An occasional paper on digital media and learning*. John D. and Catherine T. MacArthur Foundation.

Jia, Y., Xu, L., Lu, Z., & Zhang, Y. (2019). Consumers' privacy and security concerns in smart grid technology: An empirical study in China. *Energy Policy*, 131, 344–352.

Jo, H. (2023). From Classroom to Screen: Analyzing the Mechanisms Shaping E-Learning Benefits amidst COVID-19. *Journal of the Knowledge Economy*. Advance online publication. DOI: 10.1007/s13132-023-01614-0

Jones, Q. (1997). Virtual-Communities, Virtual Settlements & Cyber-Archaeology: A Theoretical Outline. *Journal of Computer-Mediated Communication*, 3(3), 0. DOI: 10.1111/j.1083-6101.1997.tb00075.x

Jones, S. G. (1997). *Virtual Culture: Identity and Communication in Cybersociety*. Sage Publications.

Joshi, Y., Lim, W. M., Jagani, K., & Kumar, S. (2023). Social media influencer marketing: Foundations, trends, and ways forward. *Electronic Commerce Research*. Advance online publication. DOI: 10.1007/s10660-023-09719-z

Jovanović, A. & Milosavljević, A. (2022). VoRtex Metaverse platform for gamified collaborative learning. Electronics. https://doi.org/mdpi.comDOI: 10.3390/electronics11030317

Kang, H. & Lou, C. (2022). AI agency vs. human agency: understanding human–AI interactions on TikTok and their implications for user engagement. Journal of Computer-Mediated Communication. https://doi.org/ oup.comDOI: 10.1093/jcmc/zmac014

Kang, J. W., & Namkung, Y. (2019). The role of personalization on continuance intention in food service mobile apps. *International Journal of Contemporary Hospitality Management*. Advance online publication.

Kantola, S., Fagerholm, N., & Nikula, A. (2023). Utilization and implementation of PPGIS in land use planning and decision-making from the perspective of organizations. *Land Use Policy*, 127, 106528. Advance online publication. DOI: 10.1016/j.landusepol.2022.106528

Kaplan, A. M., & Haenlein, M. (2009). The fairyland of Second Life: Virtual social worlds and how to use them. *Business Horizons*, 52(6), 563–572. DOI: 10.1016/j.bushor.2009.07.002

Kaplan, A. M., & Haenlein, M. (2010). Users of the world, unite! The challenges and opportunities of Social Media. *Business Horizons*, 53(1), 59–68. DOI: 10.1016/j.bushor.2009.09.003

Kapri, S. S., & Sharma, A. (2024). Digital marketing impact on rural Homestay booking and role of destination image. *Anatolia*, •••, 1–13. DOI: 10.1080/13032917.2024.2319075

Kasauli, R., Knauss, E., Horkoff, J., Liebel, G., & de Oliveira Neto, F. G. (2021). Requirements engineering challenges and practices in large-scale agile system development. Journal of Systems and Software, 172, 110851. https://doi.org/sciencedirect.comDOI: 10.1016/j.jss.2020.110851

Kassem, M., Benomran, L., & Teizer, J. (2017). Virtual environments for safety learning in construction and engineering: Seeking evidence and identifying gaps for future research. *Visualization in Engineering*, 5(1), 16. Advance online publication. DOI: 10.1186/s40327-017-0054-1

Keaton, W. & Gilbert, A. (2020). Successful online learning: What does learner interaction with peers, instructors and parents look like?. Journal of Online Learning Research. learntechlib.org

Keni, K., Wilson, N., & Teoh, A. P. (2024). Antecedents of viewers' watch behavior toward YouTube videos: Evidence from the most populous Muslim-majority country. *Journal of Islamic Marketing*, 15(2), 446–469. DOI: 10.1108/JIMA-01-2023-0008

Kernighan, B. W., & Lin, S. (1970). An efficient heuristic procedure for partitioning graphs. *The Bell System Technical Journal*, 49(2), 291–307. DOI: 10.1002/j.1538-7305.1970.tb01770.x

Khan, A. M., Soroya, S. H., & Mahmood, K. (2024). Impact of information credibility on social media information adoption behavior: A systematic literature review. *Library Hi Tech*, 42(1), 261–283. DOI: 10.1108/LHT-03-2022-0165

Khan, S., Jabeen, F., & Hussain, M. (2018). A review on security and privacy issues in smart grid communications. *Sustainable Cities and Society*, 40, 600–612.

Khan, Z. T., & Johnson, P. A. (2020). Citizen and government co-production of data: Analyzing the challenges to government adoption of VGI. *The Canadian Geographer. Geographe Canadien*, 64(3), 374–387. Advance online publication. DOI: 10.1111/cag.12619

Kharmalki, G. W., & Raizada, S. (2020). Social media marketing in sports: The rise of fan engagement through Instagram. *Annals of Tropical Medicine and Public Health*, 17(23), 1–8. DOI: 10.36295/ASRO.2020.231721

Khatib, T., Syed, A., Khan, U., & Alsharif, S. (2015). A comprehensive review on smart grid and its research challenges. *Renewable & Sustainable Energy Reviews*, 51, 1507–1518. DOI: 10.1016/j.rser.2015.07.123

Khoei, T. T., Slimane, H. O., & Kaabouch, N. (2022). Cyber-security of smart grids: Attacks, detection, countermeasure techniques, and future directions. *Communications and Network*, 14(4), 119–170. DOI: 10.4236/cn.2022.144009

Khor, E. T., & Mutthulakshmi, K. (2024). A systematic review of the role of learning analytics in supporting personalized learning. *Education Sciences*, 14(1), 51. DOI: 10.3390/educsci14010051

Kim, A., Qian, Y., Lee, H-W., Mastromartino, B. & Zhang, J.J. (2020). Growth in Sport Media and the rise of new sport fandom. *Multidisciplinary Perspectives on Media Fandom*, 150-171. DOI: 10.4018/978-1-7998-3323-9.ch009

Kim, D. J., Salvacion, M., Salehan, M., & Kim, D. W. (2023). An empirical study of community cohesiveness, community attachment, and their roles in virtual community participation. [HTML]. *European Journal of Information Systems*, 32(3), 573–600. DOI: 10.1080/0960085X.2021.2018364

Kim, H. M., Lyons, K., & Cunningham, M. A. (2008). Towards a theoretically-grounded framework for evaluating immersive business models and applications: Analysis of ventures in Second Life. *Journal of Virtual Worlds Research*, 1(1). Advance online publication. https://jvwr-ojs-utexas.tdl.org/jvwr/article/view/289. DOI: 10.4101/jvwr.v1i1.289

Kim, J., James, J., & Kim, Y. (2013). A model of the relationship among sport consumer motives, spectator commitment, and behavioral intentions. *Sport Management Review*, 16(2), 173–185. DOI: 10.1016/j.smr.2012.08.004

Kim, J., Melton, R., Min, J. E., & Kim, B. Y. (2020). Who says what?: Exploring the impacts of content type and blog type on brand credibility, brand similarity and eWOM intention. *Journal of Fashion Marketing and Management*. Advance online publication.

Kim, K., & Trail, G. (2011). A Conceptual Framework for Understanding Relationships Between Sport Consumers and Sport Organizations: A Relationship Quality Approach. *Journal of Sport Management*, 25(1), 57–69. DOI: 10.1123/jsm.25.1.57

Kim, T., Jo, H., Yhee, Y., & Koo, C. (2022). Robots, artificial intelligence, and service automation (RAISA) in hospitality: Sentiment analysis of YouTube streaming data. *Electronic Markets*, 32(1), 259–275. DOI: 10.1007/s12525-021-00514-y

Kirkman, B. L., Cordery, J. L., Mathieu, J., Rosen, B., & Kukenberger, M. (2013). Global Organizational Communities of Practice: The Effects of Nationality Diversity, Psychological Safety, and Media Richness on Community Performance. *Human Relations*, 2013(66), 333–362. DOI: 10.1177/0018726712464076

Klinkhardt, C., Woerle, T., Briem, L., Heilig, M., Kagerbauer, M., & Vortisch, P. (2021). Using openstreetmap as a data source for attractiveness in travel demand models. In *Transportation Research Record* (Vol. 2675, Issue 8). DOI: 10.1177/0361198121997415

Kloza, D., van Dijk, N., & De Hert, P. (2015). Assessing the European approach to privacy and data protection in smart grids: Lessons for emerging technologies. In Skopik, F., & Smith, P. (Eds.), *Smart Grid Security* (pp. 11–47). Syngress., DOI: 10.1016/B978-0-12-802122-4.00002-X

Knott, E., Rao, A. H., Summers, K., & Teeger, C. (2022). Interviews in the social sciences. Nature Reviews Methods Primers, 2(1), 73. https://doi.org/nature.comDOI: 10.1038/s43586-022-00150-6

Kokkini, V., Tseliou, E., Abakoumkin, G., & Bozatzis, N. (2022). "Immersed in world of warcraft": A discursive study of identity management talk about excessive online gaming. [HTML]. *Journal of Language and Social Psychology*, 41(5), 590–612. DOI: 10.1177/0261927X211067820

Kollock, P., & Smith, M. (Eds.). (1999). *Communities in Cyberspace*. Routledge.

Kong, H., & Fang, H. (2024). Research on the Effectiveness of Virtual Endorsers: A Study Based on the Match-Up Hypothesis and Source Credibility Model. *Sustainability (Basel)*, 16(5), 1761. DOI: 10.3390/su16051761

Koronios, K., Travlos, A., Douvis, J., & Papadopoulos, A. (2020). Sport, media and actual consumption behavior: An examination of spectator motives and constraints for sport media consumption. *EuroMed Journal of Business*, 15(2), 151–166. DOI: 10.1108/EMJB-10-2019-0130

Ko, S. Y., Chung, H. K., Kim, J. I., & Shin, Y. (2021). A Study on the Typology and Advancement of Cultural Leisure-Based Metaverse. *KIPS Transactions on Software and Data Engineering*, 10(8), 331–338.

Kozinets, R. V. (2010). *Netnography: Doing Ethnographic Research Online*. Sage Publications.

Kriewaldt, J., & Lee, S. J. (2021). Digital volunteerism: Missing maps: Crowd sourcing to support humanitarian responses for a better future. *Geography Bulletin*, •••, 19–21.

Kristof-Brown, A., Schneider, B., & Su, R. (2023). Person-organization fit theory and research: Conundrums, conclusions, and calls to action. Personnel psychology. https://doi.org/ wiley.comDOI: 10.1111/peps.12581

Król, K. (2020). Evolution of online mapping: From Web 1.0 to Web 6.0. *Geomatics, Landmanagement and Landscape*, 1, 33–51. DOI: 10.15576/GLL/2020.1.33

Kross, E., Verduyn, P., Demiralp, E., Park, J., Lee, D. S., Lin, N., & Ybarra, O. (2022). Social media and well-being: Pitfalls, progress, and next steps. *Trends in Cognitive Sciences*, 26(4), 293–306. PMID: 33187873

Kshetri, N., Dwivedi, Y. K., Davenport, T. H., & Panteli, N. (2023). Generative artificial intelligence in marketing: Applications, opportunities, challenges, and research agenda. [HTML]. *International Journal of Information Management*, 102716. Advance online publication. DOI: 10.1016/j.ijinfomgt.2023.102716

Kumar, P., Braeken, A., Gurtov, A., Iinatti, J., & Ha, P. H. (2017). Anonymous secure framework in connected smart home environments. *IEEE Transactions on Information Forensics and Security*, 12(4), 968–979. DOI: 10.1109/TIFS.2016.2647225

Kumpula, J. M., Onnela, J.-P., Saramäki, J., Kertész, J., & Kaski, K. (2009). Model of community emergence in weighted social networks. *Computer Physics Communications*, 180(4), 517–522. DOI: 10.1016/j.cpc.2008.12.016

Kuzma, J., Bell, V., & Logue, C. (2014). A Study of the Use of Social Media Marketing in the Football Industry. *Journal of Emerging Trends in Computing and Information. The Sciences*, 10(5), 728–738. https://eprints.worc.ac.uk/3460/1/kuzmacisoct2014paper.pdf

Lainas, S. (2023). Self-help/mutual aid groups for health and psychosocial problems: Key features and their perspectives in the 21st century. American Journal of Community Psychology. https://doi.org/ wiley.comDOI: 10.1002/ajcp.12718

Laituri, M., Luizza, M. W., Hoover, J. D., & Allegretti, A. M. (2023). Questioning the practice of participation: Critical reflections on participatory mapping as a research tool. *Applied Geography (Sevenoaks, England)*, 152, 102900. Advance online publication. DOI: 10.1016/j.apgeog.2023.102900

Lancichinetti, A., & Fortunato, S. (2009). Benchmarks for testing community detection algorithms on directed and weighted graphs with overlapping communities. *Physical Review. E*, 80(1), 016118. DOI: 10.1103/PhysRevE.80.016118 PMID: 19658785

Lancichinetti, A., Fortunato, S., & Radicchi, F. (2008). Benchmark graphs for testing community detection algorithms. *Physical Review. E*, 78(4), 046110. DOI: 10.1103/PhysRevE.78.046110 PMID: 18999496

Langley, D. J., van Doorn, J., Ng, I. C., Stieglitz, S., Lazovik, A., & Boonstra, A. (2021). The Internet of Everything: Smart things and their impact on business models. Journal of Business Research, 122, 853-863. https://doi.org/ sciencedirect.comDOI: 10.1016/j.jbusres.2019.12.035

Łapniewska, Z. (). Solidarity and mutual aid: Women organizing the "visible hand" urban commons. Gender. https://doi.org/ wiley.comDOI: 10.1111/gwao.12833

Larson, L. & DeChurch, L. A. (2020). Leading teams in the digital age: Four perspectives on technology and what they mean for leading teams. The leadership quarterly. sciencedirect.com

Lata, S., & Rana, K. (2021). WHAT ARE THE DETERMINANTS OF CONSUMERS'ONLINE REVIEWS ADOPTION FOR HOTEL BOOKINGS: A STRUCTURAL EQUATION MODELLING APPROACH. *Enlightening Tourism. A Pathmaking Journal, 11*(1), 171-193.

Lee, J. A., & Eastin, M. S. (2021). Perceived authenticity of social media influencers: Scale development and validation. *Journal of Research in Interactive Marketing*, 15(4), 822–841. DOI: 10.1108/JRIM-12-2020-0253

Lee, J., & Lee, H. K. (2024). Exploring direct and indirect cultural experiences: A study of global consumers' Hanbok experience and engagement mediated via YouTube. *Fashion and Textiles*, 11(1), 19. DOI: 10.1186/s40691-024-00385-9

Lee, J., Lim, J., Pyo, S., & Lee, J. (2023). Aerial online mapping on-board system by real-time object detection for UGV path generation in unstructured outdoor environments. *Journal of Field Robotics*, 40(7), 1754–1765. Advance online publication. DOI: 10.1002/rob.22213

Lee, M. A., Kunkel, T., Funk, D. C., Karg, A., & McDonald, H. (2020). Built to last: Relationship quality management for season ticket holders. *European Sport Management Quarterly*, 20(3), 364–384. DOI: 10.1080/16184742.2019.1613438

Le, H. T. P. M., & Ryu, S. (2023). The eWOM adoption model in the hospitality industry: The moderating effect of the vlogger's review. *Journal of Hospitality and Tourism Technology*, 14(2), 225–244. DOI: 10.1108/JHTT-08-2021-0233

Lepri, B., Oliver, N., Letouzé, E., Pentland, A., & Vinck, P. (2017). Fair, transparent, and accountable algorithmic decision-making processes. *Philosophy & Technology*, 31(4), 611–627. DOI: 10.1007/s13347-017-0279-x

Leszczyna, R. (2018). Cybersecurity and privacy in standards for smart grids – A comprehensive survey. *Computer Standards & Interfaces*, 56, 62–73. DOI: 10.1016/j.csi.2017.09.005

Levy, R. (2022). Algorithmic content curation in online platforms: An examination of echo chambers and filter bubbles. *Digital Journalism (Abingdon, England)*, 8(2), 193–211.

Li, J. & Zheng, H. (2022). Online information seeking and disease prevention intent during COVID-19 outbreak. Journalism & Mass Communication Quarterly. https://doi.org/ sagepub.comDOI: 10.1177/1077699020961518

Li, F., Larimo, J., & Leonidou, L. C. (2020). Social media marketing strategy: Definition, conceptualization, taxonomy, validation, and future agenda. *Journal of the Academy of Marketing Science*, 49(1), 51–70. DOI: 10.1007/s11747-020-00733-3

Li, K. C., & Wong, B. T. (2020). Social media in Higher Education: A Review of Their uses, benefits and Limitations. *Communications in Computer and Information Science*, 1302, 248–257. DOI: 10.1007/978-981-33-4594-2_21

Lin, M. E., Ayo-Ajibola, O., Castellanos, C. X., West, J., Luu, N., Kim, I., & Kokot, N. C. (2024). Assessing Laryngectomy Patient Education on YouTube: Investigating Quality and Reliability. *OTO Open*, 8(1), e113. DOI: 10.1002/oto2.113 PMID: 38299048

Lin, T. J., Wang, S. Y., Grant, S., Chien, C. L., & Lan, Y. J. (2014). Task-based teaching approaches of Chinese as a foreign language in Second Life through teachers' perspectives. *Procedia Technology*, 13, 16–22. https://www.sciencedirect.com/science/article/pii/S2212017314000140. DOI: 10.1016/j.protcy.2014.02.004

Lin, Z., Gukasyan, G., & Nasyrova, L. (2024). Virtual reality in cultural education: Cultural integration and academic performance of migrant students in the context of cultural capital. *Education and Information Technologies*. Advance online publication. DOI: 10.1007/s10639-024-12450-3

Liu, C., & Zhang, H. (2012). A survey of demand response in smart grid: Approaches, initiatives and perspectives. *IEEE Transactions on Industrial Informatics*, 9(3), 1484–1495. DOI: 10.1109/TII.2012.2188407

Liu, S., Xiao, W., Fang, C., Zhang, X., & Lin, J. (2020). Social support, belongingness, and value co-creation behaviors in online health communities. [HTML]. *Telematics and Informatics*, 50, 101398. Advance online publication. DOI: 10.1016/j.tele.2020.101398

Liu, X., Wang, G. A., Johri, A., Zhou, M., & Fan, W. (2012). Harnessing global expertise: A comparative study of expertise profiling methods for online communities. *Information Systems Frontiers*, 16(4), 715–727. DOI: 10.1007/s10796-012-9385-6

Livingston, E., Houston, E., Carradine, J., Fallon, B., Akmeemana, C., Nizam, M., & McNab, A. (2022). Global student perspectives on digital inclusion in education during COVID-19. *Global Studies of Childhood*, 13(4), 341–357. DOI: 10.1177/20436106221102617

Li, X. L., Johnston, K. A., & Feng, J.Xiufang (Leah) Li. (2024). Virtual community engagement: Engaging virtual communities for nation branding through sports. *Public Relations Review*, 50(3), 102440. DOI: 10.1016/j.pubrev.2024.102440

Li, Y., & Ma, H. (2020). Blockchain-based privacy-preserving energy trading in smart grid. *IEEE Access : Practical Innovations, Open Solutions*, 8, 131180–131191.

Lohtia, R., Donthu, N., & Guillory, M. D. (2013). The impact of advertising, trustworthiness, and valence on the effectiveness of blogs. *International Journal of Electronic Marketing and Retailing*, 5(4), 317–339. DOI: 10.1504/IJEMR.2013.060264

Lowenthal, P. R., Horan, A., DeArmond, M. C., Lomellini, A., Egan, D., Johnson, M., Moeller, K. N., Keldgord, F., Kuohn, J., Jensen, S., Stamm, A., & Pounds, D. (2023). Classroom community and online learning: A synthesis of Alfred Rovai's research. *TechTrends*, 67(6), 931–944. DOI: 10.1007/s11528-023-00904-3

Lucena, J., & Casaca, J. (2013). Branding no futebol: O valor económico das marcas dos três grandes do futebol português. *Revista Portuguesa e Brasileira de Gestão*, •••, 33–46. https://www.redalyc.org/articulo.oa?id=388539138005

Luger, T. M., Hamilton, A. B., & True, G. (2020). Measuring community-engaged research contexts, processes, and outcomes: a mapping review. The Milbank Quarterly. wiley.com

Lugrin, J. L., Longpré, S., & El Saddik, A. (2019). Towards ethical guidelines for virtual reality. *IEEE Transactions on Technology and Society*, 1(1), 48–58.

Lusseau, D., Schneider, K., Boisseau, O. J., Haase, P., Slooten, E., & Dawson, S. M. (2003). The bottlenose dolphin community of doubtful sound features a large proportion of long-lasting associations: Can geographic isolation explain this unique trait? *Behavioral Ecology and Sociobiology*, 54(4), 396–405. DOI: 10.1007/s00265-003-0651-y

Lynch, M., Sage, T., Hitchcock, L. I., & Sage, M. (2021). A heutagogical approach for the assessment of Internet Communication Technology (ICT) assignments in higher education. International Journal of Educational Technology in Higher Education, 18(1), 55. https://doi.org/ springer.comDOI: 10.1186/s41239-021-00290-x

Mabić, M., Lasić, M., & Zovko, J. (2019). Web 2.0 technologies in business: Why not? *Interdisciplinary Description of Complex Systems*, 17(2, 2-B), 304–314. DOI: 10.7906/indecs.17.2.7

Maderer, D., Parganas, P., & Anagnostopoulos, C. (2018). Brand-Image Communication Through Social Media: The Case of European Professional Football Clubs. *International Journal of Sport Communication*, 3(11), 1–20. DOI: 10.1123/ijsc.2018-0086

Mahan, J. (2011). Examining the predictors of consumer response to sport marketing via digital social media. *International Journal of Sport Management and Marketing*, 9, 254–267. DOI: 10.1504/IJSMM.2011.041575

Mahmoudian, A., Boroujerdi, S. S., Siyani, M. G., & Mahmoud, A. I. F. (2021). Moderating Role of Using Instagram in Relation between Involvement with the Team, Attachment and Fan Loyalty (Case Study: Persepolis Football Team). *Communication Mangagement in Sports Media*, 2(8), 103–115. DOI: 10.30473/jsm.2020.50380.1370

Mahmud, Z., Chauhan, A., Sarkar, D., & Soden, R. (2022). Revisiting Engagement in Humanitarian Mapping: An Updated Analysis of Contributor Retention in OpenStreetMap. *Conference on Human Factors in Computing Systems - Proceedings*. DOI: 10.1145/3491101.3519728

Malthouse, E. C., Haenlein, M., Skiera, B., Wege, E., & Zhang, M. (2013). Managing customer relationships in the social media era: Introducing the social CRM house. *Journal of Interactive Marketing*, 27(4), 270–280.

Mandal, A. K., Parakash, C., & Tiwari, A. (2012). Performance evaluation of cryptographic algorithms: DES and AES. In 2012 IEEE Students' Conference on Electrical, Electronics and Computer Science (pp. 1–5). IEEE. https://doi.org/DOI: 10.1109/SCEECS.2012.6184991

Manoharan, A. P., Ingrams, A., Kang, D., & Zhao, H. (2021). Globalization and Worldwide Best Practices in E-Government. *International Journal of Public Administration*, 44(6), 465–476. Advance online publication. DOI: 10.1080/01900692.2020.1729182

Martínez, P., Herrero, Á., & García-de los Salmones, M. D. M. (2020). Determinants of eWOM on hospitality CSR issues. In Facebook we trust? *Journal of Sustainable Tourism*, 1-19.

Martínez-López, F. J., Anaya-Sánchez, R., Aguilar-Illescas, R., & Molinillo, S. (2016). Types of Virtual Communities and Virtual Brand Communities. In *Online Brand Communities: Using the Social Web for Branding and Marketing* (pp. 125–140). Springer. DOI: 10.1007/978-3-319-24826-4_8

Martin, F., & Borup, J. (2022). Online learner engagement: Conceptual definitions, research themes, and supportive practices. [HTML]. *Educational Psychologist*, 57(3), 162–177. Advance online publication. DOI: 10.1080/00461520.2022.2089147

Marwick, A. E., & Lewis, R. (2017). *Media manipulation and disinformation online*. Data & Society Research Institute.

Marx, V. (2023). Method of the year: long-read sequencing. Nature Methods. nature.com

Maseko, B. & Siziba, L. (2023). On the dialectics of policy and practice: Multilingualism and the virtual linguistic landscape of a South African university. Cogent Arts & Humanities. https://doi.org/tandfonline.comDOI: 10.1080/23311983.2023.2268395

Masele, J. J., & Mwita, D. (2024). Online Television Subscription in Tanzania: Examination of the Influence of Information Quality, Video quality and technology ease of use. *ORSEA JOURNAL, 13*(2).

Massanari, A. L. (2017). Gamergate and the Fappening: How Reddit's algorithm, governance, and culture support toxic technocultures. *New Media & Society*, 19(3), 329–346. DOI: 10.1177/1461444815608807

Mastromartino, B., Ross, W. J., Wear, H., & Naraine, M. L. (2020). Thinking outside the 'box': A discussion of sports fans, teams, and the environment in the context of COVID- 19. *Sport in Society*, 11(23), 1–17. DOI: 10.1080/17430437.2020.1804108

Mathavan, B., Vafaei-Zadeh, A., Hanifah, H., Ramayah, T., & Kurnia, S. (2024). Understanding the purchase intention of fitness wearables: Using value-based adoption model. *Asia-Pacific Journal of Business Administration*, 16(1), 101–126. DOI: 10.1108/APJBA-04-2022-0166

Matzat, U. (2004). Cooperation and Community on the Internet: Past Issues and Present Perspectives for Theoretical-Empirical Internet Research. *Analyse & Kritik*, 26(1), 63–90. DOI: 10.1515/auk-2004-0104

McCarthy, J., Rowley, J., Ashworth, C., & Pioch, E. (2014). Managing brand presence through social media: The case of UK football clubs. *Internet Research*, 24(2), 181–204. DOI: 10.1108/IntR-08-2012-0154

McLean, R., & Wainwright, D. (2009). Social networks, football fans, fantasy and reality: How corporate and media interests are invading our life world. *Journal of Information. Communication and Ethics in Society*, 7(1), 54–71. DOI: 10.1108/14779960910938098

McMillan, D. W., & Chavis, D. M. (1986). Sense of community: A definition and theory. *Journal of Community Psychology*, 14(1), 6–23. DOI: 10.1002/1520-6629(198601)14:1<6::AID-JCOP2290140103>3.0.CO;2-I

Meena, S. S., & Tokekar, D. V. (2021). Community detection in social networks by incorporating the preferential selection. *Journal of Complex Networks*, 9(6), cnab040. Advance online publication. DOI: 10.1093/comnet/cnab040

Meena, S. S., & Tokekar, V. (2020). Modularity based Community Detection in Social Networks. *International Journal of Engineering and Advanced Technology*, 9(3), 564–569. DOI: 10.35940/ijeat.B3382.029320

Meena, S. S., & Tokekar, V. (2023). *A Model to Generate Benchmark Network with Community Structure.*, DOI: 10.1007/978-981-16-9967-2_23

Messinger, P. R., Smirnov, K., & Ge, X. (2021). Virtual communities. In *Springer eBooks* (pp. 1–17). DOI: 10.1007/978-3-319-98390-5_161-1

Miković, R., Petrović, D., Mihić, M., Obradović, V., & Todorović, M. (2020). The integration of social capital and knowledge management–The key challenge for international development and cooperation projects of nonprofit organizations. [HTML]. *International Journal of Project Management*, 38(8), 515–533. DOI: 10.1016/j.ijproman.2020.07.006

Miller, M. R., Jun, H., Herrera, F., Villa, J. Y., Welch, G., & Bailenson, J. N. (2019). Social interaction in augmented reality. *PLoS One*, 14(5), e0216290. DOI: 10.1371/journal.pone.0216290 PMID: 31086381

Minaei, M. (2020). Evolution, density and completeness of OpenStreetMap road networks in developing countries: The case of Iran. *Applied Geography (Sevenoaks, England)*, 119, 102246. Advance online publication. DOI: 10.1016/j.apgeog.2020.102246

Minghini, M., Sarretta, A., & Napolitano, M. (2022). OpenStreetMap Contribution to Local Data Ecosystems in COVID-19 Times: Experiences and Reflections from the Italian Case. *Data*, 7(4), 39. Advance online publication. DOI: 10.3390/data7040039

Minter, M., Mason, L. R., Burgess, M. D., Peach, W. J., & Hughes, J. (2024). Understanding stakeholder perceptions on the impacts of gamebird releasing on or near UK protected sites. Journal for Nature Conservation, 126581. https://doi.org/sciencedirect.comDOI: 10.1016/j.jnc.2024.126581

Mintz, J., Connolly, C., O'Brien, E., Daniela, L., & Ceallaigh, T. Ó. (2024). Inclusive Digital Education: Contexts, Practices and Perspectives. *Computers in the Schools*, 41(2), 115–119. DOI: 10.1080/07380569.2024.2340873

Mirzaei, T., & Esmaeilzadeh, P. (2021). Engagement in online health communities: Channel expansion and social exchanges. [HTML]. *Information & Management*, 58(1), 103404. Advance online publication. DOI: 10.1016/j.im.2020.103404

Misra, D. P. (2023). Social media for education and research: Practical considerations. *Journal of the Royal College of Physicians of Edinburgh/˜the Royal College of Physicians of Edinburgh, 53*(1), 4–6. https://doi.org/DOI: 10.1177/14782715231158008

Mlika, F., Karoui, W., & Romdhane, L. B. (2024). Trustworthy decentralization based on blockchain tools for social network architectures. *Social Network Analysis and Mining*, 14(1), 95. Advance online publication. DOI: 10.1007/s13278-024-01252-7

Mmbaga, N. A., Mathias, B. D., Williams, D. W., & Cardon, M. S. (2020). A review of and future agenda for research on identity in entrepreneurship. [HTML]. *Journal of Business Venturing*, 35(6), 106049. DOI: 10.1016/j.jbusvent.2020.106049

Mockaitis, A., Rose, E., & Zettinig, P. (2012). The power of individual cultural values in global virtual teams. *International Journal of Cross Cultural Management*, 12(2), 193–210. DOI: 10.1177/1470595812439868

Mohamed, F., & Shoufan, A. (2024). Users' experience with health-related content on YouTube: An exploratory study. *BMC Public Health*, 24(1), 86. DOI: 10.1186/s12889-023-17585-5 PMID: 38172765

Mohiuddin, M. B., & Jabot, M. (2023). Activating Education for Sustainable Development Goals Through YouthMappers. In *Sustainable Development Goals Series: Vol. Part F2734*. DOI: 10.1007/978-3-031-05182-1_8

Molinillo, S., Aguilar-Illescas, R., Anaya-Sánchez, R., & Liébana-Cabanillas, F. (2021). Social commerce website design, perceived value and loyalty behavior intentions: The moderating roles of gender, age and frequency of use. [HTML]. *Journal of Retailing and Consumer Services*, 63, 102404. DOI: 10.1016/j.jretconser.2020.102404

Molloy, M., & Reed, B. (1995a). A critical point for random graphs with a given degree sequence. *Random Structures and Algorithms*, 6(2–3), 161–180. DOI: 10.1002/rsa.3240060204

Morrison-Smith, S. & Ruiz, J. (2020). Challenges and barriers in virtual teams: a literature review. SN Applied Sciences. https://doi.org/ springer.comDOI: 10.1007/s42452-020-2801-5

Motahar, P. S., Tavakoli, R., & Mura, P. (2024). Social media influencers' visual framing of Iran on YouTube. *Tourism Recreation Research*, 49(2), 270–282. DOI: 10.1080/02508281.2021.2014252

Mousavi, S. & Roper, S. (2023). Enhancing relationships through online brand communities: Comparing posters and lurkers. International Journal of Electronic Commerce. https://doi.org/ tandfonline.comDOI: 10.1080/10864415.2022.2158596

Mpofu, P., Asak, M. O., & Salawu, A. (2022). Facebook groups as transnational counter public sphere for diasporic communities. Cogent arts & humanities. https://doi.org/tandfonline.comDOI: 10.1080/23311983.2022.2027598

Muhamad, N., Muhamad Hakimi, F. H., & Mahadzir, M. D. A. (2023). Community Activation for Disaster Risk Reduction Through OpenStreetMap: A Scoping Review. *Journal of Advanced Geospatial Science & Technology*, 3(2), 25–50. Advance online publication. DOI: 10.11113/jagst.v3n2.68

Mukherjee, S. & Narang, D. (2023). Digital economy and work-from-home: The rise of home offices amidst the COVID-19 outbreak in India. Journal of the Knowledge Economy. https://doi.org/ springer.comDOI: 10.1007/s13132-022-00896-0

Murad, A., Faruque, F., Naji, A., Tiwari, A., Qurnfulah, E., Rahman, M., & Dewan, A. (2024). Optimizing health service location in a highly urbanized city: Multi criteria decision making and P-Median problem models for public hospitals in Jeddah City, KSA. *PLoS ONE, 19*(1 January). DOI: 10.1371/journal.pone.0294819

Muralidhara Rao, P., Al-Turjman, F., & Deebak, B. D. (2022). Smart grid metering: Security, privacy, and open challenges. In Deebak, B. D., & Al-Turjman, F. (Eds.), *Sustainable Networks in Smart Grid* (pp. 255–272). Academic Press., DOI: 10.1016/B978-0-323-85626-3.00009-0

Murphy, E. (2004). Recognising and Promoting Collaboration in an Online Asynchronous Discussion. *British Journal of Educational Technology*, 35(4), 421–431. DOI: 10.1111/j.0007-1013.2004.00401.x

Mystakidis, S. (2022). Metaverse. Encyclopedia. https://doi.org/ mdpi.comDOI: 10.3390/encyclopedia2010031

Naeem, M., Malik, A. W., & Aljohani, N. R. (2017). Security and privacy issues in smart grid: A comprehensive review. *Sustainable Cities and Society*, 28, 413–427.

Nagaraj, A. (2021). Information seeding and knowledge production in online communities: Evidence from openstreetmap. *Management Science*, 67(8), 4908–4934. Advance online publication. DOI: 10.1287/mnsc.2020.3764

Na, H., & Staudt Willet, K. B. (2022). Affinity and anonymity benefitting early career teachers in the r/teachers subreddit. [HTML]. *Journal of Research on Technology in Education*, 1–18. DOI: 10.1080/15391523.2022.2150727

Nath, K. (). Evolution of the internet from web 1.0 to metaverse: The good, the bad and the ugly. TechRxiv Powered by IEEE. https://dx.doi.org/ figshare.comDOI: 10.36227/techrxiv.19743676.v1

Nazari Ardabili, D., Amin, F., & Fayyazi, B. M. (2024). Designing an Adoption Model for Electronic Human Resource Management in Service-Oriented Organizations: A Case Study of Tehran Municipality. *Journal of Information Technology Management*, 16(2), 91–111.

Neamţu, N. & Faludi, C. (2021). Learning Effectiveness of Social Work Methods With Groups, in Online and Face-to-Face Contexts. Frontiers in Psychology. https://doi.org/ frontiersin.orgDOI: 10.3389/fpsyg.2021.649691

Newman, M. E. J. (2003). The structure and function of complex networks. *SIAM Review*, 45(2), 167–256. DOI: 10.1137/S003614450342480

Newman, M. E. J. (2004). Fast algorithm for detecting community structure in networks. *Physical Review. E*, 69(6), 066133. DOI: 10.1103/PhysRevE.69.066133 PMID: 15244693

Newman, M. E. J. (2006). Modularity and community structure in networks. *Proceedings of the National Academy of Sciences of the United States of America*, 103(23), 8577–8582. DOI: 10.1073/pnas.0601602103 PMID: 16723398

Newman, M. E. J., & Girvan, M. (2004). Finding and evaluating community structure in networks. *Physical Review. E*, 69(2), 026113. DOI: 10.1103/PhysRevE.69.026113 PMID: 14995526

Newman, M. E. J., Moore, C., & Watts, D. J. (2000). Mean-Field Solution of the Small-World Network Model. *Physical Review Letters*, 84(14), 3201–3204. DOI: 10.1103/PhysRevLett.84.3201 PMID: 11019047

Ng, A., Jordan, M., & Weiss, Y. (2001). On Spectral Clustering: Analysis and an algorithm. In T. Dietterich, S. Becker, & Z. Ghahramani (Eds.), *Advances in Neural Information Processing Systems* (Vol. 14). MIT Press. https://proceedings.neurips.cc/paper_files/paper/2001/file/801272ee79cfde7fa5960571fee36b9b-Paper.pdf

Nguyen, C. Q., Kariyawasam, D., Alba-Concepcion, K., Grattan, S., Hetherington, K., Wakefield, C. E., ... & Farrar, M. A. (2022). 'Advocacy groups are the connectors': Experiences and contributions of rare disease patient organization leaders in advanced neurotherapeutics. Health expectations, 25(6), 3175-3191. https://doi.org/ wiley.comDOI: 10.1111/hex.13625

Nguyen, D. T. B., & Nguyen, V. T. K. (2024). The Impact of Electronic Word-of-Mouth on the Purchase Intention of Tourists on Online Hotel Booking Applications. [IJABIM]. *International Journal of Asian Business and Information Management*, 15(1), 1–19. DOI: 10.4018/IJABIM.342086

Nikiel, J. (2022). The Forever Now: Foretelling the Present in William Gibson's Bigend Trilogy. It Takes a Storyteller to Know a Storyteller. https://doi.org/ [HTML] DOI: 10.1163/9789004533288_004

Ni, M. (2022). *Digital Participation for Inclusive Growth: A Case Study of Singapore's Collaborative Digital Governance Model.* Design for Vulnerable Communities. [HTML], DOI: 10.1007/978-3-030-96866-3_17

Nisar, T. M. N., Prabhakar, G., & Patil, P. P. (2018). Sports clubs' use of social media to increase spectator interest. *International Journal of Information Management*, 43, 188–195. DOI: 10.1016/j.ijinfomgt.2018.08.003

Nugroho, A., & Wang, W. T. (2024). Credibility of Youtube product reviews and customers' product return intention: A product fit uncertainty perspective. *Information Technology & People*, 37(4), 1560–1586. DOI: 10.1108/ITP-11-2021-0838

Obradović, M., Alčaković, S., Vyugina, D., & Tasevski, S. (2019). Use of social media in communication strategies of premier league football clubs. *International scientific conference on information technology and data related research,* 244-249. DOI: 10.15308/Sinteza-2019-244-249

O'Keefe, L., Rafferty, J., Gunder, A., & Vignare, K. (2020). Delivering High-Quality Instruction Online in Response to COVID-19: Faculty Playbook.. Online Learning Consortium. ed.gov

Ongsakul, V., Ali, F., Wu, C., Duan, Y., Cobanoglu, C., & Ryu, K. (2020). Hotel website quality, performance, telepresence and behavioral intentions. *Tourism Review*. Advance online publication.

Óskarsdóttira, M. *, Cristián Bravob, Wouter Verbekee, Carlos Sarrautef, Bart Baesensc,d, Jan VanthienencSocial "Network Analytics for Churn Prediction in Telco: Model Building, Evaluation and Network Architecture" arXiv:2001.06701v1 [cs. SI] 18 Jan 2020

Ozaki, N., Tezuka, H., & Inaba, M. (2016). A Simple Acceleration Method for the Louvain Algorithm. *International Journal of Computer and Electrical Engineering*, 8(3), 207–218. DOI: 10.17706/IJCEE.2016.8.3.207-218

Ozora, S., & Susanto, E. H. (2021). The Use of Instagram in an Effort to Attract Fans of the PSIM Jogja Soccer Club. *Advances in Social Science, Education and Humanities Research*, (570), 818–823. DOI: 10.2991/assehr.k.210805.129

Packard, N. (2020). Three Kinds of Demand Pull for the ARPANET into the Internet. Cogent Social Sciences. https://doi.org/tandfonline.comDOI: 10.1080/23311886.2020.1720565

Packard, N. (2023). Internet prehistory: ARPANET chronology. Cogent Social Sciences. https://doi.org/ tandfonline.comDOI: 10.1080/23311886.2023.2245237

Pandya, A. & Lodha, P. (2021). Social connectedness, excessive screen time during COVID-19 and mental health: a review of current evidence. Frontiers in Human Dynamics. https://doi.org/ frontiersin.orgDOI: 10.3389/fhumd.2021.684137

Pang, L. J., & Yang, Z. (2021). The Impact of Information Interaction on User Engagement Behavior in Virtual Brand Community. *Inform. Sci.*, 39, 108–115.

Parkin, S. (2023, June 10). Who needs the metaverse? Meet the people still living on Second Life. *The Guardian*.https://www.theguardian.com/technology/2023/jun/10/who-needs-the-metaverse-meet-the-people-still-living-on-second-life

Park, J. Y., & Lee, H. E. (2024). How Consumer Photo Reviews and Online Platform Types Influence Luxury Hotel Booking Intentions Through Envy. *Journal of Travel Research*, •••, 00472875241247317. DOI: 10.1177/00472875241247317

Park, R. (1936). Human Ecology. *American Journal of Sociology*, 17(1), 1–15. DOI: 10.1086/217327

Pasta, M. Q., & Zaidi, F. (2016a). Leveraging evolution dynamics to generate benchmark complex networks with community structures. *ArXiv Preprint ArXiv:1606.01169*.

Pasta, M. Q., & Zaidi, F. (2016b). Leveraging evolution dynamics to generate benchmark complex networks with community structures. *ArXiv Preprint ArXiv:1606.01169*.

Pasta, M. Q., Jan, Z., Sallaberry, A., & Zaidi, F. (2013). Tunable and Growing Network Generation Model with Community Structures. *2013 International Conference on Cloud and Green Computing*, 233–240. DOI: 10.1109/CGC.2013.44

Patel, P. S., Desai, N. D., Shah, S. H., & Shah, S. N. (2024). Lived experiences of bereaved family members during COVID-19 pandemic in a tertiary care hospital with special reference to imposed restrictive COVID guidelines—a qualitative study. OMEGA-Journal of Death and Dying, 89(1), 404-420. https://doi.org/ sagepub.comDOI: 10.1177/00302228221075207

Pedersen, P. M., Laucella, P. C., Kian, E. M., & Geurin, A. N. (2020). *Strategic Sport Communication* (3a Edição). United States of America: Human Kinetics. https://books.google.com/books?hl=pt-PT&lr=&id=LObsDwAAQBAJ&oi=fnd&pg=PP2&dq=Pedersen,+Paul+M.,+Laucella,+Pamela+C.,+Kian,+Edward+M.+%26+Geurin,+Andrea.+N.+(2020).+Strategic+Sport+Communication+(3a+Edição).+United+States+of+America:+Human+Kinetics.+&ots=FkOzivaSRv&sig=cRVSdGOwovzqTir24hp2nUgaFjE

Pedersen, P. M. (2017). *Routledge handbook of sport communication.* Routledege Taylor & Francis Group., https://api.taylorfrancis.com/content/books/mono/download?identifierName=doi&identifierValue=10.4324/9780203123485&type=googlepdf DOI: 10.4324/9781315088556

Penn, R. (2016). Football talk: Sociological reflections on the dialectics of language. *EJSS European Journal for Sport and Society*, 13(2), 154–166. DOI: 10.1080/16138171.2016.1183931

Pennycook, G., & Rand, D. G. (2021). The Implied Truth Effect: Attaching warnings to a subset of fake news stories increases perceived accuracy of stories without warnings. *Management Science*, 67(1), 508–527.

Perez, E., Manca, S., Fernández-Pascual, R., & Guckin, C. M. (2023). A systematic review of social media as a teaching and learning tool in higher education: A theoretical grounding perspective. *Education and Information Technologies*, 28(9), 11921–11950. DOI: 10.1007/s10639-023-11647-2

Petrlic, R. (2010). A privacy-preserving concept for smart grids. B1-B14.

Petty, R. E., & Cacioppo, J. T. (2012). *Communication and persuasion: Central and peripheral routes to attitude change.* Springer Science & Business Media.

Petzold, J., Andrews, N., Ford, J. D., Hedemann, C., & Postigo, J. C. (2020). Indigenous knowledge on climate change adaptation: A global evidence map of academic literature. In *Environmental Research Letters* (Vol. 15, Issue 11). DOI: 10.1088/1748-9326/abb330

Piatkowska, E., Bajraktari, A., Chhajed, D., & Smith, P. (2017). Tool support for data protection impact assessment in the smart grid. *E&I Elektrotechnik und Informationstechnik*, 134(1), 26–29. DOI: 10.1007/s00502-017-0484-4

Ponnusamy, S., Iranmanesh, M., Foroughi, B., & Hyun, S. S. (2020). Drivers and outcomes of Instagram Addiction: Psychological well-being as moderator. [HTML]. *Computers in Human Behavior*, 107, 106294. DOI: 10.1016/j.chb.2020.106294

Poor, N., Skoric, M., & Lampe, C. (2022). Death of a child, birth of a guild: Factors aiding the rapid formation of online support communities. [HTML]. *The Information Society*, 38(3), 188–199. Advance online publication. DOI: 10.1080/01972243.2022.2071219

Popenoe, R., Langius-Eklöf, A., Stenwall, E., & Jervaeus, A. (2021). A practical guide to data analysis in general literature reviews. Nordic journal of nursing research, 41(4), 175-186. http://dx.doi.org/sagepub.comDOI: 10.1177/2057158521991949

Popp, B., Germelmann, C., & Jung, B. (2016). We love to hate them! Social media-based anti-brand communities in professional football. *International Journal of Sports Marketing & Sponsorship*, 17(4), 349–367. DOI: 10.1108/IJSMS-11-2016-018

Porter, C. E. (2004). A Typology of Virtual Communities: A Multi-Disciplinary Foundation for Future Research. *Journal of Computer-Mediated Communication*, 10(1), 00. DOI: 10.1111/j.1083-6101.2004.tb00228.x

Pöyry, E. & Laaksonen, S. M. (2022). Opposing brand activism: triggers and strategies of consumers' antibrand actions. European Journal of Marketing. http://dx.doi .org/ emerald.comDOI: 10.1108/EJM-12-2020-0901

Preece, J. (2000). *Online Communities: Designing Usability, Supporting Sociability*. John Wiley & Sons.

Preece, J., & de Souza, C. S. (2004). A Framework for Analyzing and Understanding Online Communities. *Interacting with Computers*, 16(3), 579–610. DOI: 10.1016/j. intcom.2003.12.006

Price, D. J. (1966). *NETWORKS OF SCIENTIFIC PAPERS*.

Price, W. (2017). *The Evolution of Instagram* Ads [Infographic]. Sovial Media Today. Consultado em: 4 de janeiro de 2022. https://www.socialmediatoday.com/news/the -evolution-of-instagram-ads-infographic/507628/

Proctor, D. (2021). The social production of internet space: Affordance, programming, and virtuality. [HTML]. *Communication Theory*, 31(4), 593–612. Advance online publication. DOI: 10.1093/ct/qtz036

Psyllidis, A., Gao, S., Hu, Y., Kim, E. K., McKenzie, G., Purves, R., Yuan, M., & Andris, C. (2022). Points of Interest (POI): A commentary on the state of the art, challenges, and prospects for the future. *Computational Urban Science*, 2(1), 20. Advance online publication. DOI: 10.1007/s43762-022-00047-w PMID: 35789810

Qie, N., & Kang, X. (2023). Capabilities influencing cross-cultural communication in digital contexts: Exploration with a Chinese sample. In *Lecture notes in computer science* (pp. 126–141). DOI: 10.1007/978-3-031-35939-2_10

Que, X., Checconi, F., Petrini, F., & Gunnels, J. A. (2015). Scalable Community Detection with the Louvain Algorithm. *2015 IEEE International Parallel and Distributed Processing Symposium*, 28–37. DOI: 10.1109/IPDPS.2015.59

Quill, T. M. (2018). Humanitarian Mapping as Library Outreach: A Case for Community-Oriented Mapathons. *Journal of Web Librarianship*, 12(3), 160–168. Advance online publication. DOI: 10.1080/19322909.2018.1463585

Quinn, P. (2021). Research under the GDPR – a level playing field for public and private sector research? *Life Sciences, Society and Policy*, 17(1), 4. Advance online publication. DOI: 10.1186/s40504-021-00111-z PMID: 33648586

Quintela, J. (2020). O diretor de comunicação no futebol: perfis e tendências nos "três grandes" clubes portugueses. *PODIUM Sport, Leisure and Tourism Review, 9 (1),* 21- 41. https://periodicos.uninove.br/podium/article/view/13748

Rafdinal, W., Wibisono, N., & Setiawati, L. (2024). Customer-centric virtual reality applications adoption in the hospitality industry: quality-value-based adoption model. *Journal of Hospitality and Tourism Insights.*

Raghavan, U. N., Albert, R., & Kumara, S. (2007). Near linear time algorithm to detect community structures in large-scale networks. *Physical Review E: Statistical, Nonlinear, and Soft Matter Physics*, 76(3), 036106. Advance online publication. DOI: 10.1103/PhysRevE.76.036106 PMID: 17930305

Raji, M. A., Olodo, H. B., Oke, T. T., Addy, W. A., Ofodile, O. C., & Oyewole, A. T. (2024). Digital marketing in tourism: a review of practices in the USA and Africa. International Journal of Applied Research in Social Sciences, 6(3), 393-408. https://doi.org/fepbl.comDOI: 10.51594/ijarss.v6i3.896

Rakesh, V., & Hickok, E. (2023). Cyber security of smart grids in India. https://www.dqindia.com/cyber-security-of-smart-grids-in-india/

Ramayah, T. J. F. H., Cheah, J., Chuah, F., Ting, H., & Memon, M. A. (2018). Partial least squares structural equation modeling (PLS-SEM) using smartPLS 3.0. *An updated guide and practical guide to statistical analysis*, 978-967.

Raper, J. (2020). *Progress towards spatial multimedia.* Geographic Information Research. [HTML] DOI: 10.1201/9781003062691-41

Rasheed, S. (2011). Simulation of image encryption using AES algorithm.

Raviscioni, S., Rojas Bolanos, M. A., Gaspari, F., Ponti, C., Biraghi, C. A., & Tadi, M. (2022). COLLABORATIVE MAPPING STRATEGY IN SUPPORT OF SLUM UPGRADING: THE CASE OF BOGOTÁ. *International Archives of the Photogrammetry, Remote Sensing and Spatial Information Sciences - ISPRS Archives, 43*(B4-2022). DOI: 10.5194/isprs-archives-XLIII-B4-2022-273-2022

Ray, A., Bala, P. K., & Dwivedi, Y. K. (2020). Exploring values affecting e-Learning adoption from the user-generated-content: A consumption-value-theory perspective. *Journal of Strategic Marketing*, •••, 1–23.

Redjeki, F. & Affandi, A. (2021). Utilization of digital marketing for MSME players as value creation for customers during the COVID-19 pandemic. International Journal of Science and Society. https://doi.org/ researchgate.netDOI: 10.200609/ijsoc.v3i1.264

Rheingold, H. (1993). *The Virtual Community: Homesteading on the Electronic Frontier*. Addison-Wesley.

Rickman, H. P. (Ed.). (1976). *W. Dilthey: selected writings*. Cambridge University Press.

Ritterbusch, G. D. & Teichmann, M. R. (2023). Defining the metaverse: A systematic literature review. Ieee Access. https://doi.org/ieee.orgDOI: 10.1109/ACCESS.2023.3241809

Rive, P. B. (2012). *Design in a Virtual Innovation Ecology: A Cybernetic Systems Approach to Knowledge Creation and Design Collaboration in Second Life* (Doctoral dissertation, Open Access Te Herenga Waka-Victoria University of Wellington). https://openaccess.wgtn.ac.nz/articles/thesis/Design_in_a_Virtual_Innovation_Ecology_A_Cybernetic_Systems_Approach_to_Knowledge_Creation_and_Design_Collaboration_in_Second_Life/17004709

Rizvanović, B., Zutshi, A., Grilo, A., & Nodehi, T. (2023). Linking the potentials of extended digital marketing impact and start-up growth: Developing a macro-dynamic framework of start-up growth drivers supported by digital marketing. Technological Forecasting and Social Change, 186, 122128. https://doi.org/ sciencedirect.comDOI: 10.1016/j.techfore.2022.122128

Roberson, Q. & Perry, J. L. (2022). Inclusive leadership in thought and action: A thematic analysis. Group & Organization Management. https://doi.org/umich.eduDOI: 10.1177/10596011211013161

Roblox 17+ Policy Standards. (2023). Retrieved from https://en.help.roblox.com/hc/en-us/articles/15869919570708-Roblox-17-Policy-Standards

Rogers, R. (2020). Deplatforming: Following extreme Internet celebrities to Telegram and alternative social media. European Journal of Communication. http://dx.doi.org/ sagepub.comDOI: 10.1177/0267323120922066

Rojas-Sánchez, M. A., Palos-Sánchez, P. R., & Folgado-Fernández, J. A. (2023). Systematic literature review and bibliometric analysis on virtual reality and education. Education and Information Technologies, 28(1), 155-192. https://doi.org/ springer.comDOI: 10.1007/s10639-022-11167-5

Rong, J., Liu, W., Jiang, F., Cheng, Y., Li, H., & Peng, J. (2023). Privacy-aware optimal load scheduling for energy management system of smart home. *Sustainable Energy. Grids and Networks*, 34, 101039. DOI: 10.1016/j.segan.2023.101039

Rosedale, P. (2022, July 8). Value creation in virtual worlds. *Medium.* https://medium.com/@philiprosedale/value-creation-in-virtual-worlds-696604a694d1

Roy, G., & Shrivastava, A. K. (2020). Future of gig economy: opportunities and challenges. *Imi Konnect, 9*(1), 14-27.January-March 20.cdr (imik.edu.in)

Roy, S. K., Fatema, M. R., Islam, M. J., & Huda, M. N. (2020). Reviewing YouTube as a compelling tool for the promotion of tourism. *International Journal of Managing Account*, 2(5), 96–104.

Ruangkanjanases, A., Hsu, S. L., Wu, Y. J., Chen, S. C., & Chang, J. Y. (2020). What drives continuance intention towards social media? Social influence and identity perspectives. Sustainability, 12(17), 7081. http://dx.doi.org/mdpi.comDOI: 10.3390/su12177081

Rufino, G. G.Rufino, Gilliane G. (2024). Methods Used in YouTube for Teaching and Learning English Language: A Systematic Literature Review. *International Journal of English Language Studies*, 6(1), 82–97. DOI: 10.32996/ijels.2024.6.1.9

Ryu, S., & Kim, D. (2016). *Quick Community Detection of Big Graph Data Using Modified Louvain Algorithm.* https://doi.org/DOI: 10.1109/HPCC-SmartCity-DSS.2016.167

Sağkaya Güngör, A., & Ozansoy Çadırcı, T. (2022). Understanding digital consumer: A review, synthesis, and future research agenda. *International Journal of Consumer Studies*, 46(5), 1829–1858. DOI: 10.1111/ijcs.12809

Sahlberg, P., & Doyle, W. (2019). *Let the children play: How more play will save our schools and help children thrive*. Oxford University Press., https://books.google.be/books?hl=en&lr=&id=ny8DEAAAQBAJ&oi=fnd&pg=PP1&dq=%E2%80%9CPlay+is+not+frivolous:+it+enhances+brain+structure+and+function+and+promotes+executive+function%E2%80%9D&ots=ox84L6kTb3&sig=4igeE94L3cM04W-t-btsiB0HCgs&redir_esc=y#v=onepage&q=%E2%80%9CPlay%20is%20not%20frivolous%3A%20it%20enhances%20brain%20structure%20and%20function%20and%20promotes%20executive%20function%E2%80%9D&f=false

Sahu, A. S. (2022). Assessing internet and web services based webdom and virtual web-data-centric geographical study. GeoJournal. https://doi.org/springer.comDOI: 10.1007/s10708-021-10549-5

Saleem, A. N., Noori, N. M., & Ozdamli, F. (2021). Gamification Applications in e-learning: A Literature review. *Technology. Knowledge and Learning*, 27(1), 139–159. DOI: 10.1007/s10758-020-09487-x

Sallaberry, A., Zaidi, F., & Melançon, G. (2013). Model for generating artificial social networks having community structures with small-world and scale-free properties. *Social Network Analysis and Mining*, 3(3), 597–609. DOI: 10.1007/s13278-013-0105-0

Salloum, S. A., Al-Emran, M., Habes, M., Alghizzawi, M., Ghani, M. A., & Shaalan, K. (2019). It is important to understand the impact of social media practices on the acceptance of E-Learning Systems. In *Advances in intelligent systems and computing* (pp. 360–369). DOI: 10.1007/978-3-030-31129-2_33

Salmi, T. S., Benar, N., & Honari, H. (2019). Identifying value creation strategies in the brand communities of sport clubs based on the use of social media. *Annals of Applied Sport Science*, 7(2), 55–61. http://aassjournal.com/article-1-718-en.html. DOI: 10.29252/aassjournal.7.2.55

Sands, S., Ferraro, C., Demsar, V., & Chandler, G. (2022). False idols: Unpacking the opportunities and challenges of falsity in the context of virtual influencers. [HTML]. *Business Horizons*, 65(6), 777–788. Advance online publication. DOI: 10.1016/j.bushor.2022.08.002

Santos, D., Santos, C., Santos, J., Filho, A., & Saba, H. (2024). The Importance of the Facility Location Techniques to Assist Companies in Decision-Making for the Installation of Logistics Hub. *Open Journal of Business and Management*, 12(01), 79–89. Advance online publication. DOI: 10.4236/ojbm.2024.121006

Santoso, N. P. L., Sunarjo, R. A., & Fadli, I. S. (2023). Analyzing the Factors Influencing the Success of Business Incubation Programs: A SmartPLS Approach. *ADI Journal on Recent Innovation*, 5(1), 60–71. DOI: 10.34306/ajri.v5i1.985

Saputri, M. E. (2024). Faktor-Faktor Information Adoption Model terhadap Purchase Intention: Studi pada Media Sosial Tiktok Azarine Cosmetic. *Al-Kharaj: Jurnal Ekonomi. Keuangan & Bisnis Syariah*, 6(5), 3778–3790.

Saputro, N., & Akkaya, K. (2013). On preserving user privacy in smart grid advanced metering infrastructure applications. *Security and Communication Networks*, 7(1), 206–220. DOI: 10.1002/sec.706

Sarac, H. S. (2014). Benefits and challenges of using Second Life in English teaching: Experts' opinions. *Procedia: Social and Behavioral Sciences*, 158, 326–330. https://www.sciencedirect.com/science/article/pii/S1877042814061886. DOI: 10.1016/j.sbspro.2014.12.095

Scherr, S., & Wang, K. (2021). Explaining the success of social media with gratification niches: Motivations behind daytime, nighttime, and active use of TikTok in China. [HTML]. *Computers in Human Behavior*, 124, 106893. Advance online publication. DOI: 10.1016/j.chb.2021.106893

Schott, M., Grinberger, A. Y., Lautenbach, S., & Zipf, A. (2021). The impact of community happenings in openstreetmap-establishing a framework for online community member activity analyses. *ISPRS International Journal of Geo-Information*, 10(3), 164. Advance online publication. DOI: 10.3390/ijgi10030164

Schou, P. K., Bucher, E., & Waldkirch, M. (2022). Entrepreneurial learning in online communities. Small Business Economics. https://doi.org/springer.comDOI: 10.1007/s11187-021-00502-8

Schrage, M. (1990). *Shared Minds*. Random House.

Schrage, M. (1995). *No more teams: Mastering the dynamics of creative collaboration*. Currency.

Schuetz, P., & Caflisch, A. (2008). Efficient modularity optimization by multistep greedy algorithm and vertex mover refinement. *Physical Review. E*, 77(4), 046112. DOI: 10.1103/PhysRevE.77.046112 PMID: 18517695

Selem, K. M., Shoukat, M. H., Khalid, R., & Raza, M. (2024). Guest interaction with hotel booking website information: Scale development and validation of antecedents and consequences. *Journal of Hospitality Marketing & Management*, 33(5), 626–648. DOI: 10.1080/19368623.2023.2279174

Shahzad, K., Zhang, Q., & Khan, M. K. (2024). Blockchain technology adoption in supply chain management: An investigation from UTAUT and information system success model. *International Journal of Shipping and Transport Logistics*, 18(2), 165–190. DOI: 10.1504/IJSTL.2024.137893

Shang, J., Liu, L., Li, X., Xie, F., & Wu, C. (2016). Targeted revision: A learning-based approach for incremental community detection in dynamic networks. *Physica A*, 443, 70–85. DOI: 10.1016/j.physa.2015.09.072

Shao, D. & Lee, I. J. (2020). Acceptance and influencing factors of social virtual reality in the urban elderly. Sustainability. http://dx.doi.org/mdpi.comDOI: 10.3390/su12229345

Shin, D. H., & Biocca, F. (2020). The role of privacy concerns in shaping users' social media behavior. *Computers in Human Behavior*, 102, 139–147.

Sigala, M. (2024). Social Media and Crisis Communication: Managing or Creating a Crisis? Lessons Learnt from Hotel Amarilis. In *Case Based Research in Tourism, Travel, and Hospitality* (pp. 61–82). Springer. DOI: 10.1007/978-981-97-1891-7_4

Silaban, P. H., Chen, W. K., Nababan, T. S., Eunike, I. J., & Silalahi, A. D. K. (2022). How travel vlogs on YouTube influence consumer behavior: A use and gratification perspective and customer engagement. *Human Behavior and Emerging Technologies*, 2022, 1–16. DOI: 10.1155/2022/4432977

Simpson, S., Richardson, L., Pietrabissa, G., Castelnuovo, G., & Reid, C. (2021). Videotherapy and therapeutic alliance in the age of COVID-19. Clinical psychology & psychotherapy, 28(2), 409-421. https://doi.org/ wiley.comDOI: 10.1002/cpp.2521

Sirola, A., Savela, N., Savolainen, I., Kaakinen, M., & Oksanen, A. (2021). The role of virtual communities in gambling and gaming behaviors: A systematic review. Journal of Gambling Studies, 37(1), 165-187. https://doi.org/springer.comDOI: 10.1007/s10899-020-09946-1

Sivathanu, B., & Pillai, R. (2023). The effect of deepfake video advertisements on the hotel booking intention of tourists. *Journal of Hospitality and Tourism Insights*, 6(5), 1669–1687. DOI: 10.1108/JHTI-03-2022-0094

Skaalsveen, K., Ingram, J., & Urquhart, J. (2020). The role of farmers' social networks in the implementation of no-till farming practices. *Agricultural Systems*, 181, 102824. Advance online publication. DOI: 10.1016/j.agsy.2020.102824

Sousa, B., & Vieira, C. (2018). Um Estudo Sobre a Afetividade Aplicada ao Fenómeno do Futebol: Abordagemn na Ótica dos Consumidores. *PODIUM Sport, Leisure And. Podium (São Paulo)*, 7(2), 293–312. DOI: 10.5585/podium.v7i2.282

Sports, N. (2018). *World Football Report.* Nielsen Sports. Consultado em: 16 de novembro de 2021. https://www.nielsen.com/wp-content/uploads/sites/3/2019/04/world- football-report-2018.pdf

Stander, F. W., Llewellyn, E. V. Z., & Kemiso, M. (2016). Promoting fan engagement: An exploration of the fundamental motives for sport consumption amongst premier league football spectators. *Journal of Psychology in Africa*, 26(4), 309–315. DOI: 10.1080/14330237.2016.1208920

Statista. (2023). Leading social networks worldwide as of January 2023, ranked by number of monthly active users. Retrieved from https://www.statista.com/statistics/272014/global-social-networks-ranked-by-number-of-users/

Stavros, C., Meng, M., Westberg, K., & Farrelly, F. (2014). Understanding fan motivation for interacting on social media. *Sport Management Review*, 17(4), 455–469. DOI: 10.1016/j.smr.2013.11.004

Steigerwald, E., Ramírez-Castañeda, V., Brandt, D. Y. C., Báldi, A., Shapiro, J. T., Bowker, L., & Tarvin, R. D. (2022). Overcoming language barriers in academia: Machine translation tools and a vision for a multilingual future. *BioScience/Bioscience, 72*(10), 988–998. DOI: 10.1093/biosci/biac062

Stewart, O. G. (2015). A critical review of the literature on social media's affordances in the classroom. *E-Learning and Digital Media*, 12(5–6), 481–501. DOI: 10.1177/2042753016672895

Studies, A., Relations, P., Andreea, M., Studies, A., & Relations, P. (2012). Social media and marketing of the "Popcorn" music wave: The success of Romanian commercial musicians analysed through their perceived image on. 5(2), 125-139.

Sudarshan, S., Mehrotra, S., & Thirthalli, J. (2024). Effectiveness of Blended Internet-based Self-help and Face-to-face Intervention for Depression: A Pilot Study from India. Indian Journal of Psychological Medicine, 02537176241238289. https://doi.org/sagepub.comDOI: 10.1177/02537176241238289

Sun, B., Mao, H., & Yin, C. (2020). Male and female users' differences in online technology community based on text mining. Frontiers in Psychology. https://doi.org/ frontiersin.orgDOI: 10.3389/fpsyg.2020.00806

Sundararaj, V., & Rejeesh, M. R. (2021). A detailed behavioral analysis on consumer and customer changing behavior with respect to social networking sites. [HTML]. *Journal of Retailing and Consumer Services*, 58, 102190. Advance online publication. DOI: 10.1016/j.jretconser.2020.102190

Sutcliffe, A., & Alrayes, A. (2012). Investigating user experience in Second Life for collaborative learning. *International Journal of Human-Computer Studies*, 70(7), 508–525. https://www.sciencedirect.com/science/article/abs/pii/S1071581912000262. DOI: 10.1016/j.ijhcs.2012.01.005

Sycinska-Dziarnowska, M., & Paradowska-Stankiewicz, I. (2020). Dental challenges and the needs of the population during the covid-19 pandemic period. Real-time surveillance using google trends. International journal of environmental research and public health, 17(23), 8999. http://dx.doi.org/mdpi.comDOI: 10.3390/ijerph17238999

Szymkowiak, A., Melović, B., Dabić, M., Jeganathan, K., & Kundi, G. S. (2021). Information technology and Gen Z: The role of teachers, the internet, and technology in the education of young people. [HTML]. *Technology in Society*, 65, 101565. DOI: 10.1016/j.techsoc.2021.101565

Ta, T. (2024, May 28). *Breaking the Monotony: How AR VR could Revolutionize Virtual meetings*. Travancore Analytics. https://www.travancoreanalytics.com/ar-vr-in-virtual-meetings/

Talukder, A. K. (2020). The Next Generation Web: Technologies and Services. In Big Data Analytics: 8th International Conference, BDA 2020, Sonepat, India, December 15–18, 2020, Proceedings 8 (pp. 209-229). Springer International Publishing. [HTML]DOI: 10.1007/978-3-030-66665-1_14

Taneja, B. (2021). The digital edge for M-commerce to replace E-commerce. In *Emerging challenges, solutions, and best practices for digital enterprise transformation* (pp. 299–318). IGI Global. [HTML], DOI: 10.4018/978-1-7998-8587-0.ch016

Taouktsis, X., & Zikopoulos, C. (2024). A decision-making tool for the determination of the distribution center location in a humanitarian logistics network. *Expert Systems with Applications*, 238, 122010. Advance online publication. DOI: 10.1016/j.eswa.2023.122010

Tapp, A. (2004). The loyalty of football fans – we'll support you ever more? *The Journal of Database Marketing & Customer Strategy Management*, 11(3), 225–246. DOI: 10.1057/palgrave.dbm.3240221

Tariq, M. U. (2024). Harnessing Persuasive Technologies for Enhanced Learner Engagement and Motivation. In M. Sanmugam, D. Lim, N. Mohd Barkhaya, W. Wan Yahaya, & Z. Khlaif (Eds.), *Power of Persuasive Educational Technologies in Enhancing Learning* (pp. 30-62). IGI Global. https://doi.org/DOI: 10.4018/979-8-3693-6397-3.ch002

Tariq, M. U. (2024). Multidisciplinary service learning in higher education: Concepts, implementation, and impact. In S. Watson (Ed.), *Applications of service learning in higher education* (pp. 1-19). IGI Global. https://doi.org/DOI: 10.4018/979-8-3693-2133-1.ch001

Tariq, M. U. (2024). Neurodiversity inclusion and belonging strategies in the workplace. In J. Vázquez de Príncipe (Ed.), *Resilience of multicultural and multigenerational leadership and workplace experience* (pp. 182-201). IGI Global. https://doi.org/DOI: 10.4018/979-8-3693-1802-7.ch009

Tariq, M. U. (2024). AI and IoT in flood forecasting and mitigation: A comprehensive approach. In Ouaissa, M., Ouaissa, M., Boulouard, Z., Iwendi, C., & Krichen, M. (Eds.), *AI and IoT for proactive disaster management* (pp. 26–60). IGI Global., DOI: 10.4018/979-8-3693-3896-4.ch003

Tariq, M. U. (2024). AI and the future of talent management: Transforming recruitment and retention with machine learning. In Christiansen, B., Aziz, M., & O'Keeffe, E. (Eds.), *Global practices on effective talent acquisition and retention* (pp. 1–16). IGI Global., DOI: 10.4018/979-8-3693-1938-3.ch001

Tariq, M. U. (2024). Application of blockchain and Internet of Things (IoT) in modern business. In Sinha, M., Bhandari, A., Priya, S., & Kabiraj, S. (Eds.), *Future of customer engagement through marketing intelligence* (pp. 66–94). IGI Global., DOI: 10.4018/979-8-3693-2367-0.ch004

Tariq, M. U. (2024). Challenges of a metaverse shaping the future of entrepreneurship. In Inder, S., Dawra, S., Tennin, K., & Sharma, S. (Eds.), *New business frontiers in the metaverse* (pp. 155–173). IGI Global., DOI: 10.4018/979-8-3693-2422-6.ch011

Tariq, M. U. (2024). Crafting Authentic Narratives for Sustainable Branding. In Rodrigues, P. (Eds.), *Compelling Storytelling Narratives for Sustainable Branding* (pp. 194–229). IGI Global., DOI: 10.4018/979-8-3693-3326-6.ch011

Tariq, M. U. (2024). Cybersecurity Risk Assessment Models and Theories in the Travel and Tourism Industry. In Thealla, P., Nadda, V., Dadwal, S., Oztosun, L., & Cantafio, G. (Eds.), *Corporate Cybersecurity in the Aviation, Tourism, and Hospitality Sector* (pp. 1–17). IGI Global., DOI: 10.4018/979-8-3693-2715-9.ch001

Tariq, M. U. (2024). Emerging trends and innovations in blockchain-digital twin integration for green investments: A case study perspective. In Jafar, S., Rodriguez, R., Kannan, H., Akhtar, S., & Plugmann, P. (Eds.), *Harnessing blockchain-digital twin fusion for sustainable investments* (pp. 148–175). IGI Global., DOI: 10.4018/979-8-3693-1878-2.ch007

Tariq, M. U. (2024). Emotional intelligence in understanding and influencing consumer behavior. In Musiolik, T., Rodriguez, R., & Kannan, H. (Eds.), *AI impacts in digital consumer behavior* (pp. 56–81). IGI Global., DOI: 10.4018/979-8-3693-1918-5.ch003

Tariq, M. U. (2024). Empowering student entrepreneurs: From idea to execution. In Cantafio, G., & Munna, A. (Eds.), *Empowering students and elevating universities with innovation centers* (pp. 83–111). IGI Global., DOI: 10.4018/979-8-3693-1467-8.ch005

Tariq, M. U. (2024). Enhancing cybersecurity protocols in modern healthcare systems: Strategies and best practices. In Garcia, M., & de Almeida, R. (Eds.), *Transformative approaches to patient literacy and healthcare innovation* (pp. 223–241). IGI Global., DOI: 10.4018/979-8-3693-3661-8.ch011

Tariq, M. U. (2024). Enhancing Students and Learning Achievement as 21st-Century Skills Through Transdisciplinary Approaches. In Kumar, R., Ong, E., Anggoro, S., & Toh, T. (Eds.), *Transdisciplinary Approaches to Learning Outcomes in Higher Education* (pp. 220–257). IGI Global., DOI: 10.4018/979-8-3693-3699-1.ch007

Tariq, M. U. (2024). Equity and inclusion in learning ecosystems. In Al Husseiny, F., & Munna, A. (Eds.), *Preparing students for the future educational paradigm* (pp. 155–176). IGI Global., DOI: 10.4018/979-8-3693-1536-1.ch007

Tariq, M. U. (2024). Fintech startups and cryptocurrency in business: Revolutionizing entrepreneurship. In Kankaew, K., Nakpathom, P., Chnitphattana, A., Pitchayadejanant, K., & Kunnapapdeelert, S. (Eds.), *Applying business intelligence and innovation to entrepreneurship* (pp. 106–124). IGI Global., DOI: 10.4018/979-8-3693-1846-1.ch006

Tariq, M. U. (2024). Integration of IoMT for Enhanced Healthcare: Sleep Monitoring, Body Movement Detection, and Rehabilitation Evaluation. In Liu, H., Tripathy, R., & Bhattacharya, P. (Eds.), *Clinical Practice and Unmet Challenges in AI-Enhanced Healthcare Systems* (pp. 70–95). IGI Global., DOI: 10.4018/979-8-3693-2703-6.ch004

Tariq, M. U. (2024). Leading Smart Technologies and Innovations for E-Business 5.0: Applications and Management Frameworks. In Popkova, E. (Ed.), *Smart Technologies and Innovations in E-Business* (pp. 25–46). IGI Global., DOI: 10.4018/978-1-6684-7840-0.ch002

Tariq, M. U. (2024). Leveraging AI for Entrepreneurial Innovation in Healthcare. In Özsungur, F. (Ed.), *Generating Entrepreneurial Ideas With AI* (pp. 192–216). IGI Global., DOI: 10.4018/979-8-3693-3498-0.ch009

Tariq, M. U. (2024). Leveraging artificial intelligence for a sustainable and climate-neutral economy in Asia. In Ordóñez de Pablos, P., Almunawar, M., & Anshari, M. (Eds.), *Strengthening sustainable digitalization of Asian economy and society* (pp. 1–21). IGI Global., DOI: 10.4018/979-8-3693-1942-0.ch001

Tariq, M. U. (2024). Metaverse in business and commerce. In Kumar, J., Arora, M., & Erkol Bayram, G. (Eds.), *Exploring the use of metaverse in business and education* (pp. 47–72). IGI Global., DOI: 10.4018/979-8-3693-5868-9.ch004

Tariq, M. U. (2024). Multi-Agent Models in Healthcare System Design. In Dall'Acqua, L. (Ed.), *Bioethics of Cognitive Ergonomics and Digital Transition* (pp. 143–170). IGI Global., DOI: 10.4018/979-8-3693-2667-1.ch008

Tariq, M. U. (2024). Navigating the Personalization Pathway: Implementing Adaptive Learning Technologies in Higher Education. In Minh Tung, T. (Ed.), *Adaptive Learning Technologies for Higher Education* (pp. 265–291). IGI Global., DOI: 10.4018/979-8-3693-3641-0.ch012

Tariq, M. U. (2024). Revolutionizing health data management with blockchain technology: Enhancing security and efficiency in a digital era. In Garcia, M., & de Almeida, R. (Eds.), *Emerging technologies for health literacy and medical practice* (pp. 153–175). IGI Global., DOI: 10.4018/979-8-3693-1214-8.ch008

Tariq, M. U. (2024). Smart Transportation Systems: Paving the Way for Sustainable Urban Mobility. In Munuhwa, S. (Ed.), *Contemporary Solutions for Sustainable Transportation Practices* (pp. 254–283). IGI Global., DOI: 10.4018/979-8-3693-3755-4.ch010

Tariq, M. U. (2024). Social Innovations for Improving Healthcare. In Chandan, H. (Ed.), *Social Innovations in Education, Environment, and Healthcare* (pp. 302–317). IGI Global., DOI: 10.4018/979-8-3693-2569-8.ch015

Tariq, M. U. (2024). The role of AI ethics in cost and complexity reduction. In Tennin, K., Ray, S., & Sorg, J. (Eds.), *Cases on AI ethics in business* (pp. 59–78). IGI Global., DOI: 10.4018/979-8-3693-2643-5.ch004

Tariq, M. U. (2024). The role of AI in skilling, upskilling, and reskilling the workforce. In Doshi, R., Dadhich, M., Poddar, S., & Hiran, K. (Eds.), *Integrating generative AI in education to achieve sustainable development goals* (pp. 421–433). IGI Global., DOI: 10.4018/979-8-3693-2440-0.ch023

Tariq, M. U. (2024). The role of emerging technologies in shaping the global digital government landscape. In Guo, Y. (Ed.), *Emerging developments and technologies in digital government* (pp. 160–180). IGI Global., DOI: 10.4018/979-8-3693-2363-2.ch009

Tariq, M. U. (2024). The transformation of healthcare through AI-driven diagnostics. In Sharma, A., Chanderwal, N., Tyagi, S., Upadhyay, P., & Tyagi, A. (Eds.), *Enhancing medical imaging with emerging technologies* (pp. 250–264). IGI Global., DOI: 10.4018/979-8-3693-5261-8.ch015

Tariq, M., Ali, M., Naeem, F., & Poor, H. V. (2021). Vulnerability assessment of 6G-enabled smart grid cyber–physical systems. *IEEE Internet of Things Journal*, 8(7), 5468–5475. DOI: 10.1109/JIOT.2020.3042090

Teo, L. X., Leng, H. K., & Phua, Y. X. P. (2019). Marketing on Instagram. *International Journal of Sports Marketing & Sponsorship*, 2(20), 321–332. DOI: 10.1108/IJSMS-04-2018-0028

Thalheim, B., Jaakkola, H., Nakanishi, T., Sasaki, S., & Schewe, K.-D. (2014). Conceptual Modelling of Collaboration for Information Systems. In Tokuda, T., Kiyoki, Y., Jaakkola, H., & Yoshida, N. (Eds.), *Information Modelling and Knowledge Bases XXV* (pp. 272–305).

Thompson, A.-J., Martin, A., Gee, S., & Geurin, A. N. (2018). Building brand and fan relationships through social media. *Sport, Business and Management*, 8(3), 235–256. DOI: 10.1108/SBM-04-2017-0024

Torous, J., Bucci, S., Bell, I. H., Kessing, L. V., Faurholt-Jepsen, M., Whelan, P., ... & Firth, J. (2021). The growing field of digital psychiatry: current evidence and the future of apps, social media, chatbots, and virtual reality. World Psychiatry, 20(3), 318-335. https://doi.org/wiley.comDOI: 10.1002/wps.20883

Traag, V. A. (2015). *Faster unfolding of communities: speeding up the Louvain algorithm*. DOI: 10.1103/PhysRevE.92.032801

Trivedi, M. H., Minhajuddin, A., Slater, H., Baronia, R., Blader, J. C., Blood, J., ... & Wakefield, S. M. (2023). Texas Youth Depression and Suicide Research Network (TX-YDSRN) research registry and learning healthcare network: Rationale, design, and baseline characteristics. Journal of affective disorders, 340, 88-99. https://doi.org/ sciencedirect.comDOI: 10.1016/j.jad.2023.07.035

Tseng, S. Y., & Wang, C. N. (2016). Perceived risk influence on dual-route information adoption processes on travel websites. *Journal of Business Research*, 69(6), 2289–2296. DOI: 10.1016/j.jbusres.2015.12.044

Turkle, S. (1997). *Life on the Screen: Identity in the Age of the Internet*. Simon & Schuster.

Turnbull, J., Searle, A., & Lorimer, J. (2023). Anthropause environmentalisms: Noticing natures with the self-isolating bird club. Transactions of the Institute of British Geographers, 48(2), 232-248. https://doi.org/ wiley.comDOI: 10.1111/tran.12569

Tzavella, K., Skopeliti, A., & Fekete, A. (2022). Volunteered geographic information use in crisis, emergency and disaster management: A scoping review and a web atlas. *Geo-Spatial Information Science*. Advance online publication. DOI: 10.1080/10095020.2022.2139642

UEFA. (2022). *History: Seasons*. UEFA. Consultado em: 15 de novembro de 2021. https://pt.uefa.com/uefaeuro/history/seasons/1980/

Ufholz, K. (2020). Peer support groups for weight loss. Current Cardiovascular Risk Reports. https://doi.org/springer.comDOI: 10.1007/s12170-020-00654-4

Uludag, S., Zeadally, S., & Badra, M. (2015). Techniques, taxonomy, and challenges of privacy protection in the smart grid. In Zeadally, S., & Badra, M. (Eds.), *Privacy in a Digital, Networked World. Computer Communications and Networks*. Springer., DOI: 10.1007/978-3-319-08470-1_15

Usman, J. (2021). The Discourse of Propaganda in Traveloka's YouTube Advertising Videos. *Indonesian Journal of EFL and Linguistics*, 5(1), 175–194.

Vale, L., & Fernandes, T. (2018). Social media and sports: Driving fan engagement with football clubs on Facebook. *Journal of Strategic Marketing*, 26(1), 1, 37–55. DOI: 10.1080/0965254X.2017.1359655

Valkenburg, P. M., Beyens, I., Pouwels, J. L., van Driel, I. I., & Keijsers, L. (2022). Social media use and adolescents' well-being: Developing a typology of person-specific effects. *Child Development*, 93(5), e322–e338.

Van Dijk, J. (1999). *The Network Society*. Sage.

Van Dongen, S. (2000). Graph clustering by flow simulation. *PhD Thesis, University of Utrecht*.

van Doorn, J., Lemon, K. N., Mittal, V., Nass, S., Pick, D., Pirner, P., & Verhoef, P. C. (2010). Customer Engagement Behavior: Theoretical Foundations and Research Directions. *Journal of Service Research*, 13(3), 253–266. DOI: 10.1177/1094670510375599

Van Engen, K. J., Dey, A., Runge, N., Spehar, B., Sommers, M. S., & Peelle, J. E. (2020). Effects of age, word frequency, and noise on the time course of spoken word recognition. Collabra: Psychology, 6(1), 17247. https://doi.org/nih.govDOI: 10.1525%2Fcollabra.17247

Van Esch, P., & Black, J. S. (2023). Virtual reality and social presence: The potential of VR to enhance social media engagement. *JMR, Journal of Marketing Research*, 60(1), 45–58.

Van Est, R., Van den Hoven, J., & Lokhorst, G.-J. (2017). Social and ethical implications of creating artificial moral agents for healthcare. *Science and Engineering Ethics*, 23(2), 431–448. PMID: 27380187

Ventre, I., & Kolbe, D. (2020). The Impact of Perceived Usefulness of Online Reviews, Trust and Perceived Risk on Online Purchase Intention in Emerging Markets: A Mexican Perspective. *Journal of International Consumer Marketing*, 32(4), 1–13. DOI: 10.1080/08961530.2020.1712293

Verduyn, P., Ybarra, O., Résibois, M., Jonides, J., & Kross, E. (2020). Do social network sites enhance or undermine subjective well-being? A critical review. *Social Issues and Policy Review*, 14(1), 274–302. DOI: 10.1111/sipr.12033

Vogt, A., Flacke, J., Pfeffer, K., Hoefsloot, F. I., Strugar Kolesnik, J., & Schnell, J. (2023). Development of an inclusive Mapping Application in a Co-Design Process. *AGILE: GIScience Series*, 4, 1–8. Advance online publication. DOI: 10.5194/agile-giss-4-48-2023

Vosoughi, S., Roy, D., & Aral, S. (2018). The spread of true and false news online. *Science*, 359(6380), 1146–1151. DOI: 10.1126/science.aap9559 PMID: 29590045

Wakita, K., & Tsurumi, T. (2007). Finding community structure in mega-scale social networks. *Proceedings of the 16th International Conference on World Wide Web*, 1275–1276. DOI: 10.1145/1242572.1242805

Waltman, L., & Van Eck, N. J. (2013). A smart local moving algorithm for large-scale modularity-based community detection. *The European Physical Journal B*, 86(11), 471. Advance online publication. DOI: 10.1140/epjb/e2013-40829-0

Wang, K., Tai, C. F., & Hu, H. (2023). Social influence processes within MMORPG guilds: A mixed-methods approach of nomological network analysis. [HTML]. *Information Technology & People*. Advance online publication. DOI: 10.1108/ITP-09-2022-0726

Wang, X., Sun, J., & Wen, H. (2019). Tourism seasonality, online user rating and hotel price: A quantitative approach based on the hedonic price model. *International Journal of Hospitality Management*, 79, 140–147. DOI: 10.1016/j.ijhm.2019.01.007

Wang, Y., Asaad, Y., & Filieri, R. (2020). What makes hosts trust Airbnb? Antecedents of hosts' trust toward Airbnb and its impact on continuance intention. *Journal of Travel Research*, 59(4), 686–703. DOI: 10.1177/0047287519855135

Warschauer, M. (2003). *Technology and social inclusion: Rethinking the digital divide*. MIT Press. DOI: 10.7551/mitpress/6699.001.0001

Watkinson, K., Huck, J. J., & Harris, A. (2023). Using gamification to increase map data production during humanitarian volunteered geographic information (VGI) campaigns. *Cartography and Geographic Information Science*, 50(1), 79–95. Advance online publication. DOI: 10.1080/15230406.2022.2156389

Watts, D. J., & Strogatz, S. H. (1998). Collective dynamics of 'small-world' networks. *Nature*, 393(6684), 440–442. DOI: 10.1038/30918 PMID: 9623998

Wellman, B. (1999). The Network Community. In Wellman, B. (Ed.), *Networks in the Global Village*. Westview Press.

Wenger, E. (1999). *Communities of Practice: Learning, Meaning, and Identity*. Cambridge University Press.

Wenger, E. (2000). Wenger (2000). Communities of Practice and Social Learning Systems. *Organization*, 7(2), 225–246. DOI: 10.1177/135050840072002

Wen, Y. (2020). Augmented reality enhanced cognitive engagement: Designing classroom-based collaborative learning activities for young language learners. *Educational Technology Research and Development*, 69(2), 843–860. DOI: 10.1007/s11423-020-09893-z

Whyte, C. (2023). Cyberspace is what states make of it: The social construction (and deconstruction) of strategic concepts. [HTML]. *Comparative Strategy*, 42(1), 128–151. Advance online publication. DOI: 10.1080/01495933.2022.2158031

William, J., & Chinn, S. (2010). Meeting Relationship-Marketing Goals Through Social Media: A Conceptual Model for Sport Marketers. *International Journal of Sport Communication*, 3(4), 422–437. DOI: 10.1123/ijsc.3.4.422

Williams, D., O'Brien, D., & Kramers, E. (2003). The Atlas of Canada Web Mapping: The User Counts. *Cartographic Perspectives*, 44(44), 8–28. Advance online publication. DOI: 10.14714/CP44.512

Winanda, M., Satriawan, A., & Gondokaryono, Y. S. (2014). Smart grid secure data transmission for high voltage grid. In *2014 International Conference on Information Technology Systems and Innovation (ICITSI)*. https://doi.org/DOI: 10.1109/ICITSI.2014.7048240

Wood, D. J., & Gray, B. (1991). Toward a Comprehensive Theory of Collaboration. *The Journal of Applied Behavioral Science*, 27(2), 139–162. DOI: 10.1177/0021886391272001

Wu, S., & Mariano, B. (2023). Emerging technologies and global health: A systematic review generating bibliometric evidence for innovation management. *BMJ Innovations*, 9(3), 165–176. DOI: 10.1136/bmjinnov-2022-001064

Xie, Z., Li, X., & Wang, X. (2007). A new community-based evolving network model. *Physica A*, 384(2), 725–732. DOI: 10.1016/j.physa.2007.05.031

Xu, X.-J., Zhang, X., & Mendes, J. F. F. (2009). Growing community networks with local events. *Physica A*, 388(7), 1273–1278. DOI: 10.1016/j.physa.2008.12.022

Xu, Y., An, Z., Jin, D., Liang, W., & Hu, W. (2021). Privacy-preserving data aggregation in smart grids: A survey. *IEEE Access : Practical Innovations, Open Solutions*, 9, 57122–57133. DOI: 10.1109/ACCESS.2021.3068951

Yadlin-Segal, A. & Oppenheim, Y. (2021). Whose dystopia is it anyway? Deepfakes and social media regulation. Convergence. https://doi.org/sagepub.comDOI: 10.1177/1354856520923963

Yan, Y., Feng, C. C., Huang, W., Fan, H., Wang, Y. C., & Zipf, A. (2020). Volunteered geographic information research in the first decade: a narrative review of selected journal articles in GIScience. In *International Journal of Geographical Information Science* (Vol. 34, Issue 9). DOI: 10.1080/13658816.2020.1730848

Yang, H. L., Wu, Y. Y., Lin, X. Y., Xie, L., Zhang, S., Zhang, S. Q., ... & Zheng, X. D. (2021). Internet use, life satisfaction, and subjective well-being among the elderly: evidence from 2017 China general social survey. Frontiers in Public Health, 9, 677643. https://doi.org/ frontiersin.orgDOI: 10.3389/fpubh.2021.677643

Yang, M. S., Hu, S. G., Kpandika, B. E., & Liu, L. (2021). Effects of social attachment on social media continuous usage intention: The mediating role of affective commitment. *Human Systems Management*, 40(4), 619–631. DOI: 10.3233/HSM-201057

Yin, E., & Mahrous, A. (2022). Covid-19 global pandemic, workplace spirituality and the rise of spirituality-driven organisations in the post-digital era. Journal of Humanities and Applied Social Sciences, 4(2), 79-93. http://dx.doi.org/emerald.comDOI: 10.1108/JHASS-11-2021-0177

Yoo, M., Singh, A. K., & Loewy, N. (2024). Predicting hotel booking cancelation with machine learning techniques. *Journal of Hospitality and Tourism Technology*, 15(1), 54–69. DOI: 10.1108/JHTT-07-2022-0227

Yoshida, M., Gordon, B. S., Nakazawa, M., Shibuya, S., & Fujiwara, N. (2018). Bridging the gap between social media and behavioral brand loyalty. *Electronic Commerce Research and Applications*, 28, 208–218. DOI: 10.1016/j.elerap.2018.02.005

Yuan, L., Deng, X., & Zhong, W. (2021). Encouraging Passive Members of Online Brand Communities to Generate eWOM Based on TAM and Social Capital Theory. *IEEE Access : Practical Innovations, Open Solutions*, 9, 12840–12851. DOI: 10.1109/ACCESS.2021.3050162

Yu, H., Ryoo, Y., & Han, E. (2024). Mind over matter: How biased perceptions of political knowledge influence selection and evaluation of political YouTube channels. *Internet Research*, 34(2), 474–494. DOI: 10.1108/INTR-09-2021-0677

Yulia, H. (2020). Online learning to prevent the spread of pandemic corona virus in Indonesia. ETERNAL (English Teaching Journal). upgris.ac.id

Yuna, D., Xiaokun, L., Jianing, L., & Lu, H. (2022). Cross-cultural communication on social media: Review from the cultural psychology and neuroscience perspective. *Frontiers in Psychology*, 13. Advance online publication. DOI: 10.3389/fpsyg.2022.858900 PMID: 35356358

Yu, X., Wang, C. X., & Spector, J. M. (2020). Factors that impact social networking in online self-regulated learning activities. [HTML]. *Educational Technology Research and Development*, 68(6), 3077–3095. DOI: 10.1007/s11423-020-09843-9

Zachary, W. W. (1977). An information flow model for conflict and fission in small groups. *Journal of Anthropological Research*, 33(4), 452–473. DOI: 10.1086/jar.33.4.3629752

Zahrah, I. N. (2024). Vlogger and Brand Credibility Perception: A Systematic Literature Review of Endorsement Effectiveness in Youtube Vlogs. *Jurnal Indonesia Sosial Teknologi*, 5(2), 445–459. DOI: 10.59141/jist.v5i2.905

Zaidi, F. (2013). Small world networks and clustered small world networks with random connectivity. *Social Network Analysis and Mining*, 3(1), 51–63. DOI: 10.1007/s13278-012-0052-1

Zakar, R., Iqbal, S., Zakar, M. Z., & Fischer, F. (2021). COVID-19 and health information seeking behavior: digital health literacy survey amongst university students in Pakistan. International Journal of Environmental Research and Public Health, 18(8), 4009. https://doi.org/ mdpi.comDOI: 10.3390/ijerph18084009

Zarei, E., & Jabbarzadeh, A. (2019). Knowledge management and social media: A scientometrics survey. International Journal of Data and Network Science, 3(4), 359-378. https://doi.org/Top of FormDOI: 10.5267/j.ijdns.2019.2.008

Zeadally, S., Pathan, A.-S. K., Alcaraz, C., & Badra, M. (2012). Towards privacy protection in smart grid. *Wireless Personal Communications*, 73(1), 23–50. DOI: 10.1007/s11277-012-0939-1

Zentai, L. (2013). The evolution of cartographic visualization in the Digital Era. *Sharing Knowledge*, 146.

Zhang, D., Ma, J., & He, Z. (2024). The effect of emotional changes in composite reviews on consumers' information adoption from a dual perspective. *Industrial Management & Data Systems*, 124(6), 2205–2229. DOI: 10.1108/IMDS-06-2023-0396

Zhang, H., Zhang, Y., Zhang, Q., & Tian, D. (2018). Inference attacks on privacy-preserving data publishing: A survey. *IEEE Access : Practical Innovations, Open Solutions*, 6, 29920–29936. DOI: 10.1109/ACCESS.2018.2849282

Zhang, R. Y., & Tang, C. H. H. (2024). The impact of partitioned pricing on hotel booking and the moderating effect of temporal distance. *International Journal of Hospitality Management*, 116, 103621. DOI: 10.1016/j.ijhm.2023.103621

Zhang, Y. (2023). The Influence of Game-Enhanced Communication on EFL Learners' Pragmatic Competence in Compliment Responses. [HTML]. *Applied Linguistics*, amad082. Advance online publication. DOI: 10.1093/applin/amad082

Zhang, Y., Xia, X., Xu, X., Yu, F., Wu, H., Yu, Y., & Wei, B. (2020). Robust Hierarchical Overlapping Community Detection With Personalized PageRank. *IEEE Access : Practical Innovations, Open Solutions*, 8, 102867–102882. DOI: 10.1109/ACCESS.2020.2998860

Zhang, Z., Pu, P., Han, D., & Tang, M. (2018). Self-adaptive Louvain algorithm: Fast and stable community detection algorithm based on the principle of small probability event. *Physica A*, 506, 975–986. DOI: 10.1016/j.physa.2018.04.036

Zhou, X., Xiang, L., & Xiao-Fan, W. (2008). Weighted Evolving Networks with Self-organized Communities. *Communications in Theoretical Physics*, 50(1), 261–266. DOI: 10.1088/0253-6102/50/1/50

Zhou, Z., Wang, R., & Zhan, G. (2022). Cultivating consumer subjective well-being through online brand communities: A multidimensional view of social capital. [HTML]. *Journal of Product and Brand Management*. Advance online publication. DOI: 10.1108/JPBM-12-2020-3267

Zhu, Y., & Xie, B. B. (2018). The relationship between the perceived climate of team Cha-xu and employee silence: Research on affective commitment and traditionality. *Acta Psychologica Sinica*, 50(5), 539–548. DOI: 10.3724/SP.J.1041.2018.00539

Zniva, R., Weitzl, W. J., & Lindmoser, C. (2023). Be constantly different! How to manage influencer authenticity. *Electronic Commerce Research*, 23(3), 1485–1514. DOI: 10.1007/s10660-022-09653-6

About the Contributors

Munir Ahmad is a seasoned professional in the realm of Spatial Data Infrastructure (SDI), Geo-Information Productions, Information Systems, and Information Governance, boasting over 25 years of dedicated experience in the field. With a PhD in Computer Science, Dr. Ahmad's expertise spans Spatial Data Production, Management, Processing, Analysis, Visualization, and Quality Control. Throughout his career, Dr. Ahmad has been deeply involved in the development and deployment of SDI systems specially in the context of Pakistan, leveraging his proficiency in Spatial Database Design, Web, Mobile & Desktop GIS, and Geo Web Services Architecture. His contributions to Volunteered Geographic Information (VGI) and Open Source Geoportal & Metadata Portal have significantly enriched the geospatial community. As a trainer and researcher, Dr. Ahmad has authored over 50 publications, advancing the industry's knowledge base and fostering innovation in Geo-Tech, Data Governance, and Information Infrastructure, and Emerging Technologies. His commitment to Research and Development (R&D) is evident in his role as a dedicated educator and mentor in the field.

Marta Araújo Master in Communication Sciences with a specialization in Communication, Marketing and Advertising from the Universidade Católica Portuguesa, and a degree in Public Relations and Social Communication from the Escola Superior de Comunicação Social. Academic interest in the areas of sports communication, digital and operational marketing, and e-commerce.

Andi Asrifan, S.Pd, M.Pd, a distinguished figure in the realm of education, particularly in English Language Education, has made significant contributions through his extensive research, teaching, and leadership roles. As the Head of the Institute for Cooperation and International Affairs at Universitas Muhammadiyah Sidenreng Rappang, Dr. Asrifan's academic journey is marked by a rich tapestry of achievements, including a Doctor of Education in English Language Education. His work spans various facets of education, language, and technology, reflecting the diverse topics covered in his publications and research endeavors. These include, but are not limited to, the impact of the COVID-19 pandemic on educational practices, methodologies in English as a Foreign Language (EFL) classrooms, and the integration of technology in teaching and learning processes. Dr. Asrifan's commitment to advancing educational standards and practices is further evidenced by his active participation in international conferences, webinars, and workshops across countries like India, the Philippines, and Pakistan. These events, organized by various institutions and associations, underscore his role as a global educator and thought leader. His dedication to professional development is also highlighted through his involvement in numerous courses and certifications in personal branding, public speaking, and literacy teaching. Moreover, Dr. Asrifan's leadership extends beyond academia into organizational and educational development, where he has served in various capacities, including as an external examiner for Ph.D. dissertations and a reviewer for scientific journals. His accolades, memberships in professional organizations, and roles as an ambassador for international associations speak volumes of his influence and commitment to fostering educational excellence and sustainable development goals globally.

Manuel Bolognesi is an entrepreneur and innovator in virtual-world content and experience creation, with a track record of success that started when he was a young teenager in the virtual world of Second Life. With a vast customer base of both clients and businesses, Manuel quickly became one of the top entrepreneurs in the virtual world, gaining direct access and advertising capabilities to multiple communities of active virtual-world users. Over the years, his first-hand expertise in product strategy and design has led to successful collaborations with professionals and teams across multiple virtual-world platforms, positioning him as an expert in the field. As the founder and administrator of Enrapture, Manuel brings his entrepreneurial background and expertise to the forefront, as well as his experience as a business development specialist and Metaverse Expert. He has been involved in the organization of NFT live minting projects during prominent industry events for news publishers and co-authored articles on Metaverse and Web3 topics, which have been featured by the likes of "Future of Marketing Institute," "Moonshot News," "Dialogue Agency," and "What's New in Publishing."

Anita Candra Dewi has established herself as a prominent figure in the educational sector, particularly in Makassar, where she has contributed significantly as a civil servant, lecturer, and teacher across various educational institutions. With a profound academic background, Dr. Dewi holds a doctoral degree (S-3) in Indonesian Language Education, showcasing her deep commitment and expertise in language and education. Her academic journey is a testament to her dedication to advancing the study and teaching of the Indonesian language and literature. Beyond her formal teaching roles, Dr. Dewi is actively involved in the broader educational community by participating in numerous seminars, workshops, and training sessions. These activities highlight her eagerness to stay at the forefront of educational methodologies and pedagogical innovations, particularly in the realm of language education. Her involvement in these events allows her to share her insights and expertise with fellow educators and students and enables her to learn and adapt to the evolving educational landscape continuously. Dr. Dewi's contributions to the field extend into scholarly work as well. She has authored several academic papers and books on language learning and literature. These publications serve as valuable resources for students, educators, and researchers, offering fresh perspectives and practical strategies for teaching and learning the Indonesian language and exploring its rich literary traditions. Through her multifaceted career, Dr. Anita Candra Dewi exemplifies the role of an educator who is deeply invested in both the theoretical and practical aspects of language education, making significant strides in enhancing the quality and accessibility of language learning in Indonesia.

Alexandre Duarte With a PhD in Communication Sciences from University of Minho, a Master degree in Communication & Image and a Bachelor in Markcting & Advertising by IADE, Alexandre is an Assistant Professor in Universidade NOVA de Lisboa, invited Professor in Universidade Católica Portuguesa and researcher of the R&D Unit ICNOVA (Universidade Nova de Lisboa). Throughout his career, Alexandre had the opportunity to work for several multinational advertising agencies such as TBWA, Saatchi & Saatchi, Ogilvy, W/Portugal, W/Brazil, Lowe&Partners, or BrandiaCentral as a Senior Creative Copywriter. Author of many seminars on communication, regularly participates in different conferences and lectures in both business and academic contexts. Between 2012 and 2014, was the Tutor of the EUROBEST Young Marketers Academy and in the beginning of 2014, was appointed CEO of RESTART, an Institute of Creativity, Arts and New Technologies. In 2018 was invited to teach in the UNIVERSIDADE CATÓLICA PORTUGUESA, where now Coordinates the Post Graduations Courses in Advertising&Creativity and Service Design and, in 2019 was re-elected member of the Directors Board of EDCOM.

Nabanita Ghosh Am a dedicated professional in commerce. Am a qualified Cost Accountant and having a keen interest in the field of finance Has passion for researching, learning and wish to work as an editor.

Jane Godbehear is an accomplished expert in the areas of Ethical International Commerce, BioTech, and Virtual Sustainability. With a degree in computing and information technology, as well as a diploma in small business and electronic bookkeeping, Jane has a wide-ranging skill set that allows her to bring a unique perspective to the table at Enrapture. Jane is also a 3D virtual-world artist with over 13 years of experience in creating 3D virtual-world landscapes, drafts, and project sketches for real-life projects. Her experience as a system analyst, scenario thinker, and change management professional is an asset to everyday operations at the company. She is committed to driving innovation and progress in the areas of virtual sustainability and ethical international commerce, using her expertise to help organizations achieve their goals while remaining ethically and socially responsible. In addition to her professional experience, Jane has also worked extensively with children's psychology and children learning, allowing her to bring a nuanced approach to her work that takes into account a variety of factors and perspectives, leading to great contributions when creating games aimed at a young user base.

Javier Gonzalez Nuñez He is a professor at the Strategy and General Management Department. He holds a degree in Finance from the University of Derby in England, an MBA from ENEB in Spain and a Master in Financial Management from the latter institution, as well as a Master in Finance from ICHEC Brussels School of Management in Belgium and in Innovation Management and Entrepreneurship from HEC Paris, France. He attended the Global Advanced Management Program at the Instituto de Empresa (IE) in Spain. He participated and graduated from the International Teachers Program (ITP) at Insead. He complemented his education with executive programs at Harvard, Wharton and Insead. Founding partner and CEO of Tonic Teaching, a strategy and innovation consultancy; and of HOPE (Higher Education for Disadvantaged Populations and Refugees). He has been project manager for Sanofi, Lombard (Luxembourg) and UJA (India). He is a strategy and innovation consultant for the United Nations, EUIPO (European Union Intellectual Property Agency), Governments of Belgium and the Netherlands, Airbus, Neom, among others; as well as member of boards of directors and advisory boards of several startups; and mentor of projects with social and environmental impact at MIT, USA.

Herlina, M.Pd., stands out as a distinguished academician with a comprehensive background in early childhood education. Her journey in the educational sector is marked by a blend of extensive educational qualifications and a rich tapestry of work experiences that span across various facets of early childhood education. Dr. Herlina's commitment to the field is further underscored by her active participation in numerous organizational activities and research projects, which highlight her dedication to advancing educational practices and policies. Her scholarly contributions are evident in her array of scientific publications, which not only add to the body of knowledge in her field but also serve as a testament to her expertise and scholarly rigor. Beyond her academic and professional endeavors, Dr. Herlina has also proven her mettle in the competitive arena of scientific research and innovation. Her prowess was nationally recognized when she emerged as a winner in a prestigious national scientific work competition. This accolade is not just a personal achievement for Dr. Herlina but also a moment of pride for the academic and educational communities she represents. It underscores her ability to blend theoretical knowledge with practical insights, thereby creating impactful educational solutions and innovations. Dr. Herlina's journey and achievements illuminate the path for future educators and researchers, embodying the essence of dedication, innovation, and excellence in the field of early childhood education.

Ira Irviana, S.Pd., M.Pd., is an accomplished educator and researcher specializing in primary education. Born on February 18, 1990, in Ujung Pandang, she has dedicated her career to improving educational outcomes for elementary students. Ira completed her undergraduate studies in Elementary School Teacher Education at Universitas Muhammadiyah Makassar, followed by a master's degree in Educational Administration from Universitas Negeri Makassar. Currently, she serves as a lecturer at Universitas Islam Makassar, where she has been teaching since 2018. Ira's academic journey is marked by a strong commitment to research, particularly in the areas of teaching methodologies and student learning outcomes. She has authored numerous articles in reputable journals, focusing on innovative teaching models such as Team Games Tournament, contextual learning, and reciprocal teaching with digital literacy integration. Her research is driven by a passion for finding effective strategies to enhance student engagement and achievement, particularly in the context of Indonesian elementary schools. In addition to her research, Ira has extensive teaching experience, having taught various subjects related to Indonesian language education, scientific writing, and educational methodology. Her teaching philosophy emphasizes the use of interactive and student-centered approaches, which she has successfully implemented in her courses to improve student learning experiences. Ira's contributions to education extend beyond the classroom. She has actively participated in various national and international seminars, workshops, and webinars, sharing her insights and learning from other experts in the field. Her dedication to education is also evident in her ongoing efforts to support teachers in adopting innovative teaching practices that are responsive to the challenges of modern education. Through her work, Ira continues to make significant contributions to the field of primary education in Indonesia.

Shivi Khanna is an Associate Professor in School of Business and Management at CHRIST University, Banerghatta Road, Bangalore, India. She has completed her PhD in corporate structure determinants in Indian companies. She has published articles in various international and national refereed journals. Her areas of research interests include Corporate Finance, environmental sustainability and social media usage.

Sunita Kumar A passionate educationist with 17+ years of experience (Industry: 5+ years and Teaching: 12+ years) experience. Dr Sunita area of expertise/ specialization including advertising, branding, digital Marketing, consumer behaviour, Marketing Analytics. Over the last 12 years, she has taught and received positive evaluations for many marketing units, including Brand Management, Marketing Research, International Marketing, Fundamental of Marketing, Consumer Behaviour, Marketing Management, Social Media and Digital Marketing, Data Analysis using SPSS both postgraduate and undergraduate level. She has also been actively supervising master's and Ph.D. candidates from Christ university in Bangalore. Dr Sunita also often shares her industry experience and research findings with different audiences and stakeholders, both locally and internationally. she has been actively leading and involved in numerous research project and consultancies projects, as well as published numerous indexed journals/ articles, book, chapters in a book, conference proceedings, and industry reports.

Suman Lata is associated with Amity University Noida.

Lukman was born in Kadidi on March 7, 1986. He currently resides at Jl. Mustika, Rappang, Panca Rijang District, Sidrap Regency. Lukman completed his primary education at SD Negeri No. 3 Macorawalie in 1999, followed by SLTP N. 4 Panca Rijang in 2002. He graduated from MAN 1 Mamuju in 2005. He earned his Bachelor's degree in Government Science from STISIP Muhammadiyah Rappang in 2012, a Master's degree in Public Administration from UNISMUH Makassar in 2015, and is pursuing a Ph.D. in Public Administration at UNHAS, expected to graduate in 2024. Lukman has been a lecturer at STISIP Muhammadiyah Rappang since 2016 and is now with the Faculty of Social and Political Sciences at Universitas Muhammadiyah Sidenreng Rappang, specializing in Public Administration. His areas of expertise include Public Policy, Management, and Organization. Lukman is married to Dr. Erfina, S.Sos., M.Si., and they have two children: Muh. Khaerul and Muthiah Az-Zahra.

Shyam Sundar Meena is currently working as an associate professor, the Department of Computer Science & Engineering, SVIIT- SVVV, Indore. He has obtained a Ph.D. from Devi Ahilya University, Indore, India, a Master of Engineering degree from the Institute of Engineering & Technology, DAVV, Indore in Computer Engineering (with specialization in Software Engineering) and a Bachelor of Engineering (Computer Engineering) from Shri Govindram Seksaria Institute of Technology and Science, Indore. He has 16 years of experience in the field of teaching.

Kartik Mistry is pursuing Final Year Computer Engineering in MCT Rajiv Gandhi Institute of Technology.

Jignesh Patil completed Master from SRK University and Currently working as Assistant Professor in MCT Rajiv Gandhi Institute of Technology.

Krishma Rana is a scholar in central university of Jammu.

Sreethi Rebeka R is pursuing her Ph.D in Commerce from CHRIST (Deemed to be University) & Faculty of Commerce at Mount Carmel College, Autonomous. Completed her graduation from Stella Maris College, Autonomous, M.Com from Loyola College, Autonomous, M.Phil from University of Madras, and SLET in Commerce. She has participated and presented research papers at national and international conferences and has published research papers and book chapters in reputed journals.

Prashant Kumar Siddhey is Doctorate and Master's in Management from Devi Ahilya University, Indore. He has over 16 years of experience blended with industrial and academics both. 24 publications to his credit, including Book, Research Papers, Book Chapter, Case Studies. Presently, he is working as a Professor, Chandigarh University. He has worked as with institutes and universities of repute and handled various responsibilities successfully as HoD- School of Management, Coordinator-MBA, BoS, Examinations, Training and Placements, Industrial Relations, National and International Conferences etc. He worked to transform institute to University and to establish school of management for newly established university. He is active life member of Indian Society for Training and Development. His area of interest is General Management and Human Resource Management.

Muhammad Usman Tariq has more than 16+ year's experience in industry and academia. He has authored more than 200+ research articles, 100+ case studies, 50+ book chapters and several books other than 4 patents. He is founder and CEO of The Case HQ, a unique repository for courses, narrative and video case studies. He has been working as a consultant and trainer for industries representing six sigma, quality, health and safety, environmental systems, project management, and information security standards. His work has encompassed sectors in aviation, manufacturing, food, hospitality, education, finance, research, software and transportation. He has diverse and significant experience working with accreditation agencies of ABET, ACBSP, AACSB, WASC, CAA, EFQM and NCEAC. Additionally, Dr. Tariq has operational experience in incubators, research labs, government research projects, private sector startups, program creation and management at various industrial and academic levels. He is Certified Higher Education Teacher from Harvard University, USA, Certified Online Educator from HMBSU, Certified Six Sigma Master Black Belt, Lead Auditor ISO 9001 Certified, ISO 14001, IOSH MS, OSHA 30,

Khaerun Nisa'a Tayibu, S.Pd., M.Pd., has established herself as a distinguished figure in the educational field through her comprehensive academic background, extensive teaching experience, professional training, research endeavors, accolades, and active participation in professional/scientific organizations. Her educational journey began with a Bachelor of Education (S.Pd.), then a Master of Education (M.Pd.), laying a solid foundation for her career. Tayibu's teaching experience is vast, covering various levels of education and demonstrating her adaptability and commitment to fostering student growth. She has also participated in numerous professional training programs, enhancing her pedagogical skills and staying abreast of the latest educational trends and methodologies. Tayibu's dedication to education extends into her research activities, where she has contributed valuable insights into teaching methodologies and educational psychology. Her work has enriched academic discourse and earned her several awards, recognizing her contributions to the field of education. These accolades reflect her commitment to excellence and innovation in teaching and research. Moreover, Tayibu's involvement in professional and scientific organizations underscores her commitment to the educational community. She engages with fellow educators and researchers through these memberships, sharing knowledge and collaborating on initiatives to improve educational practices. Her active participation in these organizations demonstrates her dedication to advancing education and her role as a leader in the field. Khaerun Nisa'a Tayibu's career is a testament to her passion for education, her pursuit of excellence, and her unwavering commitment to contributing to the betterment of educational standards and practices.

Rejoice Thomas holds a Doctoral Degree from Bharathiar University, Coimbatore (Tamilnadu). He has participated and presented research papers at national and international conferences and also published papers in leading journals. An astute professional having more than 12 years of experience in Teaching, Learning & Development. Possesses strong skills and abilities to provide learning opportunities to employees by proper gap analysis, structured planning, designing learning paths, and tracking mechanisms to measure effectiveness. He is also an experienced trainer specializing in Sustainable Development Goals (SDGs) with a demonstrated history of designing and facilitating impactful training programs and specializes in Environmental, Social, and Governance (ESG).

Vrinda Tokekar is a Professor of the Department of Information Technology at the Institute of Engineering & Technology and Head of the IT Center in Devi Ahilya Vishwavidyalaya, Indore. She received her Bachelor of Engineering, (Electrical & Electronics) (Hons.) from Birla Institute of Technology & Science, Pilani (Raj.), Master of Engineering (Computer Engineering) from SGSITS, Indore and Ph.D. in Computer Engineering from Devi Ahilya University, Indore, India. She has 36 years of academic and teaching experience in Graduate and postgraduate engineering programs. Her research areas are Wireless and Ad-hoc Networks, Network Security and Network Analysis. She has guided many PhDs.

Index

B

C

D

E

F

G

H

I

L

M

O

P

R

S

T

V

www.ingramcontent.com/pod-product-compliance
Lightning Source LLC
LaVergne TN
LVHW080610300926
849162LV00005B/1101